John Dee

JOHN DEE

The Politics of Reading and Writing in the English Renaissance

WILLIAM H. SHERMAN

UNIVERSITY OF MASSACHUSETTS PRESS

AMHERST

Library of Congress Cataloging-in-Publication Data
Sherman, William H. (William Howard)
John Dee : the politics of reading and writing in the
English Renaissance / William H. Sherman.
p.   cm.—(Massachusetts studies in early modern culture)
Includes bibliographical references and index.
ISBN 0–87023–940–6 (alk. paper)
1. Dee, John, 1527–1608—Library. 2. Dee, John,
1527–1608—Books and reading. 3. Scientists—Great Britain.
4. Astrologers—Great Britain. I. Title.
Z8220.9.S48   1995
001'.092—dc20   94–20149

British Library Cataloguing in Publication data are available.

An earlier version of chapter 6 appeared as "John Dee's *Brytannicae Reipublicae Synopsis:* A Reader's Guide to the Elizabethan Commonwealth," *Journal of Medieval and Renaissance Studies* 20:2, pp. 293-315. Copyright Duke University Press, 1990. Reprinted with permission.

Part titles: Plate 2 from Johannes Stradanus, *Nova Reperta* [*New Discoveries*] (Antwerp, c. 1600), illustrating the invention of the compass. Used by permission of the Folger Shakespeare Library.

To My Teachers

Contents

Acknowledgments

In a book that stresses the communal contexts of scholarship, it is an especially appropriate pleasure to acknowledge the communities that have influenced and sustained me during its production.

I want, first, to thank those who have directed my research in an official capacity. James Shapiro provided me with an exciting introduction to Renaissance Studies and, through his critical readings, taught me much of what I know about writing. Lisa Jardine nurtured my graduate study in Cambridge with her truly inimitable blend of erudition, enthusiasm, and friendship. Patrick Collinson kindly acted as a supplemental supervisor, and he remains a source of information and, indeed, inspiration. Many readers will know how fortunate I have been to learn from any one of these mentors, and they will also know that each has taught me about much more than the English Renaissance. I dedicate this book to them with respect and gratitude.

Dee demands of his students a broad-based expertise that it is no longer possible for a single person to attain. If I have approached Dee's omnidisciplinarity with any success it is due in large measure to the patient guidance of scholars from other fields. I must single out Paul Hammer's instruction in political history, Simon Schaffer's direction in the history of science, and Elisabeth Leedham-Green's indispensable assistance on matters bibliographical, paleographical, and linguistic. For more general advice and encouragement I thank David Scott Kastan, Anthony Grafton, Annabel Patterson, Bruce Moran, D. B. Quinn, Roy Ritchie, Nicholas Clulee, David Starkey, Brendan Bradshaw, and Keith Wrightson. For their camaraderie and input I am grateful to Bela Kapossy, Suzanne Reynolds, Elizabeth Fowler, Claire McEachern, Dilip Menon, G. Arunima, Marianna Cherry, and the Parkers. Joan Pau Rubiés i Mirabet, James Knowles, Stephen Johnston, Jim Alsop, Christy Anderson, Cathy Curtis, Naomi Tadmor, David Armitage, Heidi Brayman, and Bill Pidduck kindly read parts of the manuscript, and the members of seminars and conferences in Cambridge and London listened to several papers: I am grateful to them all, and particularly to Warren Boutcher, Lorna

Hutson, and Peter Miller, for their vital comments. This study has also benefited from the critical attention of Quentin Skinner and Marie Axton, who examined the thesis on which it is based. The four anonymous readers for the University of Massachusetts Press saved me from countless errors (though I'm sure I managed to slip a few by them). Alan Stewart was a gracious proofreading partner: the text and the index were greatly improved by his meticulous eye. Lastly, Claire MacDonald deserves special mention, and my fondest gratitude, for her companionship. Those who have worked on Dee and lived to tell the tale can attest that he is a particularly demanding subject, and Claire must claim most credit for the sanity that I have managed to preserve.

In the various libraries through which I have tracked Dee I have encountered an efficiency and generosity he would have envied. The librarians of the Royal College of Physicians (London), The Huntington, The New York Society, Christ Church College (Oxford), Merton College (Oxford), Queens' College (Cambridge), and Trinity College (Cambridge) were particularly kind.

This book was written in the ideal environments provided by Clare College (Cambridge), the National Maritime Museum (Greenwich), the Huntington Library (California), and the University of Maryland (College Park). It is a privilege to acknowledge the financial support of a Kellett Fellowship from Columbia University, research grants from Clare College and the Cambridge English Faculty, an American Friends of Cambridge Scholarship, a Mellon Foundation Fellowship at the Huntington, and a Caird Research Fellowship at the National Maritime Museum. Without the support (financial and otherwise) of my parents, above all, this book would have been neither begun nor finished.

Preface

Over the past four centuries, and especially the last four decades, John Dee (1527–1608/9) has proven one of the most interesting and enigmatic figures of the English Renaissance. Books from his library and from his own pen have always been treasured;[1] and since 1950 there have appeared three monographs, four doctoral theses, and countless essays devoted to his life and works.[2] He is one of the few Elizabethan figures who (like Queen Elizabeth herself) remain vivid—or at least colorful—enough to inspire historians and novelists alike.[3] Yet, while he has always been assured of a place in Britain's heritage, and in Renaissance Studies, the nature of that place has never been secure. Since his own day his activities, his works, his milieux, his influence—in short, his very identity—have been subject to fluctuation and debate.

Much of the variability of Dee's fate can be ascribed to his position as one of the great Renaissance polymaths: their aspirations toward universal knowledge and their seemingly protean characters pose peculiar historiographical problems.[4] During his long career Dee plowed a virtually boundless field of knowledge: even a list including astrology, mathematics, cartography, cryptography, alchemy, angelology, medicine, theology, and law fails to describe the full array of his activities. Like other representatives of late Renaissance "encyclopedism," he believed that his strivings in these various spheres amounted to a patterned and synthetic endeavor; that by mastering all disciplines and all books he would apprehend the mystery of God's creation.[5] As Gabriel Naudé put it, by assembling a universal library "he might know all, see all, and be ignorant of nothing," thus truly qualifying as a *"Cosmopolitan, or Habitant of the Universe."*[6]

In describing the suggestively named science of *anthropographie*, Dee asserted the need not merely for *inter*disciplinarity but for *omni*disciplinarity, and offered a tantalizing vision of its rewards:

You must of sundry professions, borow or challenge home, peculier partes hereof: and farder procede: as, God, Nature, Reason and Experience shall informe you. The Anatomistes will restore to you, some part:

The Physiognomistes, some . . . & many other (in certaine thinges) will be Contributaries. And farder, the Heauen, the Earth, and all other Creatures, will eche shew, and offer their Harmonious seruice, to fill vp, that, which wanteth hereof: and with your own Experience, concluding: you may Methodically register the whole. . . .[7]

Scholars from fields as diverse as philosophy, geography, and bibliography have been "contributaries" to the recovery of Dee and his world. Not surprisingly, they have failed to achieve the *gestalt* of either Dee or his holistic universe; and the problem of how to "methodically register the whole" remains as acute as ever. Of the strategies available, scholars have almost unanimously opted for the traditional methods of intellectual history and intellectual biography, identifying him with certain schools of thought and tracing their development into a coherent philosophy.[8] Particularly in the influential work of Frances Yates and her students, he has been chiefly associated with the occult philosophy, and has been identified as England's great "magus," or philosopher-magician. With a degree of consensus remarkable for such a complex figure, in both the scholarly and the popular imagination Dee has become the reincarnation of Merlin at the Tudor court.

This study began with the realization that Dee left behind many traces of nonmagical activities and writings, and that these traces have been played down or left out altogether in previous accounts. I set out simply to recover these scattered and neglected sources (particularly his marginal annotations and his manuscript writings) and to set them alongside the better-known works; "to fill up," in other words, "that which wanteth." But I quickly developed a sense that these sources did more than enlarge or clarify the received picture: they cast serious doubts on the packaging of Dee as—exclusively or even primarily—a Hermetic, Neoplatonic magus.

In fact, they made it increasingly difficult to assign Dee to any particular school or approach. The more I read, the more Dee seemed to confound conventional divisions of labor and belief. Not only were both Aristotle and Plato central to Dee's thought, but so were Euclid, Ptolemy, Proclus, Plotinus, Cicero, Roger Bacon, Paracelsus, and Ramus—a group that gives twentieth-century intellectual historians a strong sense of cognitive dissonance, if not schizophrenia.

What kind of outlook—or, more pointedly, purpose—could have allowed Dee to accommodate these eclectic sources? What kind of personal and cultural phenomena do his efforts to collect and combine all knowledge (the mathematical and the magical, and everything in between) represent? Taking a cue from recent developments in history, sociology, and science, I tried to shift attention from Dee's putative intellectual allegiances to the professional modes and social roles that he so carefully, almost obsessively, documented.

Gradually another Dee emerged, occupying a peculiar and significant place at the crossroads of early modern culture. By equipping himself with a humanistic education in the recovery and analysis of textual information, by pursuing all practical (and most speculative) knowledge, by assembling his country's largest and most valuable library and museum, and by developing a wide range of courtly and commercial contacts, Dee fulfilled a powerful and challenging role. Setting himself up in what was perhaps the first English think tank, he acted as a retailer of special (often secret) knowledge, an "intelligencer" in the broadest sense.

The opening section of this book offers a more detailed account of this shift from "magus" to "intelligencer," reviewing past approaches to Dee and calling for new attention to neglected sources, contexts, and configurations. The remainder of the study is a preliminary, and by no means exhaustive, attempt at such attention. It joins the recent studies of Nicholas Clulee and others in pointing toward a post-Yatesian account of Dee. Despite my title, then, this study does not claim to present "the whole Dee." It will be immediately clear where I have left materials and issues to others better suited to address them. What I offer, rather, is a range of perspectives which have not figured in previous pictures of the whole Dee and some suggestions about their implications for our understanding of Dee and his contemporaries.

In place of the standard division into "life" and "works" I have opted for what—for Dee at least—are more appropriate terms. After treating Dee's *careers* in Part I, I begin by considering Dee's *readings* and attempt to move from the question of what he read to where, why, how, and for whom he read: in Part II, I discuss the place of reading in the Renaissance and in Dee's career. Chapter 2 focuses on the physical place of Dee's reading—the extraordinary library which formed the centerpiece of his intellectual, social, and professional life. In order to contextualize Dee's information-processing methods, I then survey the theories and practices of reading in the modern and the early modern periods. Chapter 4, finally, details Dee's own elaborate methods of digesting texts. In Part III I turn my attention to the *writings* in which Dee applied his learning. After a general account of his contributions to Tudor historical thought and what might be called his "political science," I discuss his neglected writings, ranging from a proposal for the reformation of the calendar to a mediation in a rural mining dispute. I focus on his tabular synopsis of the Elizabethan commonwealth and the maps and treatises he produced as Elizabeth's "imperial geographer."

Perhaps Frances Yates was right to point to Dee's Hermetic leanings—she just stressed the wrong Hermes, or the wrong Hermetic attributes. Dee's career was not fashioned in the mold of Hermes Trismegistus:[9] the Hermetic corpus occupied, at most, a prominent corner of his arsenal of universal learning. Rather, Dee resembles the Hermes who, in the classical world, stood on the edge of the market and the city, marking space and guiding communication, commerce, and travel.[10] From the margins of the university, the city, and the court, Dee served and continues to serve—with a mixture of visibility and invisibility, openness and secrecy, and success and failure entirely appropriate to a Hermetic figure—as the mercurial messenger of the English Renaissance.

I. Introduction

ONE

Politics in the Margins

The Careers of John Dee

The workes of my handes, and wordes of my mouth . . . may bear liuely
witnesse. . . .   —John Dee, *A Letter . . . apologeticall* (1599)

A COMPENDIOUS REHEARSAL OF HIS STUDIOUS LIFE

On 9 November 1592, Anne Russell, countess of Warwick,
delivered a letter to Queen Elizabeth at Hampton Court: it
was a "supplication" from the Queen's "servant in Mortlake," John
Dee.[1] In it, Dee urgently requested an opportunity to recount his
long-standing service, and to plead for some relief from the "in-
juries and indignities" that had befallen him. His petition was
granted: less than two weeks later, on 22 November, he was visited
by the queen's commissioners, Mr. Thomas Wolley (a privy coun-
cillor and sometime secretary for French and Latin) and Sir Thomas
Gorge (a gentleman of the queen's wardrobe). Dee led the two men
to his library, where he sat them before two "great tables, being
covered; the one, with very many letters and recordes . . . and
testimonies of my studious lyfe, in and from the most famous
places and parties of all Christendome; and the other with such
divers books of my making, printed and unprinted, as I had . . .
written or devised" (4). Surrounded by what remained of Elizabethan England's largest library and facing the piles of texts that
embodied the career of the sixty-five-year-old scholar who created
it, the queen's commissioners heard Dee's lengthy presentation.

He wrote it up at their request following the tribunal, calling it
"The Compendious Rehearsall of John Dee his Dutifull Declara-
cion and Proof of the Course and Race of his Studious Lyfe. . . ."
Although it runs to over forty printed pages it was essentially, as

the title suggests, a *curriculum vitae*—that is, a running-through of
his life. It contained a chronological rehearsal of exactly half a
century of intellectual pursuits: the date of the hearing was fifty
years to the month after Dee's matriculation at the University of
Cambridge in 1542.

While it was written near the end of his life, and while its
rhetoric and argument were colored by its context (the aim being,
after all, to elicit royal support), it is a reliable and revealing
document that provides the starting point for a study of Dee's
career. Aside from offering an immediate taste of Dee's unusual
and often difficult prose style, it allows me to carry out two preliminary tasks simultaneously: to survey the often surprising details of
Dee's activities, contacts, and writings; and to convey a sense of
Dee's extraordinary self-consciousness about his social and professional status.

My account of Dee's *curriculum vitae* follows the structure of
the "Compendious Rehearsall"; but it draws heavily—as, indeed,
did the "Compendious Rehearsall" itself—upon the other major
source of autobiographical information, Dee's so-called private
diary. This is preserved in two long-term almanacs, in the margins
of which he entered memoranda of his domestic, fiscal, political,
intellectual, and medical transactions.[2] They cover the period
from the mid-1570s, when he was in his forties and at his most
integrated with the English court, through to the end of his life.
They not only fill out our knowledge of Dee and his *milieux* but also
establish him as a seminal figure in the history of English auto-
biography: Elisabeth Bourcier's definitive study of the private journal in early modern England considers Dee's diary the first "authentic journal" of the period—and one of its most interesting
specimens.[3]

In the first section of the "Compendious Rehearsall" ("The Entrance and Groundplat of my First Studies"), Dee recounts the
conditions of his birth and formal studies. He was born in London
on 13 July 1527 to Rowland Dee, a mercer employed at the court
of King Henry VIII. Rowland sent his son to Chelmsford Grammar School and then, in November 1542, to Cambridge. Mid-
Tudor Cambridge was dominated by what Winthrop Hudson has
termed "the Cambridge Connection," and especially by the "Athenian Tribe" at St. John's College.[4] At St. John's Dee was tutored by

the chief of that tribe, the influential John Cheke. While he may not have enjoyed much contact with Cheke's most important student, Prince Edward,[5] he established useful contacts with several of Cheke's other students, including William Cecil (later Lord Burghley and Elizabeth's treasurer) and William Grindal (Archbishop of Canterbury). Roger Ascham later exclaimed that Cheke "did bring up so many learned men in that one college of St. John's at one time as, I believe, the whole university of Louvain in many years was never able to afford."[6] Just to be on the safe side, Dee left Cambridge in 1547 (after receiving his B.A.) and went to Louvain itself, "to speake and conferr with some learned men, and chiefely mathematicians" (5).

When he returned to Cambridge later that year, he was appointed under-reader in Greek at Trinity College, and one of its foundation fellows. He stayed just long enough to receive his M.A. in the summer of 1548, when he went abroad once again, first to Louvain and then to Paris. At Louvain he studied under and alongside the foremost Continental cosmographers: he numbered among his teachers and friends Gemma Frisius, Pedro Nuñez, Abraham Ortelius, and Gerard Mercator. These men exercised an influence on Dee that extended far beyond the classroom and long past his visit to Louvain. When he became seriously ill in the late 1550s, Dee appointed Nuñez his executor. Ortelius—who was only a few months older than Dee—remained an active correspondent;[7] and when he traveled to England in 1577, he paid a visit to Dee.[8] That visit produced a graphic trace of their friendship, and of the Anglo-Dutch milieu within which it flourished—Dee's remarkable contribution to Ortelius' *Album Amicorum,* a collection of signatures, poems, drawings, and engravings accumulated by Ortelius from the 1570s to the 1590s as he circulated among Europe's leading scholars, statesmen, and artists.[9] In the panels left blank by the accomplished illustrator who provided many pages with unique ornamental borders, Dee expressed his love for Ortelius ("Geographer, Mathematician, Philosopher"), and provided a version of his recently granted coat of arms—see Figure 3.[10]

Dee also continued to correspond with Mercator, and in a manuscript produced in 1577 he referred to the "honest *Philosopher & Mathematicien Gerardus Mercator,*" of whom "sufficient Record is publisshed of o^r great familiarity."[11] That record was published in

1558 in the form of Dee's dedicatory epistle to Mercator from his astronomical text, the *Propaedeumata aphoristica*.[12] It provided an image—less visual but no less graphic than Ortelius' *Album Amicorum*—of Dee's years in Louvain and his friendship with its scholars. It was there that his "whole system of philosophizing in the foreign manner laid down its first and deepest roots"[13]—for which Dee had Mercator above all to thank, since "it was the custom of our mutual friendship and intimacy that, during three whole years, neither of us willingly lacked the other's presence for as much as three whole days; and such was the eagerness of both for learning and philosophizing that, after we had come together, we scarcely left off the investigation of difficult and useful problems for three minutes of an hour" (111). In fact, Dee credited Mercator with applying the pressure to publish which resulted in this, Dee's first printed work. And he concluded his letter by returning the favor: "It remains now for me to beg you earnestly to entrust to the public studies of men . . . your own remarkable discoveries both in that excellent branch of philosophy which is called physics and also in geometry and geography; for thus, certainly, you will greatly enlarge the Republic of letters with your most useful and fresh inventions. . . ."[14]

Dee arrived in Paris on 20 July 1550, and within a few days was lecturing on Euclid at "Rhemes College" to what was, by his own description, a rapt and overflowing audience. These readings brought Dee to the attention of "very many of all estates and professions [who] were desirous of my acquaintance and conference": they included the stars of the French intelligentsia, "Orontius, Mizaldus, Petrus Montaureus, Ranconetus, Danesius, Jacobus Sylvius, Turnebus, Vicomercatus, Gulielmus Postellus, Fernelius, Johannes a Pena, &c." (8).[15] During his stay he tutored William Pickering, the English ambassador to Charles V; and Pickering later mediated between Dee and Peter Ramus, bringing the former a presentation copy of the latter's *Prooemium Mathematicum,* inscribed to "his singular good friend J. Dee of London" (see fig. 4).[16]

The second and third sections of the text are concerned with establishing Dee's "good estimation and credit in matters of good learning, both abroad and at home in England" (6). The European courts were keen even from this early stage to adorn themselves with Dee's learning—and to profit from his mathematical innovations and alchemical discoveries. He was offered a place as "one of the French kinge's mathematicall readers, with 200 French crownes yearely stipend"; but he refused this, along with the private stipends offered by several French noblemen. During the next decades he refused offers from several European rulers, each one promising a higher salary than the last. By far the most generous offer came from Tsar Ivan the Terrible: in 1586 he sent a man to recruit Dee, promising that he would "enjoy at his Imperial handes £2000 sterling yearely stipende; and of his protector yearely a thousand rubbles; with my diet also to be allowed me free out of the emperour's own kitchin" (9).[17] Dee passed up Ivan's offers; but his son Arthur later became "Archiater" (chief physician) to Tsar Mikhail, on the recommendation of King James.[18]

He returned to England in 1551 and began a long and successful period of activity as a court intellectual. Dee enjoyed the patronage—albeit inconsistently—of many members of the Elizabethan administration, including the earl of Leicester, Christopher Hatton, Francis Walsingham, and Edward Dyer. More interesting, in light of recent work on the royal household, are Dee's connections with the queen's jewelers, dwarfs, and, above all, ladies-in-waiting. His wife, Jane Fromonds, was among the retainers of Lady Clinton at court, and this no doubt facilitated his close connections with the Clintons and the other leading ladies at court (especially Margaret Russell, Bridget Cooke, Mary Lewknor, and the Skidmores). He was particularly close to Blanch Parry, who was for a time Elizabeth's most intimate servant. Until recently they have been assigned only a marginal—almost ornamental— role in the English court, but these women were closest to the person of the queen, and to some degree controlled access to the space around her. They were therefore powerful court brokers, and were patently desirable to know.[19]

Over time Queen Elizabeth herself proved Dee's most consistent patron, offering him continual encouragement, occasional advancement, and sparse financial support.[20] "Her Majestie's Specially Gracious and Very Bountiful Favours" toward Dee and some of his "Dutifull Services Done unto Her Majestie" are the subjects of Chapters IV (11–19) and V (20–23) of the "Compendious Rehearsall." Dee was consulted in his astrological capacity for advice on the most propitious date for the queen's coronation (1558), in his astronomical capacity for his advice on the reform of the Julian calendar (1582) and his opinion of the comet of 1577, in his medical capacity for advice on the queen's sickness (1571 and 1578), in his legal capacity for proofs of Elizabeth's titles to foreign lands (1570s and 1590s), and in his tutorial capacity for explications of his *Propaedeumata aphoristica* (1558) and *Monas hieroglyphica* (1564). In recompense Elizabeth promised him a stipend to outdo King Edward's, a number of ecclesiastical sinecures (including the deanery of Gloucester and the rectories of Upton and Long-Lednam), and protection against the enemies of his "rare studies and philosophical exercises" (21). According to Gabriel Harvey's brother Richard, the queen gave Dee "the name of hyr Philosopher."[21]

During this phase of his career Dee was principally involved in the two activities detailed in Chapters VI and VII of the "Compendious Rehearsall"—the "Writing of Divers Bookes and Treatises" (24–27) on subjects from perspectival geometry to imperial geography, and the establishment of a monumental library of books and manuscripts (27–31).

For obvious reasons, the "Compendious Rehearsall" offers little record of the period from 1583 to 1589: these were the years of Dee's enigmatic escapades at the Bohemian court. In May 1583, the Polish prince Albrecht Laski arrived in London, and when he left for the Continent four months later Dee went with him—with his family, his spirit medium Edward Kelley, and a large proportion of his books and instruments in tow. Why Dee left when he was at the height of his influence at the English court, and what he did, and hoped to achieve, at the Bohemian court, remain for the most part mysterious. Much new research—particularly in Eastern European archives—will need to be carried out. For the time being, scholars can concentrate on teasing out two complicated strands of Dee's interactions during this period.

The first is the well-known (perhaps notorious) set of angelic and political transactions that Dee recorded in the *Libri Mysteriorum,* part of which Meric Casaubon published in 1659 under the title *A True and Faithfull Relation of what passed for many years between Dr. John Dee and Some Spirits.* These texts make for fascinating—if difficult and often disturbing—reading, packing together with little direction or demarcation Dee's devout prayers, his transcripts of the angelic voices that spoke through Kelley, and his narrative of political progress at the Rudolfine court.[22]

The other strand is closely related to that which Owen Gingerich and Robert Westman have picked up among the "less visible community of which Tycho [Brahe] was a part"—a "small, elite network of academic and court astronomers . . . that during the 1570s and '80s . . . was privately glossing, clarifying, and criticizing Copernicus' *De Revolutionibus*."[23] Among the "marginal footprints" which are the "residues of a once intense discussion" and of "a particular community's practice of reading and construing an astronomical text," some of the steps belong to Dee himself, and many others crossed his path during these years. These footprints cluster around the courts of Rudolf and the landgrave of Hessen-Kassel—the two foreign courts where Dee was most active.[24] And what provided the foundation for the community's interaction (aside from its interest in Copernican cosmology) was the textual aftermath of the new star and the comet that appeared in 1572 and 1577. Not only did Dee write a tract on the subject, but he was in contact with most of the other European astronomers who did as well—including Rudolf's physician Hagecius (Tadeáš Hájek), with whom he lodged during his time in Prague.[25] There is, finally, interesting evidence to suggest that Dee was caught up in the textual conflict (waged at these same courts) that gave birth, according to Nicholas Jardine, to the History and Philosophy of Science itself—the Tycho-Ursus controversy.[26] Dee was part of the community to which both Tycho and Ursus appealed for authority and support: the former sent Dee a copy of his work, and in the latter's *Fundamentum Astronomicum* (the text that gave rise to Tycho's and Kepler's charges of plagiarism) the final diagram is dedicated to "Ioanni Dee Anglo."[27]

Such a rehearsal of the salient features of Dee's career threatens to give the impression that his progress through the course and race of his life was smooth and unconstrained; that he contributed successfully and freely to the progress of science, accumulating in the process an impressive array of scholarly and political contacts. But the peregrinations and negotiations documented in the "Compendious Rehearsall"—indeed, the document itself and the circumstances that generated it—remind us of a crucial fact about Dee and his career, a fact that historians of early modern science have increasingly found to be characteristic of the period. Dee's career was marked by unevenness, uncertainty, and opposition; security, financial and spiritual, remained elusive; his position, intellectual and professional, was never on solid ground.

Evidence of Dee's struggle and of his self-consciousness abounds. The writings and records documenting his life are full of traces that reveal his constant need to situate himself in relation to physical places and socioprofessional configurations. Beyond *apologiae* like the "Compendious Rehearsall" itself, Dee manipulated—sometimes clumsily and sometimes effectively—a range of techniques to advertise his role. First, Dee's printed works are littered with self-referential devices which range from the blatant to the cryptic. His "Mathematicall Praeface" to the first English translation of Euclid in 1570, for instance, opens with a huge initial *D*—in which, to make sure the pun was not missed, he added his delta, his hieroglyphical monad, and a version of his coat of arms. In the same text there is a more subtle device: the signatures run from *a* to *d* and then begin again with *A*.[28] Second, Dee was obsessed with genealogy, and especially with establishing his own lineage. This was more than just an antiquarian pastime: his genealogical manuscripts concern Queen Elizabeth (with whom he allegedly shared a common ancestry among the Welsh kings), and other rulers from Europe and the Indies.[29] And Dee's most extensive genealogical roll (the manuscript stretches, over a length of almost seven feet, back to the reign of King Arthur) culminates in a potent display of self-fashioning: out of the lines and coats of arms of various noble families emerges not just Dee's place on the family tree but also the tripartite "Insignia Ioannis Dee Londinensis," which contains Dee's most detailed version of his coat of arms, and his self-portrait (see Fig. 5).[30] Finally, Dee's autobiographical supplications and defenses constantly interrupt his discourse: his texts sometimes seem to be produced in reaction to personal attacks rather than in relation to intellectual or political concerns.

Perhaps the most remarkable of these traces is the "Digression Apologeticall" which he inserted into his "Mathematicall Praeface." After praising those ingenious mathematicians who had devised the means to create illusions and to make artificial animals appear to fly (as Dee himself had done with a scarab on pullies for a production of Aristophanes' *Pax* at Trinity College) he went on to lament the suspicions and the name of "conjuror" which inevitably seemed to follow such feats (as, indeed, they had for Dee on that occasion). This gave vent to a powerful defense of his scholarly integrity against the accusations launched by his already numerous detractors:

for my xx. or xxv. yeares Studie: for two or three thousand Markes spending: seuen or eight thousand Miles going . . . only for good learninges sake: And that, in all maner of wethers: in all maner of waies and passages: both early and late: in daunger of violence by man: in daunger of destruction by wilde beastes: in hunger: in thirst: in perilous heates by day . . . in daungerous dampes of colde, by night. . . . And for much more (then all this) done & suffred, for Learning and attaining of Wisedome. . . . And in the end (in your iudgement) am I become, worse, then when I began? Worse, then a Mad man? A dangerous Member in the Common Wealth: and no Member of the Church of Christ? Call you this, to be learned? Call you this, to be a Philosopher? and a louer of Wisedome? (A2r)

These self-situating texts are among our richest resources for deep, contextual knowledge of Dee: they contain revealing pointers to sources, chronologies, beliefs, methods, and so on. But they are sources that have made students of Dee curiously uncomfortable, and as a result have been underutilized in their accounts. This scholarly embarrassment most likely results from the breach of decorum represented by Dee's polemical, autobiographical rhetoric. But perhaps we need to consider if this code of decorum is not more modern than early modern; if the breach is not caused by the intrusion of personal problems and professional maneuvers into our ideal of the solitary, detached genius. This is not to obscure the fact that Dee's struggles derived in part from personal shortcomings; that he was often unrealistic, excessively serious, and open to delusion; that his contribution to science was on the whole inferior to that of a Copernicus or a Newton (though there are important exceptions in specific fields, such as navigation and cartography). But these problems should not, in turn, obscure the fact that many of Dee's struggles derived from the difficult career path that he chose, and from the systemically problematic conditions of early modern scientific practice.[31] Dee's apologetics are crucial, then, to the recovery of his place in society; without them, Dee remains strangely disembodied.

THE MYTH OF THE MAGUS

In recent decades Dee has come closer than at any other time since his death—and quite possibly his birth—to having a stable, fixed identity.[32] From a series of studies beginning in the 1950s, Dee has emerged as a widely recognized historical character—England's great "magus."[33] The magus was a philosopher-magician who aspired through study of the arcane sciences to understand the fabric of the cosmos and to achieve union with the divine. Dee was most decisively presented in this form by Peter French, in *John Dee: The World of an Elizabethan Magus* (1972); but his account derives almost entirely from I. R. F. Calder's monumental doctoral dissertation, "John Dee Studied as an English Neoplatonist" (1952),[34] and from Dame Frances Yates, who taught both Calder and French.

During her long tenure at the Warburg Institute, Yates produced seminal essays and books on the intellectual history of the European Renaissance. She exerted such a strong influence through her works and her teaching that she has been credited with creating a whole approach to the Renaissance, which has been labeled the "Yates Thesis" (Westman) and the "Warburg Interpretation" (Clulee). Simply put, this approach argued that twentieth-century historians had lost sight of the Neoplatonic, and especially the Hermetic and Cabalistic, aspects of Renaissance intellectual and scientific culture. While Dee played a minor role in Yates's early efforts along these lines, he increasingly came to embody her vision and to appear more frequently in her writings.[35] She discovered in Dee a scientific figure who had been marginalized because of a reputation for occultism. By using him as an exemplar she was able to posit such occultism as central to the outlook and achievements of the Renaissance and, in the process, to turn Dee himself into a leading, representative figure.

The name John Dee is now difficult to dissociate from the identity of the magus: whether in the debased form of a deluded wizard or elevated to a masterful natural philosopher, this is how he has captured the historical imagination and entered the historical vocabulary. References to Dee by writers of recent generations present him in this guise as a matter of course—and this is true from the narrow circle of Dee specialists to general academic and even fiction writers. Virtually every post-Yatesian student of Dee has acknowledged her influence and pledged at least partial allegiance to her conceptual framework.[36] Dee's name rarely occurs in general works on early modern English history or literature without the identifying tag "magus." In his social history of early modern England, for example, J. A. Sharpe calls Dee the "key figure in Neo-Platonic scholarship," and "the perfect example" of "the magus, the ascetic and isolated searcher for the truth."[37] In Umberto Eco's novel *Foucault's Pendulum,* Dee makes several cameo appearances alongside none other than William Shakespeare. And Dee figures in another recent novel, John Crowley's *Aegypt,* which credits Yates herself with some inspiration. But no one has employed Dee's magical persona with such surrealistic flair as the late Victorian author "Hippocrates Junior," who published a bizarre compilation of doctored Renaissance texts under the title *The Predicted Plague.* In the "Outline of Astrologer Dee's Life" we find a Pre-Raphaelite print of Ophelia on a riverbank with the caption "A mixed medley of Shakespeare and Dr. Dee's Astrology" (312).[38]

Although it is as much a simplification as a celebration of her work, one of Yates's enduring legacies is a myth of the magus that has without doubt become part of our historical unconscious. Although some of Dee's twentieth-century manifestations have owed little to historical verisimilitude, I use the word *myth* not in the sense of an imaginary construction, to deny the reality that Yates describes: rather, I use it in the sense of a narrative and rhetorical construction, to highlight Yates's story as an interpretive strategy imposed on Dee—in order not simply to make sense of him, but also to fashion him into something useful for her larger purposes. While the story the Yatesians have spun is an exciting one (it is what initially motivated me to study Dee) and an important one (it represented a valuable departure from entrenched historical conventions,)[39] the myth of the magus is neither the only nor the most helpful way of describing Dee's activities and assessing his status. A single label—however encyclopedic its intellectual approach—is bound to fall short of encompassing Dee's wide-ranging career: but in shaping him for modern readers the myth of the magus has, in several ways, proven actively misleading, distorting or deviating from the sources that document that career.

Yates and French acknowledge in places Dee's nonmagical activities; nonetheless, their magus-framework severs Dee from his contacts and contexts, placing him in the margins of Elizabethan society and creating, if not an outcast, at least a recluse. This has not only effaced the extent of Dee's embeddedness and participation in English and European academic, commercial, and courtly circles, but deflected attention from the exact nature of the "marginal" spaces he occupied. The magus is a solitary figure who plumbs the depths of nature in the shadowy secrecy of his laboratory, communicating with others only reluctantly and through cryptic conceits. In Yates's narrative, Dee is "shunned and isolated"; and Graham Yewbrey sees Dee as an "intellectually insular man." In his intellectual background, approach, and output, then, Dee the magus is not just eclectic; he is eccentric, grounded only by the historically muddled Hermetic tradition and connected only with those sympathetic to his peculiar blend of magic, science, and religion.

Going hand in hand with this characterization of Dee has been a tendency to identify him as a "philosopher." While Dee often applied this label to himself and his contemporaries, the Yatesians have used the term—like many others—in an anachronistic sense that fails to convey the broad range of activities and approaches it signified for Dee. Yates herself was sure that Dee was not just *a* philosopher, but "the characteristic philosopher of the Elizabethan age"—and it was his Hermetic leanings that earned him this distinction. This has relegated his activities to the realm of ideas and led to a search for the single, coherent system behind them. Since Yates, Dee scholars have been inclined to search for the key to his philosophy—occult, natural, or political.[40]

The search for Dee's coherent and systematic philosophy is in itself futile: as Patrick Curry has suggested, this tends "in even the best of the [works] on science and magic" toward "the treatment of historical figures as disembodied intellects," and of historical philosophies as "the incarnations of abstract essences" rather than "contingent constructions."[41] In Dee's case, perhaps the chief detriment of this approach is that it skews his relation to the Renaissance debate on the active and the contemplative life. A description of Dee as a Hermetic philosopher of nature will inevitably assign him to a *vita contemplativa.* But this would miss the ways in which Dee's intellectual work called for and represented at least an equal measure of the *vita activa*. Like a good civic Humanist he believed that one should accompany the other: he was deeply committed to applying his scholarship (some of which was supremely speculative) to the practical needs of the English commonwealth. Dee's comments on the science of numbers in his "Mathematicall Praeface" are a case in point. For Dee numbers *did* hold the answer to the rules of the universe, and he argued that through mathematical methods "the zelous Philosopher may wyn nere this Riuerish *Ida,* this Mountayne of Contemplation" (*iv). But he went on to spell out the twenty-seven practical and mechanical sciences that benefit from a knowledge of Euclidean geometry. Contemplation and action went hand in hand in Dee's *modus vivendi,* just as (in the same text) Plato, Pythagoras, and Lull exerted their influence alongside Aristotle, Avicenna, and Gemma Frisius.

Although they are applied to Florentine Humanism, J. G. A. Pocock's words are easily and usefully transferred to the English context: "the humanist had a profound commitment to participation in human life and in concrete and particular detail. . . . The need to make the particular intelligible had given rise to the idea of conversation, the idea that the universal was imminent in participation in the web of life and language, and so the highest values, even those of nonpolitical contemplation, had come to be seen as attainable only through conversation and social association."[42] In applying this to Dee and his contemporaries we need only add that the idea of conversation often had a textual dimension: not only did Dee interact as a humanistically trained reader with other scholars and statesmen, but many of his conversations took place in the margins of his books and manuscripts (as he conversed with other authors past and present) and in the written works he prepared for a variety of audiences. Indeed, this ideal of conversation can be seen as one of the dominant *modes* of early modern intellectual, political, and scientific exchange.

Two more precise examples will illustrate the distorting effects of the myth of the magus. First, even in its more respectable form, the image of the magus has done little to challenge the conventional story of the attack on Dee's library. As he explained in the "Compendious Rehearsall," he returned from his Continental sojourn to find many of his books and instruments "spoiled." One of the most fruitful avenues of Julian Roberts and Andrew Watson's research on the library was that which led them to cast doubt on the attack by an angry mob which, in the standard version of the story, suspected Dee's magical learning. They have traced this story to Dee's first biographer, Thomas Smith, and have found that it has been uncritically repeated ever since: "Charlotte Fell Smith first spoke of the 'mob,' M. R. James embroidered the story with the social composition of the rioters . . . and in 1980 the Mortlake mob became a London crowd."[43] Roberts and Watson have suggested that the "spoiled" items were, rather, stolen by a group of Dee's former associates, who had a good sense of the collection's value.

Second, according to the Yatesian narrative, Dee's career from this point onward was marked by poverty, disappointment, and disgrace. She wrote that "Dee had fallen into deep disfavour after his return from his mysterious Continental mission in 1589. . . ."[44] Graham Yewbrey echoed Yates, calling this final period one "of neglect and of intense disappointment."[45] Accurately (if unwittingly) suggesting the genre of Yates's story, Colin Ronan wrote of "the *tragedy* of Dee's fall from grace" after his association with Edward Kelley:[46] the magus, according to the Faustian mold, meets an unhappy end.

While he was spared Faustus' gruesome denouement, Dee's last years were evidently not spent in contented repose. There are striking indications, however, that contrary to the Yatesian narrative Dee not only maintained his earlier contacts (at least those who were still alive and in favor) but continued to gain new ones: far from having fallen from grace, he seems to have reached as high a position as was possible for someone of his class and occupation. When Dee's daughter Madinia was christened on 5 March 1590, Sir George Cary, Anne Lady Cobham, and Lady Walsingham were made her godparents; and on 27 August 1595 (when Dee was sixty-eight years old!) Margarite Dee was christened with Lord Keeper Puckering, the countess of Cumberland, and the countess of Essex as godparents.[47] Diary entries from this period indicate contacts of various sorts with John Herbert (master of requests and principal secretary), Lord Anderson (justice of the common pleas), Sir Thomas Wilkes (diplomat and courtier), Sir Thomas Egerton (master of the rolls), and the earl and countess of Derby. In the 1590s Dee also lent books to Robert Beale (one of the clerks of the

Privy Council) and for several months actually housed the family of Anthony Ashley (another clerk of the Privy Council).

In 1592, in fact, Dee was ready to leave Mortlake, and he made a bold but unsuccessful attempt to turn the Hospital of St. Cross into a new space ideally suited to what he saw as his role as scientific consultant to the Elizabethan court. This takes us, once again, back to the "Compendious Rehearsall" with which we began: it is that text which spells out the details and the background of Dee's scheme, and, in fact, it is this proposal that provides the key to the entire text and the tribunal it documents. Although the story gets a little convoluted, it gives a vivid impression of the difficulties of the patronage system within which scholars like Dee had to operate, as well as the unappreciated combination of persistence and connectedness (as well, of course, as the better-appreciated futility) that marks Dee's efforts within it.

On 9 August 1592, Dee was invited to dinner with Lord Burghley and his sons Robert and Thomas. The next day they dined again, and were joined by Lord Cobham, who, after dinner, "requested the Lord Threasorer to help me to St. Crosses, which he promised to do his best in."[48] As references in the diary suggest, Dee was at this time in hot pursuit not only of the mastership of St. Cross in Winchester but of the chancellorship of St. Paul's or the provostship of Eton.

This pursuit had started back in July 1590, when Dee met with Archbishop Whitgift, who promised to "take some order for my present mainteynance."[49] No position materialized; but in November of that year Whitgift sent Dee a gift of £5. By 21 January 1591 Dee was "utterly put owt of hope for recovering the two parsonages [of Upton and Long-Lednam, which he claimed he had never been properly granted] by the Lord Archbishop and the Lord Threasorer."[50] But his hopes were renewed by Burghley in December when, during an audience at Whitehall, he gave Dee the "jentle answer . . . that the Quene wold have me have something at this promotion of bishops at hand."[51] In 1592, some time before the dinners with Burghley, Dr. William Aubrey—Dee's cousin and a master of requests—sued on Dee's behalf for some rectories and vicarages in the diocese of St. David's. Dee was granted them, but received none of the income they were supposed to generate.[52] Finally, in 1592, Dee was informed by the countess of Warwick that the mastership of St. Cross would soon be vacant. When the queen was at Nonesuch in August, "the same suite was renewed unto her Majestie by the aforesaid Countess of Warwick: as well in respecte of my incredible want of due maintenance, as for that the most Reverend Father in God, this L. Archbishop of Canterbury, his good Grace, very often times, and to diverse hath affirmed, that this Mastership of S. Crosse's is a living most fitt for me, and I fitt for it. And also the right honourable Lord Treasurer . . . is of the same mind herein."[53] This, in effect, is where the "Compendious Rehearsall" begins, with Dee passing his request for a royal tribunal to the queen via the countess of Warwick. From the structure of the presentation that he gave on the ensuing occasion it is clear that the tribunal with Wolley and Gorge amounted to an interview for the post at St. Cross. His closing statement (Chapter 13) listed the reasons why he particularly desired the mastership of St. Cross over other possible positions.

In the sixteenth century the Hospital of St. Cross was a well-established and physically attractive almshouse not far from Winchester School.[54] Dee saw the Hospital as more than merely a source of passive income: he proposed to turn the institution into an early modern scientific academy and think tank. There would be a library and a printing press, as well as a laboratory for "exercises in perspective and other works philosophicall." This institute would both attract and generate intelligence. Most important, it would cause Dee to "become of better ability and credit, and so be better able to allure . . . rare and excellent men from all parts of Christendome (and perhaps some out of farder regions)."[55]

But, as the final section of the text—"The Sequel of the Premisses"—indicates, the matter rumbled along for several years and never resolved itself satisfactorily. Dee was promised "the pension of £200 yearely . . . out of the revenues of the Byshoprick of Oxford . . . till St. Crosses were voyd" (44). And, more immediately, the queen sent Gorge back to Dee's house on 2 December with "one hundred markes, part in gold, and part in silver," along with "the Lady Howard her letter to my wife, full of courtesie and kindnes, and in it a token of six old angells of gold," which he "delivered . . . unto me on the same table in my study, where they had sat a few daies before in commission" (45). But in the end Dee was left with the disappointing wardenship in Manchester and a bitter realization that the queen's gifts were "but words onely to me" with "the fruit ever due to others."[56]

It is well known that the situation did not improve under Elizabeth's successor, James. In 1604 Dee was moved to the extreme measure of publishing a petition complaining of his condition.[57] But, once again, what has been taken as an indication of Dee's disgrace proves to contain important evidence of the continuity of his status. The *Letter . . . apologeticall* did more than reprint Dee's Elizabethan petition of the same name (first written in 1595 and first published in 1599). It added a verse epistle to James which called for an official parliamentary or royal act to clear his name: in an accompanying broadside letter published at the same time (and displayed to the king at Greenwich on 5 June 1604), Dee went so far as to offer himself for trial, "willingly, to the punishment of Death: (yea, eyther to be stoned to death: or to be buried quicke: or to be burned vnmercifully). . . ." Even more surprisingly, these petitions revealed that Dee actually served James in an official capacity, having been sworn in as "his mathematician" on 9 August 1603.[58]

These details highlight one last distortion that has appeared, in the wake of recent studies of Dee, regarding what Clulee called "the vagaries of patronage." In his review of Clulee, Stephen Clucas concluded that "Dee simply didn't know how to play the game of 'Patron and Client'" (100). And in her review of the same work Lesley Cormack went one step further, suggesting that "Dee was unwilling to play the patronage game . . ." (135). But the foregoing negotiations—which involved some of the country's highest officials and most sought-after posts—suggest that if Dee lost the patronage game it was certainly not due to an ignorance of the rules or an unwillingness to play.

REREADING DEE

The myth of the magus thus essentializes Dee by isolating him from his social and spatial circumstances—or at least by failing to treat them in all of their contingency and complexity. These effects have been supported, and to some degree concealed, by two historiographical operations.

First, in constructing a narrative so compelling that it has easily won its battle with unruly and often contradictory evidence, Yates and her students have ignored many records of Dee's activities and works that are incompatible with the myth of the magus. Second, they have identified him with historiographical categories that have more to do with twentieth-century academic concerns than sixteenth-century cultural phenomena.

My reservations about Yatesian historiography can perhaps be best introduced by considering the terms "Neoplatonism" or "Hermet(ic)ism" and their relation to both "Humanism" and "Science." The fundamental problem is that each term—Hermeticism in particular—is given more clarity and autonomy than the currents it describes, and hence an explanatory function far beyond what it can deliver.[59] "Hermeticism" is a notoriously slippery concept. "That it formed an important ingredient" in Renaissance philosophies and practices (including those of Dee) "cannot be doubted, nor has it been since the earlier work of Kristeller, Garin, Walker, and several others": however, "it still remains to show that Hermeticism ever functioned as an important, independent worldview. . . ."[60] In other words, the Yatesians have taken "the occult philosophy" as an *explicans* (a thing to do the explaining) rather than as an *explicandum* (a thing to be explained).[61]

One of the ways they have done so, and one of the ways in which any label is formulated, is by defining it in opposition to other terms. In Yatesian intellectual history the second most influential of these dichotomies—second only to the classic antithesis between Platonism and Aristotelianism—is that between Hermeticism and Humanism. Yates and her students set these two terms in such absolute opposition that they now appear to be poles of a magnet, two cores of fundamental texts and tenets toward one of which any figure will gravitate. "It cannot," wrote Yates in the classic study of the Hermetic tradition, "be sufficiently emphasized that these two Renaissance experiences are of an entirely different order . . . making their appeal to different sides of the human mind."[62]

It is not only Hermeticism that suffers in this dichotomy. Yates uses "Humanism" in its most restricted sense—that movement, initiated by Petrarch, which was concerned with "the recovery of the Latin texts, of the literature of Roman civilisation in the Renaissance, and the attitude to life and letters which arose out of that recovery."[63] It was a nonreligious, nonscientific, and (at least in its rhetoric) anti-Scholastic movement. But this movement changed as it passed through the next two centuries and into neighboring countries. While the early Humanists' bent was indeed, as Yates suggests, "in the direction of literature and history," this did not mean that rhetoric and bibliography were the be-all and end-all of Humanist scholarship. They were (at least theoretically) means to the end of improving society, and this pursuit entailed the enlistment of the philosophy, theology, and science that Yates generally reserved for Neoplatonists. If the Yatesians did not recognize anything of the Humanist in Dee, this was partly because his Humanism had changed in ways that made it no longer identifiable: it had grafted religious, medieval, legal, and even magical branches onto its literary trunk.[64]

In Dee's career, however, there are strands of Humanism even as Yates understood it. According to French, Dee was "well aware that the way to curry general favour in Renaissance England was to be proficient in ancient languages and humanistic studies, but he ignored this and sought to discover the deepest secrets of philosophy. . . . He hardly seems to have been a product of sixteenth-century Cambridge."[65] On the contrary, Dee was one of its exemplary products. He was a serious student of Greek, Latin, and Hebrew, and through his teachers, his books, and his contacts in England and abroad he became proficient in both traditional and avant-garde studies. The fact that he opted for a career outside of the universities should not mislead us: most of Tudor Cambridge's successful products were to be found in noble households, in foreign embassies, in ecclesiastical positions, in ships, on battlefields, at the Inns of Court, and at the court itself.

What studies of Dee and his contemporaries make increasingly clear is that they did not gravitate to one or the other pole: their voyages of reconnaissance and plunder in the world of knowledge took them to both poles. This is most clearly manifest in the area of science. In a recent article Owen Hannaway contrasts the laboratory plans of Tycho Brahe and Andreas Libavius in a way that highlights the Neoplatonic and humanistic imperatives.[66] Brahe's Uraniborg, a castle, observatory, and laboratory on a secluded, royally granted island, exemplifies the "secretiveness" and "aristocratic aloofness" of the occult tradition; Libavius' "Chemical

House," an urban dwelling-place with open laboratories, exemplifies his ideal of chemistry as a liberal art based upon access to
shared information and its application to the needs of the common
man. "The one evoked a life of withdrawal devoted to the contemplative study and articulation of eternal verities; the other
called forth a life of social intercourse and active engagement
pursued for the betterment of mankind" (609–10). This characterization is useful in clarifying the strategies available to Renaissance
scientists, but even in its application to Brahe and Libavius the
opposition breaks down. The two men's activities and beliefs were
less clear-cut than Hannaway, and they themselves, would argue.[67]

In Dee's scientific career the opposition proves even harder to
sustain. He has generally been considered a denizen of Brahe's
Uraniborg—and not without reason. He was in contact with
Brahe,[68] and like him was the subject of one of Libavius' attacks.[69]
The "*arbor raritatis*" in his highly arcane text, the *Monas hieroglyphica,* unabashedly outlined a doctrine of scholarly election. He
was a member of the select brotherhood of alchemical adepts. And,
like Brahe, he came to be associated with "that center of alchemical
occultism that Libavius so detested, Rudolfine Prague."[70] Yet his
house in Mortlake bore an undeniable resemblance to Libavius'
Chemical House. His "Mathematicall Praeface" to the English
Euclid and his revised edition of Robert Recorde's *Grounde of Artes*
appealed to the mercantile and mechanical classes as much as to
academics or adepts. And he would undoubtedly have applauded
Libavius' remarkable formulation of a chemical Humanism: "We
do not want the chemist to neglect the exercises of piety or exempt
himself from the other roles of an upright life, simply pining away
amidst his dark furnaces. Rather we want him to cultivate *human-
itas* in a civil society and to bring luster to his profession by an
upright household, so that he may strive for every virtue and be
able to assist with his friends as an aid and counsel to his country.
Thus we are not going to devise for him just a *chymeion* or laboratory to use as a private study and hideaway in order that his practice
will be more distinguished than anyone else's; but rather, what we
shall provide for him is a dwelling suitable for decorous participation in society and living the life of a free man."[71]

Thus we seem to be left with a paradox. But the existence of
competing methodologies, philosophies, and ideologies is only

paradoxical in the terms of traditions of ideas. If we turn our attention to the social, economic, and political frameworks of these ideas—with the help of recent work on Humanist scholarship, court politics, literary criticism, and the history of science—we find that there were *roles* for sixteenth- and seventeenth-century intellectuals that could accommodate many types of, and approaches to, knowledge.[72]

In Dee's case this has entailed, first and foremost, an attention to him as a reader—to his collection, management, and application of the information contained in Elizabethan England's largest library. Like many of his learned contemporaries he digested his textual acquisitions actively and thoroughly, creating a map to a huge body of valuable material that could meet his—and others'—future needs. Through his writings, but also through oral consultations, he put this information at the disposal of a range of governmental, commercial, and scholarly interests. These activities, of reading, writing, and conversing, were the means by which Dee mediated between textual traditions and contemporary needs. They were the basis both for his service, by which he earned a living, and for his social interaction, by which he forged and maintained links with a broad network of contacts.

In locating Dee, secondly, scholars have left spatial considerations underexplored. Yet recent work in a number of disciplines has suggested the value—even the necessity—of putting knowledge-based activities into their spatial context. Influenced by the work of (among others) Foucault and Bachelard, literary and scientific scholars are recovering the domestic, civic, and institutional spaces in which reading, writing, acting, and experimenting have been carried out.[73] Dee's own activities and, indeed, identity were in no small way bound up with his sense of place. In the next chapter I will examine the spatial complex represented by Dee's library and household. Before moving on, however, there are two further places within which Dee must be situated.

The first is his neighborhood. Mortlake was ideally placed for Dee's activities, in relation both to England's main waterway and to the hubs of government and commerce. It was bounded by the River Thames to the north, by Putney and Barnes to the east, by Richmond and Kingston to the south, and by Kew to the west.[74] When Mercator wrote to "the most famous Dr John Dee, his

Master and most esteemed Patron" [!] he addressed the letter to his "home at Mortlake on the Thames near London."[75] And Dee himself explained that "the passage and way to my house . . . is so easy, neere, and of light cost from London or court."[76] Mortlake also offered the possibility of interaction with illustrious neighbors: these included the Controller of the Household and Irish projector Sir James Croft, his associate William Herbert of St. Julians, and the Cecilian Henry Maynard.[77] Dee was associated with—and associated himself with—Mortlake: many of his writings are dated with the phrase "at my poor house at Mortlake."[78]

Dee must also be associated with the city of which Mortlake was a suburb—London. From early in his career he adopted the agnomen "Londinensis," and most references to his name include this tag.[79] He signed his own works "Joannes Dee Londinensis," and this is how he was addressed in letters, referred to in texts and catalogues, and identified in the famous Ashmolean portrait. At first the tag does not seem significant: but it signifies a simultaneously English and European identity for Dee. The tag was only necessary within a European context, and there it bound him to England and its capital (not, and this is important, to its universities).[80]

In studying scholarly roles, finally, intellectual historians have not traditionally taken into account the factor of service. Dee naturally considered himself a zealous servant of God. But, as he wrote in his *Letter . . . apologeticall,* he was also "her most excellent Maiesties very true, faithfull, and dutifull seruaunt" (B4r). And whether he was casting horoscopes or computing tables of longitude and latitude, Dee carried out most of his activity as a "seruant, to our most gratious and incomparable Queene Elizabeth, and as a very comfortable fellow-member of the body politique" (B3v).

This in itself forces us to look at Dee's intellectual activities in a different light. It opens up the questions of who his audience was and who was paying for his services (and how); in other words, it embeds him in a socioprofessional network of patronage relations. Since Lytle and Orgel's 1981 volume, the study of patronage has expanded almost beyond recognition, moving far beyond the often simplistic and inapplicable studies of the artistic spheres. In political history, for instance, the concept of the "Man of Business" has emerged to describe the junior or secondary functionaries in Parliament who "facilitat[ed] the interests and objectives of the Privy Council, or of individual Privy Councillors."[81] Scientific historiography has produced even more enlightening work for our purposes: Mario Biagioli's study, "Galileo's System of Patronage,"[82] and the volume edited by Bruce Moran, *Patronage and Institutions,* are exemplary. These considerations may seem less inspired—certainly less inspiring—than the image of a man whose "fundamental motivation" was "to know the hidden springs and ultimate reasons behind the processes and the very existence of the cosmos."[83] But while Dee's activities were delimited by his socioeconomic possibilities, the two motives—courtly or commercial service and the knowledge of nature—were far from exclusive. As I have been suggesting, the European courts of the late Renaissance fostered hybrid roles, which drew on skills from the arts and the sciences, and favored at once the polymath and the pragmatist. In describing three such figures at the Italian court, Lina Bolzoni has used the suggestive term "Neoplatonic secretaries."[84] As long as "Neoplatonic" isn't taken too literally or exclusively, this is not a bad characterization of Dee.

While his library brought him an unusual freelance status, it is important to stress that Dee was not exactly a free agent. The interests he served were not always his own.[85] He operated, moreover, within what Patrick Collinson has called "a code of public decorum."[86] As an intellectual on the fringes of the court, his activities were no less creative than those of scholars who remained in the ivory tower, nor less valid than those of more visible government functionaries. He provided the intellectual foundations for new directions in many fields of action, from applied mathematics to global exploration.

Despite the existence of social and institutional constraints, then, figures like Dee, in the "second and third ranks of the political hierarchy," had a central role to play.[87] The scientist and the Humanist scholar were increasingly useful assets of the English Renaissance court. But there was considerable confusion surrounding their institutional positions, social statuses, and means of support. Underlying this phenomenon there must have been a relatively high degree of socioprofessional mobility such as that identified by Biagioli in late Renaissance Italy.[88] But this very mobility ensured that the support they received was generally lower than the caliber of their service and, falling between the cracks of patronage and bureaucracy, they often received no support at all. Ultimately, the real paradox that made life difficult for these intellectuals was not one of incompatible philosophies but rather an inevitable by-product of the system within which they worked. The system itself was one of the most underappreciated achievements of the Elizabethan regime: it made knowledge—especially new forms of knowledge—a political commodity and created new opportunities for the application of intelligence to the management of the state.[89] But then, as now, it put the intelligencers in an impossible situation: as brokers of valuable information and subservient mediators, they were both necessary and necessarily invisible. For social and professional rather than intellectual reasons, they remained offstage; and in the text of early modern history they have been committed to the productive but obscure space of the margins.

II. Readings

TWO

A Living Library

The *Bibliotheca Mortlacensis* Revisited

It is true that a fair Librarie, is not onely an ornament and credit to the place where it is; but an useful commoditie by it self to the publick; yet in effect it is no more than a dead Bodie as now it is constituted, in comparison of what it might bee, if it were animated with a publick Spirit to keep and use it, and ordered as it might bee for publick service.   —John Dury, *The Reformed Librarie-Keeper*

To . . . condemn so many brave witts to a perpetual silence and solitude, is ill to understand the scope of a *Library*. . . .   —Gabriel Naudé, *Instructions Concerning Erecting of a Library*

THE PLACE OF READING

One of the larger projects to which this study (and particularly this part) contributes is the recovery of the place of reading in the Renaissance. Studying the place of reading means attending to the roles of readers as manifested in concrete practices and their artifactual traces—the focus of Chapters 3 and 4. But it also means attending to two interconnecting spaces—and this is the sense of place that I explore in Chapters 2 and 3—the physical place in which reading was carried out, and the cultural place of readers within the social and professional matrix.

More than fifty years ago, F. R. Johnson wrote that Dee's circle, with its center in his Mortlake library, constituted the scientific academy of Renaissance England, a center for scientific activities not yet nurtured by the universities or by other official institutions.[1] This description of Dee's library raises a series of questions that subsequent scholars have been surprisingly slow to answer—

and in many cases to ask. They have occupied themselves with specialized pockets within the library and have lost sight of Johnson's remarks. No one has followed up his claim with a study of the *context* of Dee's library, moving from questions of what he read to where, how, why, with whom, and for whom he read.[2] How did Dee finance the library's creation and maintenance, despite being of modest birth and having no ostensible source of income?[3] What did he do there? What did visitors, friends, and patrons expect from Dee and his books? What was the place of such a scholarly reader who lived and worked outside of the universities? In search of the answers to these questions we must travel back over four hundred years for a visit to Dee's house in Mortlake.

REVISITING THE *BIBLIOTHECA MORTLACENSIS:* LIBRARY, MUSEUM, ACADEMY

Dee's library, the *"Bibliotheca Mortlacensis,"* was not only a monument to his scholarly interests and achievements; it was one of the great monuments of English Renaissance culture. By the time it was catalogued in 1583, Dee had assembled England's largest and—for many subjects, at least—most valuable collection of books and manuscripts. Its dispersal, which began even while he lived, was perhaps the most significant redistribution of textual resources since the dissolution of the monasteries. The leading collectors of the late sixteenth and early seventeenth centuries scrambled to acquire what they could.[4] It was Robert Cotton, not surprisingly, who pursued Dee's books most actively and successfully.[5] According to John Aubrey, when Dee died Cotton bought the land around his house, believing that Dee had buried valuable manuscripts in an adjacent field.[6] Later in the seventeenth century Elias Ashmole launched another campaign for the recovery of Dee's textual remains, which involved some of the leading historians of the day. On 11 January 1673 he wrote to Anthony Wood, "[I] am in quest of whatsoever Doctor Dee left behind him."[7] On or around this date he sent Aubrey to Mortlake to search for Dee's grave and to collect details of his life by interviewing the elders of the community.[8] While these efforts turned up little, he met with some success when he rushed off in pursuit of Dee's *Libri Mysteriorum.* Hearing that they had turned up in a chest at the home of Thomas

Wale (a warden in the Tower of London), Ashmole was thrilled to find that the manuscripts were still in Wale's possession. But when he paid a visit to Wale he was horrified by what he found: Wale had been so bewildered by the pages of Dee's angelic conversations that he had allowed his maid to use them as waste paper to line her pie tins.[9]

For us even more than for Ashmole, a visit to Dee's house and a look around his library must rest on scholarly and imaginative reconstruction, and the pursuit of his textual remains is a difficult and often frustrating process: the books that have survived are scattered throughout Britain, Europe, and America, and the building itself was long ago buried under Mortlake's famous tapestry works. From the principal sources—particularly the 1583 catalogue—we learn that Dee's bookshelves held between three and four thousand titles, representing virtually every aspect of classical, medieval, and Renaissance learning. The library was especially rich in scientific and historical manuscripts, and its unsurpassed Hermetic, navigational, artistic, Paracelsian, and Semitic holdings have long attracted scholarly attention.[10] The aspiration toward total knowledge that characterized Dee and other late Renaissance scholars was the driving force behind the shape of the collection. Yates claimed, without exaggeration, that "the whole Renaissance is in this library."[11] Roberts and Watson's subject index tells us that, aside from the texts in the trivial and quadrivial canons, the collection included works on anger, burial, chastity, cosmetics, dogs, dreams, earthquakes, falconry, gymnastics, heresy, memory, roads, and tides. These books were in twenty-one different languages, including not only the principal classical, Semitic, and Romance languages, but also Anglo-Saxon, Armenian, Catalan, Czech, Portuguese, and Swedish.

The range and sheer quantity of the volumes was impressive.[12] But Dee was relatively unconcerned with their visual impact—unlike image-conscious collectors such as Samuel Pepys, whose beautifully and uniformly bound volumes remain in their original carved cases at Magdalene College, Cambridge.[13] Dee's books were rarely bound in distinguished, much less uniform, bindings: in fact, many remained unbound, as they would have been purchased. Nor were they stored according to any consistent method: some were shelved vertically, with either their spines or their fore-edges out, and some were piled in horizontal stacks. Even though it was something of a showpiece, then, "the library must have presented a drab, if businesslike appearance."[14] Its order, too, was somewhat haphazard. The first 1,400 entries in the catalogue—which is almost certainly a shelf list—reveal a clear distribution according to size, the most economical way of storing books. These volumes are further separated into *libri compacti* (bound) and *libri non compacti* (unbound). After this they are ordered not by size but by subject headings—"chemical books," "Paracelsian books," "Grammars," and "Historical books pertaining to navigation." In several places Dee also grouped his books by linguistic categories: in the catalogue we find the sections "Hebrew, Chaldaic, & Syriac books," "Italian books," "German books," and "English books."[15]

Dee's library thus displays a relative and rather surprising lack of organizational principles. According to Roberts and Watson, "no shelf-marks of any kind attributable to Dee are found in either the books, whether manuscript or printed, or in the catalogues," and a great number of the books have no external markings whatsoever. The library "cannot have been easy to use."[16] A visitor would have been utterly dependent upon Dee's guidance—which is no doubt just how he wanted things. The value of the collection cannot, in this sense, be separated from the presence of Dee; and the apparent disorder and inaccessibility of the library were quite possibly part of its design, since they served to make the librarian indispensable for unlocking its secrets and bringing it to life.

As for Dee himself, the tool he must have used to find certain books—whether compiling treatises, writing letters, jotting down cross-references, or advising other scholars *viva voce*—was his memory. In our age of high literacy and advanced information technology we have tended to underestimate the potential of memory and to lose sight of its role in medieval and Renaissance cultures. In these periods the design of libraries and the act of reading were crucially dependent upon the arts of memory, those mnemonic techniques and habits that were an integral part of both Scholastic and Humanist pedagogy.[17] The library was both a metaphor and an exemplary site for the trained memory of a skilled reader. In Mary Carruthers's words, "all of these [pedagogical] schemes bespeak the assumption that a good memory is a library of texts, and a thoroughly catalogued one at that." St. Jerome wrote to Meliodorus that "by careful reading and daily meditation his heart should construct a library for Christ."[18] As we shall see in the next chapter, the goal of reading was the construction of a storehouse, or library, of useful phrases, passages, and ideas. While many devices were employed in this process, a fundamental role was played by the memory in mediating between a scholar's solitary meditation or socioprofessional function and the verbal or written material at his disposal, as well as in mapping the locations of particular texts and passages. In some of the larger libraries of the period, mnemonic topics or subject headings were painted on the *arcae* (cases of shelves) to describe the collections they contained—strong evidence, for Carruthers, "of the similarity perceived between what is read and written in memory and in books."[19] But even behind a library like Dee's, in which the mnemonic system escapes us and which may not have had one at all, there must have operated a prodigious memory.[20]

One of the classic mnemonic schemes involved the assignment of objects to different places within a building, which would then be "walked through" in the mind of the speaker or writer. Dee's library was spread throughout several rooms of his house—a fact that may or may not have been related to its organization. A "Goodwife Faldo," who had known Dee in her childhood, informed Elias Ashmole that he had "4 or 5 Roomes in his house fild with Bookes"; and Roberts and Watson point out that the 1583 catalogue inventoried only his "Externa bibliotheca."[21] In Chapter VII of the "Compendious Rehearsall" Dee makes passing reference to his "chiefe and open library," confirming the existence of other library rooms and especially what might be called an "Interna bibliotheca." It is this chapter, entitled "A briefe note and some remembrance of my late spoyled Mortlake Library," which provides Dee's fullest account of the library's "furniture" and overall value.[22] Like the rest of the document, it petitioned the queen for the reparation of expenses and the restoration of losses—in this case those resulting from the "spoiling" of the library during Dee's absence from 1583 to 1589. It is therefore a negative and partial account; but, aside from the catalogue and a few references in contemporary works, it is all we have to go on.

From this "briefe note" we learn that the library was not only furnished with books but with reading equipment like cases and tables, and also with four important "appendices." The first was a collection of "rare and exquisitely made instruments mathematicall." These included a quadrant made by Richard Chancellor, which had been purchased for Dee by Mr. Bromfield (the lieutenant of the ordinance); and an "excellent *radius Astronomicus* of ten foot longe," devised by and acquired from Gemma Frisius.[23] There were also "Two globes of Gerardus Mercators best making" on which Dee had written "divers reformations, both geographicall and celestiall" (particularly the motions of the comets he had observed); a collection of sea compasses; a great "magnes-stone, commonly called a load stone"; and "an excellent watch-clock made by one Dibbley" (the use of which was "very great, more then vulgar").

A second "very necessary appendix" to the library was the extensive collection of charters, seals, and coats of arms. These were kept in "a great case or frame of boxes," and numbered in the hundreds.[24] The principal documents pertained to "divers Irelandish territories, provinces, and lands," with details of landholding, submissions and tributes, "with seales appendant to the little writings thereof in parchment." There were also "evidences antient of some Welsh princes and noblemen, their great giftes of lands to the foundations or enrichings of sundry houses of religious men," and likewise evidences "of the Normans donations and gifts about and some hundred yeares after the conquest." These documents had an obvious antiquarian value—"as antiquarians can testifie for their part; and noble heralds can tell. . . ." But, like most antiquarian matters, the deeds were a potent force in the political and legal spheres—"as her Majesties officers for her interest and titles royall may think in their consideration." In the Elizabethan period the records pertaining to the titles of crown and nobility were in a primitive state, and some of the most important collections remained in private hands. To come by their records those hands often had to search the bowels of England's medieval repositories: Dee found some of his "hardly gotten moniments," which were "as in manner out of a dunghill," in the corner of a church, "wherein very many were utterly spoyled by rotting, through the raine . . . falling on them, through the decayed roofe of that church, lying desolate and wast at this houre." When such records were needed in the course of litigation—and they often were—noblemen were forced to pay a fee for copying and citation. Many of these records were already in royal custody, and during Elizabeth's reign ministers of the crown were encouraged to search out and to copy or acquire those that were not.[25] For verification of the value of his records Dee explained that they were "well knowne to divers, who had skyll, and were of office to deale with such monimentes": they had been consulted by "some antiquaries"; several of "her Majesties heralds" had seen them and taken notes out of them; and "other of the Clerks of the Records in the Tower satt whole dayes at my house in Mortlake, in gathering rarities to their liking out of them." At that time, when they were still in his possession, Dee had bequeathed them to the Tower where, he claimed, they properly belonged and where they would be if the queen and her council would issue a "publique warning" for their restitution.

The third appendix was a motley assortment of natural wonders.[26] Dee did not enumerate these in his account. He did, however, single out one curious item which, until it was stolen, adorned the shelves, walls, or ceiling of his library:

Whosoever came by one great bladder with about four pound weight, of a very sweetish thing, like a brownish gum in it, artificially prepared by thirty tymes purifying of it, hath more then I could well affoord him for one hundred crownes. . . .

Since he was in close contact with England's most prominent explorers and travelers it is probable that he possessed at least a small collection of plants, minerals, fossils, crafts, or costumes brought from remote lands. We also know that he had a number of maps, and these may—in line with contemporary fashion—have been on display.[27] And although they receive no mention in the "Compendious Rehearsall," we should not forget Dee's famous crystal ball (which graces the cover of Nicholas Clulee's book), his sigils on wax tablets (which later belonged to Cotton), and his collection of mirrors (including an obsidian disk of Spanish-American origin used for communication with angels, and several glasses used for optical experiments and illusions).[28] This last collection was used on one occasion to amuse the queen, and on another to assist William Bourne with his "Treatise on the Properties and Qualities of Glasses for Optical Purposes."[29]

Finally, Dee's library opened out onto "three laboratories, serving for *Pyrotechnia* [that is, (al)chemical exercises]." These rooms, both in location and in function, Dee accounted "an *appendix practical* to my foresaid library and studies" (my emphasis). The construction and furniture together—including "storehouses, chambers, and garrets" and "vessells (some of earth, some of mettall, some of glass, and some of mixt stuff)"—"cost me first and last above 200 pounds." All that remained in 1592 was a few damaged containers, "hardly worth forty shillings."

The *Bibliotheca Mortlacensis* must thus be seen as much more than a collection of books. Like many of the period's larger libraries it must be considered part of a more general place of knowledge, in which the books coexisted with laboratories, gardens, and cabinets of curiosities.[30] The term that was often applied to the entire complex was *museum*. In the early modern period this flexible word denoted a study, a library, a repository, a laboratory, and even a "Public Place for the Resort of Learned Men."[31] A visit to Archduke Ferdinand II's museum at Schloss Ambras "was possible only by way of a circuit, starting with the first hall of armour, which contained equipment for tournaments, and ending with the library . . ." (29). Antonio Giganti "conceived of his collection (including the library) as a unity. . . . His museum and his library, while occupying two different though intercommunicating spaces, were unified to such an extent that the ceiling of the latter formed an exhibition space, and the former contained a table which formed a physical base for research" (19). The Elector Augustus' *Kunstkammer* existed alongside a collection of coins, an armory, an *Anatomie-Kammer,* a treasury chamber, and his famous library (69). The Munich residence of Duke Albrecht V had four related collections: the household treasures, the *Kunstkammer,* the Antiquarium, and the library (79).[32] In seventeenth-century Rome the Jesuit Athanasius Kircher established his "enciclopedia concreta," the museum of the Collegio Romano.[33] And in the *True and Faithfull Relation* Dee described the study of Emperor Rudolf's scholar Hagecius, in which Dee and Kelley carried out their alchemical experiments: it was covered with writings "and very many *Hieroglyphical* Notes *Philosophical* in Birds, Fishes, Flowers, Fruits, Leaves and Six Vessels, as for the Philosopher's works."[34]

The situation in England was slightly but significantly different: whereas the European collections were generally main-

tained by heads of state, there was not in the sixteenth century—
despite the exhortations of several scholars—a royal or national
collection of British books, manuscripts, and antiquities. The
creation of museums was left to private scholars, churchmen,
ministers of the crown, and (to a limited extent) universities.[35]
Both Dee and Robert Cotton, the possessors of Elizabethan and
Jacobean England's most valuable libraries, began their programs
of collection only after petitioning the crown to create a national
library under royal auspices, and offering their services as agents or
librarians. Dee submitted his remarkable "Supplication . . . for the
recovery and preservation of ancient Writers and Monuments" to
Queen Mary on 15 January 1556.[36] In it he decried one of the disturbing side effects of the dissolution of the monasteries—the dispersal and loss of England's textual treasures. He bemoaned the
fact that many "a pretious jewel" had already been lost (including a
manuscript of "that wonderfull work of the sage and eloquent
Cicero de Republica" at Canterbury); but suggested that, if diligent
search were made, "the remnants of such incredible store, as well
of Writers Theological, as in all other liberal Sciences, might
be saved."[37] This would not only preserve "the passing excellent
works of our fore-fathers from rot and worms"; it would serve as the
foundation of a "Library Royal" which Dee offered to enrich with
printed books from the Continent and manuscript copies of the
best works from "the Vaticana at Rome, S. Marci at Venice, and the
like at Bononia, Florence, Vienna &c." Queen Mary's rejection of
the petition had a greater impact on her nation's heritage than on
Dee's career: under his own agency he acquired the monastic and
Continental books that became England's most valuable collection
during the reign of Mary's sister and successor.[38]

Dee signed the preface to the reader of his *Propaedeumata aphoristica* "Ex Musaeo nostro Mortlacensi," and it is likely that he
meant by "Musaeo nostro" more than "my study."[39] In an entertainment written for Gray's Inn in 1594, Francis Bacon's advocate
argued for the establishment of a centralized scholarly institution
with a library, a garden, a cabinet of natural and artificial works,
and a still-house.[40] At Mortlake, during the previous decades,
Dee had created just such an institution. His library was clearly
the centerpiece of his collection and, indeed, of his life. But his
purpose-built laboratories were integral to the design of his "acad-

emy," as were the collections of charters, scientific instruments, and natural curiosities. There is evidence to suggest that Dee's house was surrounded by flora and that he took an active interest in botany: his library, for instance, was well stocked with botanical works.[41] But Dee's diary entry on 20 May 1577 would seem to indicate that his garden was quite modest: on that day he hired "the barber of Cheswik, Walter Hooper" to maintain his "hedges and knots . . . with twise cutting in the yere at the least. . . ." And though he noted that Queen Elizabeth, when she came to see him on 17 September 1580, stood for some time beside his "garden in the felde," he was clearly unlikely to have fostered an example of the emblematic or philosophical garden popular among Renaissance rulers and Rosicrucians.[42]

THE PRIVATE LIBRARY AS PUBLIC COMMODITY

With the approach of Queen Elizabeth we progress from the library's content and layout to its use and influence. These considerations follow a natural progression (which makes their virtual absence from works on Dee all the more conspicuous): they are the key to the context of the *Bibliotheca Mortlacensis,* to its place in Dee's activities, and indeed to the place of libraries in early modern society. After all, no library exists in a vacuum and, as Roberts and Watson proclaim, "A library is important and influential only in-so-far as its owner (and his associates) read its books and made use of them."[43] This was perhaps more widely believed in Dee's time than in any other: Renaissance writings on the history and theory of libraries uniformly stressed their value not for meditation or preservation but for communication and application in academic and civic activities.[44] Dee's contemporary Thomas Bodley retired from government service after being passed over for the position of secretary of state. But, wishing to remain "a profitable Member of the State," he resolved to establish a university library at Oxford, convinced that "in my Solitude . . . I could not busy my self to better purpose, than by reducing that Place (which then in every Part lay ruined and wast) to the Publick use of Students."[45] On the Continent—at roughly the same time and near the end of his own career—Justus Lipsius wrote his *De Bibliothecis Syntagma* [or *Brief Outline of the History of Libraries*], in which he surveyed the libraries of Greece, Byzantium, and Rome. At the end of his final chapter, on the "Alexandrian Museum," he concluded: "I have nothing further that seems worth saying on this subject of libraries, except for a few words about their use [*fructum*]. If they stand empty . . . , if students [*homines*] do not frequent them and make use of their books, why were they ever established . . . ?" By cataloguing and analyzing the libraries of antiquity, Lipsius hoped to move Prince Charles to follow their precedents:

I close, O MOST ILLUSTRIOUS RULER, with the wish that you, a descendant of great men and born to do great things, may long continue in that work, worthy of the highest praise, which you have already begun—the work of encouraging the production of books and the cultivation of the liberal arts [*libris & litterisque propagandis*] among men, and so make your name for all time revered.[46]

Through their libraries, then, great collectors would not only earn the admiration of their contemporaries but ensure the long life of their reputation.

When Gabriel Naudé offered his *Avis pour Dresser une Bibliothèque* to the President de Mesme in 1627 he produced an updated list of notable libraries and noble librarians as a prelude to the same message, that there is "no expedient more honest and assur'd, to acquire a great reputation amongst the people, than in erecting of fair and magnificent *Libraries*, to devote and consecrate them afterward to the use of the Publick."[47] Naudé, who presided over the massive library of Cardinal Mazarin (which became, in effect, France's first public library), went on to explain that such a collection ought to have the widest scope: "a Library which is erected for the publick benefit ought to be universal" (C2r). By collecting books meet for all purposes, "Reformed Librarie-Keepers" (as John Dury described them) could become "Agents for the advancement of universal Learning."[48] This made them supremely valuable—and, more pointedly, employable—within both the republic of letters at large and the particular commonwealth they served.

In Mortlake Dee established a universal library and put it at the disposal of a wide range of students, from craftsmen to statesmen: it became, to paraphrase Francis Johnson, "a public amenity";[49] and Dee became, like Dury's reformed librarian, "a Factor and Trader for helps to Learning, and a Treasurer to keep them, and a dispenser to applie them to use. . . ."[50] His household was a bustling one, and his *familia* was on the order of his great Humanist predecessors. Dee maintained throughout his tenure at Mortlake a steady stream of resident and visiting students: aside from his children and household servants it is possible to trace more than twenty people who spent extended periods at his house in some scholarly capacity.[51] Most of them received some sort of instruction from Dee—for which (as we know from a few documented cases) he received tutorial fees. Many clearly assisted in his work: the variety of copyists' hands in the manuscripts he produced and owned suggests that some served as amanuenses; and some acted as assistants in his laboratory. Several went on to achieve their own scholarly prominence, including Thomas Digges, Maurice Kyffin,[52] and Roger Cook, who was later to build the still-houses used by Walter Ralegh and the earl of Northumberland during their incarceration in the Tower, and to follow Dee's footsteps to the court of Emperor Rudolf II, where he assisted Cornelis Drebbel in his alchemical experiments.[53]

Not everyone who used Dee's library should be considered a student or a member of his *familia*. Some scholars and statesmen made use of the library in the course of visits. It proved such an attractive and accessible site that Dee was inundated with both wanted and unwanted visitors—so many that in 1592, when he found it necessary to advertise its status, he called his house the "*Mortlacensi Hospitali Philosophorum peregrinantium* {Mortlake Hospice for wandering Philosophers}."[54] Indeed, with fortuitous timing, it would have been possible for a visitor to bump into Francis Bacon (on a day-trip from the court with Sir Thomas Wilkes), Richard Hakluyt (learning about King Arthur's discovery of Friesland), the governors of the Muscovy Company (planning a series of voyages in search of the Northwest Passage), or—on the occasion of an extraordinary governmental field trip—the queen and her entire Privy Council.[55] The records of visitors in Dee's diary sometimes give the impression that his house was a busy annex of the court. This is especially true during the early months of 1583. On 18 February, Dee reported that "the Lady Walsingham cam suddenly into my howse very freely" and, just after her departure, her husband Francis popped in accompanied by Edward Dyer. In another episode during the previous month, Walsingham arrived to find "by good luck" Adrian Gilbert. The most revealing account of a visit to the *Bibliotheca Mortlacensis* is offered by the gunner and mathematical practitioner William Bourne. In the 1580 edition of his *Regiment for the Sea,* a popular navigational textbook, he describes this scenario: "As upon a time I being with Master *Dee* at his house at *Murclacke,* we falling in talke about the disouerie to *Cathay* & so talked as touching the shipping[;] whereupon he opened a Booke and shewed me a note what number of ships the great *Cane* had readie at one time to goe vnto the sea about his affaires, surely you would thinke it vncredible, the number was 15000[,] surely a huge armie by sea: and then I replyed againe that it might be that they were but small things, and yet they might call them shippes, and then he turned vnto another place where the great *Cane* did send one of his daughters by sea, and did appoint 14. of his ships . . . beside all the rest of his daughters traine . . . which must bee no small number."[56] No better example could be provided of the use of Dee's library; from it we get a sense of Dee's command of its contents, of its influence on his contemporaries, and of its value to those who wished to advance learning and establish an empire.

Others made use of Dee's books through borrowing and lending arrangements.[57] On the last day of July 1590, Dee presented to Richard Ca[ve]ndish a copy of Zacharius' twelve letters, "written in French with my own hand." Dee thought this no small privilege, and he extracted from Cavendish an elaborate oath of secrecy: "he promised me, before my wife, never to disclose to any that he hath it; and that yf he dye before me he will restore it agayn to me; but if I dy befor him, that he shall deliver it to one of my sonnes, most fit among them to have it."[58] And on 12 June 1591 Dee lent to Robert Beale, the clerk of the Privy Council, a manuscript of the *Chronica Hollandiae Magna*—which he had himself borrowed from his associate Thomas Webb.[59]

On two occasions Dee assembled a considerable traveling library, shifting the *Bibliotheca*'s sphere of influence from Mortlake to Bohemia and, later, to Manchester. Roberts and Watson have identified the eight hundred books that Dee probably took with him on his Continental travels of 1583–89. Although most of the books would have influenced the Eastern European intellectual scene indirectly, by guiding the alchemical, mathematical, and cabalistic studies he carried out on behalf of his courtly patrons, volumes like his Greek manuscript of Boethius' *De Consolatione Philosophiae* made a more direct impression: in 1584 he presented it to the library of the Uniwersytet Jagiellonski in Cracow, where it remains.[60] While the number and nature of the books Dee took with him to Manchester went undocumented, we know of several loans he made to local people. In February 1597 he lent to Matthew Heton the Estienne Bible Concordance (Roberts and Watson, no. 1) and Christoph Pezel's *De coena* (Roberts and Watson, no. D17). On 17 December 1597 he lent a Spanish grammar (Roberts and Watson, no. 1670) to a Mr. Barlow, and on 19 July 1600 Randall Kemp borrowed Holinshed's *Chronicles* (Roberts and Watson, no. 1681). The other known loans were all in relation to the case of demonical possession known as "the Seven in Lancashire."[61] Dee himself was consulted; but, prudently refusing to take part in the proceedings, he sent in his place several books for the education of the local justice Edmund Hopwood. On 19 March 1597, Hopwood borrowed Wier's *De praestigiis daemonum* (Roberts and Watson, no. 862) and Menghi's *Fustis daemonum* (Roberts and Watson, D14). Several months later he also took out the *Malleus maleficarum* (Roberts and Watson, no. 1551) on extended loan.[62] As in Poland, Dee enriched the local stock of books in Manchester: at least one book, and probably many more, stayed behind when Dee returned to London.[63]

Several of Dee's manuscripts formed the basis for important publications. In the summer of 1563 Dee paid a visit to the *"restaurator mathematicarum"* of Urbino, Federico Commandino. He carried with him a Latin manuscript of Machometus Bagdedinus' treatise, *De Superficierum Divisionibus.* Before leaving he presented it to Commandino, who published it seven years later, with a preface by Dee.[64] One of Dee's manuscripts of Roger Bacon (now untraceable) was responsible for an important episode in what may be called Dee's Rosicrucian afterlife. While his personal affiliations with the Fraternity of the Rosy Cross are tenuous (at best), and while his authorship of the treatise *The Rosie Crucian Secrets* published under his name in 1985 is extremely unlikely,[65] Dee did provide a significant textual impetus to the group.[66] In 1618, an edition of Bacon's *Epistolae . . . de secretis operibus artis et naturae et de nullitate magiae* appeared in Hamburg, printed in the "bibliopolio Frobeniano" and associated with the Rosicrucian movement. The title page describes the book as "Opera Johannis Dee Londinensis e pluribus castigata . . . cum notis quibusdam partim ipsius Johannis Dee, partim edentis." Many of the printed marginal notes are initialed "JD" and derive from Dee's manuscript annotations.[67] It was not only as a preserver of Bacon's text that Dee was influential: the reproduction of his reading notes implies that Dee was also valued as an interpreter. Writing during the Rosicrucian scare in France, Gabriel Naudé prefaced an apology for Bacon's mathematical theories with a deferential note to Dee: "If we had the book which John Dee, citizen of London and a very learned philosopher and mathematician, says that he composed in defence of Roger Bacon [i.e., the apparently lost *Speculum unitatis, sive Apologia pro Fratre Rogerio Bacchone Anglo* of 1557] in which he shows that all that is said about his marvellous works should be ascribed to nature and mathematics, rather than to a commerce with demons, which he never had, I protest that I would speak no more about him. . . ."[68] Thus, less than twenty years after his death, Dee's textual remains were generating competing portraits—the cabalistic magician and the Baconian mathematician—in relation to a group whose own affiliations to occult philosophy and mainstream science were being contested.

One last question regarding the use of Dee's books merits consideration, and it may provide a final and compelling example of the public utility of Dee's private library. Roberts and Watson noticed that a "striking peculiarity" of the library was its great number of duplicates (42). Although they list a number of the multiple copies found in the catalogue, including "the lavish provision of 157 copies of ninety-two editions of Paracelsus' various works," they provide neither an adequate impression nor a detailed discussion of the phenomenon. By placing numerals next to entries in the catalogue, Dee indicated that he had multiple, identical copies of sixty-two different works—usually two, but up to four of each. A careful collation of the catalogue, based on Roberts and Watson's author index, revealed a further 352 titles found in more than one copy.[69] For many authors Dee had their complete as well as single works (often in multiple copies themselves). The most extreme case was Aristotle: Dee owned four copies of his *Opera*, as well as multiple copies of the *De Anima, De Caelo et Mundo, De*

Generatione et Corruptione, De Mundo, Ethica, Mechanica, Metaphysica (eleven copies), *Meteorologia, Organon* (eleven copies, plus multiple copies of the *Categoriae, Analytica Posteriora, Analytica Priora,* and *Topica* individually), *Parva Naturalia,* and *Physica.*[70] Dee also had the *Opera* and separate works of Achillinus, Archimedes, Boethius, Cassiodorus, Cicero, Ficino, Gauricus, Joachim of Fiore, Johannes of Damascus, Josephus, Lull, Nicholas of Cusa, Philo, Plato, Pontanus, Richard of St. Victor, Seneca, Synesius, Themistius, Theophrastus, and Xenophon. Many of the multiples represent widely read or canonical texts: given their influence, particularly upon Dee, some duplicate copies of works by Roger Bacon, Paracelsus, and Euclid are to be expected. But the presence of several copies of books such as John Peckham's *Perspectiva communis,* Guillaume Rabot's *Oratio de Gente,* Hieronymus Mercurialis' *Variae lectores,* or Leonhardt Thurneysser zum Thurn's *Prokategoris* is especially puzzling.

Why did Dee have duplicates and multiple copies at all? Passing over the distinct possibility that some of the multiple entries were mistakes, the phenomenon can be explained in part by the Humanist concern with the accuracy of texts. Many marginal notes attest to Dee's philological perspicuity: for a wide range of works he collated and compared manuscript and printed editions. This explanation most likely applies to those texts with messy transmissions—particularly those of the ancient Greeks—and to those texts with which Dee was involved in an editorial capacity. Of Euclid's *Elementa Geometrica,* for the first English translation of which he wrote his "Mathematicall Praeface," Dee had twenty printed copies (representing nineteen editions, some of them incomplete but many with important commentaries) as well as seven manuscripts.

Another possibility is that Dee stocked duplicate copies, especially of books that were difficult to acquire in England, in order to sell them. The pattern of Dee's duplicates does not resemble that of a retail seller of books, though his status as a freeman of the Mercers' Company (which he inherited from his father) would have allowed him to be one.[71] A more probable reason for the multiple copies lies in the presence of students in Dee's library. As Elisabeth Leedham-Green noted in her edition of *Books in Cambridge Inventories,* "several college Fellows in this survey had libraries apparently designed to fulfill more than their own personal needs. . . . It is reasonable to suppose that the duplicate texts in particular were either lent to their pupils or sold to them and subsequently re-purchased."[72] Dee's copy of the 1541 edition of Cicero's *Tusculanae Quaestiones* is an interesting case in point. At the bottom of the title page Dee wrote, "Iste liber pertinet ad me Johannem Dee teste Barleo, Smitheo, Odell, cum multis alijs." And on the next page he wrote an inscription that turned the volume over to Roger Cook.[73] Surviving books and their marginalia do not, however, afford us much insight into the multiple uses (and users) of multiple copies. All that we can say, ultimately, is that Dee knew from his own acquisition habits that materials lent to others might never find their way back; that he kept copies of some books on hand to present as gifts to other scholars or to patrons; and that his collection was extremely well stocked for exchanges of information both inside and outside the library's walls.

We leave the *Bibliotheca Mortlacensis,* then, with three general impressions. First, Dee's base of operations was his own household, and his textual activities were carried out alongside his domestic and communal duties. His study was not only the site of his reading and writing, but of managing his properties, raising his family, and attending to the medical needs of his neighbors. Second, Dee's library should also be considered, in the senses discussed above, a museum. Like most of the larger libraries of the early modern period, it was part of a general intellectual and scientific space in which the books coexisted with laboratories, gardens, and cabinets of curiosities. Third, it represented a place where court, city, and university could meet. Ideally situated for visits from Richmond, London, or abroad, and well equipped for intellectual inquiry, it offered a space where independent scholarship could be carried out and circulated among the academic, commercial, and political communities.

HOW PRIVATE WAS THE EARLY MODERN PRIVATE LIBRARY?

As the foregoing account of Dee's library is intended to suggest, the term "private library" is not one that we can afford to take for granted. While it strictly signifies a noninstitutional collection of books and manuscripts, it has taken on modern connotations that, in relation to early modern readers, are misleadingly anachronistic. The private library has become, by most accounts, diametrically opposed to the "public"; it is a place of isolation, even insulation. Inhabiting this space is the figure of the solitary scholar or the detached reader, retiring from society into repose among books, which are the sources of entertainment or the catalysts for contemplation.

This picture depends so heavily upon the case of Michel de Montaigne that I think it is fair to call it the "Montaigne Model."[74] As the story goes, in 1571 (at the age of thirty-eight) Montaigne renounced his public duties and returned to his country château, where he set about composing his *Essais*. He established a beautiful library, on the wall of which he inscribed, "Michel de Montaigne, long since bored with the slavery of parlement and public office but still vigorous, withdrew to lay his head on the breast of the learned Virgins in calm and security; he shall pass the remaining days of his life there. Hoping that fate will allow him to perfect this dwelling, this sweet paternal retreat, he has consecrated it to his freedom, tranquility, and leisure."[75] This picture is reinforced in his essay "On the Three Kinds of Commerce,"[76] where he claims that the third and best kind is that of a man with his books—which is to say, with himself. He describes his library as an oasis from public obligation: " 'Tis there that I am in my kingdom, and there I endeavour to make myself an absolute monarch, and to sequester this one corner from all society, conjugal, filial, and civil. . . ."[77] In his recent reconstruction of Montaigne's library, Adi Ophir calls it a "solitarium," in which Montaigne's self—the mold of the modern self—was studied and reconstituted.[78] As Ophir envisions it, the early modern library was a sort of solipsistic utopia, in which books "allow[ed] the self to meet itself without the distortion of public, social life." Roger Chartier cites the same passages from Montaigne's essay and comes to a similar conclusion: "The hours spent in the library are hours of withdrawal in two senses, which define the essence of privacy in the modern era: withdrawal from the public sphere, from civic responsibility, from the affairs of city and state; and withdrawal from the family, from the household, from the social responsibilities of domestic intimacy." These comments are clearly colored by their context—they are part of a

History of Private Life which attempts to identify the emergence of modern forms of privacy in the Renaissance period—but they do tend (unlike Chartier's other work) to reproduce the Montaigne Model as a Renaissance norm.[79]

Montaigne was not alone in stressing his aloneness. Indeed, as Steven Shapin has shown, there is a "pervasive topos in Western culture, from the Greeks onward, [which] stipulates that the most authentic intellectual agents are the most solitary."[80] This has been accompanied by, or expressed through, a "rhetoric of solitude," which can be set alongside the rhetoric of civic Humanism; a conflicting repertoire which "maintained that those seeking the highest forms of knowledge must live in relative solitude." What is at stake in this rhetoric is the authenticity and validity of scholarly (and especially scientific) activity, and it has flourished, significantly, during what can be considered "crises of legitimation" in the position and status of those who traded in knowledge. It is therefore worth bearing in mind that our picture of Montaigne's library rests entirely upon his own accounts—on taking him at his word, that is, in texts that are concerned precisely and classically with the development of the rhetoric of scholarly self-fashioning.

In Dee's case, the rhetoric of solitude has been supplemented by the "myth of the magus" which, to recall the previous chapter, presents him as a lonely ascetic seeking the secrets of the universe. Our brief visit to Dee's library, however, should be sufficient to question the use not only of the magus as a model for Dee, but of Montaigne as a model for the early modern reader. Montaigne's library, rather than being exemplary, was exceptional, and even (to a certain degree) fictional.

Two historical fields help to clarify this argument, and to offer alternatives to the Montaigne Model. First, recent work in publishing history, the history of the book, and the history of reading forces us to see libraries as embedded in broader networks of textual production and dissemination. While it is naturally less evident in Montaigne's case than in Dee's (since Dee constantly draws attention to the material conditions of his study—the dirt, the long hours, the interruptions—whereas Montaigne effaces such traces, reading and writing in a pristine and suspiciously autonomous environment), collecting and processing the information contained in a library on the scale of Montaigne's or Dee's was not a leisurely pursuit. It was hard work, and it entailed many kinds of commerce besides that of a man with his books.

Two examples from Dee's library illustrate the way other "commercial" interests intrude upon the solitary intercourse between a man and his books. First, when Dee prepared his catalogue in 1583 he called upon the assistance of a man named Andreas Fremonsheim. He was not a disinterested volunteer: he was, as Roberts has discovered, the London agent of the great Birkmann booksellers of Cologne. His motives for helping Dee to compile his inventory are not entirely clear, but when Dee left shortly thereafter on his long Continental sojourn, he had an outstanding debt to the Birkmanns of over sixty-three pounds. The second example is Dee's practice of writing wish lists or notices of particularly interesting holdings directly into the margins or flyleaves of his books. On the back flyleaf of one of his copies of Geoffrey of Monmouth, now in the library of Christ Church, Oxford, he listed the names and locations of six men who had "good store of moniments" and medieval manuscripts. Among them is the historian John Stow, "who set owt the sommary of the english Chronicle"; Rice ap Howell Bedo Dee, who gave Dee "the first note of my pedigree"; "Mr Cary in chepes side"; Mr D. Cay of Oxford, who "hath Caradocus Lancarvanensis"; and a "Mr. Clyderall" of Newcastle," who "hath a barell full of old histories of this land."[81]

A more striking and elaborate record of this latter practice is found in Dee's relationship with Conrad Gesner and his various *Bibliothecae*—the sixteenth century's foremost bibliographical guides.[82] Dee visited the great bibliographer and medical scholar on 23 April 1563, signing on that occasion Gesner's *Liber Amicorum;*[83] and he possessed a fairly complete set of his works. He owned the three-volume "Pandects" of the *Bibliotheca* (1548–49) which survives, apparently without annotations, at the Newark Parish Library (see entry no. 210 in Roberts & Watson). The same catalogue entry also contains Gesner's *Appendix Bibliothecae* of 1555, which can now be found at the British Library.[84] It has Dee's underlining and notes throughout—including corrections and expansions of entries and notices of possessors of various works—and on the back flyleaf there is a handwritten list of 110 books.[85] In 1574 Josias Simler published an "Epitome" of the *Bibliotheca,* and

Dee's copy (probably Roberts & Watson, no. 282) has very recently been acquired by the Bodleian Library. It has even fuller annotations than the 1555 *Appendix,* and its margins document Dee's extensive connections with the great booksellers and book collectors of the Continent.[86] Dee's notes in these volumes were of value not only to himself: John Davis picked several of them for his haul during the "spoiling" of the library, and Simler himself hoped to incorporate Dee's comments into the second edition of the *Epitome.*[87]

The other useful body of work, which may at first appear far less relevant than the bibliographical disciplines, is the history of science—or, more specifically, the historical sociology of science. Recent studies by the likes of Steven Shapin, Simon Schaffer, and Owen Hannaway have encouraged us to put scientific activity in its context by putting it, literally, in its place; by attending to what they call, simply enough, the "place of knowledge."[88] Work in this field has been principally concerned with the observatory and the laboratory and (except for Ophir's problematic treatment of Montaigne) has not yet considered the library as a place where science is carried out and where knowledge is produced.[89]

According to Ophir, and virtually all other commentators,[90] "the object that books mediate for Montaigne" is his isolated self: it "is not out there, ready for observation, reachable through voyage or experiment," nor could books "provide a solid frame of reference" by which external objects "could have appeared . . . as an object of knowledge."[91] Even if this is true of Montaigne, this division between the book and the material world does not apply to most readers. In early modern science—and literature and politics—the book was by all means a medium of observation, voyage, and experiment, which not only provided a solid frame of reference but lent (through the authority invoked in the reference) considerable argumentative force.[92] This is most vividly represented by Dee's activities in the area of maritime expansion (to which I devote Chapter 7 below). Dee collected cosmographical texts and collections of voyages and canvassed European geographers for their opinions about countries, markets, and passages. These informed the services he provided for the men who actually made the voyages: he taught them the rudiments of astronomy, drew them maps, and helped them stock their on-ship libraries. They in turn brought back to him maps and accounts of their observations, as well as physical artifacts. And finally he wrote new texts to persuade the government and merchant backers to invest in new voyages, new experiments that would build on the experiences of earlier ventures.

In such a process the interface between library and world is complicated and blurred.[93] According to the Montaigne Model there operated in the library a rigid boundary, one that "distinguished the private from the public" and "distanced the self from others."[94] In a space like Dee's library, as in Schaffer's and Shapin's work on seventeenth-century scientific spaces, that boundary functioned more as a membrane than as a borderline: it let certain people, texts, and ideas in and kept others out. It served rather to conflate public and private by making private knowledge credible through its affiliation with the city or court or, to put it another way, valuable through its application to the public sphere.

This leads me to recommend, by way of conclusion, a shift in vocabulary from "private" to "privy." Scatological references aside, the primary connotations of this term in early modern England are suggested by its cognates such as "privileged," its synonyms such as "secret" and "proper," and its use in institutions such as the "Privy Council," the "Privy Chamber," and "secret or privy service." In Samuel Johnson's dictionary, as in the *Oxford English Dictionary,* it simultaneously implies exclusion (in the sense of secret or clandestine) and inclusion (in the sense of being "admitted to secrets of state" or "to participation of knowledge").[95] The private (or privy) library was thus less asocial and apolitical than selectively social and political. It could only be otherwise in cases where the physical space of reading was absolutely separate from its socioprofessional status, where no interest operated except self-interest, or where the reader had minimal connections or maximal privilege. Throughout the sixteenth century, at least, such situations must have been exceedingly rare, and it took Montaigne's boldness and virtuosity (as well, of course, as his status and privilege) to make it a model. The private library and the solitary scholarly reader are less representations of early modern reality than rhetorical strategies by which early modern subjects negotiated their place in society.

CODA: "BURN BUT HIS BOOKS"

Renaissance libraries were powerful sites of intellectual creativity, social status, and political influence. But they were also the focus of anxiety, resentment, and violence. The first age of printing was also an age of censorship and book burning. Early modern authorities had, perhaps, more to lose than to gain from the proliferation of printed information; and those who commanded that information were at once empowered and endangered by their textual collections and skills.

Caliban, having stored up years of resentment while subject to Prospero's textual mastery, dreamed up a violent revenge upon not just the tyrant but his books. He urged his coconspirators Stefano and Trinculo,

> . . . thou mayst brain him,
> Having first seiz'd his books; or with a log
> Batter his skull, or paunch him with a stake,
> Or cut his wezand with thy knife. Remember
> First to possess his books; for without them
> He's but a sot, as I am, nor hath not
> One spirit to command—they all do hate him
> As rootedly as I. Burn but his books.
> (*The Tempest,* III, ii, 86–93)

As Caliban tried to impress upon his cohorts, the source of Prospero's power is his books. With them he controls servants, spirits, and the very elements; without them he has no subordinates and is vulnerable.

Dee was acutely aware of the value of his library and of the extent to which his ability to command information, influence people, and shape events was bound up with his textual possessions—and it is this form of magic rather than a reputation for conjuring that connects Dee with Prospero. Being the guardian of his country's largest collection of books and manuscripts was, however, a grave responsibility, and it gave rise to considerable anxiety. On 24 November 1582 Dee was visited by an extraordinary nightmare: "I dremed that I was dead, and after my bowels were taken out I walked and talked with diverse, and among other the Lord

Thresorer who was come to my house to burn my bokes. . . ."[96]
This was to be a recurring dream: almost seven years later he again
recorded a nocturnal assault on his library, a "terrible dream that
Mr. [Edward] Kelly wold by force bereave me of my bokes." Upon
returning to England—the month after his dream about Mr.
Kelley—Dee found that his dreams had become a terrible reality:
in his absence the library had been sacked and many of his most
valuable volumes and instruments were missing or destroyed—
the work not of an angry mob suspicious of Dee's learning, but
rather (as in both dreams) of associates appreciative or envious of its
power.

Dee's worries thus proved well founded, and his was not the only
library to come under attack. Virtually every major contemporary
collection became the object of suspicion or suppression. The
Elizabethan government placed John Stow under surveillance: his
books were searched and some items were confiscated. Robert
Cotton's collection came, during the reign of Charles I, to be
perceived as more a threat than an asset to the ruling powers, and it
was closed by a royal order.[97] The same fate befell the Parisian
library of Cardinal Mazarin, and Naudé, its librarian, was forced
into exile.[98]

These darker dynamics, like the pages that lined pie tins or rot-
ted on dung piles in ruined churches, serve as forceful reminders of
the contingency—and, often, the cruelty—of historical transmission. But the attacks on libraries, and the personal condemnations
that accompanied them, betray a more significant phenomenon:
there were in the early modern period deep-seated uncertainties
about the power of information and those who possessed it. Sadly,
an abundance of modern examples—some far more atrocious than
their early modern precedents—suggests that they have not been
(and may never be) resolved.

THREE

Reading

Modern Theory and Early
Modern Practice

The story of man's travels through his own texts remains in large measure unknown. —Michel de Certeau, *The Practice of Everyday Life*

. . . in it, as in a Magazine, are stored vp abundance of both *Precepts* and *Examples*, collected out of the best Monuments of Auncient and Moderne Writers. . . . In so much that any of what degree soever shall heere readily find laid vp to his hand not onely pertinent *Precepts*, but wholesome *Examples* also accomodated and fitted for their seuerall uses and affaires. Whence it is, that this Worke may not vnfitly bee titled, *A LIVING LIBRARIE*. —Philipp Camerarius, *The Living Librarie, or, Meditations and Observations Historical, Natural, Moral, Political, and Poetical*

INTRODUCTION

The interaction of texts and readers has in recent years emerged as one of the most central subjects of theory and research in the humanities. Scholars from the many disciplines concerned with texts have converged on the question of how readers in past and present cultures "encounter and manipulate the written word."[1] There is, then, a field—though not yet a discipline, or inter-discipline—within which the study of Dee's reading practices must be situated: in this chapter I will provide a critical account of this field as a prelude to my own attempt at an "archaeology of reading practices."[2] I begin by reviewing the theoretical approaches currently available, and then move on to the processes by which, and the conditions under which, texts were consumed, read, and used in early modern England—particularly the relation of reading to pedagogical and professional practices. Finally I introduce the traces of active reading left in sixteenth-century books—marginal annotations, or "*adversaria*"—by surveying the "Adv." class in the Cambridge University Library and the marginalia of Sir Thomas Smith.

READING IN THEORY

While their specific contributions have had a variety of effects on a range of disciplines, modern theorists of reading have made an invaluable general contribution to the study of texts by questioning received wisdom on the place of reading. They have challenged the reader's subordination to the author and the text, positing the reader as more of an equal partner in the creation of meaning and value. They have explored the ways in which texts are more than frozen, transparent vehicles for ideas by calling attention to their contexts and to the processes of interpretation and appropriation that accompany their production and consumption. And, above all, they have made reading "conspicuous" and opened it to study by warning against taking it for granted and consigning it to common sense. As Robert Darnton has suggested, reading is "not always and everywhere the same. We may think of it as a straightforward process of lifting information from a page; but . . . it must be sifted, sorted, and interpreted."[3] It is, paradoxically, reading's very pervasiveness that has rendered it imperceptible: it "is such a matter of course that, at first glance, it seems there is nothing to say about it."[4] Textual scholars and *lecturers*—in effect, professional readers—ought to be most sensitive to reading techniques and strategies; yet they have often been the most susceptible to the reproduction—witting or unwitting—of regulating presuppositions and misleading assumptions.[5]

Literary criticism, which seems the most obvious place to begin a survey of approaches to reading, has witnessed in recent years a "return of the reader."[6] This has been part of an attempt to counter the formalist assumptions that prevailed in English departments through much of the century. In reaction to the rigid belief in the self-sufficiency of texts (i.e., that authors encode in texts all that is necessary for their interpretation and appreciation), there has developed a theory of "reader-response"—or, more generally, a variety of "reception theories."[7] Advocates of these approaches have sought to reassert the indispensable contributions readers make to the textual event. Reader-Response critics have attempted to level—and some even to invert—the hierarchy established by the so-called New Critics, which placed the text ("the prime mover of all meanings and emotions") at the top, the "mediating critic" in the middle, and the "invisible, mute, imperceptible, ghostly" reader at the bottom.[8] Reader-Response criticism undertakes, in short, to expose the unacknowledged assumptions and ideologies of formalist literary teaching and to make explicit the implicit hermeneutics of the reading process.

The critic responsible for the most articulated reception theory is Wolfgang Iser. His attention to the act of reading has generated a fully fledged phenomenological theory of aesthetic response.[9] This theory follows the imperative of Reader-Response criticism in that it "attempts to bring into play the imaginative and perceptive faculties of the reader."[10] But it fails, in a manner symptomatic of Reader-Response criticism in general, to provide an alternative to earlier formalist modes of carrying out, studying, and teaching readings. Iser is reluctant to renounce his faith in a privileged, almost sacred, text: in the interaction between the reader and the text it is the latter that has most control.[11] As with the New Critics, the text is carefully encoded with the keys to its meaning: the reader is a necessary but passive and anonymous presence who 'realizes' that meaning. Iser's "reading subject . . . is not a specific, historically situated individual but a transhistorical mind whose activities are, at least formally, everywhere the same."[12] Even when he and like-minded critics introduce contextual concerns, they show little interest in turning from ideal or archetypal readers to actual ones. The pages of Reader-Response works are peopled with every kind of reader except the real and historical: Freund lists the mock reader (Gibson), the implied reader (Booth and Iser), the model reader (Eco), the super-reader (Riffaterre), the inscribed or encoded reader (Brooke-Rose), and the ideal reader (Culler).[13]

Deconstruction is the most celebrated and controversial case of a literary theory that ultimately substitutes a new formalism for the old one it derides. Yet, there is no denying that its practitioners are some of the most virtuosic readers in the academy; and—at least in theory—their method calls for a close, and historicized, reading.

J. Hillis Miller, one of the leading American apologists for deconstruction, is rightly suspicious of critics who take the mechanical contextualization of a text as an end in itself: "even when the
exact relation of the text to its context has been identified, the
work of interpretation has only begun. The difficult business of
actually reading the work . . . still remains to be done."[14] For
Miller, the "fundamental task, the new rationale for the humanities is to teach reading and the effective writing that can only
come from or accompany a sophisticated ability to read."[15] Yet this
teaching is undermined by an inadequate attention to extratextual
forces—such as the conditions of production and reproduction and
the cultural baggage the teacher and the student bring to their
readings—and by a playful but ultimately crippling belief in
absolute indeterminacy.[16]

While the deconstructive act of reading may, furthermore, be
endlessly interpretive and even endlessly intertextual, it is marked
by an almost Romantic withdrawal from the interpersonal. This
may be a latent trend in the work of Miller; but it is flagrant in the
writings of Maurice Blanchot, one of the most influential forebears
of deconstruction. He has argued that textual activity—at least
when it involves literary texts—is dependent upon an "essential
solitude."[17] Reading can be an affirmative and ecstatically creative
act; but it is virtually unconstrained by history and society, and it
has no impact upon the autonomous power of the author's text.[18]
Blanchot's reader may meet and struggle with a text; but the
textual event is not a matter of communication: the reader is turned
inward and speaks neither to the author nor to other readers. For
Blanchot, "Reading is not a conversation, it does not discuss, it
does not question."[19] In an outrageous and emblematic gesture,
Blanchot contributed throughout the 1960s a number of dialogues
and interviews to the *Nouvelle Revue Française:* in each case, the two
speakers were Blanchot and himself.[20]

From several corners of the academic world—across national
and disciplinary boundaries—there has emerged a general approach that I have found more helpful in analyzing textual transmissions: it is best captured by D. F. McKenzie's phrase "the
sociology of texts." McKenzie's own studies (and especially the
manifesto delivered in his Panizzi Lectures at the British Library)
have encouraged the reorientation of the field of bibliography to

include the study of "not only the technical but the social processes of transmission."[21] This has dramatically broadened the scope of textual studies, and the arena of textual activity. As Jerome McGann put it in his review of McKenzie, "one has to take the entirety of the language event as the object of interpretation. Indeed, one has to proceed from the position that language is more properly conceived as an event than a medium: not a container or even an avenue of meaning, but an extended field of communicative action."[22] Most established bibliographers have resisted McKenzie's and McGann's program, because they feel their traditional *raison d'être* (the establishment of authorial intent through editorial methods) is discarded;[23] but there are encouraging signs that bibliography has entered into a fruitful dialogue with the other disciplines that study the lives of texts and the sociohistorical factors that shape their transmissions between people and through time.[24]

Sociological bibliography's closest neighbor is that sector of historical studies known as "the history of the book." Its main proponents, Roger Chartier and Robert Darnton, have focused on books as "an historical and cultural phenomenon," recognizing that they are "more than merely a vehicle for a text."[25] For one practitioner, the history of the book can be distinguished from printing history (and related approaches to texts) "because of its concern with readers and the act of reading"; it attends not just to "the what, but the how, or process of reading."[26] This has involved forays from bibliography into anthropology and social and economic history—in pursuit of a sense of how individuals represented and gave meaning to their world, how the written word sought to influence beliefs and actions, and how textual access and skills differed between social groups.[27] In concentrating on the "appropriation" of texts—"the differentiated uses . . . of the same goods, the same ideas, and the same actions"—historians of the book not only have stressed the importance of contextualization but have emphasized the possibilities for cultural variation and plurality within cultures.[28]

Although it is a part of a highly distinct and often downright specialized discipline, the field of "sociolinguistics" is of direct relevance to the "sociology of texts." Taking as its starting point Saussure's axiom, "Language is a social fact," it attempts to interpret language—and texts—within a sociocultural context.[29] Sociolinguists conceive of language as fundamentally interpersonal, and for most the interaction of readers and writers can be "dramatized as a communicative event."[30] Although they do not generally consider such events in past cultures—and therefore often ignore the significant differences between speakers/listeners and readers/writers—the sociolinguists' study of written discourse is clearly compatible with the sociology of texts. In his research on written discourse Martin Nystrand adopts a "social interactive position in which the text is interesting less as the means whereby speakers act on listeners and more as the functional, interpretive link between what writers have to say and readers want to know."[31]

Sociolinguistics—and particularly the work of J. L. Austin and J. R. Searle—has been instrumental in leading a number of recent historians of political thought (most prominently Quentin Skinner) in the direction of the sociology of texts. In some of the most closely argued critiques of academic reading practices, they have called for the recovery of the contexts of texts—the voices of the argument represented by every textual event.[32] With very few exceptions, however, their own work has yet to engage with the methods and evidence of the sociology of texts. Their contexts have tended to be discursive more than socioeconomic; their readings have been more concerned to establish authorial intent than to trace readerly appropriation; and the debates they recover have generally given voice only to the most canonical writers.

The question of literacy, a subject that has traditionally remained within the domain of linguistics, has been taken up to great effect by scholars from a number of other disciplines. Chartier has pointed out that our modern conception of literate reading is inadequate to understand Renaissance reading practices: "Full comprehension of that culture presupposes the view that access to the written word was a process much more broadly defined than simply the silent reading of an individual, in isolation, literacy in the classic sense."[33] This lesson has been better assimilated, however, by students of medieval intellectual culture. Mary Carruthers explains that, "as a concept, literacy privileges a physical artifact, the writing support, over the social and rhetorical process that a text both records and generates, namely, the composition by an author and its reception by an audience." Like her fellow medievalist Brian Stock, Carruthers has asserted the need to consider orality and literacy not so much as *doxis* but as *praxis*.[34]

The sociology of texts, finally, owes no small debt to sociology itself. For McKenzie sociology "directs us to consider the human motives and interactions which texts involve at every stage of their production, transmission and consumption" and "alerts us to the roles of institutions, and their own complex structures, in affecting the forms of social discourse, past and present."[35] The interpenetration of sociology and literature is hardly new. Robert Escarpit's classic study, *Sociology of Literature,* took as its purview—as Malcolm Bradbury wrote in his introduction to the English translation—"the entire environment of literary creation, distribution and consumption." And Raymond Williams's textbook, *Marxism and Literature,* is a full account, from a Marxist perspective, of the interplay between texts and sociocultural contexts. These works join with others from the sociology of texts to form a larger project to challenge the traditional conception of textual and (more generally) cultural consumption. Their concern with what Michel de Certeau called "the ideology of 'informing' through books" challenges the passivity of the reading process, and allows us to "discover creative activity where it has been denied that any exists."[36]

What all of this suggests is that reading has played an important role in society, and that it must be studied as an activity in particular contexts; as a process not only of reception but of appropriation, and an act of mediation between textual information and readers with specific skills, interests, and needs.[37] Theories of reading are important, but they must give way to, and be grounded in, histories of the reading practices of actual readers.

READING IN HISTORY

Stephen Greenblatt, according to his now-famous confession, "began with the desire to speak with the dead."[38] Those of us who share his desire have much to learn from Renaissance readings of Renaissance (and pre-Renaissance) texts. One of the best, and least explored, ways to converse with the dead is to study *their* conversations with the dead; to listen to their voices as they confronted the texts that they inherited. Any attempt to reconstruct Renaissance reading practices confronts, however, an immediate and daunting difficulty: compared with the exhaustive attention paid to Renaissance texts, Renaissance readers have been virtually ignored. There is thus little historical work of direct help in filling out the backdrop, and even less work on particular readers available for comparative study.[39] Indeed, a recent article with the promising title "Reconstructing Elizabethan Reading" restricts itself to the general strategies available to Elizabethan readers, since "we still [do not] have an individual reader to examine."[40] On the contrary, we have many individual readers, and readings, to examine—Dee and Gabriel Harvey are only the grandest examples—and it is from them that we can hope to gain detailed and intimate knowledge of how Renaissance readers confronted and manipulated the written word.[41]

Dee, like most of his contemporaries, did not passively receive information but actively "sifted, sorted, and interpreted" it.[42] He did not just read texts to learn from them in a disinterested process of self-edification: he read them to use them. This was one of the guiding principles of the educational program to which students like Dee were subjected in mid-Tudor Cambridge, and which prepared them for textual activities in a range of professional roles. It is wrong to see this program as narrowly rhetorical and grammatical: as Joan Simon asserts, "in Erasmus' and Vives' framework of reading authors . . . grammar is always seen as a means to an end."[43] At least among humanistically trained readers, reading itself was always a means to an end—or, as Jardine and Grafton put it, a "goal-oriented activity"[44]—whether that end was textual (as in the efforts of editors and philologists to improve the transmission of inherited texts) or political (as in the efforts of civically minded scholars to apply their reading to the advancement of the commonwealth). This involved, first and foremost, the surveying of available information. It had to be processed, by digesting its contents—or, to continue the geographical metaphor, mapping its contours—and by gathering, in one way or another, pieces useful for meeting the reader's future needs.

One of the key strategies guiding scholarly reading practices during the sixteenth century was the collection of a thesaurus ("treasury" or "storehouse") of useful phrases, images, and ideas. Annotations entered directly in the margins of books were a common and economical method. But Renaissance readers also used notebooks, often organized by a set of preconceived subjects or "topics" (i.e., *loci communes* or common places). As Walter Ong reminds us in his foreword to the classic study of the subject, the Renaissance was the age of the commonplace; an age when (unlike our own) imitation and the use of preprocessed materials were not only allowed but expected, and when the term *commonplace* was far from derogatory.[45] By 1627 a collector, reader, or writer could turn to "all sorts of *Commonplaces, Dictionaries, Mixtures,* several *Lections, Collections of Sentences,* and other like *Repertories.*"[46] And in 1594 Edward Vaughan published his textbook on efficient biblical reading, entitled *Ten Introductions:* it explained "How to read, and in reading, how to vnderstand; and in vnderstanding, how to bear in mind all the bookes, chapters, and verses contained in the holie Bible" (full title). In his final "introduction" he gave unusually explicit instructions for the construction and use of commonplace books: "You must digest in a writing booke of two quires, after the maner of common places: one of the same places or titles must be at the vpper end of euerie second leafe in Quarto; and be sure to place nothing vnderneath but such matter as the place and title re-quireth. And when you haue so gone ouer and written all your booke, then cast it aside, and take another after the same order. . . . Thus doe once more in another booke, and then you shall be able readily and roundly, to speake artificially and diuinely of all things necessarie to saluation . . ." (K5v–K6r).[47] The ultimate value of this method is therefore, as Rudolph Agricola suggested, that "it gathers together whatever can build up the resources of the future speaker or writer"[48]—allowing them to discourse fully and "to the purpose upon all subjects."[49]

This method is not simply a mechanistic routine: it involves "imaginative expenditure, a version of the rhetorical procedure of finding out, discovering, or inventing the potential meaning concealed in any figure."[50] It is not so much a question of cracking the code of a text as determining its relevance and applicability in contexts often very different from that in which it was produced. An anonymous student born in 1583 wrote in his commonplace book a "Compendious & Profitable Way of Studying," suggesting that a reader should "note some Rhetoricall expressions, Description, or some very apt Simile, or a very applicative story, & the most choise morrall sentences, & here a mans sense must direct him, when he considers how aptly such a thing would fitt with an exercise of his."[51] Reading thus provided resources for individual scholars, with their peculiar skills and interests, to apply textual information to the development of their discursive skills and, more broadly, to the management of their lives. Such preparation aimed at the accumulation of *copia* for the sake not only of *eloquentia* but of *sapientia* and *prudentia*; it concerned the interrelated capacities "of the prudent man to discern courses of action, and of the orator to furnish discursive motivation for undertaking courses of action."[52] The lessons gleaned from active reading, then, potentially served exercises in just about every sphere—the military, the academic, the political, and the domestic.

The culmination of this program is captured in the Renaissance trope that I appropriated in the title of the previous chapter—a "living library."[53] In the Tudor and Stuart period both books and people were pictured as animated and compendious collections of useful textual knowledge. In 1621 John Molle published a translation of Philipp Camerarius' *Operae horarum subsicivarum:* he called it *The Living Librarie, or, Meditations and Observations Historical, Natural, Moral, Political, and Poetical.* In justifying his title, Molle's preface to the reader concisely conveyed the principles of the volume: "in it, as in a Magazine, are stored vp abundance of both *Precepts* and *Examples,* collected out of the best Monuments of Auncient and Moderne Writers. . . . In so much that any of what degree soever shall heere readily find laid vp to his hand not onely pertinent *Precepts,* but wholesome *Examples* also accomodated and fitted for their seuerall uses and affaires. Whence it is, that this Worke may not vnfitly bee titled, *A LIVING LIBRARIE* . . ." (A5v).

In 1609, when he published his response to the exiled Catholic Robert Parsons, William Barlow applied these terms to King James I, describing "his Maiesties Table for the most part at times of *Repast*" as "a little *vniuersitie,* compassed with *Learned men* in all professions, and his Maiesty in the middest of them . . . *a liuing Library,* furnished at all hands, to *reply, answer, obiect, resolve, discourse, explane.*"[54] In the same year Sir Robert Dallington produced a collection of *Aphorismes Civill and Militarie,* based loosely on Guicciardini, which described James in similar terms. In dedicating the manuscript to Prince Henry, he offered the work as a means to "en-lighten by knowledge, & en-flame by Example" the "lively Sparks, in your Princely Nature." While the "books of History" that Dallington's text summarizes are but "mute Maisters" of knowledge, Henry ought to turn to his father for "a Living Booke" of example.[55] For Joseph Hall, however, the only figure to whom these terms truly applied was the Oxford don John Rainolds. In his *Epistles* of 1608, Hall claimed that "he alone was a well-furnished library, full of all faculties, of all studies, of all learning. . . ." And in his *Defensio ecclesiae anglicanae,* Richard Crakanthorpe referred to Rainolds as "a walking library of all learning and all knowledge."[56]

Naturally, the command of texts that turned people into living libraries also made them useful to others; scholarly readers, in a number of professional guises, used their methods to serve as mediators (or "facilitators") for a wide range of intellectual, governmental, and commercial interest groups.[57] They did so through writings, of course, but also through "conferences." The Elizabethan schoolmaster Richard Mulcaster asserted that "Priuate studie tied to one booke led by one braine [is] not alway[s] the best": for "iudiciall learning" one must consult an expert scholar "who hath red, and digested all the best bookes." Then, "hauing in one lecture [i.e., reading] the benefit of his *readers* vniuersall studie, and that so fitted to his hand . . . he may streight way vse it, without further thinking on. . . ." Mulcaster recommended that these scholars be maintained with a generous allowance by those who would "vse" them: the employer can spend on them what he would have spent on his books, since "his *reader* is his librarie."[58]

Throughout the early modern period reading and conference were set alongside each other as the twin means to fruitful instruction. Naudé outlined these two precepts of consultation: "The First is, to take the counsel and advice of such as are able to give it, consert with and animate us *viva voce.* . . . The Second is, to consult, and diligently to collect those few Precepts that may be deduc'd from the Books of some Authors . . . and govern ones self by the greatest and most renowned Bibliotheques which were ever erected" (B6v–B7r). And Dury advocated the consultation of scholars, since "by their mutual Association, Communication, and Assistance in Reading, Meditating and conferring about profitable matters, they may not onely perfit their own Abilities, but advance the superstructures of all Learning to that perfection."[59] Perhaps

the most explicit endorsement of the consultation and employment of professional readers was given by Robert Devereux, earl of
Essex. Among the Tanner MSS of the Bodleian Library there is a
letter endorsed "Robert Earl of Essex to Sr Foulk Grevill." It begins, "Cousin Foulke; you tell me you are going to Cambridge and
that the Ends of yor going are, to get a Scholar to yor liking, to liue
wth you, and some 2, or 3 others to remain in the Uniuersitie, and
gather for you; and you require my Opinion, what Instruction, you
shall giue those Gatherers. . . . Hee that shall out of his own
Reading gather for the use of another, must (as I think) do it by
Epitome, or Abridgment, or under Heads, and common places."[60]
And on 4 January 1595 he wrote to the young earl of Rutland, who
was about to embark on a grand tour. In this letter he described the
two stages in the acquisition of knowledge: first, "to conceive or
understand," and second, "to lay up or remember." To help with
the latter Essex prescribed the use of "notes and abridgments." For
assistance with the former he recommended that Rutland "read
with somebody . . . and to that end you must either carry over with
you some good general scholar, or make some abode in the universities." In his own education Essex had found such consultation
invaluable: "when the little that I had learned had taught me to
find out mine own emptiness, I profited more by some expert man
in half a day's conference, than by myself in a month's study." He
concluded "this point of conference with this advice, that your
L[ordship] shal rather go a hundred miles to speak with a wise
man, than five to see a fair town."[61]

The writings of professional readers typically provided learned
information and arguments to answer an inquiry or support a
cause. As we have seen, they often employed the techniques—and
the rhetoric—of summarizing, epitomizing, abridging, and collecting, which became a centerpiece of "pragmatic" Humanism.
These methods were prerequisites for further education and careers
in the legal profession,[62] and for other forms of scholarly civil service. They pervaded published expositions, from Moses Pflacher's
*Analysis Typica Omnium cum Veteris tum Noui Testamenti Librorum
Historicorum* (1587), which consisted entirely of Ramist tables, to
the *Beautifull Blossomes* "gathered by John Byshop, from the best
trees of all kyndes, Diuine, Philosophicall, Astronomicall, Cosmographical, Historical, & Humane . . . to the vnspeakable both
pleasure and profite of all such as wil vouchsafe to vse them" (Lon-

don, 1577—title-page). They governed the ambitious reading program of the Warwickshire magistrate Sir John Newdigate, who left behind a corpus of manuscripts which "consist, for the most part, of verbatim quotations from, and summaries of, authors he has read."[63] And, as Ann Blair has recently suggested, they provide the key to Jean Bodin's *Universae Naturae Theatrum* and its cultural context.[64] The employment of such techniques, finally, could serve as an advertisement of a scholar's skills. Along with his *Discourse of Western Planting,* Richard Hakluyt (then a lecturer at Christ Church, Oxford) offered Queen Elizabeth a Latin *Analysis,* or epitome, of Aristotle's *Politics.* Lawrence Ryan suggested that "since he was taking leave from the university to join the retinue of an ambassador, it was appropriate to afford some evidence of his knowledge (at least theoretical) of politics."[65] But the document was evidence less of his knowledge of politics than of his reading practices and his desire to employ them in the queen's service.

Perhaps the most general principle that emerges from these varied sources is the supreme value Renaissance writers placed on the application—particularly the political application—of reading. It is not only Harvey's reading practices that reveal a "programme to master the whole world of learning and make it readily usable in political action."[66] Dury proposed that no student should be "dismissed out of the Schools, till they are able to make use of all sorts of Books, and direct themselvs profitably in everie cours of Studie or Action. . . ."[67] After he graduated, Francis Bacon certainly possessed and exploited these abilities; and in his own writings on education he suggested that reading had to be accompanied by communication ("Reading maketh a full man; conference a ready man; and writing an exact man") and supplemented by action ("[studies] perfect nature, and are perfected by experience").[68] For one Elizabethan, this program was not only the path to understanding but the very "Highway to Honour": ". . . by reasoning, reading, and conuersing with wise men, a man may vnderstand much: yet without practise all is nothing."[69]

"ADVERSARIA" IN THE CAMBRIDGE UNIVERSITY LIBRARY

Reading, I have suggested, is adversarial: the text is the site of an active and biased appropriation of the author's material. This idea is conveyed in the very name that is formally given to volumes whose margins contain traces of active reading—*adversaria*. This term need not set reader and writer against each other in enmity: indeed, the Humanists often referred to texts as their friends—even as the disembodied voices of absent friends. But *adversaria* certainly mark an engagement, and sometimes a struggle; the marginal notes are (as the term's literal translation suggests) "opposite" the text, and sometimes in opposition to it. There is an entire collection in the Cambridge University Library devoted to such adversarial volumes—the "Adv." (for *adversaria*) classmarks.[70] These volumes were withdrawn from their original collections and joined into a new group in the middle of the nineteenth century, presumably because the annotations were thought to be of more value or interest than the texts in which they appear. Though it is neither a complete nor an entirely representative class,[71] the Adv. collection does provide a convenient introduction to the varieties of adversarial reading carried out by Dee's colleagues. While many types of reading are represented in the margins of Adv. volumes, I restrict my discussion to the categories that best represent the academic environment in which Dee was trained and the techniques he employed in his own *adversaria*.[72]

Teachers/Students

Sir Simonds D'Ewes, recalling his brief stint as a university student, drew a revealing picture of his educational experience: "Mr Richard Holdsworth, my tutor, read unto me but one year and a half of that time; in which he went over all Seton's logic, exactly, and part of Keckerman's and Molineus. Of ethics, of moral philosophy, he read to me Gelius, and part of Pickolimineus; of physics, part of Magirus; and of history, part of Florus, which I after finished, transcribing historical abbreviations out of it in my private study: in which also, I perused most of the other authors, and read over Gellius's Attic Nights, and part of Macrobius' Saturnals. Nor was my increase in knowledge small, which I attained by the ear as well as by the eye, by being present at the public commencements, at Mr Downes his public Greek lectures, and at Mr Harbert's public rhetoric lectures in the university; at problems, sophisms, declamations, and other scholastical exercises in our private college; and by my often conversing with learned men of other colleges, and the prime young students of our own."[73] In this sketch we find most of the methods by which students in early modern Cambridge acquired knowledge: private tutorial sessions, public disputations and debates, university lectures, independent reading, and conversation within the college and without.

While we know frustratingly little about the nuts and bolts of the pedagogical process, it is clear that adversarial readings played a central role in most of these methods. D'Ewes himself notes that his tutor "read unto" him: we ought to take this literally. Holdsworth would have gone through the texts listed by D'Ewes in a systematic way, simultaneously paraphrasing the argument and glossing individual words or phrases. Ideally, tutor and pupil each possessed a copy of the text in question: in cases where the text was expensive or rare, or the students poor, the tutor would lend copies or dictate the text for copying. Much the same activity went on in university, or "public," lectures, two of which are mentioned by D'Ewes. Student notebooks and texts annotated by students during lectures offer glimpses of the Renaissance classroom in action. In his case studies of two Ramist professors in France, Anthony Grafton describes how a text was discussed line-by-line by the teacher while the students copied out the analysis—including translations, elaborations, and arguments—into their own copies, which were specially produced for the purpose, printed in cheap editions and often interleaved with blank sheets.[74] The nature of the reading—at least in the arts subjects—was primarily grammatical and rhetorical, but it increasingly contained a dialectical analysis of the argument.[75] Not only did this method require adversarial reading on the part of the pupil, but the teacher—if he was to speak with authority and depth—had to be well prepared by his own reading.

Likewise, only a foolish scholar would enter a disputation or deliver an oration without sufficient textual preparation. There is evidence that disputants produced direct quotations, either from memory or from notes, in support of their arguments. In his debate with Hutton during Queen Elizabeth's visit to Cambridge, Andrew Perne quoted at least twelve different volumes. Elisabeth Leedham-Green and David McKitterick have examined those volumes that survive in his Peterhouse Library and have found that most of the quoted passages are underlined and annotated.[76]

Lastly, students carried out readings on their own, in their "private study." This process involved, as D'Ewes explained, "transcriptions" and "abbreviations." I have already described the standard Humanist technique—recommended at the beginning of the sixteenth century by Erasmus and Vives, among others—of taking notes from reading, abstracting and summarizing systematically and "under heads."[77] The last page of Randolph Cholmondeley's notebook graphically spells out the Humanist principles that directed his reading as an Oxford student in the 1570s: under the heading "Haec praecipue spectanda atque annotanda sunt, in sequendo authore aliquo" [These points are chiefly to be observed and noted, in pursuing any author], he listed seven categories of material to extract and store for future use.[78]

While it is often possible to sense when an annotated volume is the result of classroom or tutorial practice, distinguishing between the marginalia of teachers and students is highly problematic. The two sets, based as they are on the same material, will look similar and, in the ideal case, identical—that is, when the student has perfect attention, hearing, and handwriting. Even when a volume is signed, it is difficult to know if the reading(s) took place while the annotator was a student or a teacher, or both. Bearing these uncertainties in mind, there are several Adv. volumes that seem to document the pedagogical process.

With Bartholomew Dodington's Hermogenes (Adv.d.4.4) we are on solid ground. Dodington signed and dated the volume "B: Dodingtonus 1573" on the title page. From 1562 to 1585 Dodington held the Regius Professorship of Greek. Hermogenes, one of the most popular authors on style in the Renaissance, was introduced into the second-year rhetoric/dialectic curriculum in the Cambridge University statutes of 1549, and was still a required textbook in 1570.[79] The Adv. *Ars Rhetorica* is clearly the text that Dodington used in teaching. In his orderly and thorough digestion of this introductory text, Dodington not only used the margins next to the text but had his copy interleaved. Marginal notes usually refer to the passages they are next to; but when the top or bottom margins are used, or notes are written on blank leaves, reference becomes more difficult. To solve this problem, Dodington—and many of his contemporaries—used numbers and symbols as keys to coordinate the passages and the commentaries.[80]

Dodington explained individual authors, phrases, and words by putting them in a broader context. He provided a wealth of cross-references: on one leaf (that facing page 211) he copied out pertinent passages from Cicero, Aristotle, Sturm, and Plutarch. This kind of teaching could only be practiced by a scholar with a library of well-read, and well-digested, books.

A less systematic, and more problematic, reading is that contained in the margins of Adv.b.23.1—the 1566 Basle edition of Aristotle's *De Moribus ad Nicomachum.* The volume is signed three times by "Thomas Wilson" and the Adv. catalogue attributes the marginalia to Dr. Thomas Wilson (1525?–1581), author of extremely popular handbooks of rhetoric and logic and sometime secretary of state. This is almost certainly incorrect. The reading cannot date from earlier than 1566, which raises the question: Why would Wilson—already a master of Aristotelian logic, and increasingly preoccupied with matters of state—read and annotate in the last fifteen years of his life a text that he had long ago digested? Turning to the volume itself for an answer, all textual evidence suggests a more probable attribution to Wilson's nephew, also named Thomas Wilson (1560?–1629). This Thomas Wilson was a student at St. John's College from 1581 to 1584 before he migrated to Trinity Hall. It was most likely during his tenure at St. John's that Wilson acquired the book, apparently from one John Rudd.[81] This attribution makes altogether more sense. The reading itself is a basic one, probably by someone reading the text for the first time, and even the handwriting suggests someone considerably younger than Dr. Thomas Wilson.[82] The text is heavily underlined and annotated with topical headings, cross-references, summaries, and diagrams. The attention is both to the structure of the argument and to elegant and useful rhetorical sections. The 1566 edition contained printed annotations ("scholia") by Lambinus and Zwinger, and these, too, are annotated.

There is another Adv. copy of the *Nicomachean Ethics* that is possibly the most thoroughly digested volume in the entire collection (Adv.c.2.1). The reading—at least the one in the sixteenth-century hand—was executed by "John Bradley," whose signature appears in Latin and Greek. A John Bradley matriculated sizar from Trinity in Lent, 1557–58; another matriculated pensioner from Peterhouse in Easter, 1565, proceeded to his M.A. and

M.D., and became proctor in 1579–80; a third matriculated pensioner from Magdalene, c. 1593, and went on to become a lawyer and soldier.[83] Bradley's copy is not only interlineated (with translations) but interleaved: on these blank leaves he provides Latin and Greek summaries of the text, often utilizing dichotomous tables. Unlike Wilson and Rudd, who almost exclusively annotate the Latin version of their Greek and Latin edition, Bradley is especially interested in the Greek text: his translations are mostly from Greek to Latin, and his markings surround the Greek column only.

It is a copy of Aristotle's *Logica* rather than his *Ethica* that contains what is perhaps the most valuable set of marginalia in the Adv. collection. Adv.c.8.4 is Richard Hooker's copy of the 1567 edition. It is a classic pedagogical digestion, which Hooker may have produced as a student but which he almost certainly used while teaching at Corpus Christi College, Oxford.[84] Many writers have stressed the centrality of Aristotelian epistemology to *The Laws of Ecclesiastical Polity*, but evidence has been limited to Hooker's quotations in the work itself.[85] Hooker's Adv. Aristotle provides a valuable opportunity to delve deeper and to reassess, if not "The Place of Hooker in the History of Thought,"[86] at least the place of Aristotle in the history of Hooker's thought.

Anthony Nicholaus's copy of Linacre's Latin grammar (Adv.d.14.1) is annotated in a straightforward way, with all attention focused on the principles of rhetoric and grammar. There is one unusual addition, however: on the verso of the title page and on several blank leaves in the end of the text there is a list of words in Latin and English which amounts to a personal glossary.[87]

Scholars

Scholarly reading—that carried out as an activity outside of the pedagogical context—is perhaps the most difficult type to distinguish and define. There was no more uniformity among Renaissance scholars, their beliefs, and their methods than there is today. As in the case of teachers and students, it is often only biographical detail that can assign marginal scribbles to a scholar. Yet several general trends in scholarly reading are discernible: their three main directives were digesting, cross-referencing, and correcting. By supplying marginal headings (usually no more than a word or symbol to indicate subject matter) and concise summaries (often employing synoptic diagrams), scholars digested the text into manageable chunks that could be assigned to the various spheres of their knowledge and interest, and prepared them for application to their future needs. Extensive cross-referencing, both within the volume and to other volumes, is almost always in evidence in scholarly readings: no word appears in scholars' margins with a higher frequency than *vide* (except, perhaps, *nota*). By reading with all other authorities in mind, and by entering them into the margins, the scholar provided a network of, and map to, an ever-growing body of knowledge. As with the teacher, the more comprehensive the preparation, the better the scholarly production. In striving for quality scholarship, finally, scholars had to be sure that the texts they read were accurate and complete. By taking pains to acquire good editions, by tracking down and collating manuscript versions, and by entering corrections in their copies, Renaissance scholars laid the foundations for the modern science of philology.[88]

The scholar who is best represented in the Adv. collection is Isaac Casaubon, the outstanding Genevan-born classicist: there are no less than fifteen annotated books from Casaubon's library in the class. In fact, Casaubon may well have been the most thorough and complex adversarial reader in the period. A century ago Mark Pattison extrapolated Casaubon's reading process from his *adversaria*—not only his marginalia but the sixty volumes of loose-leaf reading notes preserved in the Bodleian Library:[89] "He read pen in hand, with a sheet of paper by his side, on which he noted much, but wrote out nothing. What he jots down is not a remark of his own on what he reads, nor is it even the words he has read; it is a mark, a key, a catchword, by which the point of what he has read may be recovered in memory. The notes are not notes *on* the book, but memoranda *of* it for his own use. When he had accumulated a number of sheets, he tied them up in a packet, or stitched them up in a book. . . . 'Casaubon's way,' Grotius tells Camerarius, 'was not to write out what he designed to publish, but to trust to his memory, with at least a few jottings, partly on the margins of his books, partly on loose sheets—true sibylline leaves.' The name Adversaria was given to these memoranda by Isaac himself."[90] The sibylline leaves preserved in the Cambridge University Library are covered with more than a few jottings. Casaubon read and digested his books with extreme attention. While he did have to rely on his memory for recalling particular authors or volumes of relevance to a current problem, his adversaria provided him with a detailed map to relevant passages. Casaubon was an information processor par excellence.

His huge folio copy of Herodotus' *Historiarum Libri IX* (Adv.a.3.2) is a useful introduction to his reading practices. On the first flyleaf there is a full and orderly exposition of the contents of each of the nine books: it is titled "Series historiae Herodoti." The title page reveals another common habit: Casaubon listed passages of special interest, along with their page numbers.[91] In other volumes this list continues for several pages in the margins of the prefatory material. The text itself is surrounded by topical headings, corrections, and—above all—cross-references.

Casaubon's Pliny (Adv.a.3.1), Arrian (Adv.d.3.5), and Terence (Adv.e.3.1) contain similar annotations. The title pages all have lists of references and all three texts are digested with topical, summarizing, and corrective notes. At Pliny's statement "Et immensa multitudo aperto quodcunque est mari, hospitalique littorum omnium appulsu navigat, sed lucri non scientiae gratia" [now that the sea has been opened up and every coast offers a hospitable landing, an immense multitude goes on voyages—but their object is profit not knowledge], Casaubon underlined "lucri non scientiae" and wrote "Nauigationes tempore Plinii" in the margin, no doubt enjoying (and perhaps in preparation for employing) the irony that little had changed. In his Terence, Casaubon shows that he had not outgrown the habit of noting an elegant phrase. At the bottom of page 138 (sig.I5v) he wrote, "24. elegantiss. sed siquid, nequid," a reference to the phrase in line 24, "Sed si quid, nequid." One other phrase caught his fancy: "gerro, iners, fraus, heluo, Ganeo, damnosus" [an idle, inert, cheating, gluttonous, debauched, injurious fellow]. He headed this phrase "descr. corrupti adolescentis p. 163." Throughout Casaubon pays special attention to language and rhetoric, often pointing out "syllepses" in the margin as they occur, and on the flyleaves at the end of the volume there is a list of passages under the heading "Proverbia Terentii." In the margins next to the passages indicated he has written "Pro."[92]

There are two annotated copies of Lipsius' famous edition of

Tacitus' *Opera Omnia* in the Adv. collection, one of which is Casaubon's.[93] It is annotated in the same fashion as his other books, but it illustrates one additional weapon in his annotational arsenal. He provides the usual topical summaries in the margins next to the text, but he also enters them, more or less in sequence, as a running heading to the page and a guide to its contents. It is useful to compare Casaubon's copy to the other Adv. copy: Adv.d.12.1 was owned by Richard Latewar.[94] Latewar was educated at the Merchant Taylor's school and St. John's College, Oxford, whence he proceeded doctor of divinity on 5 February 1597. His poetic gifts and ideological leanings brought him into close contact with the Sidney circle. He was later involved in the Irish interests of Charles Blount, eighth Lord Mountjoy, whom he accompanied as chaplain on an expedition to Ireland. He appears to have wielded not only the pen but also the sword, as he died of a wound received at Benburgh, County Tyrone. His reading of Tacitus is, first, much less scholarly than Casaubon's. His eye for detail and depth of reference does not compare. But Latewar had different needs from Casaubon. He read Tacitus less as a scholar than as a martialist: his most significant marginal note appears on the last page of the text, below the colophon, where he has written out lists of civic and military hierarchies under the heading "Ordo militaris provt quisque magistratus alter alteri subiicitur."

A final scholarly reading in the Adv. collection is Petrus Faber's *M. T. Ciceronis Opera* (Adv.a.6.1–2). Again, corrections, topical headings, responsa, and cross-references indicate scholarly concerns. This is to be expected from Faber, who was a professor at the College of La Rochelle, and who published a commentary on Cicero's *Academica*.[95] A comparison of that commentary with the comments in his Adv. Cicero do not, however, yield the exact correspondences we would expect. The entry on Faber in the *Nouvelle Biographie Générale* states that Faber possessed the edition of Hervet as well as that of Stephanus—the one held in the Cambridge University Library—so it is possible that his published commentaries derived from those entered in the former edition.

Practitioners

As we might expect, books of a practical nature, especially ones that guide a practitioner of an art, craft, or profession, tend to be more commonly annotated than other types of books. There is a particular case—books on medicine, physic, and surgery—in which especially heavy annotations were the norm. A copy of Galen's *Ars Medica* (Adv.b.22.1) is typical in its thorough digestion of the text. The title and index have been expanded, there are summaries and cross-references on the pastedowns and title page, and the text itself is covered with cross-references, topical headings, and diagrams. Even more thoroughly digested—indeed, the text is all but consumed by the marginalia—is Thomas Lorkin's copy of Galen and Hippocrates (Adv.e.12.1). In this small sixteenmo, which the master of Peterhouse Andrew Perne gave to Lorkin, every available space is covered with underscoring, summaries, cross-references, elaborations, and diagrams.[96] The edition itself was especially practical, consisting for the most part of concise aphorisms.[97] In copying out, condensing, and elaborating these aphorisms on the title page, on blank leaves, and in the margins, Lorkin provided himself with a handbook or reference guide for the practicing physician.[98]

A more complicated reading in the same vein is Adv.d.3.1— John Caius's copy of his own edition of Galen. Caius was the foremost medical Humanist in Elizabethan England, combining philology and anatomy in his practice and transmission of the Galenic tradition. Vivian Nutton relates that he carried a copy of the 1538 Basle edition around Italy, comparing the text with those consulted in seven different cities and jotting down discrepancies in the margins.[99] This was a "working copy" of Galen into which Caius, an "inveterate scribbler in his books," "inscribed notes and comments over a period of some twenty years." The same concern for accuracy and detail are conveyed by the annotations in the Adv. text. He not only corrected the text but added extensive notes of argument and cross-reference. The edition already included printed "annotationes" by Caius in which he glossed individual words and passages; but Caius annotated these as well, thus glossing his glosses. According to Nutton, Caius intended to produce a second edition of the text, incorporating his notes in the first edition, but it never materialized.[100]

An annotated copy of Hollerius' *De Morbis Internis Lib. II* in the Adv. collection (Adv.d.2.1) provides another specimen of a practically digested medical book. At first glance the text does not appear to be annotated at all. However, close examination reveals several long cross-references in the text, as well as several leaves bound in before and several hundred bound in after the text, which are covered with manuscript notes. The notes bound in at the beginning concern, like Book I of the text, the diagnosis and treatment of fevers. The set of notes in the end prove to be an extended set of glosses on the text for which there was not sufficient room in the margins. They are headed "Addenda to the work of Hollerius, De Morbis internis. Remedies which have an accompanying point in the margin are those which W. Butler collected out of authors: and wrote partly in his Hollerius, partly in his other books. But those which are without an accompanying point in the margin are those which we have assembled from other sources."[101] At first, these passages consist of chapter-by-chapter summaries of Hollerius. Gradually, though, they become a catalogue of medical recipes, based on Hollerius, Butler, and others. Finally, the section becomes a diary of treatments administered to various patients. The Adv. catalogue attributes these notes to William Butler (the eminent Cambridge physician) himself, but this clearly cannot be the case: the "Addenda" suggest that a group of subsequent physicians used this book as their medical diary and as a catalogue of recipes culled from their books—incorporating those that Butler left behind in his.[102]

THE MARGINALIA OF SIR THOMAS SMITH

In concluding this survey of sixteenth-century reading practices I want to take a closer look at one reader trained in Tudor Cambridge—the scholar-statesman Sir Thomas Smith. Smith is of particular interest not only because of his status as, after Lord Burghley and alongside Thomas Wilson, the most prominent Elizabethan "intellectual in office,"[103] but because his interests and activities take us very close to John Dee. Study of their careers reveals close parallels in intellectual tastes, civic applications, and— most interestingly for our present purposes—annotational habits. This is less surprising than the differences in their contemporary position and historical stature would suggest: they were among the brightest stars in the constellation around John Cheke in mid-Tudor Cambridge.[104]

After achieving high academic status as the first Regius Professor of Civil Law, Smith left the university in 1547 for private political service and public office, acting as a member of Parliament, clerk of the Privy Council, master of requests, ambassador, commissioner, and principal secretary. But throughout this distinguished political career he never abandoned his scholarly methods and concerns. He remained a lifelong student and reader of "astronomy, architecture, natural phenomena, drugs, and medicines," establishing both a substantial library and a valuable laboratory. Like Dee, Smith acquired in Cambridge a "habit . . . of annotating his books in their margins with endless corrections, underlinings, and comments": what this reveals is not, however, a "meticulous, fussy mind," but that of a scholar trained in mid-Tudor Cambridge. Dewar's claim that Smith's books "have been scattered and lost" has no doubt deterred scholars from studying his marginalia; however, a large number of Smith's books remain in the library of Queens' College, Cambridge, and they convey the full range of his interests and annotational techniques.[105]

By the early 1570s Smith had developed an active interest in practical chemistry, alchemy, and metallurgy. In 1571 he was the leading promoter of the "Society of the new art . . . for making copper out of iron, and quicksilver out of antimony and lead."[106] During his embassy to France in 1572, Smith acquired up-to-date Continental literature and sent back instructions to his laboratory technicians—one of whom was Richard Eden, better known for his translations of navigational texts. Smith may have played a part in what Charles Webster has called "the incubation of Paracelsianism" in England:[107] QCL F.10.20 is his copy of Paracelsus' *Chirurgia magna* (Argentorati, 1573). It is lightly annotated in Smith's large, clear italic hand. He employs straightforward techniques and mnemonic devices in digesting the text, including summaries, symbols, and pictures. When an author is mentioned in the text, Smith noted his name in the margin. Next to a printed marginal note about the influence of the heavens on medical cures, Smith sketched a star; next to a note about Venus, Smith provided its astrological symbol (B3r).[108]

It was his mastery of civil law that earned Smith a Regius Professorship, as well as a favorable profile for service to the state. His copy of Justinian's *Digest* survives, along with a Greek edition of the *Institutes*.[109] His marginalia are masterpieces of digestion: they are thorough, systematic, and clear. The presence of several inks suggests that they were the product of several sittings, probably separated by significant periods of time.[110] The margins contain summaries (mostly verbatim from the text), subject headings, cross-references, and, above all, symbols and pictures. Particularly striking is his use of what might be called "scroll brackets" to highlight important passages pertaining to law: he occasionally sketched a scroll in the margin, complete with handle and roller; the unrolled "parchment" varies according to the size of the passage it accompanies.[111] Like Casaubon, and others, he often provided summaries along the tops and bottoms of pages; and in the *Digest* he used the blank verso of the last page to record summaries and cross-references. At least in these legal texts, Smith's methods of digesting owe something to Continental trends: he received training in the civil law at Padua and Paris, centers of the new Humanist jurisprudence.[112]

The Queens' books afford us, finally, a glimpse at Smith the historical scholar. Both his civic activities and his writings rested on a belief in the utility of history. As secretary to Edward Seymour, a member of commissions on divorce, religion, and the coinage, ambassador to France, and colonial projector, and as the writer of tracts on antiquarian matters and socioeconomic considerations, he needed an acute sense of history—both what had happened in the past and how this shaped present situations and future possibilities. As early as the spring of 1549 he was "put in charge of a team of eight to search into the records and dig up all the evidence he could for the English claim to sovereignty over Scotland."[113] In his treatise on *The Wages of a Roman Footsoldier* he described his method of testing arguments "in such kinds of discourses and conversations which sometime I make with myself of the order of foreign estates and commonwealths." This comparative method informed his classic account *De Republica Anglorum*: he described the government of England in such a way as to make clear "the principal points wherein it doth differ from the policy or government at this time used in France, Italy, Spain, Germany and all other countries which do follow the civil law of the Romans."[114] While many scholars are reluctant to attribute to early modern writers a fully developed historical consciousness, Smith's scholarly and political needs demanded a sensitivity to the dynamics of similarity and difference, of precedent and innovation, and of continuity and change—as well as the role that texts played in these historical dynamics.

Albertus Krantzius' chronicle of the Scandinavian rulers was an important resource for researchers, writers, and drafters of foreign policy. Smith's copy of the 1561 edition is QCL D.10.22. His marginalia are straightforward and thorough, although there are large chunks of text that he did not annotate and perhaps did not read.[115] The summaries and subject headings, again in his clear italic hand, are comprehensive, with a marked but not exclusive emphasis on British history. Here again it is his use of symbols and sketches that is most striking. There are countless portraits of kings, which are more representative than representational; islands, fortresses, and cityscapes abound; ships can be found on sigs. e4r and t2r, where they accompany a discussion of piracy and are labeled "Piraticam," and, unlabeled, on sig. Ooo6r.

Smith's copy of Paulus Aemylius Veronensis' *De rebus gestis Francorum* (QCL G.3.19) is also digested by means of summaries and illustrated with towns, portraits, and coats of arms. And in the margins of his 1519 *Historia* of Tacitus we find names and subjects (with a special attention to navigation and Jews), and sketches of cities, forts, crowns (e.g., above "Tiberius Imperat." on C2r) and letters (next to "epistolae" on D6v). Although we are most inclined to appreciate the artistic and entertainment value of these pictures, they were not merely doodles: they certainly played an important mnemonic role. It is possible that this use of illustrations was advocated by Cheke and others and may even point to a general annotational style in mid-Tudor Cambridge.[116]

On the front flyleaf Smith wrote a general note about Tacitus' text which serves well as a final word on Smith's use of history: "Tacitus imperator Cor. Taciti uiri consularis historiam de Romanis imperatoribus, non modo in *omn*ibus bibliothecis iussit collocari, sed etiam edicto cauit, ut decies quot annis ad usum publicum transcriberetur [The Emperor Tacitus not only ordered that the consul Tacitus' history of the Roman emperors should be kept in all libraries, but also decreed that it should be copied ten times each year for public use]." Libraries, and historical works, are of the utmost importance in the government of an empire.

FOUR

Dee's Marginalia

. . . this booke was [John Dee's] while he lived[.] I have divers other books, both printed & some manuscript y^t came out of his study [and] in them he hath likewise written his name & notes for wch they are farre the more pretious.   —John Winthrop's note, dated 1640, in the New York Society Library's copy of Paracelsus' *Das Buch Meteororum*

U ntil very recently Dee's extensive marginalia had, for all intents and a variety of purposes, disappeared from our intellectual map of the Renaissance. Throughout the eighteenth, nineteenth, and most of the twentieth centuries, they were the subject of only passing bibliographical notice and were reduced to the status of inert artifacts. Even after Dee's library catalogue began to fuel interpretive speculation and support intellectual arguments, attention to the actual books and Dee's notes in them remained rare. Only with the publication of Nicholas Clulee's study of Dee (1988) and Roberts and Watson's edition of his library catalogue (1990) has this trend been challenged.

However messy, modest, and (as it were) marginal they at first appear, it is no exaggeration to say that Dee's marginalia are central to the recovery of his intellectual activities and, indeed, his role in society. In terms of the intellectual historian's traditional search for sources and influences, the marginalia allow us to move beyond an exclusive reliance on his library catalogue, which is not at all an adequate basis for discussion. Roberts and Watson find in the notes valuable evidence of Dee's bibliographical and biographical details, as well as an indication of his "tastes and interests."[1] But they offer much more than this. They document the ways in which Dee *interacted* with his sources: and since he was one of the most source-oriented scholars in a source-oriented age, this is essential to our appreciation of his life and livelihood. That life was, as Clulee put it, "a dialogue with received positions on various issues, a dialogue largely carried out with and through the books he read."[2] It may be difficult to imagine, but it is in Dee's marginal scribbles rather than his "shew-stone" (his medium for divination) that we catch the most vivid and intimate glimpses of him in action, doing what he must have spent most of his time doing. It is in his conversations, or séances, with other authors as much as with angels, that we clearly hear his voice. In fact, the two types of dialogue are closely related. Not only are the pages of the angelic conversations filled with references to and images of books, but their very forms (the rituals they enacted and the languages they employed) followed textual conventions, and were informed by Kelley's masterful manipulation of Dee's textual expectations.

Even in an age of intense annotational activity Dee stands out as an exceptional annotator. A huge number (it is probably safe to say the majority) of his books contain marginalia;[3] the proportion certainly dwarfed that of most contemporary libraries and was possibly only surpassed by the likes of Gabriel Harvey and Isaac Casaubon. Ben Jonson probably lagged slightly behind. Out of 537 volumes owned by the "wizard earl" Henry Percy, only 69 of them contain manuscript annotations. John Bale does not seem to have been a heavy annotator. William Camden left behind a "relatively small number of annotations"—they appear in fewer than 5 percent of his books. Even the voracious reader Robert Burton, whose library contained just over 1,700 books, annotated around 20 percent of them.[4] Dee's annotations amount to an information-processing system that cannot have been equaled by more than a handful of sixteenth-century readers.

Such claims for the value of Dee's marginalia need, perhaps, to be qualified lest they create false expectations (or, worse, hopes) about the nature of what we find in Dee's margins. Roberts and Watson are right to point out that, taken individually, "the notes are rarely more than an expression of interest and seldom a record of opinion."[5] While even the expressions of interest can take on a certain resonance, when they can be directly related to aspects of Dee's activities or writings, such "topicality" is disappointingly rare. The tools that Dee (and his contemporaries) used to digest texts and make them useful lack, for the most part, the personal, creative, and emotional intensity that modern readers have come to look for in engagements with texts. These tools—and my account of them—will inevitably seem somewhat dry in that they are less imaginative or psychological than (literally) technical: an understanding of how Renaissance readers encountered and manipulated the written word must begin with the techniques of information management that they received and developed. Thus, aside from the occasional insights into Dee's sources, opinions, and experiences, the general significance of the marginalia is to be found in their cumulative effect and overall context; in the processing activity that they document, and the active process that they allow us to recover.

HOW DID DEE DIGEST HIS TEXTS?

In digesting his books and manuscripts Dee employed a number of basic annotational techniques, general categories of marginal notes that are found not only throughout Dee's marginalia but in those of almost all sixteenth-century scholarly readers. The most basic of these is the use of nonverbal marks to draw attention to words or passages—underlinings in the text, or lines, brackets, asterisks, quotation marks, hands with pointing fingers, and so on, in the margin.[6] In most (just over 90 percent) of Dee's books containing verbal notes, some form of underlining is in evidence. Underlining, however, is almost never found on its own: Dee appears to have been reluctant to let an underlined or bracketed passage stand without a more specific, verbal indication of its nature and/or importance. Unlike some of his contemporaries, Dee does not seem to have highlighted whole passages in the text with lead or chalk.

After "Nota"/"NB"/"Nota Bene" (which Dee used emphatically—although that may seem too strong a word for such a simple and routine practice), the most common form of verbal annotation was the *topical* note which, containing simple subject headings or names, acted as a concise key to the topic of a passage. The margins of Dee's copy of Andreas Alexander's *Mathemalogia*,[7] for instance, contain the topical notes "Astronomia" (A3r), "Perspectiuus" (D2r), and "Mathematicae definitio" (A2r). A more elaborate topical note is found in a collection of alchemical tracts:[8] Dee drew attention to a discussion of Joseph's dream by writing "Expositio Imaginum Iosephi" alongside it and drawing a small pictogram in the bottom margin (6r). A related form of annotation was the *summary* note, which conveyed the gist of an author's point, often repeating parts of the text verbatim.

Renaissance readers also entered in their margins notes of a *corrective* nature.[9] In Dee's books this was usually an editorial practice (i.e., the correction of spelling, grammar, or more general corruptions of a text). In his printed copy of Geoffrey of Monmouth's history he underlined the word "Lergecia" and, in the bottom margin, wrote, "Some copyes haue here for Lergecia, Leros" (7r). Later in the same text he underlined "Sulpitii" and asserted, "This name is corrupted" (74v).[10] A similarly philological interest is indicated by *translation* notes, which in the margins beside or between lines of text suggested equivalent terms in another language. Many but by no means all of Dee's translations were into English:[11] he also translated from many languages (including English) into Latin, Greek, and occasionally Hebrew.[12] These translations were often accompanied by more general linguistic observations: next to Paracelsus' discussion of the four elements in *Das Buch Meteororum* Dee noted, "Commonly in our speche, we call only heaven the Element. as there appeared strange sights in the Element."[13] In one case Dee's translation took the form of a poetic paraphrase: at the top of folio 48v of the alchemical *Liber A.B.C.* Dee inscribed, "The lesse the water be / the rasher and Better solution shall thou see."[14]

As I explained in the previous chapter, *cross-reference* notes were very common among scholarly readers, or at least those who tried to command a large body of interrelated materials. Cross-references could be used to link passages within a single text; or they could refer to other works. They did so with a range of precision: in some instances the annotator simply mentioned an author's name, in others a particular text, and in others an exact page, section, or even line number. In Franciscus Irenicus' description of Germany, Dee copied a quotation from Strabo and wrote, "Strabo, Lib. 5, p. 204."[15] In his *Les Illustrations de Gaule . . .*, Jean Lemaire cites a couplet from Ovid but gives no source: in his copy Dee wrote in the margin, "Ouidius Lib. 4. de Ponto. Elegia vltima" (p. 287).[16] This practice again indicates the need for a sound memory, but it also suggests, especially in the case of Gabriel Harvey, that many readers worked with other texts in close proximity.[17] Dee's cross-references raise an interesting issue: as with the references in his writings, he sometimes cites texts not known to have been in his library. This could provide evidence for his possession of certain uncatalogued books, but it more likely proves that he had access to textual resources outside his own collection.

Last, readers sometimes entered notes of a *personal* nature. These could respond to the text, or record some personal experience, usually (though not necessarily) related to the text; in any case they represent the most specific and revealing intrusions of a readerly presence into the margins of an authorial text. As I noted above, however, impersonal digestion seems to have been the norm except in cases where readers had a special relationship to the text, or when they were particularly keen to situate their reading in relation to contemporary events. Dee was especially sensitive to texts that had a bearing on his "Monas hieroglyphica." In one instance he accused the author of appropriating it without acknowledgment,[18] and in another he noted that a particular symbol used for a chemical was "agreable to my Monas Hieroglyphica."[19]

Before moving on to Dee's more advanced annotational techniques, it is important to understand that Renaissance "marginalia" were entered not just alongside the text, but on virtually any available blank space, including title pages, flyleaves, pastedowns, and errata sheets. Like Isaac Casaubon in particular, Dee used these spaces to enter cross-references—both to passages within the text and to other works.[20] When Dee used these spaces for more discursive notes, they were usually but not always related to the text in some way. On the front and back flyleaves of Euclid's *Elementa* he wrote extensive notes on lines, numbers, and the name, origins, and utility of geometry.[21] And on the flyleaves of his printed Geoffrey of Monmouth he wrote out notes on points within the text, relevant material in other texts, and (most revealingly) sources for further historical research.[22] Some of the most interesting notes, however, have a much less apparent connection to the text in which they appear. At the end of a text on sculpture Dee wrote out instructions in English "on the making and polishing of steele glas," which are dated nine years after the signature on the title page.[23] At the end of Walther Hermann Ryff's commentary on

Pliny's *Historia naturalis,* Dee wrote out astrological notes and tables.[24] And the verso of the errata sheet of Cardano's *Libri Quinque* contains very rare (but, unfortunately, mostly illegible) notes by Dee, partly autobiographical, and partly relating to the Pembroke household (of which Dee was a member in the early 1550s). It is possible to make out entries on a "monstrous birth," and the birthdates of a "Mr Peche," the children of the Herberts, Anne Compton and her son, and Dee's own mother—"Anno 1509 vel 1508. on Crisxmas day my mother was borne / to whome I am very like in visaug . . . And she was maried 1524."[25]

Dee's annotational arsenal was unusually well stocked: in addition to the categories outlined above he used a broad-ranging set of techniques in digesting his texts. The first cluster reveals his (and other readers') keen interest in the provenance of volumes. Dee's books often contain information about how or where he acquired them, and where they went after they left his library. Not all of his books were signed, but many of those that were specified a date and a city. In a few instances he was more precise. His copy of a collection of historical tracts (no. M10) was "bowght vppon a stall in London."[26] A manuscript compilation of world history was "the gift of Mr Dyckensen" of "poplar by London."[27] His copies of Peter Martyr's *Decades* (no. D1) and Antonio de Espejo's *Viaje* (no. D8) were presented to him by Thomas Harriot in 1590. And while it is unclear whether Dee acquired Andreas Alexander's *Mathemalogia* as a gift or by theft (he had a habit of absorbing the books he borrowed), a note after the colophon of that text located his reading in the household of his "singular good friend" Bishop Edmund Bonner.[28] As for the subsequent history of Dee's books, they are full of other collectors' signatures and notes. But none are more revealing than those in the books acquired by the famous American colonists (and chemists) the Winthrops:[29] in his copy of Paracelsus' *Das Buch Meteororum* (no. 1482) Winthrop wrote, "The writing on ye next leaf to ye name on the top of the ffrontispice & ye marginall notes in ye booke were written by that famous and learned philosopher John Dee. warden of Manchester, with his owne hand writing, this booke was his while he lived[.] I have divers other books, both printed & some manuscript y^t came out of his study [and] in them he hath likewise written his name & notes *for wch they are farre the more pretious.* It was y^t Joh. Dee y^t wrote the learned treatise called Monas Hieroglyphica also propaideumata Aphoristica & the preface to Euclids Elements in English folio Juli 25. 1640."[30]

Dee was especially concerned with the conditions under which a text was produced. Sometimes this meant attention to its date: on the title page of an edition of Pliny's *De mundi historia* published in 1543, Dee wrote, "Scripsit hunc librum 1541 / vide f.41."[31] In several of his manuscripts there are notes that provide information about the production of the text *for Dee:* the colophon to his Pseudo-Lullian *Liber experimentorum* reads, "Ego Blasius de santulianhos librum scripsi pro dno meo Jo. Dee et consig*n*aui eum Dno Guirardo causa mittendi dicto dno meo Jo. Dee in presencia Dno Mercurii Candreuila Roma die 28 Jan. anno 1564. [In Dee's hand:] J. Dee, Recepi Antwerpiae 1564 februarij 28" (26v).[32]

Dee was interested in, and tried to provide, information about authors and authorship. *Linguarum duodecim characteribus differentium alphabetum introductio* is generally ascribed to Guillaume Postel. However, next to the title in his copy Dee wrote, "*De Gul. Postello.* Lindani Dubitant. p.16[?] Gesneri Bibliotheca."[33] And occasionally he provided information about when an author was born, died, or flourished.[34]

Many volumes (especially manuscripts) were passed along with inaccurate or incomplete titles, and some without any at all. Dee corrected and added many titles, when they could be established. In a manuscript of Roger Bacon's works (no. DM29) Dee identified the "opus maioris R. Baconi" and in the space initially reserved for the colored initial on folio 152r he wrote, "Epistola 3is Rogeri Bacon."[35] In some books—surprisingly few—Dee wrote their titles on the spine or fore-edge, for easier identification.[36] He also added to existing titles, sometimes expanding them[37] and sometimes appending extraneous information.

Several of these practices were clearly the result of the state of textual uncertainty in Dee's day. Dee had to take pains to ensure the accuracy and fullness of his copies by collating manuscripts and comparing editions of works. Many marginal notes correct or complete a text and are patently the result of such comparisons. In a collection of alchemical tracts that Dee himself compiled, there are occasional gaps in the text: at these points Dee referred to page numbers in "libri impressi."[38] In some volumes Dee commented on the completeness of a text without entering any changes. He identified item 5 in BL MS Sloane 336—"Liber subsequens ex varijs Capitibus Nicolai Florentini excerptus est" (155v)—and then referred to the "libro impresso," noting on 235v, "Hic desunt multa."[39] In several manuscripts, however, Dee amended the text according to another, more complete copy. He noticed that his Latin text of the *Leges Walliae* (no. DM160) was missing one passage: observing, "Haec omissa sunt per Interpretem quae tamen in Brytanico textu habentur," Dee copied out the section from his Welsh copy (DM30a) along the right margin (6r).[40] Dee was especially concerned with the quality of his Roger Bacon texts. His manuscript of the *Scientia perspectiva* (M72) is corrected passim.; in the *De erroribus medicorum* (DM129)—in which all of Dee's notes concern the accuracy and not the contents of the text—there are several gaps, by which Dee wrote, "The blank places [were] left without writing" (9r).[41]

On the whole, the scholarly apparatus and general aids to the reader that are standard in modern texts were neither fully developed nor consistently provided. In Renaissance texts, and especially manuscripts, tables of contents were often incomplete or altogether absent. Readers routinely processed their volumes by adding (to) descriptions of the works contained therein, sometimes even providing page or folio numbers. In some volumes Dee added his own table of contents,[42] and in others he added to existing ones.[43] The same goes for lists of sources,[44] and subject and author indexes.[45]

Another symptom of the "user-unfriendliness" of these manuscripts and early printed texts was that chapter headings tended to be obscured and sometimes effaced. Dee occasionally improved the clarity of the layout, and the accuracy of the text, by providing these headings or by simply highlighting existing chapter divisions.[46]

In an age before comprehensive catalogues were widely available, an important way of learning about new texts was to come across them in works already owned. Dee commonly underlined, or copied in the margin, the names of authors or works mentioned. This practice is especially marked in works by Roger Bacon, one of the most influential and best-represented authors collected by Dee.[47] The same is true of the historical[48] and alchemical/natural philosophical works—a particularly diffuse textual tradition in which complete texts were hard to come by and one had to follow any possible leads.[49] In his copy of Dionysius the Areopagite's *De mystica theologia,* Dee was more explicit about his desire to own, and not just to know about, other texts: on sig. A6r, next to some underlined titles, he wrote, "libri Dionysij desiderati."[50]

Increasingly during the early modern period, readers and authors alike employed consecutive numbers to order passages. They were supplied in printed texts to help readers through an argument, and when they were absent readers often provided them for clarification and ease of future reference. This practice is found throughout Dee's books—both those he wrote and those he read. In two books, however, the numbers in the margins are not sequential, and they appear to *key* rather than to order passages.[51]

Like Isaac Casaubon, Dee sometimes provided a short guide to a page's contents in its top or bottom margin. In most cases this was a list of subjects (in its simplest form, a list of the topical notes alongside that page's text);[52] in some it was a list of important or interesting words; and in one it was a list of chemicals.[53]

As I have discussed elsewhere, Dee was an expert in genealogical matters. Genealogy was neither a casual hobby nor a disinterested antiquarian study in the sixteenth century. Historical research into the descent of aristocrats and especially rulers was vital and valuable for political transactions.[54] Dee found some of his information in charters, deeds, and monuments. But he also got some from his books and manuscripts: the margins of his historical texts are cluttered with genealogical diagrams.[55] He clearly read with lineage in mind. Often it was his own lineage in both a historical and a textual sense—that is, a line of both ancestors and authors—that he sought to establish. This is most strikingly the case in his manuscript of the Welsh laws of Hywel Dda (no. DM160)—see Fig. 6. The first word of the text, which is in Dee's own secretary hand, is "Hoelus" [Hywel]: a line connects it to the margin, where it is the third name in a long genealogy which begins with "Rodericus Magnus Rex totius Cambriae" in 843 and ends with Dee himself, his wife Jane, and their eight children (the last of whom was born in 1595). In the margin of a manuscript, then, Dee boldly posited not only his lineage but his legitimacy: he made the text his own, and, at the same time, he used the text to make himself.

As I noted in relation to the reading practices of Sir Thomas Smith, Dee employed visual techniques to supplement the verbal. In only one case does his sketch have a representational quality: a passage in Niger's *Geographia* (no. 111) describes the physiognomy of East Asian peoples, and in the margin Dee drew a face with the features described (Yy5r). Most of his drawings have rather a representative, or symbolic, value. When he drew several comets in the margins of Bale's *Illustrium maioris Britanniae Scriptorum . . . Summarium* (no. 274), it is unlikely that he was depicting actual heavenly bodies (N2 and O2).[56] Likewise, in the margin of a Ripley manuscript (no. DM90), Dee drew a bust with a crown on its head: it accompanies the text, "it is the examiner of all bodies solued and not soluyd" (p. 15).[57]

In one text Dee sketched a bona fide doodle, and it is found on the blank verso of the final page rather than in the text. In Jacobus a Saa's *De Navigatione,* a text Dee annotated heavily, there is a very light pencil sketch of a breastplate adorned with Dee's hieroglyphical monad.[58]

One other practice that depended upon some artistic talent is Dee's habit of drawing what I call "face brackets." In a number of texts, he transformed a straightforward line next to a passage into a sketch of a face in profile.[59] The passages outlined never mention people or their features, so this could again be the result of boredom or a simple desire to spruce up the margins. But one peculiar pattern suggests otherwise: they only appear in alchemical or natural philosophical texts.[60] Clearly the portraits had some symbolic value to Dee, though I have not yet ascertained what it might be.[61]

One of the most visually striking techniques Dee employed was the use of lines to connect one word or passage on a page with another related (or even identical) one.[62] These "connection lines," which usually appear in manuscripts, cross boldly through the text—on a busy page appearing to cross it out—and reveal a blatant bias toward the utility rather than the aesthetic appearance of a page. The practice is most common in Dee's alchemical texts; and it is tempting to view the practice as a textual manifestation of the alchemical belief in the interconnectedness of all matter.

The final practice is probably the most pervasive: many of Dee's marginal notes in both books and manuscripts are accompanied by his name, initials, or the letter delta (which he used as a personal cipher).[63] This not only bestows some authorial status on Dee's marginalia, but testifies to the intertextual and interpersonal quality of Renaissance reading. Dee wanted his notes to be recognized, to become part of the author's text, and to be one stage in the accretion of readers' responses—in other words, to actively participate in the creation of a new, and ever-changing, text.

WHAT DID DEE *MAKE* OF HIS TEXTS?

Having provided a thorough account of the annotational tools that Dee employed, I now want to look at the marginalia from a different perspective and provide a more systematic discussion of how they fit into the patterns of his interests and activities. In what remains of this chapter I will offer some brief overviews of Dee's annotational habits—and what they allowed him to *make* of his texts—in a few of the subjects best represented in the remnants of his library. This thematic structure, rather than a chronological one, is the most convenient way to present readings both exemplary and extraordinary, and to highlight the different ways Dee approached different kinds of material.[64] It is not intended to provide anything like comprehensive coverage; but, rather, to suggest avenues for further research.

Alchemy

Alchemical texts constitute a conspicuously large proportion of Dee's library, and they are its most consistently annotated collection. There are historical and natural philosophical books with heavier marginalia, but volume for volume, they contain more writing per marginal inch than any other subject. Dee's alchemical studies began early in his life (at least by July 1556, when he drew up a list of "Authores alchymici quos perlegi")[65] and remained an abiding interest through old age (his diaries are full of alchemical transactions with students and friends, and an alchemical notebook survives from the year before his death).[66] This was for Dee a highly experimental activity, centered in his laboratory; but it also entailed great textual labor. The alchemical tradition was itself fundamentally literary, and most contemporary vignettes of alchemists at work pictured a room scattered with open books. Dee acquired his alchemical texts from a wide range of sources, reading and applying them actively. Many of the manuscripts—more than in any other subject—are even in his own hand.[67] Most of the annotated volumes have notes in several inks and hands—indicating that Dee returned to texts as time presented new opportunities, new knowledge, and new needs.

Dee's alchemical annotations are consummately practical. They are full of observations of the lengths of incubations and purifications, the signs of chemical change and progress, and the materials and equipment best suited to the production of the philosopher's stone.[68] He eagerly sought out the elusive secret that would bring his work to fruition. One such secret was the "cold and moyst place" described above (note 11). Another was temporal: in his manuscript of *Practica et accurtaciones Georgij Ryplay et Raimundi,* Dee discovered that the so-called philosophical year actually represented one "vulgar month."[69]

But alchemy was also part of natural philosophy, and Dee carefully attended to its practical and theoretical lessons pertaining to the wider natural world. For instance, in no. 1425 he drew attention to a "Comparatio Medicinae & Alchemiae" (p. 77). And in the "Codicillus Raymundi" (no. DM94), Dee filled the bottom margin of folio 171v with a diagram outlining the principles "Materialia," "demonstratiua," and "operatiua."[70]

Finally Dee's annotations reveal a concern for the entire alchemical tradition. Cross-references are very common, especially to Norton and Ripley.[71] He was also sensitive to the conditions of secrecy that marked the transmission of alchemical texts. At the bottom of a page he copied out a quatrain from "Norton in the proheme of his Ordinall": "Bachon and Raymund wth many Authors mo / Write vnder covert, and Aristotle allso / For what secret they wrothe with theyr penne / Theyr clowdy clauses, dulled many men &c."[72] He was interested in establishing the lineage of alchemical authorities—in no. 299 he displayed some neat syllogistic reasoning to determine the relative antiquity of Albertus, Arnaldus, Bacon, and Lull[73]—and, as ever, in relating himself to their authority.[74]

History

Dee's historical books are the other group that demand exceptionally thorough treatment. They are the volumes that survive in the greatest numbers, are among the most consistently annotated,

and are most relevant to my subsequent chapters on Dee's manuscript writings. They can be crudely separated into medieval,
ecclesiastical, ancient, and European.

Dee collected the most up-to-date editions of medieval histories
and also sought copies—sometimes multiple copies—of manuscripts. Dee read his medieval chronicles with an evident sense of
purpose and a biased (which is not to say uncritical) eye: they are
very selectively annotated, with the aim of collecting evidence
applicable to contemporary scholarly and political concerns. Attention to the names, dates, and pedigrees of early British rulers,
their territorial exploits, and the resources of their dominions is
most common. The texts that were of greatest interest to Dee were
those that mentioned Brutus (and early Britannia), Kings Arthur
and Edgar, and Prince Madoc—thus informing the raging debate
over the justification for union and expansion under the Tudors
(which I discuss in detail in Chapter 7).[75]

Dee's notes in these passages are rarely interesting in themselves—they usually consist of no more than a topical word or
phrase. But their value lies in the fact that he consistently drew
attention to the material that would inform his own historical and
political discourses. In a medieval historical miscellany we find a
reference to "A mine of siluer" (106r) as well as topical and genealogical notes on Arthur, topography, Troy, Britannia, and King
Edgar.[76] In Roger Hovedon's chronicle (no. DM43) Dee paid close
attention to the succession of medieval rulers. In another chronicle
he drew a pedigree of William the Conqueror in the margin, and
noted a discussion of the subjugation of England.[77]

Five volumes of medieval history are particularly revealing. In
Higden's *Polychronicon* (no. M121) Dee highlighted "Locrimes Title to all Brytayn" (46r)—a passage clearly relevant to the works on
Elizabeth's imperial titles that Dee produced during the decade
after this reading is dated. On 144r Dee noted the doubts about
the historical veracity of Geoffrey of Monmouth—a topic that
would surface in his *Famous and Rich Discoveries*. Lastly, on 164v
there is a reference to King Edgar's "Classis 4000 Nauium," which
was doubtless a source for his paean to Edgar in his *General and Rare
Memorials*.

Dee filled the front flyleaf of Matthew of Westminster's *Flores
Historiarum* (no. 290), referring to pages in the text pertaining to

the genealogies of illustrious men, and Mercator's discussion of Arthur.[78] In the text Dee read critically, correcting several misleading dates (pp. 111 and 113) and, in an eight-column table of kings, filling in some that were missing (340–41). On page 348 he noted, "The riuer of Lee that runs by Ware. which by Statute (in Quene Elizabeth her tyme made) shuld be brought to London." On page 375 he found two sources for his own lineage, both of which he initialed. On the same page he cited a reference to King Edgar—"A Kingly Pilot"—whose fleet had grown to 4800 ships. And on page 392 he revealed his interest in historical linguistics by recording that a name mentioned (Palingus) "yet remayneth 1576."[79]

A trio of books preserved in the library of Christ Church, Oxford, are arguably Dee's most important historical texts. John Bale's chronological encyclopedia of English historical resources up to the 1550s (no. 274) naturally served as an indispensable guide to Dee's own researches. The flyleaves and margins are full of notes drawing attention to various points of interest and controversy, particularly regarding the earlier period (after c. 1290 the notes are very sparse). Dee found mention of many new texts and several passages to support his arguments pertaining to the British empire. Next to a bracketed and underlined passage, "Brytanniae imperium, quod contra sacramentum militiae per tyrranidem occupauerunt, iustis dominis ac possessoribus quamprimum restituerent," Dee exclaimed, "O Lelandinam, dicendi Libertatem" (p. 64). But Dee also updated Bale: at the end of the first part he made a note about the death of Edmund Bonner, in prison, during September 1569 (p. 736). And in the second part, he expanded and corrected references to his friends Richard Chancellor and Richard Cavendish.[80] A collection of John Leland's works (no. 597) is similarly digested, with attention to an unidentified "Libellus de Imperio Brytannorum in Scotos" (2v) and an initialed note on Brutus (D3r).

Geoffrey of Monmouth's *Britanniae vtriusque regum origo* (no. 601), finally, is not just noteworthy for being—as we would expect—Dee's most influential source for material on Arthur, Nennius, and what has become known as the British History. It is also annotated in a manner that brings Dee's entire range of annotational techniques into play. On the front flyleaf, he made notes about books treating Cadwallader, Arthur, and Nennius, as well as the life of Geoffrey himself. On the title page he continued these notes, and added a choice historical motto from Cicero's *De oratore:* "Not to know that which happened before your birth is always to remain a child." The text itself is deeply digested. Dee dated an initialed note on the bottom of 7r "1574. Julij 12." Many of the more extensive notes relate to concerns he was developing at that time: indeed, Roberts and Watson connect this period with "obsessive annotation" of the history books (40). There is a discussion of the geography of "Habren" (11v), a mention of navigation into Scythia near Cathay (32r), and a reference to Mercator's *Chronologia* (37v).[81] As with Bale, Dee found material to excite his patriotism—both for England (see the reference to the "Monarchia totius Albionis" on 69v) and for Wales (on 54r he underlined a passage about the Welsh people going under the name "Bruti" and he interjected, "Shalbe called agayne"). Finally, the back flyleaf (which I discussed in Chapter 2) contains remarkable evidence that Dee—like Bale and John Joscelyn—made an in-depth, nationwide search for old English monuments and manuscripts.

Although Dee possessed some valuable manuscript sources for ecclesiastical history, they were not systematically collected or annotated; and we must assume that Dee's interest was, generally speaking, more bibliographical and antiquarian than intellectual.[82] An exception must be made for saints' lives, which contained a good deal of information about the history and geography of particular regions: Dee was especially interested in lives of St. Dunstan, for the testimonies they offered regarding Glastonbury, the supposed burial-place of King Arthur.[83] One manuscript miscellany principally devoted to ecclesiastical matters impinged on several of Dee's interests. In item 4 (*De Regibus Angliae ab Alfredo ad Henricum Quintum*) Dee predictably provided many topical notes about early rulers. In item 9 (*Definitiones virtutum et vitiorum*) Dee highlighted the Ciceronian passages on "prudencia" (65r), "[iu]sticia" (65v), "fortitudo" (66v), and "Temperance" (67r)—thus making it a possible source for his discussion of "Vertue" in the *Brytannicae Reipublicae Synopsis* (the subject of Chapter 6 below). And a note in item 15 suggests both that such histories offered valuable precedents for legal and institutional purposes (and were thus related to deeds and charters) and that Dee was in contact with ecclesiastical leaders in the early 1590s: next to a passage about the establishment of St. David's House Dee wrote, "as allso the bishop doth specify in a Dede of his A° 1592: made for my vse" (216v).

One volume, which might be considered ancient as much as ecclesiastical history, was of particular interest to Dee: Matthaeus Beroaldus' *Chronicum* (no. 86). This was a wide-ranging work on chronology, geography, and science from biblical sources. Dee displays his usual concerns: the Trojan War (e3v), early rulers (t5v), the chronology of Christ's birth (f6r),[84] and Hebrew etymology.[85]

As we should by now expect, Dee's marginalia in books of ancient history were highly selective and indicate not a general reading but a systematic plundering of particular precedents. He was almost exclusively interested in Britain and those who could even remotely be considered its founders and early rulers.[86] He attended, as usual, to geographical, navigational, and legal matters, and was especially sensitive to discussions of imperial limits: on page 816 of no. 903 he underlined ". . . imperij limites" (a phrase he used to title his collection of writings on this subject) and wrote "Limites" in the margin. In Herodotus' histories he singled out a discussion of "the Western Sea . . . agaynst Arabia" (no. 257, p. 40).[87]

Dee was not alone in concentrating on British history at the expense of other traditions: the English historiographers were almost uniformly insular. But nowhere did this show more than in the margins of Dee's books on European history.[88] He skimmed over discussions of France (nos. 72 and 360) and Flanders (no. 348), pausing only to note mentions of British geography and genealogy. On page 40 of Rene Chopin's *De domanio Franciae* (no. 360), Dee's imperialistic chauvinism (and his command of historical sources) rears its head: next to the mention of a certain region Dee objected, "That is proper to our auncient Brytains, Humfrey lloyd doth well prove in his Breuiary of Brytaine." In one European history (no. 531), however, Dee did glance across the Channel, noting a list of early Spanish kings (478ff.)—though this was no doubt read in relation to his competing list of British precedents. And in a description of Germany (no. 184), Dee clarified a geographical error pertaining to the North Sea[89] and made the linguistic observation that most of the kings mentioned had names that ended in "rich" or "mir" (XVIIr).

Mathematical Sciences

Given the magnitude of Dee's contribution to the mathematical sciences, as well as the astounding depth of his original collection in this area, his marginal remains are disappointingly spare. Most of his copies of Euclid seem to have disappeared, and the one currently held in the British Library (no. 1078) is annotated only lightly. Likewise, his *Opera* of Archimedes (no. 167) is almost note-free.[90] The notes that do survive are more in line with the approach in his "Mathematicall Praeface" to the English Euclid than his more mystical writings on numbers[91] and (since this text was in many ways conventional—much more so than has been acknowledged) therefore in line with the concerns of other sixteenth-century mathematical writers.

The supreme virtue of mathematics for Renaissance thinkers was its (relative) demonstrative certitude.[92] As Dee wrote in his "Mathematicall Praeface" to the English Euclid, "In Mathematicall reasonings, a probable Argument, is nothyng regarded: nor yet the testimony of sense, any whit credited: But onely a perfect demonstration, of truthes certaine, necessary, and inuincible: vniuersally and necessaryly concluded: is allowed as sufficient for an Argument exactly and purely Mathematical" (☞ 4v–*1r). For mathematicians like Dee, the mathematical disciplines were not only the most persuasive but the most *useful*[93] for the apprehension of natural causes and effects and the application of these principles to the benefit of humanity—and, as Dee would have added, the glory of God, whose miraculous creation it uncovered and celebrated.[94] On mathematics a huge range of other sciences depended, from astrology to surveying. Indeed, as Robert Westman suggested in relation to Copernicus, the mathematical sciences promised to lay bare the "common principles underlying all disciplines" and, therefore, offered a glimpse of the "Platonic image of the unity of all knowledge."[95]

What Dee called attention to in his mathematical readings was, then, the certitude of mathematical proofs, the utility and dignity of mathematical sciences, and the relation of mathematics to a number of disciplines or subdisciplines. All of these concerns are clearly seen in his copy of Andreas Alexander's textbook, the *Mathemalogia* (no. 79). On the opening folio Dee noted a passage on "Mathematicae Vtilitas." He wrote topical notes for the related sciences of prognostication (C1v) and perspective (D2r) as well as the applications of "Subaltern" mathematics. But throughout the text, he paid most attention to the basic principles of mathematics and especially demonstration. On A2r, for instance, he noted in the margin, "Demo*n*strationes propter quid," "Primus modus certitudinis," "Causa/effectus," and, most simply of all, "Mathematicae definitio." The most interesting of these notes accompanies Alexander's concise summary of the Aristotelian principles of demonstration (D5r).[96] Dee bracketed the passage and, in the unusually spacious margin, summarized it in tabular form.

In his mathematical thinking, as in his study of all scientific disciplines, Dee was guided above all by Roger Bacon.[97] From the start of his "Compendii Philosophiae Fragmentum" (no. DM113), Dee noted passages on "Mathematicaru*m* Vtilitas" (4r and 6r). On folios 56ff. Bacon directly addressed the application of mathematics to the other sciences: in the upper right corner of that page, Dee signaled, "Applicatio M[a]thematicaru[m] ad alias scie[ntias]." At the bottom of the page Dee recorded a sentence that not only paraphrases Bacon's teaching but captures the principle that guided Dee's scientific practice throughout his life: "bonu*m* no*n* est in mathematicis secundu*m* se: sed dum vel physice vel Theologice a Mathematicis progredimur. I.D." For Dee mathematics was not an end in itself: its benefits were only realized in application to physics and theology—and (for Dee it went without saying) astronomy.

Astronomy/Astrology

"The *data* of astronomy," as W. P. D. Wightman so concisely put it, "were the apparent motions of the heavenly bodies. The primary purpose of every astronomer was to discover or invent a rational system whereby these phenomena could be accounted for, and their past and future states determined."[98] Dee would certainly have subscribed to this description: in the books he read, in the horoscopes he calculated, and even in the more avant-garde astral theories he produced, he never deviated from the collection of data on the motions of heavenly bodies and the attempt to discover the system of their influences.

While Dee must have recorded astrological and meteorological observations in notebooks or diaries, he also used the margins of his books and manuscripts to collect data. In a few cases, he used the flyleaves for this purpose. In others he added personal observations to those of an author. In Paulus Crusius' *Doctrina revolutionum solis* (no. 546) Dee added to the title page of a set of tables notes regarding the meridians for several European cities. And in Cyprian Leowitz's compendium of eclipses Dee added to one of the diagrams notes about his sighting in London, with the resulting discrepancies in planetary positions.[99]

What emerges from a thorough reading of Ptolemy's *Quadripartitum* (no. 37) is an interest in theories of divination and prognostication, the practical problems of calculating nativities, and the philosophical issues of fortune and free will. A loose leaf bound in as a flyleaf contains a long note (dated "1551. Meloni 14 Septembris") in which Dee relates a number of theories about the relations of a body's disposition and a person's nativity to fortune. In the text there are many notes relating to the influences of heavenly bodies on terrestrial phenomena—the subject of Dee's own *Propaedeumata aphoristica*.[100] This was a guide to practice as well as theory: Dee drew a small horoscope in the margin of E8v, and on the bottom of F8v he wrote out a summary of the "Modus tradendi astrologiam." Dee acknowledged the obvious fact that it was a fundamental text: at one point he jotted, "Nota hunc locum & sequentes pro fundamento Directionum" (H2r).

As with mathematics (to which astronomy and astrology were fundamentally bound), the nature and utility of the discipline itself was a key, and much-discussed, question. Robert S. Westman explains that "humanistically inclined scholars" (including Dee) argued for the value of the sciences of the stars "by stressing the certitude of their demonstrations and their utility to practical endeavour," as well as their connections to other areas of knowledge "such as medicine and theology."[101] In Dee's copy of the Alphonsine Tables (no. 340) a particularly eloquent description of "Vtilitas huius Artis astrorum" (as Dee put it in his topical note) caught his eye: "Haec siquidem ars diuina vtilis quidem est Grammaticis, Rhetoribus, Dialecticis: necessaria Philosophis, neces-

saria [. . .] & Medicis: Agricolis praeterea, nauium gubernator-
ibus, Architectis, Imperatoribus" (a2r). Astral arts were useful for
all of these disciplines and professions. But for solving two "pressing problems of the period" in particular a knowledge of the
motions of the heavenly bodies was "necessary and sufficient . . . :
the correction of the calendar and the fixing of position at sea."[102]
These are both subjects on which Dee wrote extensively in the
1570s and 1580s: in fact, at that time he can be considered England's leading expert on applied astrology and astronomy.

Medicine

Medical books are among those most consistently annotated by
early modern readers. As I showed in the previous chapter, medical
practitioners used the margins of medical books not only to highlight useful information in the text but to record their own recipes
and treatments. Dee, himself an amateur physician, followed these
practices. In his manuscript of Johannes de Mirfeld's *Breviarium
Bartholomaei* (no. M31) he noted recipes as they occurred in the text
and entered his own in the margins, and on the blank last leaf and
flyleaf. As with Caius' Galen and the Adv. Hollerius, Dee's medical
marginalia show signs of accumulation over a long period of time:
Dee dated the *Breviarium* upon its acquisition in 1573, and entered
his recipes through the 1580s and into the 1590s. And on the
flyleaves of his copy of Galen's *Prognostica de decubitu infirmorum* (no.
951) there are notes on the illnesses of Sir Leonel Ducket and Roger
Cook, and on the treatments Dee administered.[103] Dee must have
returned to this text, too, at different points in time: it is signed
and dated 1551 on the title page, and the note of Ducket's illness is
dated 26 August 1573.

In light of Charles Webster's assertion that Dee played an active
part in the development of English Paracelsianism—and considering that he had an almost complete collection of Paracelsian
texts—it is disappointing to find so little evidence for Dee's reading of the German medical reformer. His influence on Dee can,
however, be gauged by the frequency of cross-references to Paracelsus in non-Paracelsian texts.[104] Dee's copy of Paracelsus' textbook
on water-therapies (the *De Balneis*—no. 1476) does survive and
can be taken as representative. On the front flyleaf there is a
summary of the contents of nine chapters (possibly of the *Archidoxa*

and not the *De Balneis*), the ninth of which Dee somehow knew to
be "De praxi" even though "non est impressus." Dee signed the
book on the title page (dating it 1562, the year of its publication)
and added a sentence to the effect that the work concerns not only
'common baths' (*vulgaribus Balneis*) but 'indeed the most secret
hot springs of the philosophers' (*de secretissimis etiam philosophorum
Thermis*). Although this statement might lead us to expect more,
Dee's annotations reveal mostly practical interests. He attends to
the composition of certain chemical baths (E4r) and twice adds
notes about English equivalents to Paracelsus' German materials.
At the bottom of D3r he wrote, "In england, at Knaesborowgh, by
Wetherby in the York shyre, is a well by the river syde which in the
space of a wynter turneth any wood to stone"; and on H2r he
suggested, "Try our salt witches in England." On the back flyleaf,
finally, Dee made notes on 31 May 1594 about some of his associates and a vicar who "hath Raymund Lully his works in a skroll."

BY WAY of conclusion, I want to consider one final reading from
one final subject. In Dee's copy of Cicero's *Opera Omnia* (no. 246),
one page in the "De Natura Deorum" had particular significance
(p. 213)—see Fig. 7. On it Cicero argues for the presence of a divine intelligence behind the created world. This alone would have
been enough to interest Dee, and we see from the topical notes, as
well as the list of words at the top and bottom of the page, that he
was engaged by the argument and enchanted by much of its language. [105] But what gave this passage an almost uncanny resonance
for Dee was Cicero's use of astronomical and navigational examples.

In a passage that Dee naturally bracketed, and keyed with a
picture of the "Posidonij Sphaera," Cicero asks, "Suppose a trav-
eller to carry into Scythia or Britain the orrery recently constructed
by our friend Posidonius, which at each revolution reproduces the
same motions of the sun, the moon and the five planets that take
place in the heavens every twenty-four hours, would any single
native doubt that this orrery was the work of a rational being?" [106]
Here we have a celebration of the technical mastery of the astronomer, and a connection between Scythia and Britain, as well as
compelling proof of the divine providence ("Prouidentia") that not
only brought the wondrous world into being but allowed its highest inhabitant to enjoy its wonders.

But the page touches on another kind of "Prouidentia"—the providence that justified the "discovery" of "barbarians" and endorsed their indoctrination with the knowledge of the heavens and the Christian God who ruled them.[107] Twice on the page Dee underlined passing references to ships ("classium nauigatio" and "cursum nauigii") before coming to the *pièce de résistance:* in Accius' *Medea* the shepherd, "who had never seen a ship before, on descrying in the distance from his mountaintop the strange vessel of the Argonauts, built by the gods, in his first amazement and alarm cries out:

> so huge a bulk
> Glides from the deep with the roar of a whistling wind:
> Waves roll before, and eddies surge and swirl;
> Hurtling headlong, it snorts and sprays the foam. . . .

Dee was evidently moved by this speech, not only to underline it and give it a topical note, but to sketch a remarkable drawing of a carrack—with Jason's crew peering over the railing through the "spraying foam." In the margins of one of Dee's books, then, we are given access to an intellectual response, an act of mediation and appropriation, which is both personal and providential.

Figure 1. Engraved portrait of Dee: detail from the frontispiece to Meric
Casaubon's *A True and Faithfull Relation* (1659). [By permission of the
Syndics of Cambridge University Library]

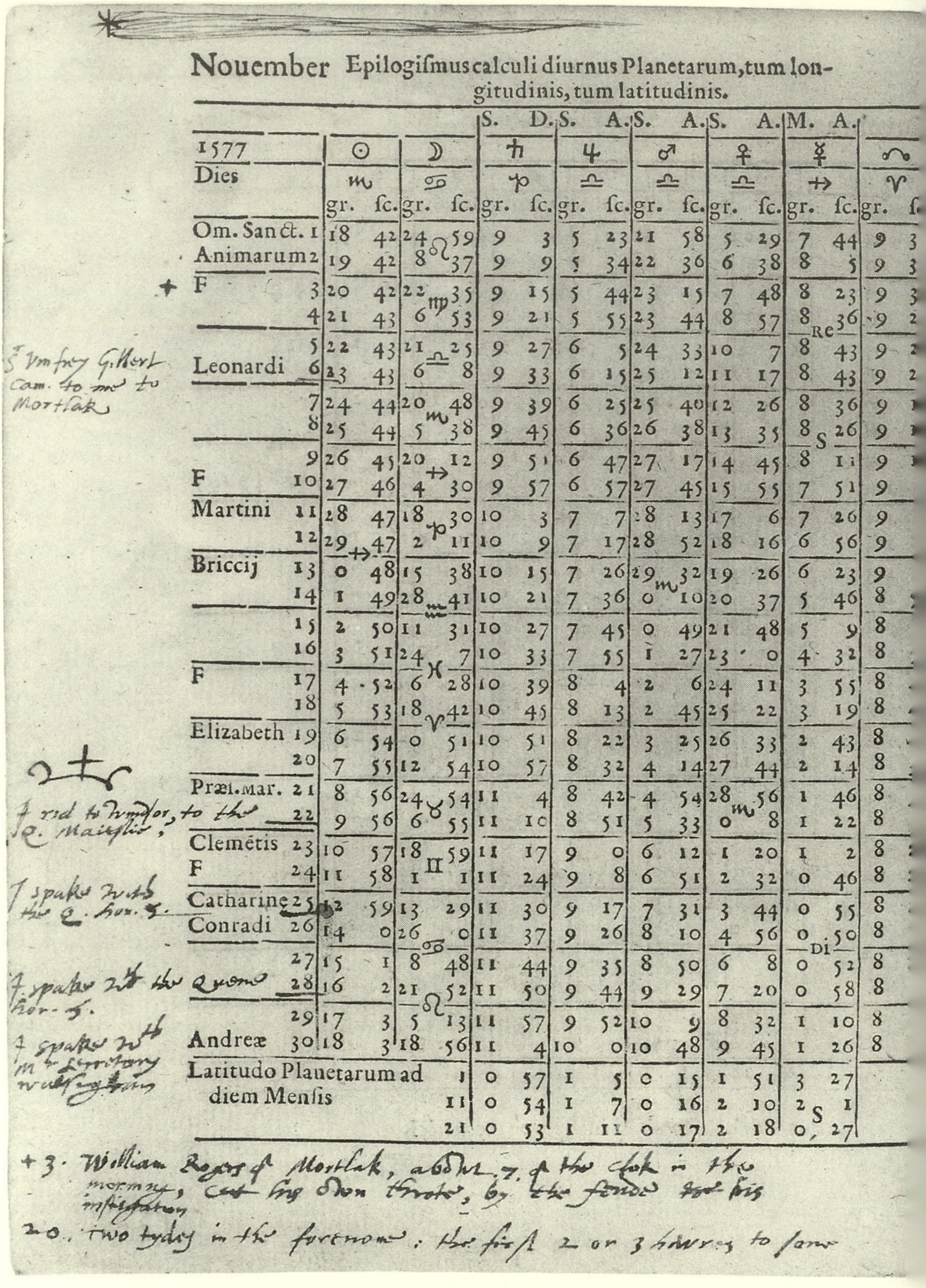

1577 Dies	S. ☉ ♏ gr. sc.	D.S. ☽ ♋ gr. sc.	A.S. ♄ ♑ gr. sc.	A.S. ♃ ♎ gr. sc.	A.S. ♂ ♎ gr. sc.	A.M. ♀ ♎ gr. sc.	A. ☿ ♐ gr. sc.	♊ ♈ gr. s
Om. Sanct. 1	18 42	24 59	9 3	5 23	21 58	5 29	7 44	9 3
Animarum 2	19 42	8 37	9 9	5 34	22 36	6 38	8 5	9 3
F 3	20 42	22 35	9 15	5 44	23 15	7 48	8 23	9 3
4	21 43	6 53	9 21	5 55	23 44	8 57	8 36 Re	9 2
5	22 43	21 25	9 27	6 5	24 33	10 7	8 43	9 2
Leonardi 6	23 43	6 8	9 33	6 15	25 12	11 17	8 43	9 2
7	24 44	20 48	9 39	6 25	25 40	12 26	8 36	9 1
8	25 44	5 38	9 45	6 36	26 38	13 35	8 26 S	9 1
9	26 45	20 12	9 51	6 47	27 17	14 45	8 11	9 1
10	27 46	4 30	9 57	6 57	27 45	15 55	7 51	9
Martini 11	28 47	18 30	10 3	7 7	28 13	17 6	7 26	9
12	29 47	2 11	10 9	7 17	28 52	18 16	6 56	9
Briccij 13	0 48	15 38	10 15	7 26	29 32	19 26	6 23	9
14	1 49	28 41	10 21	7 36	0 10	20 37	5 46	8
15	2 50	11 31	10 27	7 45	0 49	21 48	5 9	8
16	3 51	24 7	10 33	7 55	1 27	23 0	4 32	8
F 17	4 52	6 28	10 39	8 4	2 6	24 11	3 55	8
18	5 53	18 42	10 45	8 13	2 45	25 22	3 19	8
Elizabeth 19	6 54	0 51	10 51	8 22	3 25	26 33	2 43	8
20	7 55	12 54	10 57	8 32	4 14	27 44	2 14	8
Prael. mar. 21	8 56	24 54	11 4	8 42	4 54	28 56	1 46	8
22	9 56	6 55	11 10	8 51	5 33	0 8	1 22	8
Clemetis 23	10 57	18 59	11 17	9 0	6 12	1 20	1 2	8
F 24	11 58	1 1	11 24	9 8	6 51	2 32	0 46	8
Catharine 25	12 59	13 29	11 30	9 17	7 31	3 44	0 55	8
Conradi 26	14 0	26 0	11 37	9 26	8 10	4 56	0 50 Di	8
27	15 1	8 48	11 44	9 35	8 50	6 8	0 52	8
28	16 2	21 52	11 50	9 44	9 29	7 20	0 58	8
29	17 3	5 13	11 57	9 52	10 9	8 32	1 10	8
Andreae 30	18 3	18 56	12 4	10 0	10 48	9 45	1 26	8
Latitudo Planetarum ad diem Mensis 1			0 57	1 5	0 15	1 51	3 27	
11			0 54	1 7	0 16	2 10	2 1	
21			0 53	1 11	0 17	2 18	0 27	

Marginal notes (left):

☿ Umfrey Gilbert cam. to me to Mortlak

♃ ☌ ♀

I rod to Windsor, to the Q. Maiestie

I spake with the Q. hor. ♄

I spake with the Q hor. ♄

I spake with Mr Secretary Walsingham

Bottom notes:

+3. William Rogers of Mortlak, about 7. of the clok in the morning, cut his own throte, by the fende & his instigation

20. two tydes in the forenone: the first 2 or 3 howres to sone

Figure 2. Dee's diary for November 1577, kept in the margins of Joannes Stadius's *Ephemerides novae* (Bodleian Library, MS Ashmole 487, sig. Pppp2v–Pppp3r). The opening includes entries for meetings with Queen Elizabeth and Sir Humphrey Gilbert and a sketch of the comet which appeared in that month. [Courtesy of The Bodleian Library, Oxford]

+ Declared to the Q. her Title to Groenland &
Estotland
Frisland.

November — Syzygiæ Lunares. — Syzygiæ Planetarum mutuæ.

7 s		☉	♄ Occid.	♃ Orient.	♂ Orient.	♀ Orient.	☿ Occid.	Syzygiæ Planetarum mutuæ
1				✳ 17		✳ 22	△ 23	
2	□ 22							
3					✳ 3			✳ ♀ ☿
4			△ 5				□ 4	□ ♄ ☿
5	✳ 4							
6			□ 5	♂ 1		♂ 11	✳ 5	☽ ～
7					♂ 10			☽ περιγ.
8			✳ 6					
9	♂ 6 54							
10				✳ 3		✳ 4	♂ 5	
11					✳ 18			✳ ♃ ☿
12			♂ 15	□ 10		□ 8		
13								
14	✳ 7			△ 16	□ 3		✳ 13	
15						△ 22		
16	□ 22				△ 8		□ 7	♂ ☉ ☿
17			✳ 8				Orient.	
18								
19	△ 13		□ 10	♂ 15			△ 4	☽ ～
20								☽ απογ. ✳ ♃ ☉
21			△ 4		♂ 22	♂ 9		
22								
23							♂ 22	
24			△ 19					
25	♂ 1 17							
26						△ 19		
27			♂ 3	□ 2	△ 0			
28								
29			✳ 9		□ 10	□ 6		
30							△ 3	☉

Sexto Idus Nouembris ♃ ἀπγειότατος.

18º. Bordered of Mr Edward Hynde of Mortlak 30ᵗʰ to
be repayed at Hallontyde, next yere
PPPP 3

Figure 3. Dee's entry in Abraham Ortelius's friendship album.
[Reproduced by kind permission of the Master and Fellows of Pembroke
College, Cambridge]

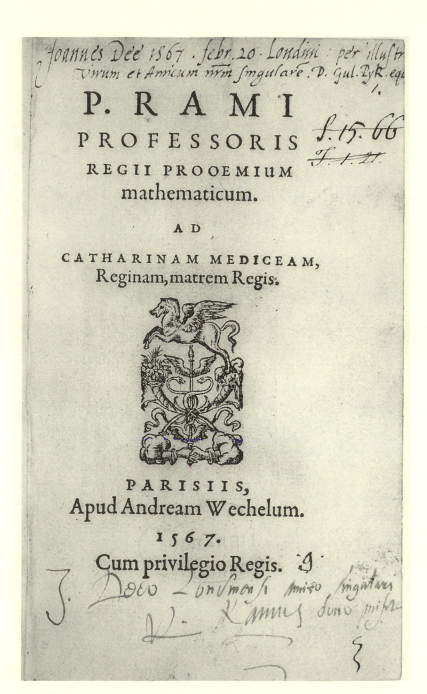

Figure 4. Title page of P. Ramus, *Prooemium mathematicum* (1567),
bearing Ramus's dedication to Dee. [By permission of the Master and
Fellows of Trinity College, Cambridge]

Figure 5. Detail from Dee's genealogical roll (British Library, Cotton Charter XIV article 1), showing the final section of his lineage as well as his self-portrait, motto, and coat of arms. [By permission of the British Library]

106

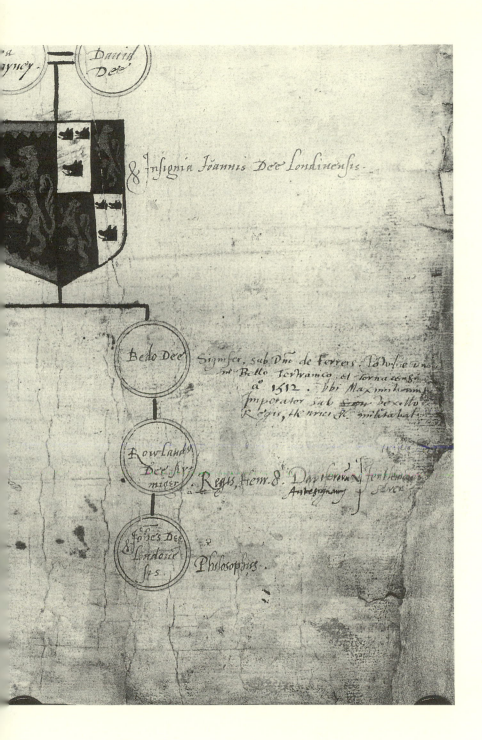

&Insignia Joannis Dee Londinensis.

Bedo Dee   Signifer, sub Dño de Ferrers Wolsie. nñ
          nī Bello Terwancō, et Terna ēnsī
              aͦ 1512. Jbi Maximilianus
          Jmperator sub bexillo
          Regis, Henrici R. militabat.

Row lands
Dee Ar-
miœr.   Regis, Hen. 8. Dapiferoru Gentlewaer
          Antesignaun of serve

Joπes Dee
& Londini
fis.   Philosophus.

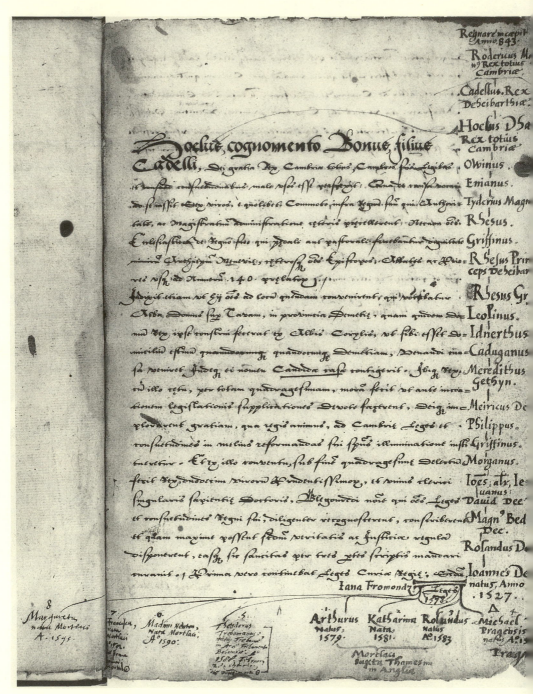

Figure 6. Genealogical marginalia in Dee's autograph copy of *The Laws of Hywel Dda*. [By permission of the Warden and Fellows of Merton College, Oxford]

108

ſtirpes enim terræ inhærent,animantes autē aſpiratiōe aeris ſuſtinentur,ipſéque aer no-
biſcum videt,nobiſcum audit,nobiſcū ſonat. nihil enim eorum ſine eo fieri poteſt.Quin
etiam mouetur nobiſcum.quacunque enim imus,quacunque mouemur,videtur quaſi locum dare & cedere:quǽque in medium locum mundi, qui eſt infimus, & quæ à medio in
ſuperum,quǽque conuerſione rotunda circū medium feruntur,ea continentem mundi efficiunt, vnámque naturā.Et quum quatuor genera ſint corporum,viciſſitudine eorū mun
di natura eſt cōtinuata.Nam ex terra aqua,ex aqua oritur aer,ex aere æther,deinde retror-
ſum viciſſim ex æthere aer,inde aqua,ex aqua terra infima. Sic naturis his ex quibus omnia conſtant,ſurſum deorſum, vltro citróque cōmeantibus,mundi partium coiunctio con
tinetur,quæ aut ſempiterna ſit neceſſe eſt hoc eodem ornatu quem videmus,aut certe per-
diuturna permanens ad longinquum & immenſum penè tempus:quorum vtrunuis vt ſit,
ſequitur natura mundum adminiſtrari.Quæ enim claſſium nauigatio, aut quæ inſtructio
exercitus:aut rurſus(vt ea quæ natura efficit,conferamus)quæ procreatio vitis,aut arboris,
quæ porrò animantis figura, conformatióque membrorum tantam naturæ ſolertiam ſig-
nificat,quantā ipſe mundus?Aut igitur nihil eſt quod ſentiente natura regatur,aut mundum regi confitendum eſt . Etenim qui reliquas naturas omnes earúmque ſemina conti-
neat,quí poteſt ipſe nō natura adminiſtrari:vt ſiqui dentes & pubertatem natura dicat exi-
ſtere,ipſum autem hominem cui ea exiſtant non conſtare natura,non intelligat ea quæ effe-
rant aliquid ex ſeſe,perfectiores habere naturas quàm ea quæ ex iis efferātur.Omnium au
tem rerum quæ natura adminiſtrantur ſeminator,& ſator,& parens,vt ita dicā,atque edu-
cator & altor eſt mūdus,omniáque ſicut mēbra & partes ſuas nutricatur & cōtinet.Quòd
ſi mundi partes natura adminiſtrantur,neceſſe eſt mūdum ipſum natura adminiſtrari. Cu
ius quidem adminiſtratio nihil habet in ſe quod reprehēdi poſſit.Ex iis enim naturis quæ
erant,quod effici optimum potuit effectum eſt.Doceat ergo aliquis potuiſſe melius,ſed ne
mo vnquam docebit. & ſiquis corrigere aliquid volet,aut deterius faciet: aut id quod fieri non potuerit,deſiderabit.Quòd ſi omnes mundi partes ita conſtitutæ ſunt, vt neque ad
vſum meliores potuerint eſſe,neque ad ſpeciem pulchriores, videamus vtrum ea fortuita-
ne ſint, an eo ſtatu, quo cohærere nullo modo potuerint niſi ſenſu moderante, diuináque
prouidentia.Si igitur meliora ſunt ea quæ natura,quàm illa quæ arte perfecta ſunt,nec ars
efficit quidquam ſine ratione, ne natura quidem rationis expers ſit habenda . Quí igitur
conuenit ſignum aut tabulam pictam quum aſpexeris,ſcire adhibitam eſſe artem: quúm-
que procul curſum nauigii videris,non dubitare quin id ratione atque arte moueatur: aut
quum ſolarium,vel deſcriptum, aut ex aqua contemplare, intelligere declarari horas arte
non caſu:mundum autem,qui & has ipſas artes,& earum artifices,& cuncta complectatur,
conſilii & rationis eſſe expertem putare?Quod ſi in Scythiam aut in Britāniam ſphæram
aliquis tulerit, hanc quam nuper familiaris noſter effecit Poſidonius , cuius ſingulæ con-
uerſiones idem efficiunt in ſole & in luna & in quinque ſtellis errantibus,quod efficitur in
cælo ſingulis diebus & noctibus:quis in illa barbarie dubitet quin ea ſphæra ſit perfecta ra
tione?Hi autem dubitant de mundo,ex quo & oriuntur & fiunt omnia,caſúne ipſe ſit ef-
fectus,aut neceſſitate aliqua,an ratione,ac mente diuina. & Archimedem arbitrantur plus
valuiſſe in imitandis ſphæræ cōuerſionibus,quàm naturam in efficiendis,preſertim quum
multis partibus ſint illa perfecta,quàm hæc ſimulata ſolertius.Atque ille apud Accium pa
ſtor qui nauem nunquam ante vidiſſet,vt procul diuinū & nouum vehiculum Argonau-
tarum è monte conſpexit,primo admirans & perterritus hoc modo loquitur,

Tanta moles labitur
Fremebunda ex alto ingenti ſonitu & ſtrepitu,
Præ ſe vndas voluit,vertices vi ſuſcitat,
Ruit prolapſa,pelagus reſpergit,profluit:
Ita dum interruptum credas nimbum voluier,
Dum quod ſublime ventis expulſum,rapi
Saxum aut procellis,vel globoſos turbines

Oo.iii.

Figure 7. Dee's annotations in Cicero's *De Natura Deorum*. [By
permission of the Royal College of Physicians, London]

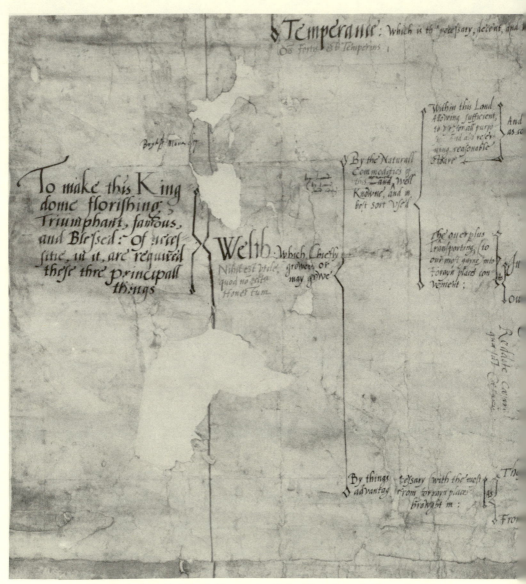

Figure 8. Detail of Dee's *Brytannicae Reipublicae Synopsis (Synopsis of the British Commonwealth)* (1570; British Library, Cotton Charter XIII article 39). See next page for full image. [By permission of the British Library]

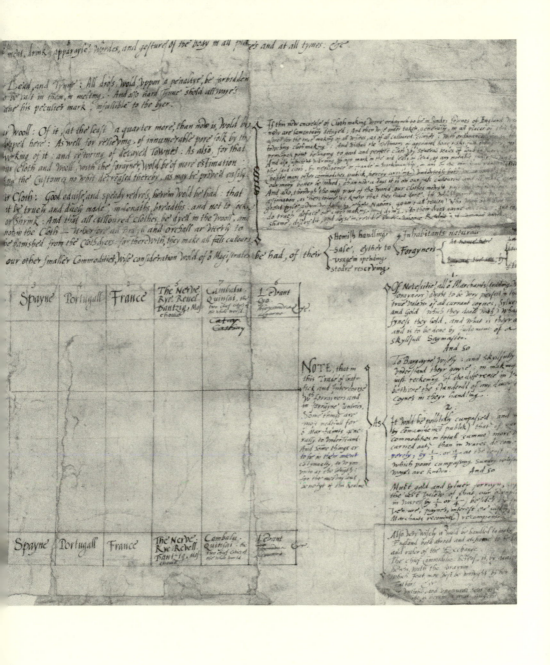

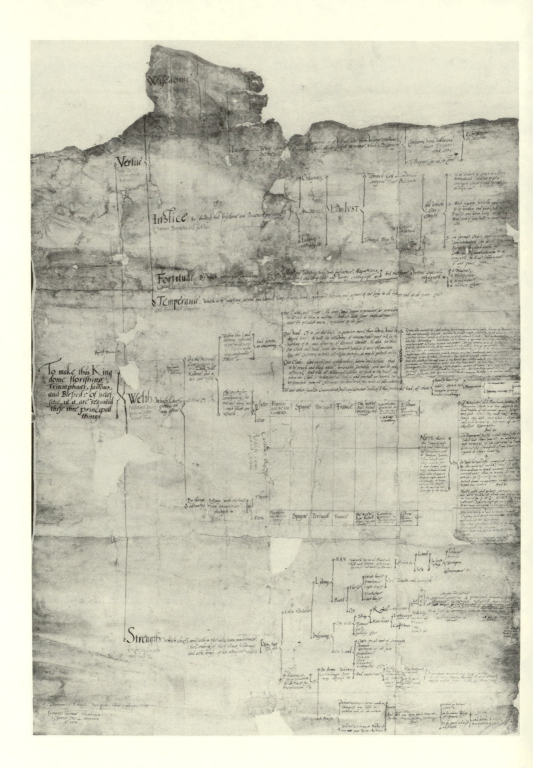

III. Writings

Ioan. Stradanus invent.   Phls. Galle excud.

FIVE

Dee's Political Science

An Introduction to the Manuscript Writings

Reading maketh a full man; conference a ready man; and writing an exact man. —Francis Bacon, "Of Studies"

Dee's manuscript writings have received attention inversely proportionate to their bulk and importance within the corpus of his works. Studies of Dee have concentrated overwhelmingly on his printed works: with few exceptions, the manuscripts have not figured as a whole, and some have been excluded altogether.[1] The historiographical problems this has created are made instantly apparent by a single statistic: of the seventy-six items in Clulee's bibliography of Dee's writings and the forty-four items in Dee's own account of "My labors and paines bestowed at divers tymes . . . by writing of divers bookes and treatises,"[2] the vast majority circulated, during his life, in manuscript. He published only four complete books: in his few remaining publications he played an editorial role, providing prefaces, introductions, emendations, or annotations. Accounts that do not consider the manuscripts are not simply incomplete; they are misleading. Dee's manuscripts address a whole range of subjects not found in his printed works and, further, they represent different kinds of authorial activity and different modes of socioprofessional interaction. My brief discussions, in the following chapters, of Dee's *Brytannicae Reipublicae Synopsis* and his writings on navigation and "imperial geography" are intended to restore a broader and more accurate sense of his textual and political agency; to assess his contributions to Elizabethan historical scholarship and his efforts to advance the English commonwealth and the British Empire.

The exclusion of Dee's manuscripts can be attributed in part—as I suggested in my Introduction—to the "blinkers" worn by those in the Yatesian tradition. In order to present Dee as a magus, and to do so in such a compelling fashion, the Yatesians have been forced to ignore those materials which are peripheral or, worse, contradictory to that story. Yates herself seems to have believed that there were few manuscripts to study: she acknowledged that in Dee's lifetime "there were many works by Dee passing from hand to hand in manuscript," but she added that "many, indeed most . . . are unknown to us."[3] On the contrary; not only do many of the manuscripts that Dee inventoried in 1592 survive, but so do some that he did not mention.[4] The exclusion can also be attributed to a more deeply seated and widely held set of assumptions concerning the relation between script and print. These add up to a discernible antimanuscript bias, a (usually) tacit belief that the manuscripts that *have* survived are less significant than the printed works. Graham Yewbrey lamented that "Despite the great number of his manuscripts presently extant, research in the life and thought of John Dee . . . is frequently hampered by the non-survival of important works."[5] While many works with tantalizing titles are apparently lost—such as *Cabalae Hebraicae compendiosa tabella; The Originals, and Chiefe points, of our auncient Brytish Histories;* and *De modo Euangelij Iesu Christi publicandi, propagandi, stabiliendique, inter Infideles Atlanticos*—research opportunities are far from exhausted. The antimanuscript bias reaches its most blatant form in the entry on Dee in the *Dictionary of Welsh Biography,* which declares that "it is not possible to assess the value of Dee's works, as most of the seventy-nine he composed still remain in manuscript form."[6]

Such blanket assumptions of a linear progression from script to print, with a concomitant escalation in the importance of a work, are untenable—particularly for the early modern period. As Harold Love and others have shown, many texts (especially poems) circulated as manuscripts in a private fashion, among a coterie for whom the work would have a special meaning, value, and use.[7] This was not only the case with literary, nor with occult or scientific, material.[8] Political, social, and economic debate, too, was largely confined to "private," manuscript circulation: many projects and position papers were submitted directly to the government under highly controlled conditions. These political manuscripts, which is how many of Dee's writings must be classified, were never intended for—indeed, would have been inappropriate for—a wider reading public. Finally, we must treat the script-print interface as complex and bidirectional: manuscript features continued to appear in printed texts, and many printed texts were subsequently reproduced and circulated in manuscript. Some of Dee's works remained in manuscript, then, because they never reached the finality of form demanded of general publication; but most did so not because they were unsuccessful but because that was the conventional form for the writings of a well-connected scholarly adviser.

A case in point—and an unusually well-documented one at that—is Dee's proposal for the reform of the Julian calendar.[9] On 24 February 1582, Pope Gregory XIII ordered the use of the reformed (i.e., Gregorian) calendar: during the month of March the English court was deliberating over its response. A commission of mathematicians and theologians was enlisted, and Dee was approached for a report. By the 25th of March he had finished his "playne discourse . . . concerning the needfull reformation of the vulgar Kalender."[10] Building up a case based on astronomical and arithmetical calculations and informed by classical and medieval sources (including Julius Caesar, Hipparchus, Ptolemy, Simon Bredon, and Roger Bacon), Dee came to the conclusion that there was a discrepancy of eleven rather than ten days between England and the Continent, and devised a schedule for absorbing them in the course of the following year.

Dee submitted the text directly to Lord Burghley and, in the most elaborate copy, it opens with his clever dedicatory poem to the "Lord Threasorer of Englande":

> . . . I shew the thing, and reason why:
> At large, in breif, in middle wise,
> I humbly give a playne Aduise
> For want of tyme, the Tyme Vntrew
> Yf I haue myst, Commaunde anew
> Your Honor may: So shall you see,
> That Loue of Truth, doth govern me.[11]

Burghley seems to have headed the commission, and it was he who consulted Thomas Digges, Henry Savile, and a Mr. Chambers for their opinions of Dee's proposal (which were all favorable). But Dee's voice was not represented only by the "playne discourse," nor was he excluded from the inner circle of debate. Two of Burghley's memoranda on Dee's discourse—one very positive, one much less so—survive among his papers, and they reveal that he "conferred also by speche with [Dee] at good length thearin."[12] But it was Secretary Walsingham who took on the more difficult (and ultimately unsuccessful) role of mediating between Dee and the stubborn council of bishops, as well as between Dee and Lord Burghley. The copy of the proposal now held in Corpus Christi College, Oxford, contains three letters from Walsingham to Dee (fols. 182, 184, and 186). One of these is a short note from Richmond, dated 25 March 1582, expressing Burghley's urgent desire for a consultation. This may have resulted in the meeting that Burghley records, but Walsingham gives a more precise sense of Burghley's pragmatic concerns: "he is appointed to conferre with the Iudges about it least the alteration may breed some error in the return of writtes."[13] In a short postscript Walsingham promised to meet with Dee himself regarding another project (one on which the two had worked together during the previous decade), as if to reassure him of his connectedness and the value of his service, despite the impending failure of the calendar proposal: "On thvrsdaye I woulde be glad to confer w^t yow towching the grawnt y^t is passte from the Compagnye of Moscovia vnto Mr Adrian Gilbert."[14]

The most under-studied—and therefore the most unexpected—aspect of Dee's career which emerges from his manuscript writings is his significant contribution to the historical scholarship of Tudor England. This development, which by most accounts was stimulated by the arrival of humanism (with its methods for recovering and processing texts and its belief in the utility of the past for present governments), was marked by new sources, techniques, and attitudes. Most strikingly, it gave rise to a new field of antiquarian research.[15] With the encouragement of powerful patrons, scholars and statesmen began a "laboryouse journey & serche" for the traces of ancient and medieval Britain.[16] They listed manuscripts, catalogued monuments, gathered records, reconstructed genealogies, collected coats of arms, and mapped the remote corners of the kingdom. The fathers of this movement were John

Leland and John Bale: the dangers confronting English antiquities after the dissolution of the monasteries—which provoked Dee's petition to Queen Mary and his own efforts of preservation—stirred them to search out and inventory forgotten manuscripts and unnoticed monuments. "In attempting thus to furnish a guide to the manuscript sources of English history, in supplying biographies, bibliographies, and word lists," Leland and Bale laid the foundations for all subsequent work.[17]

As we have seen, Dee collected, copied, and constructed manuscripts, records, genealogies, and coats of arms. He was in close contact with most of the principal antiquaries, heralds, historiographers, and book collectors of his day. He was a member of William Camden's extraordinary circle of correspondents (alongside Mercator and Ortelius): Dee's surviving letters include one addressed to his "singular good friend," William Camden, "learned in pure philosophy and true history."[18] This remarkable letter was dated from Mortlake in 1574 (when Camden was only twenty-three years old), and—in response to queries from Camden, presented to Dee via John Stow—expounded the mysteries of the number 120, the letter delta, and Dee's genealogy. During the following year Camden was appointed master of Westminster School, and in 1592 Dee returned his son Arthur to Camden's care with a letter begging him to "alter [Arthur's] natural Courage to true Fortitude."[19] In the same year Dee wrote Stow, with whom he had long acquaintance, to discuss antiquarian matters and to report on the progress of his mediation on Stow's behalf with Edward Dyer.[20] Finally, materials from Dee's library were used by Raphael Holinshed in the third volume of his *Chronicles*.[21] Considering Dee's interests and friends, it is surprising that he was not (as it seems) a member of the Elizabethan Society of Antiquaries.[22]

Perhaps the most interesting evidence of Dee's antiquarian activities is the diary he kept during his journey to Chester and Wales in 1574.[23] This small notebook bears the title "Certaine verie rare observations of Chester; & some parts of Wales: wth divers Epitaphes Coat Armours & other monuments verie orderlie & laboriouslie gathered together," and is Dee's modest version of the "perambulations" or "itineraries" in the tradition of Giraldus Cambrensis, John Leland, and William Lambard.[24] For the many places he visited, Dee, in the words of French, "noted the condition and position of various edifices, copied down coats of arms, listed the pedigrees of local gentry, and recorded local history and topography."[25] He availed himself of every possible source of information: he visited sites, interviewed local inhabitants, took in folklore, examined church windows, recorded etymological curiosities, and plumbed city archives. He even met with a pewterer in "Snedgreen," who recommended an improved method for making pewter vessels and brass pots.

The efforts of the Tudor historians and antiquaries were grounded, above all, in England's ancient and medieval textual heritage.[26] The period of Dee's researches and writings is flanked—and to some extent overshadowed—by Bale's and Leland's compendious catalogues and Cotton's unrivaled library of historical materials. But the Elizabethan years were by no means lean ones for historically minded textual scholarship. In producing his great national history, *Britannia,* William Camden "read every Greek and Roman writer who had mentioned Britain and many of the medieval authors also (later, he edited a batch of chronicles). He consulted public records, ecclesiastical registers, many libraries, the archives of cities and churches, monuments and old deeds."[27] And Archbishop Matthew Parker drew together not only an impressive collection of medieval historical—especially Anglo-Saxon—manuscripts, but a whole team of scholars who helped him to edit, digest, and apply them.[28] May McKisack has shown that virtually all of these manuscripts contain marginalia and addenda in the hands of Parker and his scholars.[29]

I have already surveyed Dee's valuable collection of historical texts and the techniques and interests that guided his reading. But a vivid and instructive sense of his participation in Elizabethan historical scholarship is conveyed by a modest manuscript prepared in 1576 (and subsequently preserved by Cotton) entitled *Correctiones et Supplementa in Sigeberti Chronicon.*[30] This text is divided into three sections, each of which treats in some way Sigebertus Gemblacensis' chronicle of German history.

The first part (3r–5v) is a list of editorial variants (or *correctiones*) by page and line number. Which texts was Dee comparing? From the form of his references it is clear that he was collating a printed text with a manuscript copy. His library catalogue tells us that he had two printed editions of the chronicle, one from 1513 and one

from 1566:[31] examination reveals that the folio and line numbers
match the latter edition.[32] What about the manuscript? Dee himself provides no indication. The answer can be found, however, on
a scribbled note interpolated between folios 55 and 57. It is signed
"John harpsfeld" and dated "21° Martij 1576"; there is no addressee. It reads: "Simon Dunelmes[. . .] is not emong the bokes.
by all likelehood my brother lent it, but he know[s] not yet to
whom. I hope hee shall shortlie cume by it & than wyll I reserve
hym [i.e., Simon] for yow. In the meane season I send yow Sigebertus Gimlacensis. . . . It is told me y[r] M[r] Stow hath Henrie
huntyngdon, who beyng yo[r] frynd wyll lend it yow if yow requyre
it of hym. My brothers huntyndon is not where it was." This note
was undoubtedly addressed to Dee, and was probably found with
his manuscript when it was bound by Cotton. Clearly, Dee had
written to Harpsfeld, requesting several historical texts. Unable
to satisfy his requests, Harpsfeld sent instead a manuscript of
Sigebertus—with the above note as a cover letter. Dee took the
opportunity to check the text of his printed edition, and no doubt
turned to his "frynd" Stow for the other material.

Harpsfeld and Dee had been long acquainted: they probably
first met when they served together as chaplains to Bishop Edmund Bonner. Harpsfeld was only one year older than Dee, but did
not fare as well at the hands of the Elizabethan reformers. He sank
into obscurity after some imprudent theological writings, and
died in 1578.[33] It is clear, however, that he remained an active
historical scholar and an associate of Dee (and others). Not long
after writing his note Harpsfeld must have located his brother's
Henry Huntingdon: in September 1576, he lent Dee a compilation of Huntingdon's tracts, and on the flyleaf of his copy of the
Flores Historiarum[34] Dee listed several books (including Huntingdon) and noted, "All these ar ioyned wth his 9 bokes of historie: in a
fayr copy, which I borrowed of M[r] John harpsfeld a° 1576 [i.e.,
1577] feb. 23."[35] Traces of Harpsfeld's continuing scholarship are
a commonplace book (in BL MS Royal 8.B.XX.) and a compilation of historical writings (in the same collection as Dee's *Correctiones*)—at the beginning of which Harpsfeld listed Dee alongside Theodorus Beza, Gemma Frisius, and Gerard Mercator as his
chief authorities.

In the second part of the text (6r–19v) Dee wrote out a tabular summary, organized chronologically, of British matters from 876 to 1100, which he gathered out of Sigebertus. This was the first section of the "Supplementa," and was in effect a loose-leaf version of the digestion he usually carried out through the marginalia in his history books—it dealt with the same subject matter, and fulfilled the same function. In the second section (the third and final part of the manuscript) Dee copied out "Robertus'" continuation of the chronicle to 1174 (or at least those parts which were not included in the printed edition), underlining and adding marginal notes on Brutus and Gildas.

Inevitably, the development of a national historical consciousness in the late medieval and Renaissance periods gave rise not just to new forms of scholarship, but to new forms of writing. It is essential to realize that the form, method, and purpose of many of Dee's manuscript works were vitally influenced by these approaches to written material.[36] First and foremost, these doctrines and attitudes had profound ramifications for the idea of authorship itself, and serve as a corrective to our modern assumptions and expectations. We generally conceive of authorship in terms of an originality that is in many ways anachronistic. As Terence Cave explains, "The establishing of sources has usually been the prelude to a definition of the 'originality' of an author as the residue which remains when the source-materials have been subtracted from his text. And such residue is thus seen as having its source or origin in the author's mind, as being produced by an act of creation (virtually *ex nihilo*)." This approach fails to recognize that "the production of any discourse is conditioned by pre-existing instances of discourse," that "the writer is always a re-writer":[37] this tenet, which we have come to associate with poststructuralism, was a basic premise of historical scholarship and pedagogy in general from at least the thirteenth century.

There are few texts among Dee's written output which it is appropriate to describe in terms of originality: in most cases he depends so heavily upon his sources that if we subtracted them from the text all that would remain would be the traces of his scholarly cutting and pasting, his zealous rhetoric, and his unique sense of syntax. As I have suggested, Dee inherited—and came to exemplify—the humanistic strategy of composing texts (oral or written) by retrieving and sifting predigested materials. This strategy had its counterparts in medieval historiographical traditions of reading and writing. Neil Hathaway has called the Middle Ages "the age of compilation": most writing was the result of "legitimate borrowing," of "plundering the authoritative material of antiquity and patristic times."[38] And Alistair Minnis has explained that there was a sharp distinction between the *auctor,* a term reserved for writers with absolute *auctoritas* (e.g., the Church Fathers, or the canonical texts of a discipline), and those who commented on (the *commentator*), compiled (the *compilator*), copied (the *scriptor*), or taught (the *lector*) the texts of the *auctores.*[39] Naturally, absolute originality was the province only of *auctores*—all other readers and writers were in some way dependent on, and derivative of, their authority.[40] Interestingly, Minnis gives the example of Euclid as an *auctor* who was classically explicated in "intrinsic" prologues (which introduced the work itself) and "extrinsic" prologues (which set it in the context of the discipline as a whole—its terms, methods, and utility.[41] It is not only possible but apropos to consider Dee's "Mathematicall Praeface" to the English Euclid of 1570 as an elaborate, but nonetheless conventional, extrinsic prologue.[42]

These ideas are "closely reflected" in "classical and medieval notions of history writing," and Hathaway suggests that they can be considered a " 'genre' of the wider activity of compiling."[43] As Joseph Levine put it, the role of the medieval hagiographer "was to compile and rewrite": Ranulph Higden, for instance, proceeded "by assembling a string of quotations drawn from his wide reading."[44] This activity, and the terms used to describe it, remained present and, indeed, remarkably consistent in the sixteenth and seventeenth centuries. The Elizabethan parliamentarian Arthur Hall described his historical study thus: "In reading, I have gathered many flowers out of Mr. William Lambarde's garden, a gentleman, after my verdict, though unknown to me, for his painful, rare and learned collection worthy to be known."[45]

When approaching early modern scholarship it is often more useful to think in terms of "adaptation" than "authorship": "Adaptation was characteristic of sixteenth-century scholarship—scholars borrowed and adapted each others' ideas almost as freely as they 'imitated' the ancients. Accretion, or the collecting of information and manuscripts, was not confined to the early humanists; many

Tudor scholars and gentlemen made collections on particular topics, some of which paved the way for revisions of accepted opinion."[46] "Collector, non auctor, ego sum" [I am a collector, not an
author], declared one of Dee's contemporaries, acknowledging the
extent to which he was merely reorganizing existing information,
and reflecting a situation in which terms like "collection" and
"gathering" were used as often as "creation" to describe authorial
activity. With Dee we can go one step further: his declaration, had
he made one, would surely have been "Lector, non auctor, ego
sum." This is to suggest that the rhetoric he employed to describe
his scholarly activities and their value needs to be put in context.
He did, granted, occasionally proclaim that he was the only, or
the first, author to produce a particular idea or work: but this was
more of a marketing ploy than a boast; an attempt (and a conventional one at that) to sell his processing skills over those of his
competitors.

One of the by-products of this great age of compilation, which
continued well beyond the Middle Ages, was a genuine, critical
historiographical method. As Dee asserts with monotonous reg-
ularity in his compilation *Of Famous and Rich Discoveries*,[47] he was
sensitive to the need not just to compile but to compare sources
and weigh evidence. He prefaces a citation of Pliny with "I will
now . . . note vnto you some Auncient & Credible Information, of
part of the Sea coastes, and Navigation thereabouts" (33r).[48] He
then offers a striking defense of the truth of this "bold" passage: "I
will evidently, by good Authority, kepe me w^th^in the bownds of
honest reason: vnpartially labouring for the preferment of that
noble Empres *Lady Verity*" (34v). A bit later he states his method
with less hyperbole: "for my better warrant & allso for the more
easy perswading you the truthe herein I will (as my manner hath
byn in all this *Discovery Volume* hitherto) [offer] testimony of the
likelyest good Authority that is publisshed" (62v). The errors of
previous writers had to be corrected: "[The] manifold errors of
many other writers of Scythien, Tartarien, Cathay, & China matters, (as now) being left vntowched of purpose, onely the *Truthe*
intended in o^r^ affaires, chiefly made probable & expressed, may (as
the Cosmopoliticall pollicy procedeth at this present) be iudged a
matter worthy of *Memory* & very nedeful to be listened vnto,
credited and put in execution" (169r).[49] He graphically pictured

himself sifting the good sources from the bad: "I entend to examyn lightly diverse Records, so as they may somewhat tend toward Information, w^t discrete choise & allowance of the Corne: & suffe[ring] the sup*er*flous chaf to fly in the Ayre of vayne Report" (41v). But Dee found some authors particularly trustworthy: on folio 125 he provided a long list of the "pryncypall Authors . . . vsed & creditted."[50]

What Dee hoped to achieve with his collection was to "bring the force of good Authoryty, toward the perswasion" of those who needed persuading (27v). "Credit" was clearly the operative word in this procedure: his guarantees of impartial, neutral scholarship were patently part of the rhetorical packaging of his nationalistic and ultimately imperialistic program. His truth was a "Truthe . . . sufficient for . . . humayne & Cyvile Service" (65v)—service on behalf of the British Empire, which Dee's text was intended to justify and render both attractive and lawful.

It is a commonplace in both Renaissance historical writing and the history of the Renaissance that the purpose of reading and writing history is didactic—and that those who have most to learn are the governing class. In dedicating the *Historie of Cambria* (1584) to Sir Philip Sidney, David Powel exhorted him to "Labour by the example of your father to discouer and bring to light, the acts of the famous men of elder times, who with conference of the estate and gouernment of all ages, will bring you to the perfect experience of those things that you haue learned out of *Aristotle, Plato,* and *Cicero,* by your trauell in philosophie."[51] And Myron Gilmore noted that Pier Paolo Vergerio made history the foremost of the liberal arts for its utility, and concluded that, in the Renaissance, "there was no gulf between the study and the market place, no divorce between culture and politics."[52]

In Tudor and Stuart England the lessons of history were to be applied in making and remaking it, in actions that consolidated the commonwealth and expanded the empire. As Thomas Norton put it, a man's "hearing or reding the actes of men and monumentes of times [and] the employeng and directing of knowledge therby gotten . . . maketh the difference of time wel or ill bestowed . . . to the benefite of his own life & of the common weale," by which "he is him selfe susteined, his neighbours releved, his posteritie preserved, & by common conference the whole societie

mayntained."[53] Arthur Ferguson has described the factors condu-
cive to the development of this historically informed "commonwealth literature": "the historical orientation already a marked
characteristic of humanist scholarship . . . ; the various problems of
contemporary life . . . which elicited the attention of a sequence of
scholars more than ordinarily ready to put their learning to the
service of the state and increasingly capable of recognizing those
forces of cause and effect which linked past and present; the influence of continental antiquarianism and geographical scholarship;
and, above all, an intense national consciousness."[54] Dee's political
writings are firmly within this tradition: as we shall see, they take
the conventional forms and use the established vocabulary, and
they are marked above all by a desire to apply historical research to
the advancement of England and Britain.

Dee knew, both from his informal legal training and from the
current practices of historical scholarship, that his historiographical projects would have to be supported by an exhaustive search for
precedents: this was the ultimate source of authority, both rhetorical and political, and it is one of the keys to Dee's role as a historical
writer. As Alsop and Stevens have suggested, "in an age which
placed great emphasis on past precedent as a guide to present
action and basis for assessing legitimacy, the antiquary was truly
the 'expert in politics.' "[55] The Henrician (and then Elizabethan)
Reformation encouraged scholars to become "experts in politics"
and to provide historical foundations for the changes wrought
within the church;[56] and many statesmen, soldiers, and scholars
(Dee's patrons and friends among them) were involved in advocating the active extension of this Reformation in territorial, anti-
Spanish interventions (particularly in Ireland and in the Netherlands, but increasingly in the New World).

During the Reformation and at least until the Restoration,
then, historical scholarship was regularly put to partisan purposes.
The political circumstances within which it was generated meant
that early modern historical discourse was in large measure polemical. Most of the texts—and this is the case with virtually all of
Dee's—were produced under pressing conditions to meet precise,
usually political, needs: in his "Mathematicall Praeface" he could
not help but convey a sense of this pressure to his readers: "Lyfe is
short, and vncertaine: Tymes are perilouse: &c. And still the

Printer awayting, for my pen staying . . ." (d4v). This introduced biases and imposed a variety of constraints on early modern historians. What we must be wary of is the application of anachronistic standards of historical truth and scholarly objectivity. When approaching texts produced in a period (like early modern England) when the boundaries between public and private and between scholarship and politics were blurred, if not obliterated, we need to be acutely aware of the terms that we, as modern readers, bring to them.

Ultimately Dee's writings must be read on their own terms—which is emphatically not to say divorced from the conventional terms of his period—and not made to conform to a grand, prefabricated version of his intentions. We may well lose sight of the great magus, the original (though eccentric) genius, the "characteristic philosopher of the Elizabethan age";[57] but we gain an appreciation of his extraordinary scholarship and its place in the Elizabethan polity. During his life Dee labored to advertise this role: "whereas (in my tyme of 30. yeres studious race) I haue wth no little care, and small charges, both fare, and nere, made manifold search . . . for the pure verity understandinge and Recoveringe of divers secret, ancient, and waightie matters; and some of them, appertaininge to histories, and discoveris of the world vniuersalie"—therefore, "Yt maie please [you] to consider the few Notes ensuinge. . . ."[58]

SIX

Brytannicae Reipublicae Synopsis (1570)

A Reader's Guide to the Elizabethan Commonwealth

> I haue declared summarily as it were in a chart or mappe, or as Aristotle termeth it, 'as in an outline' the forme and manner of the gouernement of Englande . . . this being as a proiect or table of a common wealth truely laide before you. . . . —Sir Thomas Smith, *De Republica Anglorum* (1583)

A mong the rows of oblong blue boxes that contain Sir Robert Cotton's collection of maps, charters, and genealogical rolls lies one of the most important contemporary analyses of Elizabethan England.[1] Compared to the classic texts of Sir Thomas Smith, William Harrison, and Thomas Wilson the document is extremely obscure: it has rested virtually undisturbed, except by the fire that consumed several inches along its upper edge. Its full title reads, *Brytannicae Reipub{licae} Synopsis: libris explicata tribus. Synopseos* ~~*Politicae*~~ *Adumbratio. à Joanne Dee. L{ondinensis}. Designata: Aº. 1570.* In a large table, now taking the form of a roll measuring just over 3½ × 2½ feet, its author, John Dee, anatomized the English commonwealth (Figure 8).[2] The words *synopseos, adumbratio,* and *designata* describe the text both physically and conceptually: Dee designed the *Synopsis* to outline the current state of the realm and suggest means for curing its ills.[3] The catalogue describes the text as "a table of matters belonging partly to ethics and partly to political economy." Dee's title originally advertised an attention to "politics," but in a confusing revision, providing neither a rationale nor a replacement, he crossed out *politicae*—

ironically prefiguring what many twentieth-century readers would make of his writings.

The most immediate question raised by the *Synopsis* is that of its obscurity. For a variety of reasons—which, as much as the text itself, are the subject of this chapter—it has been left out of the historical accounts of the early modern period, and it has made a minimal impact on assessments of Dee's career. Yet it has much to teach us about Dee and the commonwealth he served and sought to advance. The *Synopsis* is an interesting and unusual specimen of late-Tudor commonwealth literature, and as such offers valuable insights into the social, economic, and political issues faced by the Elizabethan regime, as well as the mechanisms and vocabularies of analysis deployed by its advisers. More specifically, the form and function of the *Synopsis*—a *reader's guide* to the commonwealth— offer valuable insights into Dee's intellectual methods and so-cioprofessional roles.

The *Synopsis* represents Dee's scholarly mediation between a body of knowledge (England's administrative, fiscal, and military strengths and weaknesses) and a body of political readers (an elite group of government officials). Combining the most up-to-date techniques and discourses from pedagogical and political spheres, it was designed to convey a concise and comprehensive view of the state of England to those readers responsible for engineering its administration. The fact that Dee was able to offer this synopsis, and the fact that he did so with the encouragement of the Privy Council, is perhaps surprising: he has not been considered realistic or even very knowledgeable about political affairs, and the Eliz-abethan government has not for its part been considered very receptive to criticism from those outside the inner circle of the crown. Yet the *Synopsis* ought to occasion some reconsideration, not only about Dee's qualifications and inclinations, but about his place in the Elizabethan political process.

IN APPROACHING the text of the *Synopsis* it is reasonable to begin with whatever illumination—and confusion—Dee himself pro-vides as to its composition. He first referred to it in his *General and Rare Memorials pertayning to the Perfect Arte of NAVIGATION* (pub-lished in 1577; written in 1576). With his argument for the establishment of a permanent coast guard in full flow, Dee broke off with a personal note to the addressee of the work—"*M. Christopher Hatton* Esquier: Capitain of her Maiesties Garde, and Ientleman of her priuy Chamber" (A1r): "But, such matter as this, I iudge you haue, or mought haue hard of, ere now, (by the worshipfull *M. Dyer,*) and that, abundantly: Seeing, *Synopsis Reipub. Brytanicae,* was, at his Request (six yeres past) contriued . . ." (B1v). This passing reference is telling. First, it provides an occasion for the *Synopsis:* in 1570 it was solicited by Edward Dyer, who acted as a go-between for members of the Privy Council—especially Hatton and the earl of Leicester.[4] He was associated with Dee throughout his life and has been considered Dee's most consistent patron.[5] His relationship to Dee was, however, more complex and more symbiotic than this word usually implies. He acted as Dee's "agent," commissioning at least two other political manuscripts and promoting these (and other) writings at court.[6] Through these writings the status of both men was enhanced: Dee gained access to the most powerful members of the governing class, and Dyer's reputation was boosted by his association with Dee's valued learning. On more than one occasion he was a more direct beneficiary of Dee's knowledge. He was a frequent visitor to Dee's library and was present during his famous natural philosophy tutorials to Philip Sidney.[7] The most striking evidence for their special relationship, however, is the fact that Dyer was made godfather to Dee's son Arthur in 1579.

Second, the comment to Hatton suggests the milieu of the text's circulation: it was presented directly to the governmental inner circle and was most likely read by several of its key officers. Third, it explains that Dee considered such matters as naval policy and national security—the subjects of his *General and Rare Memorials*—to have been foreshadowed in the *Synopsis.* Finally, it sheds some light on the confusion that has arisen from Dee's other reference to the *Synopsis.* In the inventory of his works that formed part of his "Compendious Rehearsall" of 1592, Dee lists "*Reipublicae Britannicae Synopsis*" among his unpublished manuscripts. The problem is that he dates it "Anno 1565." The petition was prepared in great haste and the dating is most likely a mistake.[8] It has, however, driven Clulee—in turn informed by Yewbrey—to postulate the existence of a book-length *Synopsis,* of which the 1570 manuscript is merely a summary.[9] The claim is perhaps supported by the phrase *"libris explicata tribus"* in the full title of the 1570 text: while *libris* need not mean 'books,' it probably does not denote divisions as short as Dee's. And at the end of his "Mathematicall Praeface," prepared in the same year, Dee provided a similar synoptic table (or "Groundplot"): in that case it merely summarized the contents of the preceding pages. Ultimately this hypothesis, whether right or wrong, is unnecessary. The *Synopsis* as we have it is a complete text in its own right: it is the version that was presented to the Privy Council, and the fact remains that Dee thought enough of it to refer to it—six years after the fact instead of twenty-two—as **the** *Synopsis*.

THE CONTENT and the purpose of the text are suggested most clearly by the large caption on its left edge: "To make this Kingdome flourishing, / Triumphant, famous, and Blessed: / Of necessitie, in it, are required / these thre principall things."[10] The "thre principall things," detailed in the three principal branches, are "Vertue," "Welth," and "Strength." Dee's middle section requires the most elucidation: it contains by far the most detailed and topical arguments. The heading "Welth" is accompanied by the Latin epigram *"Nihil est vtile, quod non sit Honestum"* [Nothing is expedient which is not honest].[11] In his attention to home industries and foreign trade, Dee touches on many of the classic issues of early modern social and economic analysis, and all are familiar to modern scholars—lapsed standards in the cloth industry, debasement of the coinage, decayed towns, and the idleness of the poor. Dee is overtly critical, suggesting ways to improve England's position internationally and the commons' position at home. His remedy, too, is familiar: these ends are to be achieved by the increase of wealth. This wealth logically proceeds either from the "Naturall Commodities of this monarchy"—themselves either used "Within this Land" or from "The ouerplus Transporting (to our most gayne) into foreyn places convenient"—or "by things . . . browght in." Dee intended to provide a tabular overview of British foreign trade: he outlined seven regions and left spaces, presumably to be filled in later, for the income gained in "Custom Royall" from trade with those areas.[12] His presentation culminates in a classic statement of what C. H. Wilson has called "the central principle" of late Tudor economics—"the balance of trade."[13] Wilson cites the well-known definition from the *Discourse of the Common Weal* (1549): ". . . we must alwaies take care that we bie no more of strangers than we sell them. . . ." Dee's version is more ambitious: "It wold be pollitikly cumpassed . . . that of our Commodities (in totall summe) more be carried out, than in waies do come in [sic], yerely; by $\frac{1}{3}$: or $\frac{1}{4}$ at the least. . . ."

Wilson concludes his survey of early mercantilist theory with the suggestion that "Perhaps the most important thing about the mercantilists was that they believed that material change was possible and desirable and supported their belief with an unprecedented concentration on organized human energy."[14] Whether or not Dee is to be considered a mercantilist, this comment is certainly true of his analysis of the cloth trade. That he considered material change to be possible and desirable is clear from his proposition, "If this new encrease of Cloth making were ordayned to be in sundry townes of England, which now are lamentably decayed," then ("besides many other commodities publik, hereby arrising") British money would be better spent and British cloth would be of higher esteem abroad. More explicitly, "Our Wooll: Of it, (at the least) a quarter more, than now is, wold be dr[a]ped here: As well for relieving of innumerable pore folk by th[e] working of it: and restoring of decayed Townes: As also, for that our cloth and wooll, with the forayner, Wold be of more estimation." His twofold suggestion for reforming the corruptions in the industry also involves the deployment of human resources in mercantilist fashion: "And withall the Testimony of appointed honest skylfull overseers, for eue[ry] principall point belonging to good and perfect cloth, by Severall Seales of lead to euery cloth [ms. faded] And also sufficient warning, by apt mark in the said Seales of lead, of any notable fault fownd in the said cloth, by negligence or fraude in workmanship, in any of the principall points. . . ."

What is most striking in Dee's analysis of the cloth trade—and, indeed, in the entire manuscript—is its currency: that is, the extent to which it corresponds to contemporary problems, practices, and discourses. *Leake's Treatise on the Cloth Industry, with Proposals for the Reform of Abuses* (1577) makes the need for reformed legislation emphatically clear: "I am fullye of opinion that, for all Colored Clothes dressed and dyed within this realme, and generallye for all other Clothe, the lawes were never yet observed in any one place with in the Realme. . . . And therefore I conclude that these deceiptes vsed by the makers is the Cause whye our commodityes are the lesse sett by in forraine nations. . . ."[15]

Leake's complaints echo Dee's, both in substance and in style—implying not that Dee was a source for Leake but that they both felt the same pressures, had access to similar knowledge, utilized recognized discourses, and wrote for similar audiences. This is even more apparent in his suggestions about "The best waye to reforme these abuses." First, "I suppose no way so meete as the findinge out and appointinge of one meete man to be a Supervisor . . . and giuinge him sufficient power and authority. . . ." Second, "The weaver [ought] to present his Clothe wouen before the Masters of his Companye, and ther to be proved, the Fullier or Clotheworker likewise, and the Dyer for his parte also; which beinge founde perfect euery of them might sett to their seales particulerly, with a Confirmation of the town seale wher it was made. And if it be faultie in any pointe materiall, then the seales wherin the offence is shall wante, and therby give knowledge to the buyer. . . ."[16]

These are not chance correspondences; nor was Dee's choice to treat the cloth trade at such length an arbitrary one. As Ramsay explains, "From the point of view of the government, especially with the raising of the cloth export duty in 1558, the yield of taxes from the woollen industry was vital." It was, in fact, the prime source of income: "Customs receipts, mostly connected with the cloth trade in one way or another, continued to provide the major source of royal revenue. . . ."[17] The textile industry was not just any industry, therefore: it was "the largest and most important of the country's manufacturing industries."[18] But this had been true for some time. The importance of the convergence in the 1570s of suggestions for reform (of which Dee and Leake were only a part) is that it testifies to a crisis—or at least a critical point—within the industry. Both P. J. Bowden and G. D. Ramsay have presented a picture of extreme pressure within the Staplers' Company—responsible not only for wool exports but for lead as well, a trade that Dee also mentions briefly—which reached its worst proportions around 1570.[19] The most immediate cause was the loss of the thriving Antwerp market in 1569:[20] that year saw a "brusque rupture of the traffic to Antwerp, which was never fully resumed."[21] This is not to suggest, then, that Dee was a radical and innovative economic theorist; it is to suggest that he provided, in a schematic nutshell, a topical and informed critique of England's crucial— and recently threatened—cloth trade.

Dee concludes this section on trade with general advice for merchants regarding the handling of money: "Of Necessitie, all o^r Marchants (trading with forayners) owght to be very perfect in the true valew of all currant coynes, Syluer and Gold . . . And So To Bargayne wisely: and Skyllfully to vnderstand theyr gayne: in marking with reckoning of the difference in vale[w] bethwene the standerds of any diuerse coynes in theyr handling."[22] This may seem like common sense, but it responds to the substantial confusion—and loss—that had resulted from shifting metal standards and general debasement of the coinage. The Doctor in the *Discourse of the Common Weal* explained in no uncertain terms what he felt had been the result of these changes: ". . . what oddes soeuer theare happen to be in [exchaunge] of thinges, youe that be merchauntes can espie it anone; ye lurched some of the coyne as sone as euer ye perceived the price of that to be enhaunced; ye, by and by perceivinge what was to be wonne theare in beyond the sea, raked all the old coyne for the moste parte in this realme, and founde the means to haue it caried ouer; so as little was lefte behind within this Realme of such old coyne at this daye; which, in my opinion, is a greate cause of this dearthe that we haue now in all thinges."[23] An "enhancement" of the exchange rate had led directly to the drainage of precious metal from the realm, which in turn had led to the renowned mid-Tudor economic crisis.[24]

As with the cloth trade, Dee presented his material on the exchange of currency in terms of commodious reform. The education of merchants in the dynamics of currency would serve to make "England both abroad and at home to be Lord and ruler of the Exchange." It is likely that he also had more modest, pedagogic motives; that this was part of his broader program for the scientific education of England's unlearned (and specifically merchant and mechanical) subjects. This project was more clearly articulated in Robert Recorde's mathematical textbook, *The Ground of Artes,* first published in 1542 and reprinted in 1582 with additions by Dee and John Mellis. Most of the arithmetical examples, significantly, use current English coins as units. Moreover, the second edition added the "practical" section entitled *The Rules of Practice for Merchants. . . .* Chapter 14 of this section, for example, "entreateth of exchanging of money from one place to another, with diuers necessarie questions incident thereunto." Even more to the point is Chapter 16: "a brief note of the ordinarie Coines of moste places of Christendome for traffique. . . ." Finally, Dee refers in a section on mixed numbers to "An example of mixture of Gold and Siluer." A manuscript marginal note in the Cambridge University Library copy suggests that this addresses the "pollution of the currency" (sig. KK.4.r).

The top section of the *Synopsis,* "Vertue," is accompanied by the Latin phrase *"Sola Virtus vitam efficit Beatam* [Only virtue brings about the prosperous life],"[25] and is broken down into "Wisedome," "Iustice," "Fortitude," and "Temperance." This section of the manuscript has been severely damaged (it is, in fact, impossible to discern further divisions within the topic of Wisedome). Fortunately, it is the section that requires least development, as it is the most conventional. It is included, in the first place, because of the ancient convention that makes a discussion of politics impossible without reference to ethics. Significantly, Dee's four virtues correspond exactly to the classical "cardinal" virtues: these were outlined most influentially in Cicero's *De officiis,* which Dee's presentation follows closely.[26] It is here that Dee's participation in a more or less conventional civic Humanism becomes most apparent: the four cardinal virtues (and the emphasis on virtue itself) were a commonplace of Renaissance commonwealth literature,[27] and the *De officiis* was a cornerstone of Renaissance arguments in favor of the *vita activa.*[28] In her dissertation on the impact of the *De officiis* on English Humanism, C. A. L. Jarrott outlines Cicero's program for the application of contemplation in civic action, and suggests that this ideal was prevalent among sixteenth-century English scholars and, increasingly, scientists (179).[29] Dee's religious and scientific activities were, then, by no means incompatible with his participation in contemporary politics: while Cicero (and the English Humanists, particularly those of the "Pragmatic" variety) channeled contemplation into action, the two were integrally connected; the service to the commonwealth prescribed by the *De officiis* by no means excluded Christian meditation or scientific experimentation.

Dee's treatment of the concept of "Iustice" is especially noteworthy, both for its criticisms and for its clarity. He suggests, first, that all laws "Ought to be ordred to gither in a Body Methodicall: and not to be a Confused Chaos (and Worse) as they are." This can be taken as a critique of the state of English law in terms of one of the qualities that Dee, and his Humanist contemporaries, valued most—method. His second and third suggestions are that the laws ought to be made more readily available and that they should be authorized—and amended, when necessary—by Parliament. One might assume that these were derivative or amateurish recommendations, since most studies of Dee do not indicate any training or experience in legal matters. However, Dee claims that he studied civil law, at least informally, and it is clear that Dyer—and others—respected him for it. While visiting the University of Louvain, he claimed, "I did, for recreation, look into the method of the civile law, and profited therein so much, that in the antimonys, imagined to be in the law, I had good hap to finde out (well allowed of) their agreementes; and also to enter into a plaine and due understanding of divers civill lawes, accounted very intricate and darke."[30] Furthermore, he argues in a pertinent section of the "Mathematicall Praeface" that an expert mathematician has much to offer in the exposition of the law: "Wonderfull many places, in the Ciuile law, require an expert *Arithmeticien,* to vnderstand [them]," whereby, "easily ye may now coniecture: that in the Canon law: and in the lawes of the Realme [i.e., the Common Law], Iustice and aequity might be greately preferred, and skilfully executed, through due skill of Arithmetike. . . ."[31] To back himself up Dee refers to passages connecting mathematical proportion and justice from "many bookes *De Republica*" or "How the best state of Common wealthes might be procured and mainteined," quoting Aristotle's *Ethics* and Plato's *Epinomis* ("which boke," Dee claims, "is the Threasury of all his doctrine"). The quotation from the latter goes on to connect the science of numbers with "*Prudentia,*" which Dee translates "*Wisdome.*"

Two aspects of the *Synopsis'* final section, on Strength, merit special attention. First, Dee provides a figure on the size of the Royal Navy and more general descriptions of the deployment of defense resources that have not, as far as I know, been measured against contemporary realities. For the navy Dee recommended the maintenance of twenty-five ordinary ships and twenty-five extraordinary, in addition to the ships of merchants. According to the figures supplied by Michael Oppenheim, Dee's ordinary ships would have amounted to over twice the number in commission in 1570.[32] Second, this section provides the clearest example of the efficiency and clarity afforded by the diagrammatic form Dee has used. It is a classic use of an expository form Dee inherited from his Humanist predecessors, a form described by Walter Ong as "tidy bracketed tables of dichotomies."[33]

Having briefly read the *Synopsis* for its content, I now want to examine this form. It is not just the product of what appears to be an obsessive harping on method:[34] it is the product of Dee's education in and mastery of *the* Humanist method of pedagogical presentation. In presenting his material in a system that scholars have found in frequent use by Humanist writers and have labeled the "divisive technique"—characterized by "a series of dichotomous synoptic tables"[35]—Dee once again proves the product of his times. As the Cambridge scholar William Temple asserted in a debate with Everard Digby over the nature and uses of dialectical method, "the divisive technique . . . is indeed the one and only *methodus*."[36] The *Synopsis* was written within what Ong has characterized as a "cult of dichotomies."[37]

Dee's use of the dichotomous method is in absolute accord with the Ramist tradition.[38] Lisa Jardine's description of this method is particularly useful: "Ramus' dichotomous method is a procedure for displaying material . . . in the most clear and most easily grasped fashion for comprehension by the student. The teacher commences with the most general definition of the subject . . . followed by the division of that subject into two parts . . . with explanations and examples. . . . He then proceeds to key down each arm of the array in turn, conveniently displaying the material under each head in a tabular form. . . . Dichotomous keying became an extremely voguish way of proceeding. . . ."[39] Walter Ong, in a discussion of "The Method of Method," quotes Ramus' own description: "The method of teaching . . . is the arrangement of various things brought down from universal and general principles to the underlying singular parts, by which arrangement the whole matter can be more easily taught and apprehended."[40] This movement (of "bringing down") is clear in Dee's diagram: he progresses—to follow one "arm of the array"—from "Strength" to the category of things "Moveable" to things "Lyving" to "MAN: trayned vp in all Martiall skyll and feates: necessary against all kinde of Enemyes." Another feature of the dichotomous method is that, "theoretically, no material is omitted."[41] This comprehensiveness can be sensed by following another part of the same branch in the subject of Strength: from things "Lyving" (as opposed to "Vnlyving") to "Beast" (as opposed to "MAN") to "Horse" (as opposed to "Ox") to "Great Horse/Dimilance/Light horse/Hackenye/Cart horse."

The dichotomous method was not without its problems, and even those who employed it had misgivings.[42] It is not hard to imagine—and Dee's diagram provides abundant examples—how the presentation will fall short of the total coverage of its subject: this is dependent both on the comprehensiveness of the subject headings and on their pairings into absolute dichotomies. In a case such as Dee's necessarily incomplete analysis of British industry, or in his division of all English subjects into either "Students" or the "Vulgar," we can see that the treatment is neither complete nor completely natural. Furthermore, as Francis Bacon pointed out, the method was limited both in range and effect: he saw that dialectic and rhetoric are "very properly applied to civil business and to those arts which rest in discourse and opinion" but that they are unsuitable for exploring the truth in any area of natural knowledge. This is to suggest that "dialectic . . . is concerned with the presentation of ideas which are already fully formed."[43] These points add to the appropriateness of Dee's dichotomizing: in the *Synopsis* he organizes his already acquired knowledge of "civil business."[44] Despite its practical faults and limitations, the dichotomous method was both an effective and an apt choice for Dee's *Synopsis*. In the final analysis, the dichotomous method is simply one of those techniques which are "particularly effective as vehicles for transmitting new or difficult knowledge to an audience."[45] This, I am suggesting, was the service Dee provided to a range of clients from Martin Frobisher, Humphrey Gilbert, and William Bourne to Edward Dyer, Christopher Hatton, and the queen herself.

WE ARE NOW in a position to assess not only Dee's role as a reader's guide, but our own capacity (as late twentieth-century scholars) to understand it. It may be that this task requires new skills; that we need to learn what Francis Bacon, in describing scholarly and scientific methods, referred to as the *"Wisdom of Transmission."* As Jardine interprets this idea, "There should be set up, according to Bacon, a separate study of the varied conventions used in transmitting a body of material to others."[46] Transferred to the modern field of textual studies, this would entail the recovery and analysis of all stages in the complex process of the writing (production), dissemination (circulation), and reception (consumption—or, to use a more active word, usage) of texts. In this section, then, I will return to the question of exclusions and biases in previous Dee studies, and point to some of the larger implications for Renaissance texts in general.

As I suggested in the preceding chapter, it is important to appreciate that the *Synopsis* is a manuscript, and to appreciate it *as* a manuscript. It should now be obvious why it circulated in manuscript form: not simply because it was privately commissioned, but, more important, because it outlined political material and therefore demanded the secrecy of a privileged document. It was not a text that was ever intended for a reading public. This clearly does not detract from its value: in fact, it increases its historical importance, both for contemporary politicians and modern historians.

This points to a fundamental aspect of texts in general and Dee's *Synopsis* in particular: they are by nature communicative. I have outlined the specific way in which Dee's text taps into a tradition of effective pedagogic communication and I want, further, to suggest how, in studying the solitary conception and static reproduction of ideas, many twentieth-century historians have effaced the intersubjectivity, intertextuality, and contextual specificity of communicative texts. Walter Ong has done much to highlight this problem. He calls it "the paradox of human communication" and explains, "Human communication is intersubjective. The media model is not."[47] At various times this media model has guided the readings of both intellectual and literary historians. Ironically, Ong has also done much to perpetuate the paradox in applying it to an unacceptably dichotomous argument on orality and literacy, using "media" to represent all written (as opposed to purely oral) forms.[48]

In order to understand the "textual event" of the *Synopsis* it is necessary to challenge this dichotomy and look at writing in more subtle ways. In an article proposing that "writing is a technology that restructures thought," Ong represents writing as a "time-obviating, context-free mechanism" that effects "the physical reduction of dynamic sound to quiescent space" and "the separation of the word from its living present, where alone real, spoken words exist."[49] This description cannot hold up to the type of communicative textuality that Dee's *Synopsis* represents. Nor can I accept Ong's apparent implication that written texts (composed of "unreal" words?) never have a "living present." Rather, as D. F. McKenzie suggests, they always have one: the "sociology of texts," like the "Wisdom of Transmission," "directs us to consider the human motives and interactions which texts involve at every stage of their production, transmission and consumption."[50] Moreover, in using the term "writing" as a catch-all category (defined in opposition to speaking), Ong fails to make crucial distinctions within that activity, such as that between script and print. He claims that, "Once reduced to space, words are frozen and in a sense dead."[51] Dee's "spatial reductions," however, not only bring ideas to life and initiate further discussion, but they make speech (and action—something missing entirely from Ong's scheme) possible.

Other students of literacy and orality have presented more sophisticated models that prove more useful in approaching the texts of transitional cultures like Elizabethan England. A common ground of these studies is their attention to the coexistence and interaction of orality and literacy within specific cultures. In his introduction to a recent collection of essays on "literacy in transition," Gerd Baumann suggests that, "Taking [these studies] together, it seems possible to distinguish the practices of literacy according to a distinction of cultural domains in which literate and oral practices relate to each other in culturally specific ways. . . ." In Baumann's neat formulation, this type of study "allows us to see the dialectical relationship between literacy as a social fact and an individual act."[52] Brian Street's critique of traditional literacy studies is exemplary in this respect, for he suggests replacing the "autonomous model" of literacy (rather like Ong's media model) with an "ideological one": "What the particular practices of reading and writing are for a given society depends upon the context; . . . they are already embedded in an ideology and cannot be isolated or treated as 'neutral' or merely 'technical.' "[53] What this ought to suggest to the student of Dee's texts is that they have a culturally specific, "ideological" context and that, in reading them, we must not reduce his "methods" to techniques and his specific communication to timeless, neutral ideas.

IN MANY respects, then, the *Synopsis* proves an illuminating object lesson in the Wisdom of Transmission: perhaps the most intriguing of these, and the one with which I will end this discussion, is what might be called the "transmission of Wisedome." This topic especially concerns the uppermost section of the text but entails a general consideration of what has, and what has not, been said about Dee's political approach.

In his doctoral dissertation on Dee, Graham Yewbrey used the *Synopsis,* and particularly the treatment of Wisdom, to excavate a fully articulated political philosophy called "Cosmopolitics." This concept—which, for Yewbrey, gives coherence to Dee's various activities and writings—offers a unique vision of a pan-European, Platonic city-state governed in accordance with divine law. The Wisdom section, "As well as being the most complex part of Dee's system . . . is also its most important area, containing that knowledge of divine truth which it was the task of Cosmopolitics to implement"; it "encompasses the whole range of Dee's religious philosophy."[54] While Yewbrey's claims are based on sensitive, detailed, and pioneering attention to the manuscript, they are incautious and somewhat overblown—not least because the section in question is almost completely missing, having been reduced to ash centuries ago.

Although what we can say about Dee's text and its politics is thus constrained, we are not limited to the point of silence. Since (as I noted above) the three other cardinal virtues are conventionally Ciceronian, it is a relatively safe assumption that Dee's treatment of "Wisedome" followed that of the *De officiis*—at least in its general drift. For the best evidence of Dee's debt to Cicero (whose *Opera* he annotated in more detail than perhaps any other surviving volume) we must turn to his *General and Rare Memorials* of 1576. Decrying the degeneration of "Publik Behauiour, *Et officijs Ciuilibus,*" Dee suggested, "Let *CICERO,* his Golden Book,

DE OFFICIIS, be the Euidence against them, to the Contrary: And that, in those Poynts, by the Heathen Orator expressed, which both greatly are agreable to the most Sacred Diuine Oracles, of our IEOVA [i.e., are compatible with Christianity]: and also, for the Common-Wealths Prosperity, right Excellent" (G3v). In 1592 Cicero remained Dee's model: in his "Compendious Rehearsall" he wrote, "the blinded lady, Fortune, doth not governe in this commonwealth, but *justitia* and *prudentia,* and that in better order, then in Tullie's *Republica* or bookes of Offices they are laid forth . . ." (38). However, its general influence notwithstanding, Cicero's discussion of the virtue took on an almost infinite variety of colorings during the Renaissance: wisdom became the arena within which the natures of truth and good government, and the relationship between them, were debated. Within the bounds of Ciceronian wisdom there was room for widely divergent views. At its simplest, this wisdom was "concerned with the bonds of union between gods and men and the relations of man to man."[55] It was at the heart of Cicero's program for bringing speculative knowledge to bear on contemporary political needs.[56] But the issues of who had access to what kind of wisdom, and the ends to which wisdom was to be applied (e.g., divine knowledge versus ethical virtue), were left open-ended.[57]

Dee's other writings have generally landed him in the "Platonist" camp; but the ground on which to pigeonhole Dee is as shaky as that lying beneath the categories themselves.[58] All that we can conclude from the *Synopsis,* and from relevant sections in other texts, is that Dee subscribed to the encyclopedic *prisca sapientia,* which was the creed of diverse intellectual approaches and which is described in the *De officiis* as *"rerum divinarum et humanarum scientia* [the knowledge of things human and divine]" (I:153). Earthly *and* divine knowledge were, for Dee, the achievable aims of human intelligence.[59] Enough of the text of the *Synopsis* survives to indicate that he made the conventional division between the ruler and his or her subjects. As for the ruler, we can only assume that he or she was empowered with the highest intellectual directive— knowledge of *both* the bonds of union between gods and men and the relations of man to man—although there is nothing to indicate how that knowledge was to be acquired. It is simply arbitrary to assume that Dee exalted and advocated (to the extent that one could) divine revelation. It is more probable that he assigned a prominent mediating role to the "Students" (i.e., the small number of philosophically, though actively, minded scholars and statesmen): they were presumably able to attain, or at least approach, *omniscientia,* and to apply it to the government of the commonwealth. Again, the text's mutilation prevents corroboration.

The only sector of the population whose wisdom was not molested by fire is the "Vulgar" (which should be taken in its Latinate and not its vernacular sense): if their "Capacitie, Talent, or Industrie . . . will not giue them Wisdome profownd, yet the next b[es]t to Wisedome must they be Carefull for to haue; which is Prudencye." The populace is here credited with two unusual powers. The first is "prudencye," which was for the Stoics (particularly those of the sixteenth century) the central virtue guiding the performance of one's civic duties. *Prudentia* was most important, of course, for rulers—in some schemes it is exclusive to them—and we can be fairly certain that one of the leaves on Dee's Ruler branch concerned some form of prudence. Six years later, in the *General and Rare Memorials,* Dee held King Edgar up to Queen Elizabeth as a mirror of prudence: in circling the country with a fearsome navy and in traveling to its different regions to hear the complaints of the commons, Edgar had displayed not only "Fortitude" and "Iustice" (H1r) but "wisdom Imperiall" and "marueilous Politicall and Princely Prudency" (G4r). The second is what appears to be historical consciousness. The members of the commonwealth ("Eche Man, in his vocation")[60] are to acquire knowledge of the past (now missing from the manuscript) and, "Comparing Words Works and things Present . . . To Prepare, for all, to Comme." This form of *sapientia* was closely related to *prudentia:* from its inception, Humanist historiography was marked by a didactic imperative which applied to rulers and subjects alike. Edgar's prudence had rested in the wisdom, "in tyme of Peace, to Foresee and preuent . . . all possible malice, fraude, force, and mischief Forreyn" (G4r): Elizabeth's would be realized by learning the lesson of Dee's historical examples and acting in similar fashion.

In view of this modest reading of Dee's "Wisedome," several elements of Yewbrey's "Cosmopolitics" must be qualified. First, for Yewbrey the *Synopsis* advocated a *European* project, outlining "the international arrangement which Dee saw as being necessary for the achievement of a Cosmopolitical Europe."[61] Dee's brief, however, was concerned with domestic politics and only ventured beyond the Channel in advocating the development of English trade. Dee did, of course, enter elsewhere into discussions of foreign policy—where he usually towed an uncompromisingly nationalistic line[62]—but neither the *Synopsis* nor the political thought it represents can be said to be European.

There is, second, too much of the "cosmic" in Yewbrey's Cosmopolitics. Dee's use of the term *cosmopolites* (and the related "cosmopolitics") no doubt derived from the Greek *kosmopolitis,* which is usually translated as citizen of the world (*kosmos*) and which formed a cornerstone of Stoic political philosophy.[63] For Yewbrey, "Dee's self-image as the Cosmpolites" involved "his certainty of his own predetermined destiny as the prophet of a universal religious reformation."[64] But for the Stoics it was simply a matter of engaging the individual in the world and of stressing one's membership in (and responsibilities toward) a global community.[65] A dual allegiance was thus required of the Stoic philosopher: to humanity as a whole and to the commonwealth in which he was born. Such a dual allegiance is flagrantly displayed in the *General and Rare Memorials.* Dee claimed that "I haue oftentymes . . . and many wayes, looked into the State of Earthly Kingdoms, Generally, the whole World ouer . . . being a Study, of no great Difficulty: But, rather, a purpose somewhat answerable, to a perfect Cosmographer: to fynde hym self, *Cosmopolites:* A Citizen, and Member, of the whole and only one Mysticall City Vniuersall. . . ." This is immediately followed, however, with the intensely patriotic conclusion, "I finde . . . that if this Brytish Monarchy, wold heretofore, haue followed the Aduantages, which they haue had, onward, They mought, very well, ere this, haue surpassed (By Iustice and Godly, sort) any particular Monarchy, els, that euer was on Earth, since Mans Creation" (G3v).

Guillaume Postel, with whom Dee shared a drive for global travel, universal knowledge, and scholarly civil service, also called himself a "Cosmopolite": according to William Bouwsma, this was in recognition of his "sense of dedication to the service of the whole human race."[66] In this respect one of Dee's marginal notes takes on particular significance. In his copy of Postel's *De Originibus,* Dee underlined the phrase "ciuis mundi" and wrote "Cosmopolites."[67]

In assessing the nature of Dee's political service it is more useful to consider the "commonwealth" than the "cosmos." The key to the politics of the *Synopsis* is Dee's use of the word *respublica* (commonwealth). This puts him in line with a humanistic tradition of political analysis, one that had verbal, textual, and ideological conventions.[68] The general approach of those writers who invoked the "ideal of the commonwealth" is best conveyed by W. R. D. Jones, who calls it "the mid-Tudor equivalent of the Welfare State."[69] Both criticism and reform tended toward the relief of the poor and the defense of communal interests. But, as Jones asks of earlier commonwealth literature, did Dee's *Synopsis* offer "mere lip-service" or "conscious pursuit" of these interests? Dee's concern for the state of the commons is apparent in his comments on the cloth trade; but for a full sense of his participation in the ideal of the commonwealth we must look beyond the *Synopsis* to the *General and Rare Memorials*. There we find him repeatedly discussing the "Commodity Publik" (△1r), the "Wealth-Publik" (B1v), and "the Politicall Body of this Brytish Common wealth" (B2r). The "Necessary Advertisement" which prefaces the treatise proper reveals Dee's interests in its very title: "A Necessary Aduertisement . . . giuen to the modest, and godly Readers: who also carefully desire the prosperous State of the Common Wealth, of this BRYTISH KINGDOM, and the Politicall SECVRITIE thereof" (△2r). This title contains the fundamental argument of commonwealth literature: not only is the well-being of the commons to be sought by all "godly Readers," but this will in turn guarantee the wealth and security of the entire kingdom. This intent is supported in two (printed) marginal notes: "O, godly Intent: O long looked for Common wealth" (B3r); and "This brief Aduertisement doth express but some of the principall poynts, most behoofull for the Common-Wealth at this tyme" (D4r). Finally, Dee's "principall Intent . . . Is (as it ought to be, of duty) to be found faithfull, seruisable, Comfortable, and profitable to the Political Body of this Brytish Common wealth" (B2r).

Yet this might still be considered lip service. It is not until we appreciate that Dee addresses the classic matters of commonwealth policy—to those outlined in the *Synopsis* should be added discussions of dearths, fisheries, wasted lands, and piracy in *General and Rare Memorials*—that it becomes clear that he was one of those who "thought coolly, secularly and constructively about the problems of the common weal and who faced the practical tasks involved in turning aspiration into action."[70] The commonwealth ideas and ideals of Dee and his contemporaries—Elton has suggested Thomas Smith and William Cecil, but writers like Robert Hitchcock and the Hakluyts should also be included—have not received adequate attention. The vast majority of work on the Tudor commonwealth has focused on the reigns of Henry VIII and Edward VI (and especially on the administration of Protector Somerset). Indeed, Jones selects 1559 as the terminal date of his study because it marks "the end of the 'crisis period' which had given to discussion of the Commonwealth ideal particular urgency." He does not follow the ideal through to Elizabeth's time because of a view of her reign that has since come under attack. He suggests that "in many ways the ideals of the Commonwealth were now achieved, 'gradually, carefully and, within human limits, effectively, under the long rule of William Cecil . . .' " and that "the complex crisis in the nation's affairs which was the subject of that composition [i.e., the *Discourse of the Common Weal*] was a thing of the past."[71]

Dee's *Synopsis* does much to dissolve this idealized picture.[72] It has been clear that Dee's text owed its content and its very existence precisely to a "complex crisis in the nation's affairs"—one that corresponds extensively to the mid-Tudor crisis represented in the *Discourse.* Jones suggests that the ideal of the commonwealth evolved into a "rather platitudinous synonym for 'society' or 'body politic,' free of any challenging social implications";[73] but one could hardly deny the state of crisis or the social challenge contained in the following statement from the *General and Rare Memorials:* "the self same Brytish and English Commons, Man, Woman, and Childe, with wringing hands, most pitifully lamenting a Remediles Inconuenience, and haynous Absurdity, already, and to long, committed: wold, most humbly and Dutifully, make Petition, that Presently, such vnparciall prouidence may be vsed: That, from henceforth, The Private Commodity of a few, shall not cause the Braynes of many a thousand, of the true and faithfull English Subiects, to fly in the Ayre" (E1v). In justifying the reform of merchant companies, further, Dee suggests that "so, shall such Dooings, be asmuch auaylable to the Common-wealth, then, as now they are to the Priuate Lucre of a Few: And that, with Publik

Dammage" (D.2.v). The examples could be multiplied—but not without giving a false impression of Dee as a socialist reformer.

Clearly, there are political and textual practices and theories in Dee that have been overlooked because of the cumulative textual assumptions of those who have—and have not—read him. In conclusion, I suggest that it is only with an awareness both of the practices of past readers and of the assumptions in our reading practices—in effect, an attention to the Wisdom of Transmission—that we can start undoing the unreading.

SEVEN

"This British Discovery and Recovery Enterprise"

Dee and England's Maritime Empire

Nowe (at length) ame I come to my chiefe purpose, of some Records settinge downe; which wilbe found sufficient, for to stire vpp yor Ma^{tis} most noble hart, and to directe you^r Godlie conscience, to vndertake this Brytish discovery, and recovery Enterprise, in yor owne Royall Interest: for the great good service of God, for yor highnes immortal fame, and the marvailous Wealth Publick of yor Brytish Impire.   —John Dee, *Brytanici Imperii Limites*

It is in his capacity as one of Tudor England's leading maritime advisers that the Dee I have been sketching takes on a clear shape. While his services on behalf of the British Empire have been consistently overshadowed by the more public legacy of Richard Hakluyt, Francis Drake, and Sir Walter Ralegh, he has always been assured of a place in this crucial chapter of maritime history and the history of geography. In 1930 Eva Taylor made him the central figure in her pioneering study, *Tudor Geography, 1485–1583;* and in 1973 Antoine de Smet claimed for Dee a seminal role in the development of Elizabethan cartography.[1] If we assemble all of the available sources—which requires us both to set aside our prejudices and to invest some serious textual labor—it becomes evident that Dee could hardly have held a more prominent place in what Kenneth Andrews described as the Tudor conjunction of "maritime enterprise and the genesis of the British Empire."[2] He is traditionally credited with coining the very term "British Empire,"[3] and he was one of its earliest, boldest, and most ingenious advocates.

In a series of maps, treatises, and conferences from the 1550s to the 1590s, Dee developed an expansionist program which he called "this British discovery and recovery enterprise." Supporting both the discovery of new lands and the recovery of territories that once arguably belonged to the British crown, Dee gradually claimed for the queen a vast imperial dominion covering most of the seas and much of the land in the Northern Hemisphere.

In the Age of Expansion, according to one of the standard accounts, Dee's "influence . . . can scarcely be set too high."[4] It can, however, be misrepresented, and careful historical reading is needed to do justice to his unique contributions. Dee's "imperial vision" has figured in the work of Yates and her successors; but by isolating it from his writings and activities and by viewing it through Yatesian lenses, they have colored it with two questionable shades. First, it is often assigned a *propagandistic* role. Yet the forms of Dee's writings and their intended audiences were quite distinct from those normally associated with propaganda. There is no doubt that his rhetoric was thoroughly nationalistic and his praise of the monarch absolute. But his texts were directed inward, to an extremely restricted circle; they were preparatory rather than celebratory; they informed policies more than they spread doctrines.

Second, in its recent incarnations Dee's imperialism has been inflated into a full-blown political, religious, and even mystical mission. In Gwyn Williams's words, Dee was interested in "establishing a quasi-mystical, quasi-scientific, quasi-religious world order, under that British-Protestant fraternity of chivalry . . . [and] the Hermetic, Platonic, and Cabalistic tradition."[5] Aside from the general implausibility of a man in Dee's position advocating or even contemplating the establishment of a "world order," these aspirations are closer to Yates's field of vision than Dee's.[6] This version of Dee's imperialism goes hand-in-hand with the myth of the magus and, like it, fails to appreciate the complex relationship between religion, politics, the occult sciences, and the New World in his writings and his era. According to Peter French, for instance, Dee had two principal motives for promoting English exploration: first, the Far East "represented one of the great repositories of occult knowledge"; and second, he had "an apocalyptic vision of England's future" that was inspired by a mythical view of England's past.[7] Renaissance voyages to the East had more to do with the dissemination of Christianity, the acquisition of riches, and a general "cosmopolitical restitution,"[8] than with the revelation of occult mysteries. And while Dee did use the "quasi-historical" exploits of King Arthur to glorify Queen Elizabeth, this vision was by no means "apocalyptic"—on the contrary, it was standard Tudor historical practice. Readers like French and Roy Strong have read too much into his imperialist rhetoric: the mythical conquests that charge his pages have all too often taken on mystical coloring.

These points are meant rather to qualify than to nullify Dee's contribution to England's nascent imperialism. As we shall see, during the 1570s in particular no one did more to promote an English "maritime monarchy"[9]—to put England, in other words, on the map. In 1581, Charles Merbury registered Dee's impact on the geopolitical consciousness of the Elizabethan court: "it is no small comforte vnto an English Gentleman, finding him selfe in a farre countrey, when he may boldly shew his face, and his forehead vnto any forren Nation: sit side by side with the proudest Spagniard: Cheek by cheeke with the stoutest Germane: set foote to foote with the forewardest Frenchman: knowing that this most Royall Prince (her Maiesties highnesse) is no whitte subiecte, nor inferiour vnto any of theirs. But that shee may also (if shee plaise) chalenge the superioritie both ouer some of them, and ouer many other kinges, and Princes more. *As maister Dee hath very learnedly of late (in sundry tables {i.e. maps} by him collected out of sundry auncient, and approued writers) shewed vnto her Maiestie, that shee may iustly call her selfe LADY, and EMPERES of all the Northe Ilandes.*"[10]

In the series of texts that are the subject of this chapter, Dee offered the queen and other courtly readers an "imperial formula" of mathematical simplicity and certainty: ". . . in Totall Somme, of all the foresayd Considerations, vnited in one: *Yt seemeth to be (almost) a Mathematicall demonstration* . . . for a faesable Policy, to bring or praeserue this Victorious Brytish Monarchy, in a marueilous Security. . . ."[11] The formula itself might be represented as: domestic and international security + territorial expansion = an "Incomparable *Ilandish Monarchy,*" this "BRYTISH IMPIRE."[12] The first, and prior, ingredient was a well-ordered commonwealth with defensive force sufficient to secure its boundaries. The second was a process (offensive, potentially, in both senses of the word) of geographical discovery and historical recovery—in Dee's felicitous phrase, "this Brytish discovery and recovery enterprise."

It is this program that earns Dee his special place in the history of the British Empire. With it he attempted, albeit mostly in vain, to make the English Renaissance an "Age of Reconnaissance";[13] and through it we can better understand the nature of that Age. The British discovery and recovery enterprise entailed, first, a *spatial* or *geographical reconnaissance.* Space was explored and conquered in the names of individuals and rulers. Travel became increasingly integral to Humanist education and service, and monarchs became increasingly dependent upon geographical knowledge for control of their dominions.[14] For his part Dee called for a "Geographicall" or "Cosmographicall Reformation"; and in the foreign policy of Dee and many of his compatriots this reformation was as decisive as the one concerning religion. The Geographical, like the Protestant, Reformation was a matter more of interpretation than of truth: new maps had to be drawn, justified, and enforced, and this required the cooperation of politicians, adventurers, and scholars.

The British discovery and recovery enterprise entailed, further, a *temporal* or *historical reconnaissance.* In order to persuade the queen and her council to pursue an imperial policy, as well as to persuade other countries to tolerate it, Dee needed to build his vision on historical foundations. In accordance with Tudor historiographical convention, he amassed a collection of precedents for territorial (re)possession and for empire itself.[15] He confronted no shortage of precedent: "Before ever Elizabethan adventurer set foot in the New World there were five centuries (or more) of precedent stored away in the minds and archives of English officials."[16] In his maritime writings Dee used these precedents—ancient and medieval, English and foreign—to picture the British Empire as it "hath bene: Yea, as it, yet, is: or, rather, as it may, & (of right) ought to be. . . ."[17] In this clumsy sentence Dee struggles with the appropriate *tense* of the imperial outlook; and he reminds us that it was as much retrospective as prospective.

Finally, Dee's discovery and recovery enterprise entailed a *textual reconnaissance.* Richard Schoeck has suggested that, during the Renaissance, textual discoveries were as exciting as geographical discoveries, "the illumination of an ancient author as stirring as the voyages of Vespucci, or Drake, Raleigh, and Frobisher."[18] But in

Dee's age the real excitement was to be found in the *relationship between* the textual labor and the geographical voyage. As John Parker put it, "An empire is the work of many hands, and editors, I like to believe, are not the least significant."[19] In the sixteenth century the hands of textual experts—not only editors but professional readers, antiquaries, and publicists—did most to shape England's embryonic empire. They conjured with considerable imagination a vision of sea power and global colonization from the pages of books and manuscripts.[20] This vision was embodied in the position papers and anthologies of Dee, Hakluyt, and their successors. Alongside these textual enterprises there were the probing voyages of merchants, pirates, soldiers, and colonizers. But as long as Elizabeth reigned—and for some time after—the British Empire remained a textual affair.[21]

A. *GENERAL AND RARE MEMORIALS* (1576/77)

Dee's *General and Rare Memorials pertayning to the Perfect Arte Of Navigation* (henceforth *Memorials*)[22] initiated the period of his most intense historical and geographical research and his most influential participation in the government of the Elizabethan commonwealth. In advocating the development of maritime resources as a means of relieving the ills of the commonwealth and enlarging the dominions of the crown, it consolidated his role as a leading maritime adviser and set the tone for the works that followed.

Despite the importance of *Memorials* to Dee's career and to English maritime history, scholars have rarely penetrated beyond the title page, which is dominated by an arresting and elaborate image labeled the "British Hieroglyphic."[23] It was one of the finest emblematic title pages of its time and has attracted bibliographical admiration for centuries.[24] The "British Hieroglyphic" is the proper point of entry into the text: Dee used it both to convey the essence of and to serve as a mnemonic aid to the project outlined in the text. But many scholars have been content to speculate on the basis of the image alone, and it has generated theories that the rest of the text cannot support.

The most useful measure in recovering the meaning of *Memorials* is not a meditation on Dee's hieroglyph but rather a consideration of what he meant in calling the text a *"Plat Politicall"* ($\triangle$1r). The term "plat" is now obsolete, and most of its connotations are covered by the related term "plot"; but during the Renaissance, "plat" was an integral term with a significant set of interconnected meanings. First, it meant a physical area of land. Second, it meant a visual representation of an area or building—a map or an architectural diagram. Third, it meant an outline or summary. And fourth, it meant a scheme or plan of action in some undertaking. On the broadest level, a "plat" was a (re)presentational strategy in which the visual, verbal, and mental were inextricably linked. A "Plat Politicall" like Dee's addressed a practical problem by simultaneously laying out the issues and suggesting lines of action.

Specifically, Dee's *Memorials* is a "Plat of a Pety-Nauy-Royall" (A4v). The scheme it forwards—the establishment of a small naval force roughly equivalent to the modern coast guard—is presented as the "Maister Key" (A4v) to the perennial problem of Tudor administrations: the interrelated needs for wealth and security. These concerns are explicitly invoked in the title of the prefatory epistle: "A necessary Aduertisement, by an vnknown freend, giuen to the modest, and godly Readers: who also carefully desire the *prosperous State* of the Common wealth, of this BRYTISH KINGDOM, and the *Politicall SECVRITIE* thereof" (sig. $\triangle$ 2r; my emphasis). Considering the scope of his subject, Dee was not unjustified in calling his plat a *"Plat Politicall, of the Brytish Monarchie"* ($\triangle$1r).[25] This should make it immediately clear that the context of Dee's plat is not so much occult, scientific, or even political philosophy: it offers pragmatic counsel for the development of British naval power as a remedy to problems facing the Elizabethan administration in the 1570s.

This is to make three separate claims for *Memorials:* that it addresses sociohistorical concerns that were conventional (even commonplace); that it does so in a conventional textual form and in relation to other "plats political"; and that, as counsel, it was not just "read" but "used" by contemporaries. I will substantiate these claims by reading, in three stages, outward from the text. First, I will summarize the book's contents and contexts; second, I will supply its intertextual situation by comparing it to several related plats. And, finally, I will provide several episodes from the book's circulation and reception in order to illustrate the uses that were made of it.

I

The contents of *Memorials* can be divided into three sections: the introductory material, the plat proper, and the two supporting orations from George Gemistos Plethon. The introduction consists of a "Brief Note Scholasticall," a "Necessary Aduertisement," and (despite its placement at the end of the book) a dedication to Sir Christopher Hatton. The "Brief Note" contains Dee's cryptic but descriptive self-introduction, while the "Necessary Aduertisement" launches a detailed defense against a series of accusations and defamations. Throughout the "Aduertisement" Dee harps on his service to his country, and his *apologia* culminates in the assertion, "It will appeare, hereafter, in due tyme, that, greater, furder, and of longer Continuance, hath bin [my] doings, and very well liked of, Aduertisements and Instructions, in sundry affayres Philosophicall, and Cosmopoliticall, FOR VERITIE, IVSTICE, AND PEACE FVRDERING, than hath . . . bin (as yet) perceiued" (є*1v).

It is here, too, that Dee outlines the ambitious original plan for *Memorials*.[26] It was to consist of four volumes, which would go under the astonishing title *The Brytish Monarchy*. The first, *Memorials*, was to be a prologue to the others and to introduce Dee's scheme for a small naval force. The second, entitled *THE BRYTISH COMPLEMENT, OF THE PERFECT ARTE OF NAVIGATION*, was to consist mainly of *QVEENE ELIZABETH, HER TABLES GVBERNAVTIK*, which would "contein many Quires of Paper." In fact, "so great, is the Volume therof, that, to haue it fairely and distinctly printed, with all the Appertenances, it would be, (in bulk) greater than the English Bible . . ." (є 4r). These "tables gubernautik" sound more spectacular than they were: they seem to have been tables of longitudes and latitudes computed according to Dee's invention—which he advertised on the title page of *Memorials*—the "paradoxal compass."[27] The third volume is a complete mystery, as it was "vtterly suppressed, or deliuered to Vulcan his Custody" (є 4v)—that is, it was burned—for reasons unknown. The fourth and final volume was to be called OF FAMOVS AND RICH DISCOVERIES, and was to contain "not only . . . the Generall Survey Hydrographicall, of all the whole world . . . but also, a particular and ample examination, of King Soloman his Ophirian three yeres voyage: And also, the lawfull and very honorable Entitling of our most gratious and Soueraigne Lady, QVEENE ELIZABETH . . . to very large Forrein Dominions . . ." (€4v). Dee spoke in enthusiastic terms of this text, claiming that, "in the Secret Center therof, is more bestowed and stored vp, than I may, or (in this place) will express." There is, however, nothing secret and little that is surprising in the text that survives: it is a straightforward collection of materials on geography, particularly of the areas to be explored in voyages to the northeast and northwest.[28] Dee's search for patronage for the project forced him into a cautious publishing strategy: "though, the Inuentions, and Collections be . . . of great Value . . . yet (by Order, taken by him, who hath the chief Interest therin [i.e. Dee himself]:) the same, are not to be printed, VNTIL THE PROOF BE PAST, How, this Mechanicien [again, Dee himself] his zealous, dutyfull, and humble Aduertisement Politicall shall be liked of, and accepted . . ." (€*2r).

He clearly hoped to gain that support by dedicating the first book to Hatton. Several scholars have pointed out that the dedication appears to be an afterthought.[29] This is beyond doubt, since Dee says as much in his "Brief Note": *The Epistle in Meter, (annexed in the end of this Book), was by the* Mechanicien *sent, after that the* vnknown Freend *had . . . put the foresayd two Treatises, in Print: & deliuered again into the hands of the sayd* Mechanicien *the whole Impression therof"* (△1v).[30] What is more interesting is why he should have done so, and what effect it had on the production and circulation of the book. When we consider that 1577 was the *annus mirabilis* in Hatton's career, Dee's motivation becomes clear. While Dee's treatise was being typeset, Hatton was appointed vice-chamberlain of the queen's household, given a seat on the Privy Council, and knighted at Windsor.[31] Furthermore, as I mentioned in the previous chapter, Hatton was already acquainted with Dee and his work.[32] The additional material introduced by the dedication caused some difficulties for the printer, resulting in an unusual and confusing collation.[33]

If the production of the book was altered by the dedication, so was its circulation. Hatton was not a passive, honorary recipient of a single copy but (as Dee hoped) an agent of politic distribution:

Vnto the Gardians, most wise,
And Sacred Senat, or Chief Powr,
I durst not offer this Aduise,
(So homely writ), for fear of Lowr.
But, at your will, and discreet choyce,
To keep by you, or to imparte,
I leaue this zealous Publik voyce:
You will accept so simple parte. (L2r)

In the closing paragraph of the text itself Dee couched his request in more detailed, and more tactful, terms: "And I beseche you (Right Worshipfull Sir,) not onely to take these my speedy Trau-ailes and Collections in good parte, your selfe: But also, to whom so euer you will deliuer any one of the Copies, (wherof, only one Hundred are to be printed . . .) You would be my Carefull Ora-tor . . ." (K4r). This gives us some idea of the unusual control Dee had over his text and suggests the audience he hoped to reach: *Memorials* was not a pamphlet published for public debate but a very limited production for a very privileged readership. This control over distribution, along with the fact that Dee hovered over the printing of the texts (entering emendations by hand), suggests that *Memorials* is better considered as a manuscript than a printed book.

As the first volume of the series, *Memorials* represents but an "Entrance into the matter of Nauigation" (ε3v). In the "Aduertise-ment" Dee introduces his scheme and outlines its expected bene-fits: the queen ought to establish a naval force, "contynually to be mainteyned, for manifold great Commodities procuring to this BRYTISH MONARCHIE: (which, no other way, can be brought to pas:) and among them all, the PERPETVALL POLITIK SECV-RITY and better preseruation of this famous Kingdom, from all Forrein danger, or Homish disorder . . . and most needfull Publik Benefit . . ." (ε3v). This statement contains in a nutshell all of the sociopolitical concerns that Dee's plat addresses. It implies that England's security was threatened on two fronts, from "beyond the seas" and "at home." What is needed to secure preservation is increased wealth; and the exclusive means to this, Dee argues, is a Petty Navy Royal consisting of "Threescore Tall Ships, and eche of them, betwene eightscore and two hundred, Tun of Burden: and Twenty other smaller Barks, (betwene 20, and 50, Tun)" (C1v).

It is important to stress from the outset that Dee's domestic perspective is usually that of the commons (or "Publik," "communaltie," "common wealth," and so on). Thus the problems that are stressed are shortages of food, land, and jobs and the social disorder that inevitably followed. Christopher Clay has explained that, in a period of drastic "population growth, inflation, agrarian change and industrial expansion," the overriding concern for peasants and policy makers alike was "the preservation of internal tranquillity" through "the upholding of the traditional order."[34] Dee's Petty Navy Royal answered precisely this concern: "The Publik Commodities wherof, ensuing: are, or would be, so great and many, as the whole Commons . . . would (for euer,) bles the day and houre, wherein such good and politik Order, was . . . established: And esteme them, not onely most worthy and Royall Counsailers, but also Heroicall Magistrates, who haue had so fatherly Care for the Communaltie: and most wisely, procured so *Generall Brytish Securitie* . . ." (A2v).

The other factor in this general British security was the danger of foreign invasion—in the form of soldiers, pirates, or even workers. Dee's international perspective rested on two fears about the boundaries of Britain: they seemed alarmingly permeable by foreigners while at the same time the natives and their rulers were all but bound in, failing not only to compete for global resources but to take advantage of those which filled the seas surrounding them on all sides.

Wealth and order at home and strength abroad are, then, the two overarching benefits that will result from Dee's plat and have been advertised before he reaches page 4. The remainder of the plat details, with more realism and less rhetoric, the ways and means of establishing a Petty Navy Royal. Dee begins with an expanded list of the resulting "Publik Commodities," setting forth thirteen items, extensively elaborating on the wealth and security theme. Proving himself—as in the *Synopsis*—well briefed on his country's most pressing political and economic problems, he outlines measures to reduce unemployment, suppress piracy, advance military science, exploit natural commodities (especially fish), and improve the skill of British mariners. If Dee begins to appear not only repetitive but paranoid about the security of England, we would do well to remember that "it was most important of all for an island nation . . . to be strong at sea, and no other strand runs more consistently or more conspicuously through the actions of the state in the economic sphere. . . ."[35] Indeed, the most pronounced factor in England's international—and particularly maritime—relations in the 1570s and 1580s was the escalation of adversity with Spain. While Elizabethan policy makers were notoriously cautious and insular, the English did not adopt a purely defensive strategy: the early 1570s saw "the opening of hostilities on a small scale, veiled as private efforts. . . . Private Englishmen were now striking at Spain at sea in the sources of her wealth."[36] Dee's plat engages not just a psychological fear, then, but a political strategy. "And, So," he concludes, "the End of Ends, and vttermost scope of the sayd Arte of Nauigation, is such Publik Commodity" (B2r).

Yet, in all of this talk of commodities there is something missing: the fact that no returns can be expected without initial capital investment. As the Tudors suspected, and the experience of the Stuarts emphatically proved, the navy would not support itself.[37] Therefore, Dee's plat of a Petty Navy Royal necessarily proceeds to "Considerations, for the Charges thereof bearing and mainteyning" (B2r). Dee was eager to assure his readers that the Petty Navy Royal would "be mainteined, without any Cost or Charge to the Queene" (ϵ*2r). While customs revenue and confiscations from convicted pirates would play their part, the maintenance would ultimately rely on one source—taxation. Dee initially resorts to euphemisms by calling for every subject "to be, after a most easy manner, Contributary thereunto: vnder the name of A perpetuall Beneuolence, for Sea Security" (B3r). But whatever name Dee hides it under, he outlines a taxation scheme in the established terms of Elizabethan fiscal machinery, the manner of which was anything but easy.

His "valuations" are to be carried out according to "the Act, of the last Subsidie, granted, Anno Eliz. 18" (B3r, in margin). During Elizabeth's reign, such "subsidies" were fairly common: "few of her years of rule were entirely free of the activities of subsidy commissioners."[38] The principles of Tudor taxation are complex, but one thing is clear: they were the source of many administrative and political problems.[39] First, even in Elizabeth's time there was a great deal of resistance to the whole idea of ship money: "The forced assessments for the ship levies . . . had never been popular with the country at large, and were often met by transparent evasions, or open refusals on the part of various towns, counties, groups and individuals."[40] Second, there was great sensitivity about the distribution of the burden. For instance, there was drastic variation in the amounts different counties were expected to pay.[41] Furthermore (as with all taxes) the poorer sort had trouble meeting the requirements. Therefore, "Although the earliest subsidies . . . attempted to tax almost the entire community, from the mid sixteenth century onwards there were exemption limits which excluded the poorer sections of it."[42] Finally, there were notorious problems with inefficient and corrupt collectors.

Dee kept all of these problems in mind when attempting to justify his scheme. He was careful to introduce detailed exemption clauses, and he intended that foreigners living in England or in some way receiving British benefits would also pay what he called a "Petty Forreyn Courtesy" (B3v). To ensure full and orderly payment, Dee suggested that two "Petty-Navy-Exchequers" be appointed and posted near the main ports (H2v). Finally, Dee pointed out that, in comparison to the price of spiritual security (for which "God challengeth the Tenth yerely, and First frutes, continually") national security (requiring only "the Tenth of the Tenth, I mean, the Hundredth parte of our Reuenues") was a bargain.

As in most plats political, Dee fills the bulk of his space with a discussion of possible objections to his scheme. In answer to the first objection (16–30)—that the navy's funds will be insufficient—Dee explains that the taxes alone would raise, "Yerely, aboue an Hundred Thousand pounds." He then lists "Ten Generall, and Extraordinary means, of increasing the Threasory of the Petty Nauy Royall" which "may be thought sufficient, for the probable Dissolution of the first Dowt" (D3v). Some of these are quite practical and some were already in practice. But he forcefully argued that the foreign fishermen who plunder Britain's seas should be forced to give "The Tenth . . . of all their yeerly Fishings . . . In Token, of their reasonable Acknowledging the ROYALTY of this Brytish Monarchy, in the selfsame Brytish Seas . . ." (C4v). This would serve to increase not only wealth, but security and food supplies as well. Even more to the point is his suggestion that all pirate ships should be captured and their goods confiscated. Less attractive, and no doubt less realistic, is his call for

temporary, voluntary contributions—such as "Legacies" (C1r)—
or the "Extraordinary" measure of requiring those of higher in-
comes to contribute an additional "Six hundredth peny" to the
normal rate. Dee is confident that not only "a sufficient masse
of Threasor, will easily and spedily be contributed," but a "great
Ouerplus also" (D2r). This treasury will cover more than the
charges of the maintenance of the navy and its mariners, which
would not exceed 200,000 pounds yearly (C2r): it will also provide
a pension for mariners after they retire, a fund for the "poore
Widdowes, and Orphanes of such Men," a stipend for "4 Petty
Pylots Publik . . . ready to serue, Mathematically and Mechani-
cally," and funds to repair decayed "Hauens, Harboroughes, Ports,
Blockhouses &c." (D2r–v).

In answering the doubt regarding the scarcity of food and resources (31–50), Dee by no means denies that such a scarcity
exists. What he argues is that the supplies sent to the navy will not
decrease the store for the rest of the commonwealth. Rather they
will, in the ways outlined above, secure many resources that are
now wasted or absorbed by foreigners. In a passionate "Supplication of the Commons," Dee condemns those subjects who "trans-
port vittayles to forreyners" with their own "priuate lucre" in mind
(E1v). In a key section of this supplication, he singles out for
particular scorn the "enclosers of commons."[43]

The third and final doubt is: "That the Threasor Contributed,
may sundry wayes be abused" (G2r). Dee's answer is simple, if
unpersuasive (51–53): he calls on God to "finde all of those Officers, so wise, faithfull, Iust, Carefull, and Diligent" who will
enforce the lawful use of the naval treasury (G2v). With men like
Francis Shaxton of Lynn in office, divine intervention would have
been necessary to straighten out a hopelessly corrupt system.[44]
Shaxton carried out his illicit export trade under the nose of the
customer of Lynn, Thomas Sydney. Sydney, too, became rich
through illegal private trading, and in 1575 he appeared before the
Privy Council on the charge of sending grain cargoes to Spain. He
was rebuked, but he kept his office—perhaps because he was
married to Sir Francis Walsingham's sister.[45]

It is only in the seven pages before Dee concludes the plat proper
that his "imperialism" emerges from his current events. In these
pages (54–60) Dee discusses the historical precedents for the naval

expansion of the British Empire. His focus is on the Saxon king "EADGARVS PACIFICVS." While his sources are the state of the art in terms of sixteenth-century historiography, his account is more patriotic than scholarly. With this example Dee hoped to do more than persuade the readers of his plat of a Petty Navy Royal: he hoped to persuade them to "valiantly recouer, and enioy, if not all our Ancient and Due Appertenances, to this Imperiall Brytish Monarchy, Yet, at the least, some . . . Notable Portion therof" (G4r).

The third and final section of *Memorials* presents another imperial precedent, this time not so much historical as analogical. In what at first appears to be a curious move, Dee appended to his plat two orations by the Byzantine scholar George Gemistos Plethon (c. 1355–1450). It was Dee's hope that they "might be a good Aduise for the framing of an Analogical Ciuile consideration" (I1r, in margin). This appendix gives rise, indeed, to a series of analogies, which go well beyond the contents of *Memorials*.

Like Dee, Gemistos has been chiefly known for his contributions to the Neoplatonic revival in the Renaissance: his visit to Florence in 1439 marks the single most important moment in the transmission of Platonic texts and thought to the Italian Humanists. But C. M. Woodhouse's recent biography shows that scholars have lost sight of a major part of Gemistos's activity and significance.[46] In a striking parallel to Dee, Woodhouse has presented a scholar who, while deeply committed to philosophical and natural philosophical study, functioned preeminently as a peripatetic scholarly civil servant. He was a regular adviser on economic, military, and philosophical matters to the emperors and despots of the Morea.[47]

While Dee was certainly aware of Gemistos's Neoplatonic contributions, it is revealing that the Gemistos whom he invokes in *Memorials* is the pragmatic political adviser. The second (though the earlier) of the two orations Dee prints is the *Address to the Despot Theodore on the Peloponnese* (c. 1415).[48] The other oration, of which Dee printed only a short extract, is the *Address* to Theodore's father, Manuel (c. 1418). There was nothing philosophical about these texts: they addressed problems in imperial security and expansion, and constituted what Dee called a "Plat for Reformation of the State" (I1r). They addressed the same concerns as occupied Dee in

Memorials: "the object that Plethon had in view . . . [was] to equalize the burdens of the state, and to maintain an efficient military force."⁴⁹ Like Dee, Gemistos began by affirming monarchical rule: recalling the "hieroglyphic" frontispiece to *Memorials,* he argued that it is best to have a single ruler at the helm of the ship of state. He went on to prescribe systematic and historically grounded constitutional provisions, including the establishment of a standing army, the restructuring of the system of taxation, and the improvement of the legal system—especially the regulation of religion and land tenure. It is not surprising, then, that Dee found these plats complementary to his own.

There was one major divergence, however: in the *Address to Theodore* Gemistos clearly stated his preference for "land forces" over "sea-men." This prompted Dee's marginal qualification, "all here, contained is not to be . . . imitated: But, here and there, the Idea generall, is to be answered with due application, particularly, for our Cuntry, and these our Dayes" (K1r).

II

Dee was by no means the only one to address the security and wealth of England in the 1570s. The first stanza in Dee's verse epistle to Hatton makes not only a proposition about the English commonwealth, but a call to those who would improve it:

> Yf Priuat wealth, be leef and deere,
> To any Wight, of Brytish Soyl:
> Ought Publik Weale, haue any peere?
> To that, is due, all Wealth and Toyl.

Within a few years, Robert Hitchcock had written a plat about which his brother wrote, as if in answer to Dee,

> Amongst the rest that well deserue,
> Account the Author one:
> Who by his toyle hath here offred,
> To all excepting none. (*4r)

The full title of Hitchcock's plat will suggest that he was entering the same argument as Dee: "A Pollitique Platt for *the honour of the Prince, the greate profite of the publique state,* relief of the poore, preseruation of the riche, reformation of Roges and Idle persones, and the wealthe of thousandes that knowes not howe to liue." Like Dee,

Hitchcock invoked the Ciceronian commonplace that "euery man is rather borne to profite his natiue soile and common weale . . . then to seke after his owne priuate gaine" (**1r). And like Dee's plat, "this little booke . . . prouideth for the poore, in honest and decent maner, brynging them to a good and a Godly vocation of life: with many other speciall benefites, to this kyngdome and common wealth . . ." (**2r). His "remedie" was put in the same terms as Dee's. In advocating an increased fishing industry, Hitchcock explains that "almightie GOD by the most comodious scituation of this Ilande . . . hath prouided a moste conuenient meane, bothe for labor for the Idle: and for food, benefite, and ritches . . ." (a1r). Even the form of Hitchcock's plat resembles Dee's: after outlining the benefits of his scheme, he raises and answers eight objections.

Hitchcock's primary complaint recalls and outdoes Dee: "The aduantage and profite whereof, this Realme and Subiects . . . for the moste parte haue loste: and suffered strangers . . . to take, who seeyng our carelesse dealyng, haue not onely taken this beneficiall fishyng from vs: but verie warely doeth sell the same commoditie vnto vs" (a3v). He advocates the establishment of a fishing fleet of four hundred ships, "70 tunne the Shippe," with one "skilfull Maister to gouerne it, twelue Marriners or fishermen, and xii. of the strong lustie Beggars, or poore men" (a2r). This, in sum, "amounteth to the number of tenne thousande persones" (a2r). And the employment of the poor as mariners will not be the only benefit: "Her Maiesties Customes and Subsidies [will be] greatly augmented: Her Nauigation greatly increased. The Tounes borderyng vpon the Sea coastes now in ruine, and voide of English inhabitauntes, [will] bee inhabited by her maiesties owne peculer Subiectes: to the greate strength of this Realme, and terror of the enemie" (a1v). As with Dee, Hitchcock claimed that "this Platte shalbe brought to passe . . . without coste or charges": the way this was to be accomplished was "by borowyng of fower score thousande pounde for three yeres" (a4r). Clearly, the problem is not deciding which plat belongs in which argument, but rather determining where one plat ends and another begins.

Yet there are differences between Hitchcock's plat and *Memorials*. While Dee's is a large volume with an extravagant variety of typefaces, Hitchcock's—with its black letter print and much smaller size—looks like a popular pamphlet. Further, Dee dedicated his treatise to a privy councilor and intended it for a governmental audience, while Hitchcock's is a "Newyeres gift to Englande" and opens with an "Epistle to Englande" (*2r). Finally, Dee had completed his writing by August 1576, and Hitchcock's plat was not printed until January 1580. It appears, then, as if the two books kept different company.

This turns out not to be the case. On the final page of his work, Hitchcock explains how his plat developed: "To further the same I gaue a Copie hereof to my Lorde of Leicester, sixe yeares paste, one other copie to the Queenes Maiestie, fower yeares paste. Also to sundrie of her Maiesties priuie Councell certaine copies. And in the ende of the last Parliament [i.e., 1576] I gaue twelue Copies to Councillors of the lawe, and other men of greate credite, hopyng that God would stirre vppe some good men to set out this woorke" (f4r). God did "stirre vppe" a good man, one who happened to be Dee's close friend: "Maister Leonerd [a mistake for Thomas] Digges . . . had one Copie, who (being a Burgesse of the house) tooke occasion there vppon, to desire license to speak his mynd, concerning this Plat, saieyng he spake for the common wealthe of all England, and for no priuate cause. . . ." In other words, Hitchcock's plat was only presented to a larger audience after circulating (and finding approval) in precisely the same environment as Dee's *Memorials*. There is, in fact, concrete evidence of close contact between the two plats and their authors: at the British Library there is a copy of *Memorials* which bears the inscription, "Captan Hichcok. book. the gift of Doctor Dee. [15]77."[50]

An author who entered the same argument with a more aggressive stance was Sir Humphrey Gilbert. With Gilbert the connections to Dee become more intimate, and more complex. On 6 November 1577, Gilbert visited Dee's house at Mortlake.[51] In the state papers there are two letters addressed to the queen by Gilbert that are dated 6 November 1577. These do not mention Dee, but the matching dates and stylistic similarities suggest that he was involved in their composition. The first is entitled "A discourse how her Majestie may annoy the king of Spayne"; the second, "A discourse how hir Majestie may meete with and annoy the king of Spayne."[52] In these closely related documents, Gilbert's goal is what he calls "securities to the immortall fame of your

Majestie." His general suggestion for "hitting the mark" reads almost like a parody of early modern political theory: "The safety of Principates, Monarchies, and Common Weales rest chiefly in making theire enemies weake, and poore, and themselves strong and rich."[53] When he adds that both of these "god hath specially wrought for your majesties safety, if your highness shall not overpas good opportunities for the same," he sounds undeniably like Dee. But Gilbert comes into his own when he suggests his actual means: "the way to worke the feate is to sett forth under such like colour of discoverie, certayne shippes of warre to the [New Land] . . . in which place they shall . . . meete in effecte all the great shippinge of Fraunce, Spayne, and Portyngall, where I would have take and bring away with theire fraygthes and ladinges, the best of those shippes and burn the woorst. . . ." This is an unabashed scheme for royally sanctioned piracy, one that Dee was unlikely to have supported. Much more conventional was Gilbert's plan to exploit "Newland Fish," "by the gayne thereof, shipping, victuall, munition, and the transporting of five or six thousand soldiors may be defrayed." But where Dee and Hitchcock hoped merely to relieve with fish, Gilbert hoped to conquer with them.

A plat attributed to Gilbert's half-brother Sir Walter Ralegh but certainly devised by Thomas Digges not only enters the argument but epitomizes it. This plat delivered to the queen "A brief Discourse, declaring how Honourable and Profitable to your most Excellent Majesty, and how Necessary and Commodious for your Realm, the making of *Dover Haven* shall be, and in what sort, with least Charges in greatest Perfection the same may be Accomplish'd."[54] This at first seems a more local concern than the grand schemes of Dee and Gilbert; but Digges's larger claim is that "There is no one thing . . . of greater necessity to maintain the Honour and Safety of this Your Majesty's Realm, than by all convenient means to encrease Navigation, Shipping and Mariners, these being a strength in time of war; and in time of Peace, Members most Profitable and Commodious." He points out that the Low Countries had followed a comparable plat with overwhelming results; yet, "with us . . . lamentable Relation hath been made of the great Decay of Mariners and Fishermen . . . And also of the present Poverty, and Desolate Habitation of many Frontier Towns" (B1v). When Digges sets out to list "The Commodities that thereby both to Your Majesty and Realm shall ensue," it is hard to avoid the feeling that we know them before reading them. And, indeed, they prove almost identical to those we have seen. First, "A Marvellous Number of Poor People both by this Work, till the *Haven* is made, and after by the Shipping, Fishing, &c. will be Employ'd, who now for want of Work are Whip'd, Mark'd, and Hang'd" (C1r). Further, "The encrease of Navigation, Fishing and Traffick that hereby will grow, and the great Wealth and Commodity thereof ariseing will not be contain'd in one Shire alone, but pour'd forth into all parts of the Realm, to the great Relief of the Poor, and Contentation of all Degrees . . ." (C1r). And there will also be increased trade, royal revenue, and defense against pirates.

These are not the only, nor indeed the best-known, voices in the Elizabethan arguments regarding security, wealth, and sea power. The writings of the Hakluyts contained highly influential plats that were related to Dee's in complicated ways.[55] Much more obscure, though no less relevant, is John Montgomery's *Treatise concerninge the mayntenance of the nauie*.[56] And it is tempting to hear an echo of Dee in Sir Philip Sidney's advice to the queen "to keep a strong successive fleet all seasonable times of the year upon this pretty sleeve or ocean of hers." As Fulke Greville described it, Sidney's reasoning was remarkably close to Dee's: "to keep them as provident surveyors [of] what did pass from one state to another, wherein the law of nature or nations had formerly given her interest to an offensive or defensive security: a regal inquisition, and worthy of a sea-sovereign—without wronging friends and neighbours—to have a perfect intelligence . . . in particular, a clear perspective glass into her enemy's merchant or martial traffic. . . ."[57] My intention has not, however, been to provide a "Compendious Rehearsall" of the entire argument. The foregoing will be sufficient to show that Dee's plat was one of many related texts that arose out of a particular historical situation.

III

One of the keys to appreciating both the nature and the impact of Dee's plat is careful study of its circulation and reception. The evidence lies in contemporary readings of the book, most of which are represented in marginal notes in surviving copies. But the earliest reading, by Dee's cousin William Aubrey, took place before the work was printed, and Aubrey's notes are recorded in a letter he sent to Dee on 28 July 1577.[58] As a judge of the Court of Admiralty Aubrey was well placed to assess the merits or defects and probable reception of the plat; and Dee was well advised to send it to him while it was still in manuscript.[59] While he pointed to several problems with the execution of Dee's project, he gave it his unequivocal support. In fact, he did not know what to praise first, the "matter" or the "manner": "I am in dowt, whether I shall prefer the matter for the substance, weight, & pythynes of the multitude of Arguments & Reasons: or the maner, for the Method, order, perspicuity, & Elocution, in that heigth & loftynes, that I did not believe oᶠ Tung . . . to be capable of" (116r). Aubrey agreed with Dee that a Petty Navy Royal would "be a better Watch for the Security of the State, than all the Intelligences or Beacons that may be devised" (116v). He was especially taken by Dee's "insertion" of the "Two Orations of *Georgius Gemistus Pletho* . . . for the worthynes & variety of many wise & sownd advises . . ." (117r). In the end Dee could claim to have contributed to the English navy more than not only Plethon to the Byzantine but Homer and Virgil to the Greek and Trojan (116r).

Of the six printed copies of *Memorials* I have personally examined, four contain extensive manuscript markings—which in itself suggests that when Dee's plat was published it found interested readers. While one of these (the Grenville copy in the British Library) contains only profuse underlinings and another (the copy in the Pepys Library of Magdalene College, Cambridge) utilizes an as yet undeciphered system of lowercase letters to indicate the nature of particularly interesting passages, two copies (the Hitchcock copy mentioned above and the one in the Cambridge University Library) contain substantial and revealing annotations.

The notes in the Cambridge University Library copy begin on page 6 (A3v) and end—apart from one note on page 56—on page 39 (E4r).[60] This suggests at once that—unlike Aubrey—this reader either only read or only found especially noteworthy the early parts of the plat proper, and paid less attention to the introductory material, the account of King Edgar, and the Latin orations. The first three notes, all on page 6, further indicate the interests of the reader. Next to Dee's "commodity" of discouraging

foreign treachery is written, "[We?] shall also cut of from [S]cot-
land al foreine [. . .]des whereby they [h]aue in tyme passed [. . .]
finalie annoied vs. And furdre cut of [. . .] others landinge in
Scotland. whereby from thence to envade [v]s," and also "[T]hat
prince that will dwel [long?] moost [i.e., must] be provided of
[s]oldie^{rs} bothe for Sea and land, if he ioyne w^t ye Sea." Near the
bottom of the page, next to Dee's ninth commodity, is written,
"[H]e may dwel longe [i]n peace that is well prouided for the
warres" (A3v). Not very subtle reasoning, but an accurate and
pithy rendering of Dee's political message. On the next page, Dee's
discussion of the fishing industry is summarized, "surelie o^r fissh-
inge moughte not onlie gyve vs greate wealth but make vs also
ver[y] stronge and o^r enemies weake by Sea" (A4r). In this discussion, Dee suggests that many foreign ships come under the pre-
tense of fishing, but in fact they are familiarizing themselves with
the British coastline—a practice much like that suggested by
Gilbert—"And, (so, making perfect Chartes of all our Coasts,
rownd about England, and Ireland) are become (allmost) perfecter
in them, then the moste parte of our Maisters, Loadmen, or Pylots"
(A4r). A note in the margin indicates the reader's agreement that
this is "a daungerous matter."

While the identity of this reader remains elusive, we can conclude several things about him and his reading. First, by looking
at the hand, we can be all but certain that the reader was a "him."
Second, we know that the reading took place not long after the
book was released.[61] Third, we know that the reader, if not actually a policy maker, at least pretended to be one: "[I] woulde wisshe
these artes of ye nauie to be [g]overned euery of them [b]y a verie
sufficient [g]entle man. and [. . .] their departur[e]s, meetings,
suits and [c]ircuits vnder ye highe [A]dmirall of this Realme"
(B1v). The most important clue is found in the fact that this copy
came from the contemporary library of John, Lord Lumley—it has
been signed by Lumley on the title page.[62] This may create more
puzzles than it solves, however, for Lumley was well out of favor at
the time *Memorials* appeared and is unlikely to have been included
in that privileged group selected by Hatton (or Dee) to receive a
copy. Yet, however puzzling, it is undeniable that he had one, and
we are left with a tentative identity for the reader as someone
attached to Lumley's household—perhaps even Lumley himself.

More important than his identity, however, are the facts that he read with political concerns and that he found "meet matter" in Dee's plat.

A more extensive reading—or set of readings—can be traced in the copy of *Memorials* bearing the dedication to Hitchcock. Again the notes do not appear until page 6 of the plat proper. They continue, however, right up to the orations of Plethon. The majority of the notes are of a summarizing, organizing, or clarifying nature and do not offer any glimpse into the reader's interests. For instance, next to Dee's section on the overseeing of foreign fishermen he copies out Dee's phrase verbatim, "to ouersee the forrayne fishermen" (B1r). At the beginning of Dee's scheme for taxation, he notes, "The plat how to haue the Nauy mayntayned" (B3r). The first indication of the reader's personal perspective and the date of his reading is a note on page 23: "In our way betwene St Christofers and Virginia in the Island *Cacus* all of salt most fitt for our i[. . .] this Island now possesseth yer noat that salt made in salt [. . .], such as wer made at Newcastel, and other coasts of England is not good for salting of Herring but there be a sharper salt as Spanish salt, or salt vpon salt but for other fish o^r salt is good" (C4r). This note is nominally related to Dee's text, in that Dee mentions herrings. But the references to and information about salt are purely the observations of the reader. Clearly, they come from someone with experience both in sailing and in the business of salting herrings. More clearly, they date from several years (and maybe even several generations) after Dee: the references to Virginia and Cacus could not have been made until well after 1577. This latter fact rules out Hitchcock himself as the "author" of the notes, although this reader was someone with very similar interests and experiences.[63] By Dee's discussion of "societies of trade," moreover, the reader has noted, "Example in the East India company" (D3v), which was not established until the turn of the century. But the most convincing—and extraordinary—evidence of all is the group of eight loose leaves that are bound in before and after Dee's text. They are covered with notes (in the same hand as the marginal notes) concerning everything from "gunpowder in Maryland" to a collection of one hundred points about "A navigable passage to be made." These notes are interesting in themselves and have not to my knowledge been studied. It is tempting to attribute the notes to John Pontois. Pontois (1565–1624) was Dee's executor and the Virginia Company's vice-admiral and representative before king and council.[64] Perhaps the volume made its way back into Dee's library during his life and passed into Pontois's hands after Dee's death. For our purposes, however, the notes are of most interest for their relation to Dee's text. It is clear that this copy was owned by a succession of seamen who found it practical and useful—indeed, a note found on the flyleaf offered a final judgment, calling *Memorials* "one of the best plates for England. yf it had bene then *per*formed honnorabell & proffitabell fore prynces & subie*c*tes."

Epilogue

During the Anglo-Dutch hostilities of the 1670s—a century after *Memorials*'s initial appearance—Dee's voice could once again be heard in the debate over English maritime policy. In the Protestant polemicist Henry Stubbe, *Memorials* found its most appreciative reader of all. Stubbe's *Further Justification of the Present War* (1673) renewed the call for national security and imperial expansion based on dominion of the seas. He grounded this policy in classical and particularly Athenian practice. But for those readers who would not regard Greek and Roman precedents, he "call[ed] to minde the *glorious Reign* of Queen *Elizabeth*," when "Sundry *Councils* were formed for the *security* of Her *Majesty* . . . and for advancing the *Royal Revenue*."[65] Foremost among these was that of "*Dr. John Dee*" who, "being looked upon as a *curious* and *intelligent* person, and very much honoured by many of Her *favourites*, communicate[d] a *project* . . . showing that the *onely way for the Queen to be secure of Her subjects at home, and against Her Enemies abroad . . . was to encrease Her Fleets* . . . ; that hereby *She* would multiply *Her Mariners* and *Sea forces*, (the best *offensive* and *defensive* strength of *Islanders*) encrease *Navigation* and *Commerce* . . . and augment the *Crown revenue* . . ." (79). While Stubbe did not in this place identify the source of Dee's project, he referred on page 133 to "Dr *Iohn Dee's* Brittish Monarchy"—the running title of *Memorials*.[66] Stubbe was attracted to the patriotic and potentially aggressive implications of Dee's project, as well as to Dee's command of precedents: "He urged the President [i.e., precedent] of K[ing] *Edgar*, who, though He were surnamed the *Peaceable*, did ensure

His Tranquillity by a constant *Navy Royal* of 4800 Ships. . . . He inculcated the *Glory* of *Pompey,* whose *Honour* had this for its *principal foundation,* that *He had restored to the Romans the Dominion of the Sea.* But above all He pressed the *advise* and example of *Pericles* and the *Athenians,* and by the glory thereof He excited *Her Majesty* to fix upon the course of strengthening *Her Navy Royal.* The *Queen* did embrace the advise, and within the compass of a *few years,* (not full *four*) Her *reputation* grew great, the *trading* and *tillage* infinitely did encrease, *Her Coffers* began to replenish, [and] Her Subjects were *rich,* loved and reverenced Her" (79–80). It was Elizabeth and her adviser, above all, who provided precedents for Stubbe: "no doubt Stubbe saw himself as following in Dee's footsteps, playing the role for Charles II that he had played for Elizabeth, instructing the monarch in the ways of ancient prudence."[67] Thus Elizabeth and Dee himself were subsumed into the pool of precedent, to be applied (with selective hindsight and rhetorical enhancement) to the pressing political needs of the British Empire.

B. *OF FAMOUS AND RICH DISCOVERIES* (1577)

During the reign of Queen Elizabeth the prospects of a British Empire were—to put it mildly—pretty grim. This may come as some surprise; and not just because of the magnitude of the empire that Britain went on to establish in the following centuries. The patriotic writers and artists of Elizabeth's court celebrated her power in explicitly imperial terms;[68] and, furthermore, even before she died there was a tradition crediting her with pioneering patronage of English sea power. But the fact is that Spain and Portugal had dominated global exploration and had long since secured the most accessible and profitable trade routes. Many were content to leave the global supremacy of the Iberian powers unchallenged; and others adopted a parasitical position, hoping both to profit and to undermine Spain and Portugal by intercepting their plunder en route from the New World to the Old. But there were those who believed that England could become an imperial power in its own right, enriching its coffers with new trades and expanding its dominions with territorial conquests.[69]

Some efforts were made in the sixteenth century to claim parts of North America for England. And the Elizabethans continued to pursue the conquest, and reformation, of Ireland. But the hopes of most Elizabethan commercial and imperial advocates rested largely on islands to the north of England and lands beyond America, in the Far East—in Southeast Asia, Japan, and, above all, Cathay (the East Coast of Asia).[70] During the Elizabethan period Cathay and its neighboring regions exerted a magnetic force on navigational theorists and adventurers.[71] In a series of pamphlets and projects the Far East was evoked with an optimism, even a faith, that sometimes verged on the mystical: quasi-historical legends, speculative geography, and religious providence conspired to produce a Cathay that was not only miraculously commodious but easily accessible. With Spain and Portugal dauntingly established in the southern sea routes and overland channels, generations of English explorers were driven north, expecting to find navigable passages through arctic waters and even through the American continent itself. No more than a glance at the maps and narratives used to support this expectation is needed to reveal its naïveté:[72] their wide, direct straits bear little relation to the circuitous and icy reality that awaited the unfortunate seamen.[73] The story of what can be called the Cathay Campaign is one of persistent, and almost entirely futile, effort to find a feasible "way thither."[74] The results are the stuff rather of tragicomedy than romance or epic. But, in the short term, it united some of the realm's best scholars, wealthiest financiers, and most skilled sailors; and, in the long term, it (like Francis Drake's circumnavigation) "greatly inflated English maritime prestige and ambition" and helped direct it "towards oceanic power and overseas empire."[75] The history of the Cathay Campaign and its search for a Northeast or Northwest Passage is thus a major factor in England's nascent imperialism and provides an essential backdrop to the study of Dee's role as England's maritime adviser.

The fates of Dee and the Cathay Campaign were intertwined from the very beginning. In 1527, the year of Dee's birth, the Bristol merchant Robert Thorne communicated his plan for northern discovery to King Henry VIII. While his letter made less of an impact than the earlier projects of John Rastell and John Rut, and the associated efforts by Roger Barlow and Sebastian Cabot,[76] it was to exert a decisive influence on the Elizabethan Campaign. According to Taylor, Anthony Jenkinson drafted his northeast project of 1565–66 with Thorne's letter before him.[77] And in the 1570s Cyprian Lucar, the son of one of Thorne's associates and the author of a mathematical treatise called *Lucarsolace,* presented copies of the letter to (among others) Dee and Hakluyt.[78] Hakluyt printed it in his *Divers voyages touching the discouerie of America* (1582).

Dee was also involved in the venture that in several ways laid the foundations for the Elizabethan Campaign—the 1553 voyages to the northeast of Hugh Willoughby and Richard Chancellor. Their chief patron was John Dudley, duke of Northumberland, whom Dee was serving and probably living with. The already considerable expertise of Chancellor was enhanced through consultations with Dee.[79] His probings along the northern Eurasian coast were sufficiently fruitful to lead to the establishment of the Muscovy Company—which employed Dee on several occasions—and to encourage several later projects which Dee advised.[80]

By 1580 Dee was, alongside William Borough and the Hakluyts, the leading adviser on ventures to the northeast and northwest. In May of that year, at Borough's instigation, Arthur Pet and Charles Jackman were commissioned by the Muscovy Company to search anew for the Northeast Passage.[81] On 17 May 1580, when a meeting of those concerned was convened at Muscovy House, Dee was among them.[82] He advised the navigators on the use of instruments and tables, and he provided an elaborate set of instructions, prepared two days earlier and accompanied by a chart and sailing directions.[83] Both Hakluyts were also engaged as advisers, and in the first edition of the *Principal Navigations* (1589) the younger Hakluyt printed most of the pertinent documents—including the Company's Commission, the instructions of Borough and Dee, a letter from Mercator, and the narratives of Chancellor and Hugh Smith. Dee closely followed the outcome of the voyage: he possessed an original manuscript of Chancellor's account (on which he added marginal annotations) and he personally interviewed Smith, who drew for him a little sketch-map of the region in which the ships were stopped by "Infinite yse."[84]

Dee played an even more important role in the next great project of northern exploration. According to his own account, he was actually responsible for initiating the series of voyages for the Northwest Passage that would follow Frobisher's. As he wrote in his diary on 23 January 1583, "the Ryght Honorable Mr. Secretary Walsingham cam to my howse, where by good lok he found Mr. Awdrian Gilbert, and so talk was begonne of North-west Straights discovery."[85] The "master pilot" for these voyages was John Davis, who spent some part of his upbringing in Dee's household.[86] On the next day they were joined by Davis himself for a private conference at the house of Robert Beale, clerk of the Privy Council, where "all charts and rutters were agreed uppon in generall." Dee's involvement continued until at least 6 March when he, "Mr. Adrian Gilbert and John Davis, did mete with Mr. Alderman Barnes, Mr. Townson and Mr. Yong and Mr. Hudson, abowt the N.W. voyage."[87] In the following months Dee mysteriously withdrew from the project and from England; but the seeds were sown, and Davis carried out three voyages between 1585 and 1587.

The crucial years, however, both for the progress of the Cathay Campaign and for Dee's contribution, were the mid-1570s. No venture better represents the drive to the northwest, with its bravery and buffoonery, than the three voyages of Martin Frobisher in 1576–78.[88] Once again, the build-up to the project began many years earlier. It was in the mid-1560s that Humphrey Gilbert, dissatisfied with the Muscovy Company's complacent monopoly of exploration, petitioned the queen for a license and drafted a pamphlet entitled *A Discourse for a Discovery for a new Passage to Cataia.* At this time the tract remained unprinted and the petition apparently failed.[89] But in 1574 the campaign was rekindled by the seasoned pilot (and pirate) Frobisher: by the end of the year he had been granted a license from the Muscovy Company, and his partner, the Company's agent Michael Lok (son of the London magnate Sir William Lok and a learned cosmographer), began drumming up support.[90] Within five years they had founded the "Company of Kathai," launched three voyages, mined shiploads of worthless ore, and wasted a vast sum of money.[91]

It is Lok's documentation that preserves the details of the enterprise, and captures Dee's participation in it. Looking back on the entire venture in 1581 from the uncomfortable vantage point of the Fleet prison (where he was landed for thirty-five hundred pounds in outstanding debts),[92] he described how Dee had heard about the preparations on 20 May 1576, after which he "came vnto me, desyring to know of me the Reasons of my fowndation

& purpose in this enterprise & offering his furderance thereof with such Instructions & Advise as by his learning he could geve therin." Lok then arranged a meeting at his own house with Frobisher, Borough, Hall, and others where Lok laid before Dee "my Bokes & Authors, my Cardes & Instruments, & my Notes therof made in writing as I had made them of many yeres Study before." Dee was moved in sympathy to instruct "the Masters & Marriners in the vse of [in]struments for Navigation in their voyage . . . which did them servi[ce] whereby he deserveth iust commendation."[93] Several of Lok's other memorials, preserved among the State Papers, reveal that Dee was an "Adventurer" in the voyages (and, like most of them, had not paid his pledge by November 1578) and was involved in the trials of Frobisher's ore at Muscovy House.[94]

Dee's version of the chain of events was, predictably, somewhat divergent: differences in chronology and emphasis served to foreground the importance of his support.[95] In his account—rehearsed in the self-promotional preface to *Memorials*—he praised Lok's initiative, which came to his attention (he claimed) in the *early* months of 1576. Soon afterward Dyer presented Dee with a copy of Gilbert's Cathay discourse (published, at last, in April 1576), which favorably mentioned Dee in its preface. Dee read Gilbert's treatise, "And perusing throughly all reasons and allegations . . . in the sayd Pamphlet expressed: did," adopting his familiar pose as a reader-adviser, "by euery Article therof, in the Margent, Note their value, or imperfection." Just before the first voyage Dee was summoned, at the request of Frobisher and Sir Leonell Ducket, to Muscovy House: there he resided for a short time, instructing Frobisher and Hall in the science of mathematical navigation. Two weeks after their departure the two mariners wrote to Dee: as it appears in the preface to *Memorials,* their letter is addressed to "the worshipfull and our approued good friend M. Dee," and thanks him for his "frendly Instructions," which "when we vse we doo remember you and hold our selues bound to you as your poore disciples, not able to be Scholers but in good will for want of learning . . ." (A2r).

In the spring and summer of the following year Dee prepared what was to be his most substantial (if not his most influential) contribution to the Cathay Campaign—the nearly 250 folios of his manuscript volume *Of Famous and Rich Discoveries* (henceforth *Discoveries*). Dee's autograph copy made its way into the Cottonian collection and is preserved (albeit thoroughly and tragically damaged by fire) in the British Library.[96] It consists (by my reckoning) of twenty-eight chapters of varying lengths. Most are dated—the earliest from 24 March and the latest from 8 June 1577. While there is a great deal of revision, the layout of the text is close to that of a printed book—and we know from the preface to *Memorials* that Dee intended to publish the work as soon as financial assistance could be found. The text is full of fascinating detail that merits close study; but even a cursory treatment of its composition affords a revealing glimpse of the sources, methods, and concerns of a scholar on the cutting edge of geopolitical scholarship.

As it survives, the text opens with Chapter 6.[97] It does not suffer badly, however, from starting *in medias res:* the chapters are organized chronologically and not according to any thematic or structural progression—they were written as new materials and free time became available. *Discoveries* is thus more like a scrapbook than a treatise; and while some topics are pervasive, they are raised and dropped almost haphazardly. What emerges from the miscellaneous considerations of the first chapters and remains throughout is an attempt to amass the historical and geographical details of a general "Periplus [or circumnavigation] Scythian & Asiaticall" (69v).

Chapter 6 concerns the "Sowtherne & Asiaticall Sea Coasts" (26r). Dee cites several precedents for "Indian Navigations," including the frequent voyages of Kings David and Solomon, the "sea Travayll of *Iambolus* by *Dionysius Siculus* recorded & accownted Auncyent," and a "pithy discourse" which Ramusio (Dee's most important source throughout the volume) received from "a Portugale" (26r–v). In Chapter 7 Dee enlarges upon the naval exploits of King Solomon and argues for the reinstitution of regular "Ophirian" voyages. One of his principal sources was Dominicus Marius Niger's *Geographia;*[98] but there were many other contemporary discussions.[99] During the sixteenth century, "The Ophirian Conjecture" (as Colin Jack-Hinton has termed it) occupied scholars and inspired adventurers throughout the countries of Europe, and to the wealth of the East Indies and Cathay were added the legendary riches of Ophir. The problem of how to get there was in this case compounded with uncertainty about where "there" was. Again, the Spanish were a step ahead of the English: the Islands of Solomon were actually discovered during the voyage of Alvaro de Mendana y Neyra to the Southwest Pacific in 1567–69.[100] But King Solomon and Ophir remained attractive to the Elizabethans. In 1586, when Philip Jones outlined his project "Concerning a Passage to be made from our North-Sea, into the Southe-Sea," he opened his argument with the example of Solomon, who "did send everie three yeres a Navie . . . from the red sea, for golde, silver, precious stones, Elephantes teethe, and Peacockes."[101] Dee's discussion in *Discoveries* was the most significant in Elizabethan England, and it influenced Purchas, Hakluyt, and (most likely) Drake.[102]

In an abrupt transition within Chapter 7, Dee shifts his focus northward to the Scythian and Caspian seas, rehearsing Pliny's records of "Navigation thereabowts" (28–41; 33r) and digressing on the "King of Sueden his dominions" (31v). In Chapter 8 he attends more closely to the Caspian Sea and assesses current measures of the distance between it and the "Scythian and Oriental [coasts] of Asia" (42r), noting in passing the probable freshness or saltiness of the sea.

In Chapter 9 Dee returns to the northern coasts of Chapter 7 and considers whether certain islands belonged to Sweden or to Germany. This is virtually the only section that gives any indication that there were European competitors for the great northern empire he envisaged.[103] He does not lose sight of British interests, however: when he mentions the North Cape above Muscovy he refers to the early English traveler in those regions, "my derely beloved *Richard Chancelor* father to Nycholas Chancelor, whose . . . service is known both in the Muscovy Region & now in the *Atlanticall Northwest attempt* [i.e., Frobisher's voyage]" (56v), and the chapter ends with an appeal for British merchants to advance Scythian exploration for new trade routes to the East (60r). In Chapter 10 Dee considers "whether Moscovia City be in Asia or Europ" and, comparing "my friend Mr. Stephen Borough his plat" with several of Mercator's maps, attempts to determine "a place in the Isy Ocean answerable to the mouth of Tanais . . ." (60v). Having raised the question of northern rivers, Dee moves on in Chapter 11 to a more general "Revew of Ryvers."

It is not until Chapter 12 that Dee introduces what have been considered his most influential sources for the geography of the Far East—Abulfeda Ismael and Marco Polo (both printed in Ramusio's *Viaggi*). These are offered as "expres Authority for the Periplus of the Northern Ocean, as from China to Russia" (75v). What Dee found so exciting in Abulfeda was his assertion that, from Vaygach on the Muscovy coast (where Englishmen had sailed) the coast ran smoothly to the southeast until it reached Cathay. This, Dee thought, was "A record worthy to be printed in gold," for it apparently confirmed the Rubruck and Planocarpini narratives used by Roger Bacon in his *Opus Majus*, corrected Ortelius and Mercator, and, most important, brought Cathay easily within reach. Although this interpretation turned out to be misguided, it at least encouraged the English adventurers and gave Hakluyt and Mercator pause for thought.[104] It also fired Dee with the desire to execute "one or t[wo] compleat Surveyes, after this," so that "the Northeast parte of *Asia* wᵗ the two principall Cityes therof, *Cambal*[u and] *Quinsay,* will become to the Brytish & natura[l] Inhabitants of this Monarchy, so well known, a[s] ar the Coasts of Denmark or Norway . . ." (80r).

In this and the following chapters Dee drew heavily on Marco Polo in describing Cambalu and Quinsay, adopting his nomenclature (e.g., "the City of Heaven" for Quinsay), his cartographical coordinates, and his assessment of the commodities of Cathay. Marco Polo's narrative was old, but it was by no means out of date: "The representation of Central and Eastern Asia by mapmakers of the sixteenth and seventeenth centuries, often curiously reconciled with new data, continued to be drawn from Marco Polo. . . ."[105] While he was working on Chapter 13 Dee was given (by God, he believed) the opportunity to reconcile new data of a very curious—in fact downright exotic—nature. On 24 March he was visited at Mortlake by Mr. Alexander Simon, a "Ninevite," born in Mosul near the river Tigris. Simon (a.k.a. Scander) had traveled extensively in "the Orientall India," amassing there a great fortune, which was later wrested from him by "the rigor of the Religious Inquisition" in Portugal. He gave Dee details of an overland route to Cathay and offered him (as he recorded in his diary) "servise into Persia."[106]

During the writing of Chapter 15, a collection of ancient notices of Cathay, Dee was given even more important (if more mundane) data to reconcile. On folio 104r he breaks off a quotation mid-sentence and writes, "even at the writing of this lyne I receyved letters from the famous Gerardus Mercator . . . of such strange Reporte of Cathay that [. . .] I think my labor the better & more nedefully bestowe[d] in this Scythian Ocean discovering. . . ." The letters are copied out at the end of the collection (264v et seq.) and have been fully transcribed and discussed by Taylor. [107] Although, as Taylor suggests, they raise more questions than they answer, they do show that Dee was one of Europe's leading scholars on Northeast Asia—and they convey the state of geographical and (especially) textual confusion that these scholars had to contend with.

From this point forward Dee does deliver on his initial promise, bestowing most of his labor on the Scythian Ocean periplus: apart from a few digressions, Chapters 16 to 26 all concern the northeast corner of Asia—the Scythian Ocean, "Moschovie Iurisdiction," "some Inland Scythian places," and the "Straits of Anian," which in the geographical thought of the day separated Northeast Asia and Northwest America. [108] Chapters 24 and 25 do most to sub-stantiate Dee's claims for the novelty of his efforts; they are most explicit in their attempt to offer a "Reformation of the Asiaticall Topographie" (217v). Foremost among the sources he subjects to such reformation is Julius Caesar Scaliger, whose discussion of the Great Arctic Gulf from the *De subtilitate* he considers at length, judging it in the end impressive but "not circumspect enough" (223r). [109]

Dee's own method set circumspection above all else—or (as he put it in *Memorials*) the "Circumspect Collection, or discrete Ap-plication, out of former or present writers" (ε*1r). In no other text is his tireless, if sometimes tiresome, deployment of the art of *compilatio* more apparent: Dee himself considered the volume not a "work" or a "treatise" but a "Collection" and a "Memorial." His range of sources could hardly have been more circumspect: his authorities include Pliny, Ptolemy, Strabo, Arrian, Aethicus, Al-bategnius, Herberstein, Olaus Magnus, Albertus Krantzius, João di Barros, François de Belleforest, André Thevet, and mercantile or ambassadorial explorers from a variety of countries and cen-turies. [110] Dee found some authors especially trustworthy: on folio

125 he provided a long list of the "pryncypall Authors . . . vsed & creditted."[111]

The so-called discretion that guided his "application" of these writers consisted mostly of partisan selection. But it also involved philological methods and rigorous textual standards. In the margin next to a citation from Marco Polo, for instance, he notes, "In the Latin 1.b.2 Cap. 11. But it semeth to be extracted out of the 7.b. 17 Chapter [?] as the Italien copy is; Where it is not expressly so but as may by circumstances be gathered" (169v). The need for caution and comparison when dealing with Marco Polo was the result of extreme textual variation and corruption: in another marginal note Dee lamented the "Great Imperfection in such copies of M. Paulus Venetus, as yet are come to our hands" (171r).[112]

Why, over a period of several months, did Dee repeatedly turn his attention to northern navigation, funneling old and new information into a large volume? Considering the manuscript's contents and the events in which Dee and his compatriots were enmeshed, it seems clear that Dee had been employed (quite probably by Dyer or the Muscovy Company) to be the Cathay Campaign's voice of scholarly persuasion. It was his express hope that *Discoveries'* "Cosmopoliticall, [and] Political Provision" would "reasonably require, perswade, or delight, such [Naviga?]tion to be vndertaken" (250r).

The argument was a local one; but the frame of the argument transcended the question of Cathay and contained the elements of Elizabethan expansionism as a whole. Dee intended the volume "not onely to haue accomplisshed & made perfecte the Periplus Schythian & Asiaticall," but also that "*Brytish* wisdome, Manhode & Travaile" would "procede vpon the farder discovery of that part wch yet is least knowen to Christian men, & les in the eye of *Envy,* of other great Conquerous Christians" (69v). The English could proceed "not onely to the Periplus of the Scythian Sea from Moscovia to the Ile of Giapan, but allso [to] the Periplus of *Atlantis* Northern Ocean to the sayd yle and so farder to the Iles of Spices." Having achieved so much after being forced north by the Iberians, this would be, much to England's credit, "To begin w^t the greatest inconvenience and to make *VERTU OF NECESSITY*" (174v).[113]

It is in *Discoveries* that the pragmatic foundations for Dee's imperial project are most evident. He advocated the development of "Merchants trade, in the meane space allso, of Cambalu, Quinsay, and all the Orientall partes of Asia & the Ile Chryse [Japan]" (69v).[114] And such global reconnaissance would allow confirmation of "the Auncient Terms of Habitable & Inhabitable," which were "devised by imagination . . . and vpon Schole talk probably continued; rather than by due experience either than or sins so tryed" (76r).[115] But Dee's imperialism ultimately rested on more universal premises. It was justified by the international "law of Nature": "for, the whole Ball & Sphericall frame of the erth & water is given *Filij hominum:* no part excepted: vnto them to vse & enioy" (76r). In return the law of nature demanded only that man "be to the O*m*nipotent Creator, syncerely thankfull & to the humayn society, frendly & comfortable" (76v). Needless to say, many of Dee's contemporaries (such as Hawkins, who was active in the slave trade, and Drake, who had an unquenchable pyromania) did not keep their share of the bargain.

The final purpose of *Discoveries*—and the content of its final chapters—marks a transition from imperial discovery to recovery and foreshadows the argument of the text discussed in the next section. In the course of the Northwest Passage there lay "Northern Iles, & Regions Septentrionall" which were, Dee claimed, "fully appertinent to the Crown of this *Brytish Impire*" (264v). In reasserting its claim to these regions, and making them available for trade and even colonization, England would create a vast northern empire and would thus become "the Inco*m*parable Island of the Whole World" (206v, margin). This step was at least one beyond what most of Dee's contemporaries were willing to take, and several steps beyond what the government would actually pursue. But it was firmly grounded in history and in historical scholarship. The territorial claims depended upon the documented precedents of early English conquests: in *Discoveries'* two final chapters (which in the Cotton MSS catalogue are listed as a separate item, "On the Iles Appertaining to the British Crown") Dee summarized this recovery project, with reference particularly to the adventures of King Arthur. The imperial idea itself was based on historical precedent: Dee's discovery and recovery enterprise would bring a return to origins and amount to a dramatic rebirth of the British Empire. In the patriotic (though scholarly) rhetoric of *Discoveries,* the Age of Elizabeth was potentially a second Age of Brutus.[116]

C. *BRYTANICI IMPERII LIMITES* (1576–78)

In the commercial world Dee figured as a leading advocate of northern exploration; but in governmental circles, he was best known for his work on the queen's titles to foreign lands and sovereignty over the "British Seas." It is possible to say, with only slight simplification, that in the City he emphasized the discovery component, and at court the recovery component, of his imperial enterprise. In the previous section I concentrated on the former aspect of his career; in this section I will pick out the latter, parallel, strand from his diary and his manuscript writings.

I will focus on a text that was all but unknown until it was recently acquired by the British Library. This manuscript, a compilation entitled *Brytanici Imperii Limites* (henceforth *Limites*), contains Dee's earliest surviving contribution to the imperial cause, and makes it possible to unravel some of the textual knots that have formed among Dee's manuscripts.[117] The largest section of material is dated 22 July 1576. This places it just before *Memorials*, which was completed in August 1576. There is no evidence, however, that the work passed from Dee's hands until at least two years later; it was not, at any rate, until late in 1577 that his views were heard at court. On 22 November he "rod to Windsor to the Q[ueen's] Majestie" and stayed there, it seems, for ten days. On 25 November he spoke with Elizabeth, and again three days later, when he also spoke with Secretary Walsingham. During this second royal audience he "declared to the Quene her title to Greenland, Estotiland and Friseland."[118]

Dee's next conference on the queen's titles was in the summer of 1578, and can just be glimpsed behind a misleading diary entry. On 15 August of that year he recorded, "I went toward Norwich with my work of Imperium Brytanicum."[119] His itinerary was provincial but his target was, nevertheless, the court: the queen was then making a ceremonial circuit of East Anglia and, on 16 August, entered Norwich.[120] The text Dee carried was not *Memorials*, as the editor of Dee's diary suggests, but rather *Limites*, which he had completed only two weeks before.

On 25 September 1578 Dee noted that "Her Majestie cam to Richemond from Grenwich."[121] On 8 October he joined her there and she "had conference with me . . . inter 9 et 11."[122] In 1579 Dee did not record any royal conference, but that year he penned a work for the queen, the title of which—all that apparently survives—suggests that it was closely related to his imperial program: *De imperatoris nomine, authoritate, et potentia* ["On the name, authority, and power of the emperor"].

By 1580 his claims on the queen's behalf had been fully elaborated, and that year he was given the opportunity to present his entire case in person. Between 3 and 10 October he recorded in his diary an extraordinary series of intellectual and social transactions.[123] At 11:00 A.M. on 3 October Dee delivered his "two rolls of the Quene's Majesties title unto herself in the garden at Richemond." They piqued her interest and, after a break for lunch, Dee was summoned to the inner sanctum of the Elizabethan court—the Privy Chamber—where he was joined by the lord treasurer. Burghley, "having the matter slightly then in consultation," was characteristically skeptical; so Dee elaborated his argument for Burghley in his chamber on the fourth and the fifth, "where he used me very honorably on his behalf." On 7 October, however, Burghley shut him out: "he being told of my being without, and allso I standing before him at his comming furth, did not or would not speak to me, I dowt not of some new greif conceyved." Dee returned to Mortlake, in what must have been a dejected state, only to find new grief in the death of his mother. On the tenth, however, "the Quene's Majestie, to my great cumfort (hora quinta), cam with her trayn from the court and at my dore graciously calling me to her, on horsbak, exhorted me briefly to take my mother's death patiently. . . ." Elizabeth also took pains to reassure him that Burghley "had gretly commended my doings for her title, which he had to examyn, which title in two rolls he had browght home two hours before."[124]

About the imperial claims contained in the two rolls there is little question; but their textual history has been difficult to illuminate. What do Dee's references to "two rolls" and "12 Velam skins" describe, and how do they relate to *Limites?*

As it survives, *Limites* is a small quarto, with a contemporary vellum binding on which is written (in bright red ink) "BRYTANICI IMPERII, LIMITES. JO: D: 1576." It is a copy—made (according to the catalogue) by someone other than Dee circa 1593—of several tracts outlining Dee's imperial geography. It opens with six blank flyleaves; the text then follows on ninety-five numbered and ruled pages, after which there are approximately one hundred blank and unnumbered leaves. The written pages can be divided into five sections, all of which are addressed (in the second person) to the queen.

The first two are short discussions of particular geographical points of contention—"Concerning a reformed location for the island of Estotilant & the region of Drogio," and "Concerning this example of geographical reform."[125] These brief accounts introduced Elizabeth to current opinion on the geography of the North Atlantic. Dee described—and in the process laid claim to—the land mass of Estotiland (roughly equivalent to northeast Canada), the island of Drogio (off the coast of Labrador), and even the "New World" of Atlantis (as he called America).[126] From his geographical and ethnographical details it is clear that he took as his inspiration "the recently published and widely accepted evidence of the Zeno brothers' apocryphal fourteenth-century journeys into Arctic regions."[127] This was offered as a direct rebuttal of Spanish claims to Atlantic territories and, also, as a "geographical reformation" of Gerard Mercator and Abraham Ortelius, "the two most celebrated geographers of this age, and both of them my singular good friends" (7). Internal evidence points to two important facts about these sections of the text. First, after referring to the northern and Scythian seacoasts, Dee claims that "an accurate, comprehensive, and full account is being undertaken, written lately in a large book in our vulgar tongue. . . ." The description matches *Discoveries* and suggests that these texts were written at roughly the same time— i.e., the spring or summer of 1577. Second, they must have been originally accompanied by a map, since Dee writes that "until this volume [*Discoveries*] can be elegantly and conveniently completed by the arts of the pen and the printing press, I thought that it would be not displeasing to your Serene Highness, if . . . I explained briefly what is worthy of your attention among the rare and novel features *shown in our Diagram*" (7).[128]

The next section (13–21) is headed "Vnto you*er* Ma:^tis tytle Royall to these forene Regions, & Ilands do appertayne .4. poyntes," and is a version of what is now generally known as "The Brief Remembrance." This name derives from its prefatory heading: "A briefe Remembraunce of Sondrye foreyne Regions, discovered, inhabited, and partlie Conquered by the Subiects of this *Brytish Monarchie:* And so your lawfull Tytle . . . for the dewe Clayme, and iust recovery of the same disclosed. . . ." As this passage suggests, the text is a short summary, or memorial, of the imperial claims that Dee spells out at length elsewhere—both in *Limites* and in *Discoveries.*[129] Dee cites the voyages of Madoc, Arthur, Saint Brendan, Malgo, "A Frier of Oxford," John and Sebastian Cabot, Stephen Borough, and Martin Frobisher to support his bold conclusion that "Of a great parte of the sea Coastes of Atlantis (otherwise called *America*) next vnto vs, and of all the Iles nere vnto the same, from *Florida* Northerly, and Cheiflie of all the *Ilands Septentrionall,* great and small, the Tytle Royall and supreme government is due, and appropriate vnto yo[r] most gratious Ma[tie] and that partlie *Iure Gentium,* partlie *Iure Civilis,* and partlie *Iure Divino,* No other Prince or Potentate els, in the whole world being able to alledge therto any Clayme the like" (21). There exists a simplified and slightly abridged version of this text. Not only is it accompanied by a map; it appears on the back of one—Dee's 1580 map of the Northern Hemisphere, now part of the Cottonian collection.[130] Writing fifteen years ago, Yewbrey had to read closely and cleverly to discover that the "Brief Remembrance" was written prior to the map and dated from early in 1578.[131] Now we can simply turn to the end of the section in *Limites,* where it is dated 4 May 1578. We can also find, in a passage omitted from the Cotton copy, Dee's most striking statement of the imperial rationale he offered to the queen (and most likely expected her to offer to others): "cheiflie this recovery & discovery Enterprise, ys speedely and Carefully to be taken in hand, and followed, With the intent of settinge forth the glorie of Christ, And spreadinge abrode the heavenly Tydinges of the gospell among the heathen" (20–21).

The fourth section (25–74) constitutes the bulk of the manuscript, and is the tract "Brytanici Imperii Limites" proper. This was a collection of literary, historical, legal, and cartographical material which Dee offered as a "recorde [of] y[t], w[ch] appertaineth to continewe the memorie of yo[r] Ma[tis] iust title Royall" (25), or, in more forward terms, "memoriall Records, of such Lands, Provinces, and Territoris, as remayne vnduly alienated from the *British Crowne* . . ." (26). It is this section that accounts for the title and the date on the volume's cover: it is signed and dated at the end,

"Yo:ʳ Ma:ᵗⁱˢ most Humble and Obedient servant. John Dee. Anno Dominj 1576; Julij 22" (74).[132] Dee's provision of sources proves to be at least as "circumspect" as in *Discoveries*. He refers to classical histories, medieval chronicles, Renaissance cosmographies, letters, maps, papal bulls, Tower records, genealogical charters, and even a pamphlet published by Henry VIII concerning the wars with the Scots. Dee had made a complete search of English sources and was careful to throw in some foreign accounts for balance. He hoped, though, that monuments within the British Isles, as well as "some libraries, publicque, or Private, in Norwaye, Denmarke, or Sweden" would turn up "very marveilous histories, to the *Brytish* antiquities, and yoʳ highnes Royalties, greatlie appertayninge" (26).

The section's two most important textual questions are raised in its opening and closing lines. The first regards the relationship of *Limites* to visual—specifically cartographical—materials. The text begins, "For as much as one parte of the Title prefixed to the litle Charte of *Geography* to be reformed, was *Imperij Brytanici Limites . . .*" (25). Here, then, is a sure indication that the text originally accompanied a map; indeed, that its primary purpose was to justify Dee's geographical reformations. He goes on to refer to "this other parte," in which he will justify the "Lawfull bowndes" he has "laid out" (25). The other regards the relationship of *Limites* to the "British Monarchy" tetralogy. The final page launches Dee's usual plea for royal assistance, and includes a rehearsal of his recent efforts in the service of commonwealth and empire. The passage contains his most detailed and coherent account of his written output during 1576–77: "I have of late byn stranglie, & vehementlie stirred vpp, and . . . byn ordered, to pen divers advises, and Treatises, in the English language. . . . I meane first of the little Booke, which by yoʳ Ma:ᵗⁱˢ order is yet staied in my handes, beinge the last yeare printed . . . as concerning the politik preservation of yoʳ Ma:ᵗⁱˢ Britishe Monarchie in theis perelous tymes, by the spedie service, of a Pety Navy Royall. . . . And secondlie, because neither famous and Riche discoveries far hence: Nor the preservation of this yoʳ Ma:ᵗⁱˢ British Monarchy, by the order of the pety Navy Royall, continuously gardinge the same: No nor this British Impier revived, and in these 2 Recordes brieflie demonstrated, can well be made, performed, recovered, and arteficially described, w^{th}out good skill in the feat of Ship government, And the Appertenances, I did therfore two years sithens . . . write also a great booke, whose Title is The British Complement of the perfect Arte of Navigation . . ." (73). [133]

The fifth and final section (75–94) of *Limites* is a simple appendix to the preceding treatise, consisting of records that appeared in the original alongside the text. The heading to this section contains an important clue about the original form of *Limites* and allows me to reach the conclusions to which I have been pointing all along. It mentions that the additional material in section five was originally "noted in the margents of the *Longe Rolle*" (75; my emphasis); it is only because this copy (in book rather than roll form) lacked sufficient space in the margins that the relevant passages were keyed with "certain markes, and figures, naming the folio" in the appended section where they were copied out. What this suggests is that Dee's *Limites* took the form of a "long roll," perhaps even one constructed from twelve pieces of vellum. If we add to this roll an accompanying geographical diagram—which would have been very similar to Dee's 1580 map—we have a plausible package of "two rolls of the Queen's Majesties title." [134]

Thus far I have silently passed over the extraordinary nature of Dee's imperial claims. What he urged on the queen was sovereignty over a considerable portion of the Northern Hemisphere; a "title Royall to all the Coasts, and Ilands beginning at or about *Terra Florida*, and so alongst, or neere vnto *Atlantis*, goinge Northerly: and then to all the most Northen Ilands great and small, And so compassinge about *Groenland*, Eastward and Northen Boundes of the Duke of Moscovie his dominions. . . ." [135] In order to convince the queen and her council—and (potentially) the international community—of the validity of this "great British maritime empire in the high latitudes," [136] Dee needed more than the patriotic rhetoric that flowed so easily from his pen. He needed to deploy an elaborate set of persuasive techniques, entailing several categories of proof.

The first and foremost of these was *historical*—that is, the force of precedent. I have already described the broad range of "records" that informed and constituted Dee's argument. But he gave two of Elizabeth's predecessors special weight: Arthur and Madoc. In the early modern "Battle over the British History" (which T. D. Kendrick has vividly reconstructed) Dee must be placed in the camp of the supporters. [137] He admits at the outset of *Limites* that his precedents "depende cheiflie vppon our kinge *Arthur*" (26). He proudly cites the pro-Arthurian texts of John Leland, John Price, John Major, and (most important of all) Geoffrey of Monmouth, and refutes skeptics such as Polydore Vergil. He was fully aware of the problems that accompanied Arthurian history and expressed his desire to separate the truth from the fiction: "I my selfe ame assured, that some ignorant or negligent copiers of Written Bookes, and some overbould writters of ther coniectures, or Opinions . . . and other fonde fainers, vaine flatteringe paynters, (as concerninge ye wonderous Actes, and prowesses, of the *Brytish* King Arthure,) haue by sundrie . . . meanes, both confounded the truth, with vntruthes: and also, haue made the truth yt selfe to be doubted of, or the les regarded, for the aboundance of their fables, glosinges, vntruthes, and Impossibilities, incerted in the true historie, of King Arthure . . ." (27). [138] There could be no illusion, however, that an objective truth could be located: due to the nature of the sources, the truth of Arthurian history was necessarily relative, and was determined by each scholar's needs and inclinations. Dee's argument, like that of his successors Selden, Boroughs, and Prynne, was "for the most part drawn from scattered passages or even phrases . . . to which a strained and improbable significance was assigned." [139] This is by no means grounds for dismissing or ridiculing the efforts of these men. Their stance required, in contrast to the relatively simple task of "purging the preposterous legends," "real learning, ingenious arguments, and an intense and emotional patriotism." [140]

The same was true of the legend of Madoc, the Welsh prince who allegedly discovered America in 1170. In this case Dee was the principal propagator. He "snatched what had been a marginal . . . story and thrust it into the centre of Elizabethan enterprise." [141] In Dee's 1576–78 manuscripts Madoc became the linchpin of claims for North America. Not long after, the material he had gathered found its way from "confidential parchment" to "public print," via Sir George Peckham. In 1582 Peckham drafted a remarkable proposal to settle English Catholics in America. For historical ammunition against the Spanish—whose territorial ambition, Peckham feared, would outweigh their religious sympathy—he turned to Dee, consulting him in July and learning of the Madoc myth. This project was not realized, but in the next year he published an account of Sir Humphrey Gilbert's voyages, in Chapter 3 of which he discussed England's "lawfull tytle" to North America. Dee's influence is readily apparent in Peckham's argument that "no other Nation can truelie by any Chronicles they can finde, make prescription of time for themselves, before the time of this Prince Madocke."[142] Insofar as it rested on the search for precedents (in Peckham's delightful phrase, on "making prescription of time"), the early modern imperial contest was a Battle of the Books; and Dee was for a time commander in chief of the Cambro-Britannic forces.

The second category of proof, which is closely linked to the first, was *legal*. While the precedents in *Limites* did not have the legal force of those in Dee's *THALATTOKRATIA BRETTANIKI* (which invoked the international law of territorial waters), they were presented within a legalistic framework. The "Brief Remembrance" employs what Dee calls a "quadripartite method," which examines "1. The Clayme in perticuler; 2. The reasons of ye Clayme; 3. The Credit of the Reason; and 4. The Value of ye Credit by force & Lawe" (13). Dee's discourse is not as methodical as this suggests, and it never quite reaches the fourth point. But some of his sources are explicitly legal, such as the volume *Priscis Anglorum Legibus*, or the *De Nobilitate* of Felix Maleolus (whom Dee calls a "very Ingenious, discreet, and zealous Doctor of Lawe" [41]).

Questions of sovereignty were intrinsically bound up with legal considerations and Dee would not have ventured into them without some knowledge of legal conventions. One did not, however, have to be a lawyer to make such arguments. Thomas Digges also produced "Arguments proouinge the Queenes Maties propertye in the sea landes, and salt shores thereof."[143] Digges's interests and qualifications were almost identical to Dee's. He does not seem to have had official legal training—though late in his life he complained that he was so occupied with "lawe-brables" that he had to set aside his mathematical studies.[144]

The final, and perhaps the most important, category of proof was *cartographic*.[145] Maps were not simply neutral representations of particular areas. They were "part of a visual language by which specific interests, doctrines, and even world views were communicated. Maps were one of a number of instruments of control by landlords and governments; they were spatial emblems of power in society; they were artefacts in the creation of myth; and they influenced perceptions of place and space at a variety of geographical scales."[146] Cartographical representations, like visual representations in general, had a persuasive power that went far beyond their descriptive functions. It is thus as inappropriate (or irrelevant) to ask of maps as of Arthurian histories whether they are true or false. It is more useful to ask about the use to which they are put; to consider maps "as *actions* rather than as impassive descriptions."[147]

From the beginning of European imperial enterprise, cartography played an indispensable role. Maps could monitor—and at the same time celebrate—the progress of a monarch's dominions. Such was the purpose of the Spanish *padron general:* it was "a kind of 'inventory' of the lands discovered, settled, or claimed by Spain" and "was kept up-to-date by continuous addition and correction."[148] Renaissance palaces were often adorned with maps intended to impress the visitor with the extent of a government's territorial power. The best chance to see this practice in action today is at the vast Cartographical Gallery in the Vatican, painted in the sixteenth century and representing the extensive papal dominion. While no examples from the English Renaissance survive, we know that Whitehall Palace had a large picture of fifteenth-century battles, a sea chart of the whole world, a painting of Palestine, and maps charting and celebrating the great voyages of Sebastian Cabot and Francis Drake.[149] As Victor Morgan points out, "These shared the palace with, among other things, a moor's head in stone . . . , a black metal figure of Moses . . . , musical mechanisms from Cologne, trick mirrors and a clockwork globe."[150]

It is even more instructive to look at the studies and galleries of Lord Burghley. Burghley's cabinets were not so much spaces for collections of curiosities as for the business of political administration. Thanks to the efforts of R. A. Skelton, we now know that Burghley had an exhaustive collection of maps, which he organized in volumes and annotated thoroughly with practical and administrative details. These volumes survive at Hatfield and Burghley Houses, and in cataloguing them Skelton suggestively called them Burghley's "cartographical commonplace books."[151]

While a number of scholars—most recently and importantly Richard Helgerson[152]—have focused on Queen Elizabeth's relationship to maps, it is Burghley rather than the queen who reveals the ways in which the government's management and colonization of space, ranging from estate surveying to military surveillance, depended upon the use of geographic representations and cartographic intelligence.

Maps could be used to support—to justify through representation—a monarch's imperial claims. On Emery Molyneux's 1592 terrestrial globe, the first printed in England, the queen's arms were superimposed on Atlantis and "were clearly designed to proclaim England's rights to the possession of the American continent north of Florida." But this same globe was also designed to act on the queen; to persuade her to pursue a policy of imperial (specifically naval) expansion. At the presentation of the globe to the queen there was a Florentine observer, Petruccio Ubaldini. In reporting the occasion to the grand duke of Tuscany he wrote, "it must be remembered that the Dedication to the Queen has to be printed with the royal arms and its wording suggests that he gave her the globe *to let her see at a glance how much of the seas she could control by means of her naval forces.*"[153]

Dee's maps acted in the same complex ways. Some were guides to mariners, or records of the routes of explorers. Others, such as the one that originally accompanied *Limites,* were used, like Molyneux's globe, both to support territorial claims on behalf of the monarch and to persuade the monarch herself. Dee's cartographic rhetoric and its role in Elizabethan imperialism emerge most dramatically from the fascinating passage that concludes the first section of *Limites.* After "reforming" Ortelius' and Mercator's charts of the arctic region around Cathay, Dee maps the Asian and American regions he wishes England to explore onto the queen's body itself: "the single little black circle shown on the left hand side of your majesty's throne, represents Cambalu, the chief city of Cathay. Meanwhile by a wonderful omen (as I hope) the City of Heaven (that is, of course, Quinsay) happens to be located at the middle joint of the index finger which encircles the hilt of your sword. And there are other things, extremely noteworthy, which, as if by Divine will, adorn the surroundings of your imperial seat. For under your Crown (the most glorious in the whole world), almost in the middle of it, is concealed an island; once known as Chryse, but now commonly called Japan. . . . Thirdly, at the right side of your Majesty, the coast of Atlantis is pleased to have its place—almost opposite Quinsay. But about the feet of your supreme highness lies the Strait of Anian, which your British subjects, voyaging in the Northern Seas both to the east & the west, were the first to sail through, to the honour of yourself & to the benefit of the common weal. And if those things are true which we have hitherto heard reported, those 4 places which I have named have thus their own geographical symmetry. But concerning these things & others related to them (which are known hitherto to have lain hidden under the shadows of your wings) before the next *septenium* [?] many wonderful Arcana will be revealed by you, if it pleases, our august & blessed Brytannic Empress, Almighty God willing."[154]

This was a bold, graphic, and (to my knowledge) unique way to persuade the queen of her imperial opportunities; and it conveys a vivid sense of Dee at work as an imperial conjurer. Once again, he offers his patron advanced and aggressive geographical scholarship, and enhances it with the rhetoric of revelation: secrets are shared and imperial arcana are disclosed.

Dee was not the only Elizabethan to mobilize cartographic rhetoric in the service of maritime imperialism. In the famous "Armada portrait" Elizabeth's hand rests on a globe, while over her shoulder Spanish ships crash and burn. In the equally famous "Ditchley portrait" the queen stands on a map of England, protecting and in some way embodying her realm. In a Dutch engraving from 1598 she is represented as a map of Europe, holding a sword over the Spanish Armada.[155] But no one went as far as Dee in combining geographical exploration, geometrical symmetry, divine will, and the royal person to justify England's nascent maritime empire.

D. *THALATTOKRATIA BRETTANIKI* (1597)

In 1597, his seventieth year, Dee had little cause for contentment. His aspirations—both for himself and for his nation—had not been realized, and his years of hard work had failed to purchase him a comfortable retirement. His heyday as England's maritime adviser was long gone and, indeed, his whole mode of life was altered—mostly for the worse. His disastrous appointment as warden of Christ's College, Manchester, meant that his hours were spent grappling with the administrative and financial difficulties of a college that (as he put it) was "allmost, become No College, in any respect." He seems to have ended up very far from the court culture that had nurtured his career as a freelance scholarly adviser.

Yet, a document survives that suggests this was not entirely the case. Sometime in the early autumn of 1597, Sir Edward Dyer— now elevated to chancellor of the Order of the Garter—wrote to Dee. His letter is no longer extant; but its message can be extrapolated from the text that Dee wrote in response on 8 September 1597. It is entitled *THALATTOKRATIA BRETTANIKI; Miscelanea quaedam extemporanea; De imperij Brytanici Iurisdictione, in Mari* [THE BRITISH SEA-SOVEREIGNTY; or an Extemporaneous Miscellany on the Sea-Jurisdiction of the British Empire].[156] Dee's treatise, which is written in epistolary form, begins with a direct address to Dyer: "I thank yoᵣ Wurship highly, that you still contynue yoᵣ true love & good will toward me: and allso remayne firmly perswaded of my constant redines, to do any thing of service, or pleasure, unto yoᵣ Wurship, that doth, or shall lye in my power, to performe" (95r). Dee thus foregrounded the service relationship that bound him to the court and stressed the continuity of his relationship with Dyer.

What he "performed" for Dyer in the text that follows took him (and takes us) full circle, back to his activities in the years 1576 to 1583: it was a consideration "of her Ma.ᵗⁱᵉˢ Title Royall and Sea Soveraigntie in Sᵗ Georges Chanell; and in all the Brytish Ocean" (95r). He began, in fact, by revisiting "the Rhapsodicall Treatise of the Brytish Monarchie" that he had written twenty-one years earlier—*Memorials.* Instead of writing an entirely new account, Dee (in his accustomed role as reader's guide) asked Dyer to look again at his original discussion:[157] "There, in the 20th page of that boke, (against the figure, 9, in the margent) begynneth matter, inducing the consideration of her Ma:ᵗⁱᵉˢ Royall Sealimits. . . . And herevppon, in the 21st page, both in the Text, and allso in the Margent, is pregnant matter conteyned. . . . Then, peradventure, the Consequences of the matter, will lead you on, to read the 22, 23, 24, 25, 26, and vnto the middle of the 27 page. . . . Afterward, you may passe ouer, to the 37 page: and there (in the

.15th. lyne, from the ende of that page) you may begin againe, to reade . . . and so you may hold on, till you haue attentifely, red ouer the 38th page, wholy; and so much of the 39th, as will bring you, to the Conclusion of that extraordinarie discourse: (almost abowte the middest of that page,) ending with this worde, *Opportunitie.* . . . Returning againe, to yor present purpose; Yt will not be impertinent to your Consideration, to procede consequently, in reading of the 54th, 55, 56, and 57 pages. . . . Yet, a little more, your paynes takinge, will gete you some more matter, here & there, till you comme to the end of the boke. The Marginall Notes, sometimes, are of great moment" (fol. 95r–v).[158] This was a remarkably precise "directed reading" (the term is Dee's) through the pertinent material in the earlier text.

It amounted to a collection of passages from the civil law pertaining to the considerations *"De Confinio in Mari statuendo"* (95r) and *"De acquiendo rerum Dominio"* (96r). Dee hoped that this would provide a sound legal basis for the ensuing claims, and he cited a long list of Roman lawyers as authorities.[159] But what Dee had to offer was not an exercise in civil law. Having referred Dyer to the requisite legal sources he went on to outline his peculiar perspective on the questions at hand: "it were good, that some expert Mathematicien, or Mechanicien (somwhat skillfull in Iure gentium et Ciuili, and in the true Idea of Iustice, and of aequum and Bonum,) wold, viua voce, explane vnto you, and allso practically demonstrate some of those lawes, and lawyers intents . . ." (95r). Dee's combination of mathematics and law may have invited problems of both credibility and marketability; but it granted him a certain intellectual license and opened for him certain rhetorical avenues. The resulting text utilized (as had Dee's previous writings on the subject) a unique package of historical, legal, and cartographical proofs that enabled him to appropriate the civil law on territorial waters in a way that furthered the imperial claims of the English crown.

As in his other writings on the subject, and—indeed—in most early modern geopolitical texts, Dee's focus is not on the centers of state power but on the boundaries or limits. Accordingly, it is often on these fuzzy edges and disputed margins that we can find the most interesting scholarly and political negotiations. Dee's claims for English sea sovereignty rested on a distinction between

Limits Absolute and Limits Respective. The former term applied whenever a body of water was flanked by the same monarch's dominions. In this case the ocean simply became the jurisdiction of that monarch. The latter term applied whenever a body of water separated the territories of two or more monarchs. In this case the sea jurisdiction would be determined either by the classic one-hundred-mile limit, or by a line drawn midway between the coasts in question.[160] These rules guided Dee's policy of *mare clausum*, and were intended (as he had argued as early as 1576 in *Memorials*) to guarantee the security of English coasts and the profitability of English maritime enterprise. This was not necessarily an aggressive or an isolationist stance: Dee hoped that there would be cooperation in drawing the lines "betwene vs, and our foresaid next Opposite Sea partners, As I may (in frendely respect,) terme them" (96v). But he was aware that some countries would view this as an encroachment and would be reluctant to grant Elizabeth her sea sovereignty. He therefore enlisted the classic imperialist rationale to justify the use of force: "yf they do, or will mislike, therof: Then, (Seeing, our *Right,* is grownded vppon Christian Aequitie, and warranted . . . by Law,) We may, by the vigor of the same our *Right,* vse *Might,* sufficient to Garde & enioye the same . . ." (96v).[161]

In the 1630s, John Selden responded to the Dutch assertion of a *Mare Liberum* with his famous argument for a *Mare Clausum,* justifying Charles I's aggressive policies. As T. W. Fulton explained in his classic work *The Sovereignty of the Sea,* Selden conceived of a four-quartered British Sea, to which Charles could lay claim: this he represented in a map, which served as a frontispiece to the second book.[162] What has gone unnoticed by almost everyone except Fulton is that during the preceding century Dee had drawn a similar, though even bolder, map of the British Seas.

In the bulk of the treatise (if one can speak of bulk in a text that is only twenty-odd pages long) Dee takes Dyer through a periplus of the British Isles, delineating in every direction what he considers to be the "British Seas." He begins with the southern coast and sets out to prove the English sovereignty over the entire Channel or "Narrow Seas." Few would have challenged this claim, and Dee treats it as a simple Limit Absolute. He concludes, without much ado, "That the whole sea or seas, betwene all the Southern

Shoares of England (aunciently called Brytan) and these Northern next Opposite shoares, of the aunciently named Celtica (generally, now, named France . . .) are vnder her Maties Sea Iurisdictione, and Soveraigntie Absolute" (98r). This depended, of course, on the principle of the queen's supremacy over France, which Dee asserted on the basis of "Direct inheritance [from King Henry V], by conquest, and by free gift and composition Royall" (98r).

The question of sovereignty over St. George's Channel was certainly raised in Dyer's letter; and it was at the heart of the English government's renewed fears about the security of the realm. On 15 November 1597 Francis Bacon delivered a speech in Parliament that outlined "four accidents or occurents of state . . . by every one whereof it seemeth to me, in my vulgar understanding, that the danger of this realm is increased." The second of these concerned Calais, which in April 1596 had been surrendered to the Spanish. Thus they "have possessed themselves of that avenue and place of approach for England . . . ; in common understanding it is a knocking at our doors."[163] What Dee was asked to provide was, in effect, the means by which to lock those doors.

Dee quickly passed northward along the western coast, stopping only to note that "her Maties large kingdome of Ireland" (which he silently appropriated) greatly increased the "portion of Sea Royalltie [which] falleth due to her Matie, in the Western Mayn Ocean Sea" (99v). He soon reached the "western shoare of Scotland, or of the Scottish Iles" (99v). Scotland took on special importance for Dee—much more than for Selden—not only because of its potential to unite the kingdom of Great Britain but because of its position opposite "that famous, and very Ancient *Platonicall* or *Salonicall Atlantis.*" Having in his earlier writings claimed the queen's title to North America, Dee's claim to Scotland would result in another case of Limits Absolute.[164] He had before him many precedents for the Scottish kings' "Homage doing to her Maties most puyssant & Triumphant progenitors and predecessors" (99v), and drew attention particularly to the homage of King James to Henry VI "at Windsor A° 1423, in the presence of three dukes, two Archbisshops, twelve Erles, twenty Barons, & two hundred Knightes & esquiers" (100r). Dee urged Elizabeth to reenact this scene with James VI, and even provided part of the script: he drafted a "Corporeall oath," which read,

I, Carolus Iacobus, king of Scots, shall be true and faithfull vnto you Lady Elizabeth, by the grace of god, Quene of England france *and Ireland,* the Noble and Superior Lady of the kingdome of Scotland: And to you, I make my fidelitie, for the same kingdome of Scotland: Which I holde, and clayme to hold of you: And I shall beare to you my faith and fidelitie of Life Lymme and worldly honor against all men: And faithfully I shall Knowledge and shall do to you Service, due vnto you. . . . (99v–100r)

Rounding the northern tip of Scotland, Dee came to the coast facing Norway. Here he reluctantly conceded a Limit Respective, and drew the line in the "Mydseas." In a marginal note he hinted that the claim could be "challendg[ed] farder" but, with a degree of restraint absent from his previous pronouncements, admitted that "all things in due tyme must be handled" (100r).

Finally Dee traveled "forward & sowtherly down" along "the east side of our Brytish Albion" (100v). Here there could be no objection to a Limit Respective, at least: "You can not, Now, dowte of her Ma[ties] Sea Iurisdiction royall . . . half the Seas over" between England and "denmark, holland, or Zeland." But Dee felt that it was "due tyme" to advance a larger claim: "I am sure that her Maiesties Brytane Monarchie, hath given name to all those seas, and to that whole eastern Ocean" (100r). In other words, Dee argued that the entire North Sea fell under British sea sovereignty.

In the period before Selden this claim was unique, and contentious in the extreme. It ran counter to received historical and cartographical wisdom. From Ptolemy onward, *Mare Brytannicum* referred to the English Channel, while the North Sea was universally known as *Mare Germanicum.*[165] But Dee wanted to conflate the two under the larger name of the British Seas: he hoped that "never here after (so far as I may perswade, or performe) shall that Sea be any longer misnamed *Germanicus Oceanus* but be restored to his true & auncient name of *Mare Britannicum*" (100v). To support what he called this "revived veritie" (101r), Dee made (as usual) an in-depth search of textual records, looking for any references to *Mare Britannicum*—especially those that used it to describe the waters between England and Europe. Knowing that English writers would be considered unacceptably biased, he paid special attention to ancient historians and German chroniclers.

First he cited Albertus Krantzius, "a great Antiquary, a Wary and carefull historiographer, a man of great Credit . . . [and] a German, who would vse all due & true means to ennoblize the name of his nation" (101r).[166] Next he cited Krantzius' neighbor, Helmoldus Presbyterus.[167] At this point he paused for a restatement of his conclusion: "Ergo, (a primo ad vltimum) All the Whole Ocean betwene Englands Esterly shoares, and the westerly opposite shoares of Denmark, Friseland, & Holland may be named OCEANUS BRITANNICUS: or MARE BRITANNICUM" (102r). Yet, "Because This veritie, (duely reuiued) will seeme a strange Paradox, to all our Geographers, Antiquaries, and many other Studentes," Dee went on to cite passages from Hadrianus Junius ("a most exquisite examiner and Censurer of very many auncient historiographers").[168]

This was virtuoso scholarship, but it would not have convinced geographers, antiquaries, or any other students. In the first printed map of the British Isles (Rome: George Lily?, 1546), "Mare Britannicum" appears between England and France, while "Mare Germanicum" is found off the east coast of England. The same nomenclature was adopted by Mercator, Hondius, Speed, and, indeed, apparently all contemporary mapmakers: I have not yet found one who adopted Dee's terms.[169]

The reason Dee fashioned these terms is, however, to be found outside the objective standards of pure scholarship; it is connected, again, to the concerns of those on whose behalf Dyer spoke. In the summer of 1597 the Privy Council was engaged in the escalating conflict between the English Merchant Adventurers and the merchants of the Hanseatic League.[170] During these months England's commercial relations with Northern Europe had degenerated: the Merchant Adventurers were accused of monopolizing trade and of harassing the Hanseatic merchants in England. The conflict had been waged on a petty level for over twenty years,[171] but in August 1597, Emperor Rudolf II was moved to issue a decree that effectively banned trade with the English merchants.[172] During the next months the interested parties exchanged diplomats at a furious pace. To support the English negotiators and buttress the English claims, the government clearly consulted outside experts. Several of their reports survive in the State Papers: an anonymous paper offered "Reasons to prove the Merchant Adventurers cloth trade on the River Elbe,"[173] and Laurence Thompson produced a comprehensive Latin treatise entitled "Assertio veritatis de legitima Interceptione Ansiaticarum Navium, contra anonymum calumniatorum."[174] In claiming for the queen the sovereignty over the North Sea, Dee was only doing his part in a campaign to counteract Rudolf's decree.

In 1652 Marchamont Nedham published his translation of Selden's *Mare Clausum,* calling it *Of the Dominion, Or, Ownership of the Sea.* As the frontispiece to the volume he offered a poetic address from "Neptune to the Common-Wealth of *England.*" The last few verses seem to look back past Selden to Dee's Elizabethan project for a maritime empire:

> What wealth or glorie may arise
> By the North-West discoveries
>   is due unto thy care.
> Th'adopting them with English names,
> The greatness of thy minde proclaim's,
>   and what thy actions are.
> New Seas thou gains't; & to the antient FOUR
> By *Edgar* left, thou addest many more.
>
> . . . For Sea-Dominion may as well bee gain'd
> By new acquests, as by descent maintain'd.
>
> Go on (great STATE!) and make it known
> Thou never wilt forsake thine own,
>   nor from thy purpose start:
> But that thy wilt thy power dilate,
> Since Narrow Seas are found too straight
>   For thy capricious heart.

As late as 1597, then, some members of the government still called on Dee as the court's leading imperial geographer. There *had* been a sea change, however, and Dee's nationalistic perspective seemed a little pointless. But it was Dee, rather than the government, who was disillusioned. The closing pages of his letter exude a sense of resignation. Dee was deeply depressed by his situation in Manchester: he was overcome by "the most intricate, [c]umbersome, and (in manner) lamentable affayres & estate, of this defamed & disordred Colledge" which deprived him of his time for study and which offered in compensation only a paltry stipend inadequate to feed the eighteen members of his household (104v).

On the page bearing this complaint the running title—which had been "THALATTOKRATIA BRETTANIKI"—reads "EX MANCESTRIANO LABYRINTHO."

Yet Dee's frustration stemmed from more than the deterioration of his living conditions. He had used much "care & diligence" to promote the British discovery and recovery enterprise and had run out of patience waiting for his advice to take effect. "I can not, as yet, vnderstand, [why] . . . (for these 21 years last past) . . . the said Landes, nor yet the Seas Iurisdiction, (duely & dutifully, declared & manifested) hath byn, or owght to haue byn made so little accownt of: And so my labors (after a sort) vaynely employed" (104r). Clearly, this was more than the usual rhetorical plea for assistance and advancement. It was the reflection of a man who had been a "Carefull, expert, & faithfull Politicien Subiect" of English kings and queens for seventy years and whose poverty and disappointment had forced him to shift his faith from Queen Elizabeth to "the king of heven & erth": "either God will give me grace sufficient, & send me mighty help (tempore opportuno) to end [my Cumbers]: Or els they will help to hasten my deliuerance, from these and all other vayne, & earthly Actions Humane" (105r). On this last page the running title consists of a single word, which seems to signal the end of more than Dee's letter—"EXITUS."

Notes

PREFACE

1. Witness the large number of volumes in the British Library that were once part of Dee's collection—and, for that matter, his letter to Queen Elizabeth displayed in the British Library's textual hall of fame, the Manuscripts Gallery.

2. My bibliography should be supplemented by that of Nicholas Clulee.

3. Peter Ackroyd's novel *The House of Doctor Dee* was published as this book went to press: I discuss Dee's other fictional cameos in my introduction. With a synchronicity that would have amused Dee himself, Ackroyd's novel explores precisely those spatial and cultural contexts that I attempt to reconstruct historically in the following chapters.

4. For three different perspectives on polymathy see Donald R. Kelley and Richard H. Popkin, eds., *The Shapes of Knowledge from the Renaissance to the Enlightenment;* Wilhelm Schmidt-Biggemann, *Topica Universalis: Eine Modellgeschichte humanistischer und barocker Wissenschaft;* and Menachem Fisch and Simon Schaffer, eds., *William Whewell, a Composite Portrait.*

5. Anthony Grafton, "The World of the Polyhistors: Humanism and Encyclopedism," 31–47; 37–38. Cf. Kelley and Popkin, eds., *The Shapes of Knowledge* (esp. Kelley, "History and the Encyclopedia"), and William J. Bouwsma, *Concordia Mundi: The Career and Thought of Guillaume Postel (1510–1581)* (esp. ch. 4). R. J. W. Evans has usefully described this "pansophism," which flourished particularly at the Bohemian court of Rudolf II (*Rudolf II and His World,* 253).

6. Gabriel Naudé, *Instructions Concerning Erecting of a Library,* B5v. In Chapter 6 we shall see that these are precisely the terms that Dee applied to himself; and since elsewhere Naudé proved himself intimate with Dee's legacy, it is not out of the question that he had Dee in mind.

7. The "Mathematicall Praeface" to Euclid, c4r.

8. For a cogent critique of these standard biographical strategies see Morson and Emerson, *Mikhail Bakhtin,* Introduction.

9. See Frances Yates's *Giordano Bruno and the Hermetic Tradition,* passim.

10. The most useful account is Garth Fowden, *The Egyptian Hermes,* but also see the suggestive essays of Michel Serres assembled in the volume *Hermes: Literature, Science, Philosophy.* In " 'To Know, To Fly, To Conjure,' " Julie Robin Solomon traces some interesting connections between Hermes, reading practices, and the new science in late sixteenth-century England.

ONE. POLITICS IN THE MARGINS

1. The text of this letter and of Dee's description of the entire episode to which it gave rise are preserved (in a slightly damaged form) in BL MS Cotton Vitellius C.VII, fols. 1–13. There are two manuscript copies in the Bodleian Library, MS Ashmole 1788, fols. 7–34, and MS Smith 96, art. 2. It has twice

been printed in its entirety: as an appendix to Thomas Hearne's *Johannis Glasto-niensis Chronica* (II:497—551), and as "The Compendious Rehearsall" in *The Autobiographical Tracts of Dr. John Dee,* ed. James Crossley (1—45). I quote from the last of these, and abbreviate it henceforth "Compendious Rehearsall." All unidentified citations in this chapter derive from this text.

2. These are Bodleian MSS Ashmole 487 (Ioannes Stadius' *Ephemerides novae . . . ab anno 1554 vsque ad annum 1600*) and 488 (Ioannes Antonius Maginus, *Ephemerides coelestium motuum . . . ab anno Domini 1581 vsque ad annum 1620*). The notes were edited by J. O. Halliwell and printed by the Camden Society in 1842. Halliwell missed many entries and misread many names, and his text needs to be checked against the original: unless otherwise stated, however, I cite the printed edition (and abbreviate it henceforth *Diary*). I have reproduced a sample page from the original as Figure 2.

3. Elisabeth Bourcier, *Les journaux privés en Angleterre de 1600 à 1660,* 27.

4. Winthrop Hudson, *The Cambridge Connection and the Elizabethan Settlement of 1559.*

5. By the time Edward became king, however, Dee had enjoyed enough courtly contact to earn a royal pension.

6. Cited in Hudson, *Cambridge Connection,* 54.

7. What remains of their correspondence can be found in J. H. Hessels, ed., *Abrahami Ortelii . . . epistulae.*

8. Dee recorded this event in his diary on 12 March 1577, but, surprisingly, this is omitted from Halliwell's edition.

9. Pembroke College, Cambridge, MS 2.113. There is an annotated facsimile of this extraordinary volume, edited by Jean Puraye et al. As we shall see, Dee shows up in several other similar volumes. For an exhaustive inventory of sixteenth-century European "friendship albums" see Wolfgang Klose, *Corpus Alborum Amicorum.*

10. Dee scholars have apparently not been aware of the fact that this coat of arms was officially granted by Robert Cooke, Clarenceux King of Arms from 1567 to 1593 (see Thomas Woodcock and John Martin Robinson, *The Oxford Guide to Heraldry*).

11. *Of Famous and Rich Discoveries* (BL MS Cotton Vitellius C.VII), fol. 265v—see my account in Chapter 7.

12. I cite Wayne Shumaker's facing-page translation in *John Dee on Astronomy,* though his renderings of some phrases (such as the one discussed in the next note) are questionable.

13. Dee's phrase is *"mea peregrina philosophandi ratio,"* and I would suggest that *peregrina* signifies more than simply "foreign." Given Dee's physical and mental travels/travails during those formative years, as well as his shared interest with Mercator in geography, he is more likely playing on the term's sense of "wander-ing" or "traveling" or even "surveying."

14. Ibid., 119; I have slightly altered Shumaker's translation.

15. Among this group are: Oronce Finé, professor of mathematics at the Royal College and pioneering cosmographer; Antoine Mizauld, author of astro-nomical works and Finé's collaborator; Petrus Montaureus, who produced com-

mentaries on Euclid (which Dee owned); Aimar de Ranconet, literary author and collaborator with Cujas; Pierre Danès, royal counsellor and professor of Greek; Jacques Dubois (Sylvius), professor of medicine at the Royal College; Adrien Turnèbe, chair of Greek at the Royal College; Franciscus Vicomercatus, commentator on Aristotle; Guillaume Postel, orientalist and polymath, on whom see William Bouwsma, *Concordia Mundi: The Career and Thought of Guillaume Postel;* Jean Fernel, doctor and cosmographer; and Joannes Peña, editor of Euclid.

16. Trinity College, Cambridge, Adv. d.1.26.

17. This offer can be corroborated by a copy of "The Contents of Mr Garlands Commission vnto Tho: Sinkinson for the bringing of Mr John Dee to the Emperour of Russia his Courte" (PRO, SP12/196, fol. 143r, dated 18 September 1586). Somewhat surprisingly, Hakluyt saw fit to publish Simkinson's and Garland's invitations in volume 3 of the *Principal Navigations* (1599–1600). According to him, at least, it was Dee's geopolitical as much as his iatrochemical knowledge that attracted the emperor and his protector: "It seemeth that this princely offer . . . was made vnto the learned and famous Mathematician *M. Iohn Dee,* partly to vse his counsell & direction about certaine discoueries to the Northeast; and partly for some other weighty occasions: but because their conquest to *Siberia* was not as then fully settled, & for diuers other secret reasons, it was for yᵉ time with al thankfulnes refused" (Vv2v).

18. N. A. Figurovski, "The Alchemist and Physician Arthur Dee (Artemii Ivanovich Dii)," 1.

19. Linda Levy Peck, *Court Patronage and Corruption in Early Stuart England,* 68ff. I am grateful to Charlotte Merton for her guidance on this subject.

20. One of the most fascinating features of Dee's diary is his relationship with Elizabeth: she is mentioned over fifty times, and many entries give detailed descriptions of the elaborate protocols (and tantalizing equivocations) marking the queen's behavior, even in the more intimate encounters.

21. Richard Harvey, *Astrological Discourse,* A3r. When in Prague Dee demanded a like title from Rudolf: he sent him a letter "requesting . . . the title of Imperial Philosopher and Mathematician" (Nicholas Clulee, *John Dee's Natural Philosophy,* 224).

22. The best attempt so far at making sense of this set of texts is Clulee, *John Dee's Natural Philosophy,* Part IV. Although I have not seen it, C. L. Whitby's recently published doctoral dissertation also discusses Dee's actions. His essay, "John Dee and Renaissance Scrying," begins to set them in their intellectual context.

23. Owen Gingerich and Robert S. Westman, *The Wittich Connection: Conflict and Priority in Late Sixteenth-Century Cosmology,* 2. This fascinating study contains suggestive discussions of the role the collection and annotation of books and manuscripts played in early modern scientific communities. See also Westman's essay, "Proof, Poetics, and Patronage: Copernicus's Preface to *De Revolutionibus.*"

24. On the former see R. J. W. Evans, *Rudolf II and His World.* On the latter see the studies of Bruce Moran—especially his essay, "Privilege, Communica-

tion, and Chemiatry," in which he discusses some of Dee's traces. One that Moran does not mention is Dee's signature in Christopher Rothmann's *Album Amicorum:* as Edward Rosen explains, he was the landgrave's mathematician and (like Dee) received a presentation copy of Tycho's *Stella Caudata* (*Three Imperial Mathematicians: Kepler Trapped Between Tycho Brahe and Ursus*).

25. On the comet and its aftermath see C. Doris Hellman, *The Comet of 1577: Its Place in the History of Astronomy.* On Hájek see Evans, *Rudolf II,* and Josef Smolka, "The Scientific Revolution in Bohemia."

26. See N. Jardine, *The Birth of History and Philosophy of Science: Kepler's 'A Defense of Tycho against Ursus';* also Rosen, *Three Imperial Mathematicians.*

27. Ursus, *Fundamentaum Astronomicum,* K4v. For brief biographies of the dedicatees of the other nineteen diagrams—who include William of Hessen-Kassel and Gerard Mercator—see Rosen, *Three Imperial Mathematicians* (66–80).

28. In the *General and Rare Memorials* of 1577 Dee employed a variation on this trick, using the character delta as one of the preliminary signatures. These offer one source of evidence, to which others shall be added in the course of this study, of Dee's unusually close control over the printing of his works.

29. BL MS Cotton Charter XIII, art. 38 (also MS Harley 5835, art. 2) traces his ancestry to the earliest Welsh kings. Cotton Charter XIV, art. 1 traces the ancestry of Dee and Elizabeth, side-by-side, back to the same Welsh rulers. Another version of Dee's pedigree is found in the margins of his Latin manuscript of the *Leges Walliae* (now Merton College, Oxford, MS 323). And in Corpus Christi College, Oxford, MS 255, a collection of miscellaneous notes, Dee recorded the pedigrees of "The Indian prince Altabalipa" (137r), the kings of Mexico (142r), and, in parallel columns, the kings of Spain and England (139r).

30. BL MS Cotton Charter XIV, art. 1.

31. It is in the more difficult cases like Dee's, where the careers tend to be less smooth and the personal polemics more fraught, that these conditions come into clearest focus.

32. I borrow the title for this section from E. M. Butler's classic study, *The Myth of the Magus.*

33. For comprehensive historiographical surveys see the introduction to R. W. Barone's thesis, "The Reputation of John Dee" (covering the pre–1950 situation), and the first chapter of Clulee's *John Dee's Natural Philosophy,* "John Dee and Renaissance Intellectual History" (covering the most recent trends).

34. Had Calder's compendious study of nearly fifteen hundred pages been boiled down to a publishable form, it would have preempted much that has been written since.

35. A progression in Frances Yates's work can be traced from *Giordano Bruno and the Hermetic Tradition* (1964), through her essay, "The Hermetic Tradition in Renaissance Science" (1967), and on into *Theatre of the World* (1969), *Shakespeare's Last Plays* (1975), and—her final work—*The Occult Philosophy in the Elizabethan Age* (1979). Yates was often at her boldest and most interesting when writing or speaking about other people's works, and it is instructive to look at

her discussions of Dee in the series of review essays she wrote from the late sixties to her death in 1981 (assembled in the third volume of her collected essays, *Ideas and Ideals in the North European Renaissance*).

36. Clulee must be singled out for his considerable (and salutary) ambivalence: while carrying out a project that is undeniably Warburgian, he carefully maintains his distance from Yates and not only avoids but highlights many of the pitfalls of her approach.

37. J. A. Sharpe, *Early Modern England: A Social History, 1550–1760*, 305; cf. John S. Mebane, *Renaissance Magic and the Return of the Golden Age: The Occult Tradition and Marlowe, Jonson, and Shakespeare*.

38. Three pages later the image of "Dr. Dee's Hounds" chasing a fox into its hole curves around the margin.

39. See Lisa Jardine's review essay on Yates's work in *History Workshop* 21, and, more generally, Patrick Curry, "Revisions of Science and Magic."

40. Again, Clulee proves an important exception: shunning the search for a totalizing system, he unravels many of the aspects of Dee's contributions to natural philosophy, as it was understood by Dee and his contemporaries (*John Dee's Natural Philosophy*, passim).

41. Curry, "Revisions," 317–18.

42. J. G. A. Pocock, *The Machiavellian Moment*, 64.

43. Julian Roberts and Andrew Watson, *John Dee's Library Catalogue*, 52.

44. Frances Yates, *Shakespeare's Last Plays*, 95.

45. Graham Yewbrey, "John Dee and the 'Sidney Group,'" 1–3; cf. 25–26 and 333, and Clulee, *John Dee's Natural Philosophy*, 195 and 238.

46. Colin Ronan, *Their Majesties' Astronomers*, 29 (my emphasis).

47. The selection of godparents in early modern England signaled (and cemented) different ties than it does for us: in initiating (or maintaining) a patronage relationship it indicated a strong social and economic bond—one that implicitly and explicitly approached actual kinship (Peck, *Court Patronage*, passim).

48. *Diary*, 40–41.

49. "Compendious Rehearsall," 14; cf. *Diary*, 35.

50. *Diary*, 37. Contemporary ecclesiastical records seem to tell a different story about Dee's loss of Long-Lednam. He was evidently instituted rector on 22 March 1558/9; but on 20 August 1576 it was noted that he "does not reside, neither is he in holy orders; vehemently suspected in religion, an astronomer, not a theologian." On 15 June 1584, in his absence, he was declared contumacious (see C. W. Foster, ed., *Lincoln Episcopal Records*, 140, 201, and 216; I am grateful to Jane Ladley for this reference).

51. *Diary*, 39.

52. "Compendious Rehearsall," 15.

53. Ibid., 16; cf. *Diary*, 40.

54. William Thorn Warren, ed., *St. Cross Hospital, Near Winchester*, contains a concise history of the institution, a list of its masters from the twelfth to the nineteenth century, and illustrations of the buildings (including the Master's House).

55. "Compendious Rehearsall," 41. Some of these would be, according to Dee's mysterious phrase, "special men" who "would be loath to be seene or heard of publickly in court or city."

56. "Compendious Rehearsall," 12. In one poignant episode Dee tells how the queen heard of his financial problems just before Christmas 1590. On 4 December he entered in his diary, "the Quene's Majestie called for me at my dore . . . as she passed by, and I met her at Estshene gate, where she graciously, putting down her mask, did say with mery chere, 'I thank thee, Dee; there was never promisse made but it was broken or kept'. I understode her Majesty to mean of the hundred angels she promised to have sent me this day . . ." (37). When the queen delivered on her promise two days later she managed both to keep and to break it (or, more precisely, to keep half of it): as Dee recalled with barely restrained bitterness, she "sent unto me fiftie poundes to keepe my Christmas with that yeare" (14).

57. A Letter, Nine yeeres since, written and first published: Containing a most briefe Discourse Apologetical . . . (London, 1603/4).

58. The relevant texts are STC 6460, 6460.5, 6461, 6465, and 6466. The two facsimile editions of the Letter . . . apologeticall reproduce only STC 6460, the 1599 edition; and Dee scholars have not, it seems, examined the Jacobean additions. Incidentally, the Huntington Library's copies (RB 41808–41810) provide another instance of Dee's careful manuscript correction of the printed text.

59. Charles B. Schmitt, "Reappraisals in Renaissance Science," 202. Cf. Gary Hatfield, "Metaphysics and the New Science." Hatfield warns that "the fact that an early modern author adopts a mathematical approach to nature is sometimes taken as providing sufficient grounds for ascribing to him a Platonic metaphysics" (98) and goes on to challenge—with explicit reference to Dee— the oppositions between the "metamathematical" and "mathematical" and, more generally, the "metaphysical" and the "scientific" (99).

60. Schmitt, "Reappraisals," 202 and 208. This is the tenor of Clulee's conclusion, as well: see his closing pages, subtitled "Magic and the Occult in the Renaissance" (John Dee's Natural Philosophy).

61. This formula was employed by Mario Biagioli to criticize Paul Rose's use of the term "humanism"—see "The Social Status of Italian Mathematicians," 56–57.

62. Yates, Giordano Bruno and the Hermetic Tradition, 159.

63. Ibid., 159 and part 2 of chap. 9 (entitled, "Against Magic: The Humanist Tradition").

64. Not only was biblical scholarship greatly enhanced by Humanist methods (and in some respects the centerpiece of Erasmus' "Christian Humanism"), but after the point when scholars were put to the service of the Protestant Reformation it also becomes impossible to speak of a Humanism for which religion is not a—or even the—vital question. In the fields of history and law, especially, Renaissance Humanists relied for their authority upon medieval monuments as much as ancient. For legal Humanism, see J. W. Binns's account in Intellectual Culture in Elizabethan and Jacobean England. The work of Mordechai Feingold has

established that both occult and scientific mentalities infiltrated the Renaissance universities (and London, the "third university") more deeply than has been thought. See especially "The Occult Tradition in the English Universities of the Renaissance," in Vickers, ed., *Occult and Scientific Mentalities in the Renaissance*. The best general account of the ramifications of these humanistic developments is Grafton and Jardine, *From Humanism to the Humanities*.

65. Peter French, *John Dee*, 22.

66. Owen Hannaway, "Laboratory Design and the Aim of Science: Andreas Libavius versus Tycho Brahe"; see also Jole Shackleford, "Tycho Brahe, Laboratory Design, and the Aim of Science: Reading Plans in Context."

67. This is especially true of Libavius. In an earlier study, (*The Chemist and the Word*), Hannaway examines Libavius's debate with Oswald Croll, the Paracelsian chemical philosopher. Though he again assigns Libavius (in many aspects convincingly) to the Humanist side of the great divide, he is more ambivalent, acknowledging that he ultimately embraced many elements of the chemical philosophy he condemned.

68. See Wilhelm Norlind, *Tycho Brahe*, 122–27, 232– 37, 286–93, and 295–96.

69. In defense of which he planned to pen a major work, *De Horizonte Aeternitatis* (*Letter . . . apologeticall,* B2). This text would explain the mathematical, theological, physical, metaphysical, and "Hierotechnical" applications of his *Monas hieroglyphica*.

70. Hannaway, "Laboratory Design," 599. For an excellent discussion of the meeting of Humanism and science in late sixteenth-century Prague, see Anthony Grafton, "Humanism and Science in Rudolphine Prague: Kepler in Context," in *Defenders of the Text*. On the meeting of Humanism and science in general see Grafton, "Humanism, Magic, and Science"; Barbara Shapiro, "History and Natural History in Sixteenth- and Seventeenth-Century England: An Essay on the Relationship Between Humanism and Science"; Antonia McLean, *Humanism and the Rise of Science in Tudor England;* and Robert S. Westman, "Humanism and Scientific Roles in the Sixteenth Century."

71. Cited in Hannaway, "Laboratory Design," 599.

72. My emphasis on roles is especially indebted to the work of Robert Westman and Mario Biagioli.

73. Steven Mullaney's influential study, *The Place of the Stage: License, Play, and Power in Renaissance England,* attempted to move "toward a rhetoric of space in Elizabethan London" (see chap. 1). In 1991 the journal *Science in Context* devoted a special issue to "the place of knowledge." And in June 1993, a conference was held at Queen Mary and Westfield College (University of London) entitled "Renaissance Topographies of Knowledge."

74. E. W. Brayley, *A Topographical History of Surrey*, III:188.

75. E. G. R. Taylor, "A Letter Dated 1577 from Mercator to John Dee," 56.

76. "Compendious Rehearsall," 40.

77. Dee's diary records dealings with all three of these men. He was probably closest with Herbert, who wrote an apology for Irish colonization and named it after Croft: he sent Dee notes on his *Monas hieroglyphica* and exchanged with Dee

both texts and servants. They joined their children Mary and Arthur in a mock wedding: Mary, however, went on to make a more socially acceptable match with Lord Herbert of Cherbury. Dee's relationship with the Maynards is not clear; but on the flyleaf to his diary he listed the four sons of Maynard and their birthdates (not printed in Halliwell's edition).

78. For example, the "Mathematicall Praeface" to the English Euclid and the "Compendious Rehearsall."

79. Occasionally we find "Mortlacensis," or simply "Anglus." He signed a letter to John Stow "Joannes Dee Cambrobrytanus Anglus" (Bodleian MS Ashmole 1788).

80. It is possible that Dee's geographical self-consciousness was acquired from, or associated with, his cosmographical colleagues from Louvain. One of their agnomens supplanted their surname: Cornelius Gemma, Frisius, became known as Gemma Frisius. And while they were not routinely addressed this way, Dee called Ortelius "Abrahamus Ortelius Antwerpianus" (see the page from the *Album Amicorum*), Mercator "Gerardus Mercator Rupelmundanus," and Nuñez "Petrus Nonius Salaciensis" (for those two see the dedicatory epistle from *Propaedeumata aphoristica*).

81. See Patrick Collinson's critical review, "Puritans, Men of Business and Elizabethan Parliaments," 192. Two other recent contributions from political history have been especially useful: R. G. Asch and A. M. Birke, eds., *Princes, Patronage, and the Nobility,* and Antoni Mączak, ed., *Klientelsysteme in Europa der Fruhen Neuzeit*—particularly, within the latter, Victor Morgan's essay, "Some Types of Patronage, Mainly in Sixteenth- and Seventeenth-Century England."

82. See also Biagioli's essays, "The Social Status of Italian Mathematicians," and "Scientific Revolution, Social Bricolage, and Etiquette."

83. Clulee, *John Dee's Natural Philosophy,* 235.

84. Lina Bolzoni, "Il segretario neoplatonico."

85. See the classic work of Barry Barnes, *Interests and the Growth of Knowledge,* and Barnes and Donald MacKenzie, "On the Role of Interests in Scientific Change."

86. Patrick Collinson, "De Republica Anglorum: Or, History with the Politics Put Back," 27.

87. Kevin Sharpe, *Sir Robert Cotton,* 149.

88. Biagioli, "The Social Status of Italian Mathematicians," 42.

89. Cf. Julian Martin, *Francis Bacon, the State, and the Reform of Natural Philosophy;* Charles Webster, *The Great Instauration: Science, Medicine and Reform, 1626-1660;* and Stephen Clucas, "Samuel Hartlib's Ephemerides, 1635-59, and the Pursuit of Scientific and Philosophical Manuscripts: The Religious Ethos of an Intelligencer."

TWO. A LIVING LIBRARY

1. Francis R. Johnson, *Astronomical Thought in Renaissance England,* 137-39. Johnson's picture of a Dee circle is misleading in one sense: Dee must be positioned in several overlapping knowledge-power grids, and in none of these

can he be considered the center. On Dee's place in London's scientific community see Mordechai Feingold, *The Mathematician's Apprenticeship: Science, Universities, and Society in England, 1560–1640,* and Christopher Hill, *The Intellectual Origins of the English Revolution,* passim.

2. To be fair, it would have been extremely difficult to carry out such a study before the publication of Julian Roberts and Andrew Watson's monumental edition of *John Dee's Library Catalogue,* which assembles virtually all known data pertaining to the creation, contents, and provenance of Dee's collection. It has been an indispensable guide in my own research and will be of lasting value to all students of Dee— and, indeed, of early modern books and libraries. Subsequent references will refer to this work as Roberts and Watson.

3. In fact, although she did not attempt to answer it, Yates put her finger on precisely this question in *Theatre of the World* (3).

4. Roberts and Watson, 1, 58, and 64–67. Henry Savile and Thomas Allen were just a couple of those who acquired books before the final sale of the library in 1625–26. It was at that time that Simonds D'Ewes, Ralph Starkey, Brian Twyne, and James Ussher procured chunks of Dee's collection.

5. Cotton's interest in Dee's library is indicated by a "wish list" that is preserved with Dee's library catalogue in BL MS Harley 1879; by a letter to Cotton from Nicholas Saunder (possessor, by theft, of several hundred of Dee's books) which is reproduced as Plate VIa in Roberts and Watson; and, of course, by the large number of Dee's volumes among the present Cotton collection.

6. See the article on Cotton in the *DNB.*

7. C. H. Josten, ed., *Elias Ashmole's Autobiographical and Historical Notes, His Correspondence, and Other Contemporary Sources Relating to His Life and Work,* IV:1293.

8. Ibid., I:188.

9. BL MS Sloane 3188, 3ʳ. The entire episode is recounted in Josten, *Elias Ashmole's Autobiographical and Historical Notes,* I:184–87. Ashmole also received some materials from Sir Thomas Browne, who had been a friend of Dee's son Arthur.

10. In Chapters 1 and 2 of *Theatre of the World* Yates highlighted the Hermetic holdings. E. G. R. Taylor listed Dee's navigational texts in an appendix to *Tudor Geography, 1485–1583.* Lucy Gent discussed treatises on the arts in Renaissance English libraries (including Dee's) in *Picture and Poetry 1560–1620.* Charles Webster listed Dee's Paracelsian books in an appendix to his essay "Alchemical and Paracelsian medicine" (cf. Appendix 5 to Roberts and Watson, a chronological concordance between Dee's catalogue and Sudhoff's *Bibliographia Paracelsia*). And Gareth Lloyd Jones inventoried Dee's Semitic books in Appendix II to *The Discovery of Hebrew in Tudor England.*

11. Yates, *Theatre of the World,* 12.

12. Although the 1583 catalogue lists under three thousand volumes, Dee's own estimate in the "Compendious Rehearsall" was closer to four thousand. There are several possible ways to account for this discrepancy. Dee's estimate was made a decade after the 1583 inventory, and he had doubtless acquired new volumes. He may also have figured in works that were omitted from the

catalogue—perhaps because they were borrowed or stolen, dangerous or forbidden. He may have counted his charters or titles within manuscript collections individually. And, finally, he may have simply been stretching the truth for effect.

13. For further comparisons see Anthony Hobson, "English Library Buildings of the 17th and 18th Century."

14. Roberts and Watson, 22.

15. This last group, the *"libri Anglici,"* was oddly eclectic and remarkably small, forming less than 5 percent of the total; see ibid., 12.

16. Ibid., 23 and 42.

17. See Frances Yates's *The Art of Memory* and, more recently, Mary Carruthers's *The Book of Memory: A Study of Memory in Medieval Culture.*

18. Cited in Carruthers, *Book of Memory,* 116, 33. Perhaps the most notorious instance of such a library is the encyclopedic work of the Jesuit Antonio Possevino. His *Bibliotheca selecta* (Rome, 1593) provided, within the most pious of frameworks, a bibliographical and analytical summary "De ratione studiorum in Historia, In Disciplinis, In Salute omnium procuranda" (as the full title claimed). But like every other Renaissance project carried out in Christ's name, Possevino's selection had a significant ideological underpinning: as an implement of the Counter-Reformation it was designed to purge monastic libraries of their problematic volumes. Albano Biondi has called it "a project for cultural hegemony" ("La *Bibliotheca Selecta* di Antonio Possevino: Un progretto di egemonia culturale").

19. Carruthers, *Book of Memory,* 121. These tagged *arcae* still survive in the libraries of many academic and religious foundations: see J. W. Clark, *Libraries in the Medieval and Renaissance Periods.* Perhaps the best-known example is Cotton's library of manuscripts. Although they are now stored in the shelves of the British Library, they retain Cotton's shelf-marks: these incorporate the names of Roman emperors, which originally correspond to cases topped by their busts.

20. Not all Renaissance librarians were convinced of the need for sophisticated mnemonic systems. Dee may well have been in the camp of Gabriel Naudé, who offered a remarkable simile in disparaging such systems: "as the Eele escapes, by being to hard pressed . . . *Artificial Memory* spoils and perverts the natural [and] seems not to have any other scope but to torture and eternally crucifie the Memory, under the Thorns of those frivolous *Punctilios* and *Chymerick* subtilties . . ." (*Instructions Concerning Erecting of a Library,* F6v).

21. Roberts & Watson, 10.

22. BL MS Cotton Vitellius C. VII, fol. 9r–v. Printed in Roberts and Watson, Appendix 4; Thomas Hearne, ed., *Johannis Glastoniensis Chronica,* II:529–33; and James Crossley's *Autobiographical Tracts of Dr. John Dee,* 27–31. In the next few paragraphs I cite *Autobiographical Tracts.* Because it occupies only four pages, I have not considered it necessary to supply page numbers.

23. In 1547 Dee returned to Cambridge from his first visit to the Low Countries, bringing to England the first astronomer's staff. This was among several instruments that Dee left to Trinity College for the use of the fellows and

scholars. Dee owned two copies of Gemma's treatise on its use, *De radio astro-nomico* (Roberts and Watson, nos. 362 and 967).

24. An inventory was made by William Camden in 1573 and is now in BL MS Lansdowne 229, fols. 98v–100r. It is printed in Roberts and Watson as part of List D (184–87).

25. This movement generated a great deal of correspondence and activity and is one of the most important indicators of the growth of a centralized, bureaucratic government. See R. B. Wernham, "The Public Records in the Sixteenth and Seventeenth Centuries," and F. Smith Fussner, *The Historical Revolution,* esp. 32–37 and 60–91. The correspondence generated by the suits of William Bowyer and William Cordell, regarding the management of the records in the Tower, is especially noteworthy. A letter to Lord Burghley on this subject, dated 15 June 1573 (BL MS Harley 94, art. 3), has been ascribed to Dee, though I find the attribution dubious: not only are the hand, syntax, and spelling uncharacteristic, but the writer refers to "Master Randolphe" as "my *Master*" (margin of fol. 41v).

26. On the general significance of such a collection in early modern culture see Krzysztof Pomian, *Collectors and Curiosities;* A. Regond-Bohat and A. Loechel, "Les Cabinets de curiosités au XVIe siècle"; Simon Welfare and John Fairley, *The Cabinet of Curiosities;* Steven Mullaney, "The Rehearsal of Cultures," chap. 3 in his *The Place of the Stage;* and Paula Findlen, "The Economy of Scientific Exchange in Early Modern Italy."

27. Aside from the maps that Dee himself produced, there survives a map in the Cotton Charter collection (XIII, art. 48) with the legend, "The Counterfet [or copy] of Mr Fernando Simon his sea carte which he lent unto my M^r at Mortlake A° 1580 Novemb. 20." Dee himself penned the passage that is usually cited to describe the Elizabethan fashion of displaying maps: "some, to beautifie their Halls, Parlers, Chambers, Galeries, Studies, or Libraries . . . liketh, loueth, and vseth, Mappes, Chartes, & Geographicall Globes" ("Mathematicall Praeface," a4r).

28. The obsidian speculum, crystal ball, and wax sigil—all of which are currently housed at the British Museum—are reproduced as Figures 8.1, 8.2, and 8.7 in Clulee, *John Dee's Natural Philosophy.*

29. Ibid., 69. Bourne's treatise is found in BL MS Lansdowne MS 121, and is printed in J. O. Halliwell-Phillipps, ed., *Rara Mathematica.*

30. This paragraph is largely based on Oliver Impey and Arthur MacGregor, eds., *The Origins of Museums: The Cabinet of Curiosities in Sixteenth- and Seventeenth-Century Europe;* subsequent references are noted in parentheses in the text and in the next two notes.

31. See Michael Hunter, "The Cabinet Institutionalized," in Impey and MacGregor, eds., *The Origins of Museums:* Hunter's essay has an appendix on the development of the word *museum.* A more detailed account is given by Paula Findlen, in "The Museum: Its Classical Etymology and Renaissance Genealogy."

32. These details are taken from the following contributions to Impey and MacGregor: Elisabeth Scheiner, "The Collections of Archduke Ferdinand II at

Schloss Ambras"; Laura Laurencich-Minelli, "Museology and Ethnographical Collections in Bologna During the Sixteenth and Seventeenth Centuries"; Joachim Menzhausen, "Elector Augustus's *Kunstkammer*"; and Lorenz Seelig, "The Munich *Kunstkammer, 1565–1807*." In the same volume there are accounts of similar collections at Rudolf II's residence in Prague (50), the Faesch museum in Basle (67), the Moritz building of 1593 in Kassel (104), the Brandenburg Kunstkammers (111), and the house of Don Bernardino Fernandez de Velasco, Constable of Castile (145).

33. M. Casciato, M. G. Ianniello, and M. Vitale, eds., *Enciclopedismo in Roma Barocca: Athanasius Kircher e il Museo del Collegio Romano tra Wunderkammer e Museo Scientifico.*

34. Cited in R. J. W. Evans, *Rudolf II and His World*, 204 n. 3.

35. Although they paled in comparison to most of the museums under discussion, libraries at both Oxford and Cambridge housed considerable collections of coins and antiquities throughout the sixteenth and seventeenth centuries; and when Oxford's Ashmolean Museum opened in 1683, the building contained a chemical laboratory in the basement, a lecture room on the ground floor, and two libraries (Impey and MacGregor, *Origins of Museums*, 221; cf. A. MacGregor, ed., *Tradescant's Rarities: Essays on the Foundation of the Ashmolean Museum*).

36. The text (from Hearne's *Johannis Glastoniensis Chronica*, II:490–95) is printed and discussed in Roberts and Watson. The only new light that I can shed on this petition is its appearance as the first entry in the *Calendar of Treasury Papers, 1556/7–1696* (1). This possibly suggests that the project was considered (and rejected) as a request for state funds, even though Dee claimed that the library would be erected "without any charges to the Queen's Majestie."

37. Roberts and Watson, 194. Cf. C. E. Wright on "The Dispersal of Monastic Libraries," and Ronald Harold Fritze, " 'Truth hath lacked witnesse, tyme wanted light': The Dispersal of the English Monastic Libraries and Protestant Efforts at Preservation."

38. Roberts and Watson found that Dee's library contained forty or fifty manuscripts from around eighteen religious houses (20; cf. 14–15).

39. See Wayne Shumaker's translation in *John Dee on Astronomy: 'Propaedeumata aphoristica' (1558 and 1568)*. This phrase appears only in the second edition of 1568: when the first edition was published in 1558 Dee was not yet settled in Mortlake. He also signed the preface to the printer Willem Sylvius in his *Monas hieroglyphica* (1564) "Ex Musaeo nostro": this probably refers to Sylvius' household, where Dee was staying.

40. Julian Martin, *Francis Bacon, the State, and the Reform of Natural Philosophy*, 69–70.

41. Roberts and Watson, 36.

42. Roy Strong, *The Renaissance Garden in England;* Terry Comito, *The Idea of the Garden in the Renaissance.*

43. Roberts and Watson, 26. The most extensive evidence of Dee's use of his books is preserved, of course, in the margins of surviving volumes; but I reserve discussion of his marginalia for Chapter 4.

44. For a concise guide to the relevant literature see André Stegmann, "Comment constituer une bibliothèque en France au début du XVIIe siècle."

45. *The Life of Sir Thomas Bodley Written by Himself*, 57. This text, written in 1609, was first printed in 1703 in Thomas Hearne's *Reliquiae Bodleianae*.

46. Justus Lipsius, *A Brief Outline of the History of Libraries*, 111, 120. I have supplied the original Latin, for some important and contestable words, from the first edition (Antwerp, 1602).

47. I cite Naudé's text as translated by John Evelyn (fellow of the Royal Society and author of *Public Employment and an Active Life prefer'd to Solitude*) and published in 1661 as *Instructions Concerning Erecting of a Library* (B4v).

48. John Dury, *The Reformed Librarie-Keeper*, 16–17. In the 1640s Dury, along with Hartlib and Comenius, tried to reform educational and governmental institutions—in fact, to forge a more fruitful partnership between them. The group's proposals grew out of the developments in information management, civic Humanism, and natural philosophy that emerged from the previous century (which Francis Bacon, their greatest influence, fused in his project for "The Advancement of Learning").

49. The paraphrase is Roberts and Watson's (41).

50. Dury, *The Reformed Librarie-Keeper*, 18.

51. See Roberts and Watson, 42–45, and Dee's diary, passim.

52. On Kyffin, see Roberts and Watson, 44, and my article in the *Dictionary of Literary Biography: Sixteenth-Century Non-Dramatic Authors*, s.v. Kyffin.

53. Roberts and Watson, 71 n.41. It is possible that Cook, who served Dee from 1567 to 1581, had played some role in the construction of Dee's laboratories, or that Dee's house was where he had learned his trade.

54. "Compendious Rehearsall," 40.

55. These episodes are recounted in the diary and in "Compendious Rehearsall."

56. E. G. R. Taylor, ed., *A Regiment for the Sea and Other Writings on Navigation by William Bourne*, 313–14. Incidentally, this account of a book-based knowledge transaction is one of the very few passages annotated in the copy belonging to Gabriel Harvey (BL C.60.f.8).

57. The web of borrowing and lending that runs through Dee's diary in particular involved not only books but money and servants as well.

58. *Diary*, 35, where Zacharius is mistranscribed "Paracelsus."

59. Ibid., 38. Some time earlier Beale—who was involved with Dee in promoting voyages of exploration—had borrowed Joachim of Fiore's *Opera*, which he returned in 1590 (Roberts and Watson, no. 706).

60. The manuscript also contained Cato's *Distichs* and Aphthonius' *Progymnasmata*. For the details, with an excerpt from Dee's dedicatory inscription, see Roberts and Watson, no. M47.

61. John Darrell, *A True Narration of the Strange and Grievous Vexation by the Devil of 7. Persons in Lancashire* (1600).

62. See Roberts and Watson, 56–57.

63. Roberts and Watson, no. 1448.

64. Paul Lawrence Rose, *The Italian Renaissance of Mathematics*, 200. The

manuscript survives in the Bibliotheca Ambrosiana (MS P.236 sup.) and bears Commandino's marginal notes. It was a copy, made by Dee himself, of his older codex, now BL Cotton MS Tiberius B.IX. Cf. Rose's article, "Commandino, John Dee, and the *De superficierum divisionibus* of Machometus Bagdedinus"; Clulee, 123; and Roberts and Watson, nos. M95q and DM92.

65. BL Harley MS 6485; *The Rosie Crucian Secrets*, ed. E. J. Langford Garstin.

66. Bruce Moran has reconstructed the fascinating reception history of the *Monas hieroglyphica* at the German court: see Part II of his study, *The Alchemical World of the German Court.*

67. Roberts and Watson, 62–63.

68. Naudé, *Apologie pur les grands hommes soupçonnés de Magie* (Paris, 1625); cited in Frances Yates, *The Rosicrucian Enlightenment,* 110.

69. These sometimes represent identical editions, but I have also counted copies of different editions, languages, and formats, as well as manuscript versions. My doctoral dissertation on Dee contains a comprehensive list of multiple copies in Dee's library.

70. It would have pleased Charles Schmitt (the Warburg Institute's great student of Renaissance Aristotelianism) to know that Dee, who has been considered the greatest representative of Neoplatonism in the English Renaissance, owned what was surely its most comprehensive private collection of the works of Aristotle.

71. Roberts and Watson, 42.

72. Elisabeth Leedham-Green, *Books in Cambridge Inventories,* I:xx. Cf. Roberts and Watson, 42.

73. This is BL 8461.b.13. It does not appear in Roberts and Watson. I am grateful to Alan Stewart for bringing it to my attention.

74. This label emerged during a conversation with David Starkey.

75. Cited in Roger Chartier, "The Practical Impact of Writing," in Chartier, ed., *A History of Private Life, Volume 3,* 134.

76. Montaigne, *Essais* III:3.

77. Cited in Raymond Irwin, *The English Library.*

78. Adi Ophir, "A Place of Knowledge Re-Created: The Library of Michel de Montaigne."

79. Roger Chartier, "The Practical Impact of Writing," in *The History of Private Life,* 136.

80. Steven Shapin, " 'The Mind is its Own Place': Science and Solitude in Seventeenth-Century England." See also Shapin's " 'A Scholar and a Gentleman': The Problematic Identity of the Scientific Practitioner in Early Modern England."

81. Christ Church, Oxford, class-mark Wb.5.12. See Roberts and Watson, 19 n. 15, for details about this list and others like it. One they neglect to mention is found in BL MS Harley 473 (Dee's diary of a journey to Chester and Wales): "Remember if I can not get Saynt Walburgs Life at London among the inglish stationers: or at Mr Steuensons: than to write to Mr Griffith the porter of the Mynster at Chester for a copy of it . . ." (1*r).

82. See Archer Taylor, *Renaissance Guides to Books*. The 1555 *Epitome Bibliothecae* contained an interesting "Apologia Bibliothecae" in its preface (*5r), and a wonderful advertisement on its title page: "HABES hic, amice Lector, catalogum locupletissimum omnium fere scriptorum, a mundi initio ad hunc usque diem, extantium & non extantium, publicatorum & passim in Bibliothecis latitantium. Opus non Bibliothecis tantum publicis priuatisque instituendis necessarium, sed studiosis omnibus, cuiuscunque artis aut scientiae, ad studia melius formanda utilissimum."

83. Richard J. Durling, "Conrad Gesner's *Liber Amicorum* 1555–1565," 138.

84. BL 616.m.2. Roberts and Watson incorrectly identify this volume with the "Josiae Simleri Epitome Bibliothecae Gesneri" of the same year which is, in fact, entry no. 170.

85. On this list, which seems to be in Nicholas Saunder's hand and to derive from Dee's collection, see the reproduction and discussion of List E in Roberts and Watson.

86. Regrettably, my examination of this volume has so far been severely limited, but I am grateful to Julian Roberts for bringing it to my attention. It will be instructive to compare Dee's notes with those of Gabriel Harvey, whose annotated copy survives at Harvard (Lisa Jardine and Anthony Grafton, " 'Studied for Action,' " 76).

87. On 8 July 1575, Simler wrote to Bonaventura Vulcanius, "Subjicietur prelo appendix Bibliothecae mox a proximis nundinis, expecto enim notas et auctaria ad priorem editionem cum ab aliis tum a clarissimis viris Gulielmo Cantero et Joanne Dee Londinensi" (H. de Vries de Heekelingen, ed., *Correspondance de Bonaventura Vulcanius,* 302).

88. See, for instance, the special issue of the journal *Science in Context* entitled "The Place of Knowledge" (Spring 1991).

89. See Owen Hannaway, "Laboratory Design and the Aim of Science: Andreas Libavius versus Tycho Brahe"; Steven Shapin, "The House of Experiment in Seventeenth-Century England"; and Steven Shapin and Simon Schaffer, *Leviathan and the Air-Pump: Hobbes, Boyle, and the Experimental Life.*

90. Most notably, Richard L. Regosin, *The Matter of My Book: Montaigne's Essais as the Book of the Self.*

91. Ophir, "A Place of Knowledge Re-Created," 170.

92. Cf. Anthony Grafton, *New Worlds, Ancient Texts.*

93. A library like Dee's functions as what Bruno Latour has usefully described as a "centre of calculation." For Latour, the question we must ask of such a center is, how does it act at a distance on unfamiliar events, places, and people? He answers in terms that can be suggestively applied to early modern reading practices: it renders them "mobile," "stable," and "combinable" (see his *Science in Action,* 223ff.).

94. Ophir, "A Place of Knowledge Re-Created," 165.

95. Samuel Johnson, *A Dictionary of the English Language,* sig. 20M1r.

96. *Diary,* 17–18. It is interesting that Dee's disemboweling may represent the rite of violence usually reserved for subjects guilty of high political crimes.

97. Kevin Sharpe, *Sir Robert Cotton,* 80. The real damage, of course, was done after Cotton's death, when the library was tragically mutilated by fire.
98. See Naudé, *News from France.*

THREE. READING

1. Roger Chartier, *The Cultural Uses of Print in Early Modern France,* 8.
2. Ibid., 346.
3. Robert Darnton, "First Steps Toward a History of Reading," 24.
4. Tzvetan Todorov, "Reading as Construction," in Susan R. Suleiman and Inge Crosman, eds., *The Reader in the Text: Essays on Audience and Interpretation,* 67. Cf. Roger Säljo's introduction to *The Written Word: Studies in Literate Thought and Action:* "Relating to written discourse has become such a deeply interiorised and natural activity in life that it escapes our conscious attention" (1).
5. See Pierre Bourdieu's conversation with Roger Chartier, "La lecture: une pratique culturelle," 218. This remarkable exchange is the most concise and suggestive account of recent developments in the study of reading.
6. Elizabeth Freund, *The Return of the Reader: Reader-Response Criticism.*
7. Robert C. Holub, *Reception Theory: A Critical Introduction.*
8. Freund, *Return of the Reader,* 4.
9. See Wolfgang Iser, *The Act of Reading: A Theory of Aesthetic Response;* also *The Implied Reader: Patterns of Communication in Prose Fiction from Bunyan to Beckett.* He contributed an essay "Interaction between Text and Reader," to Suleiman and Crosman, eds., *The Reader in the Text,* and the editors offer a critical assessment of his theories on pp. 22−26 of their introduction.
10. Iser, *The Act of Reading,* x.
11. In the first sentence of Iser's "Interaction between Text and Reader" he describes the interaction as a meeting between the "structure" of a literary work and its "recipient." This alone reveals how his approach is grounded in an outmoded structuralism and suggests that his readers—as in most reception theories—are simply too "receptive."
12. Suleiman and Crosman, *Reader in the Text,* 25.
13. Freund, *Return of the Reader,* 7. Only Hans Robert Jauss's "actual reader" and Stanley Fish's "interpretive community" begin, as categories, to account for the agency of readers and the specific constraints on their interpretive acts.
14. J. Hillis Miller, *The Ethics of Reading,* 7. The section I have excised, however, reads, "and showing how the adduced historical context inheres in the fine grain of its language." This betrays Miller's neoformalist principles and suggests that his attack is directed at an almost positivistic view of both history and historicism.
15. J. Hillis Miller, "The Function of Literary Theory at the Present Time," in Ralph Cohen, ed., *The Future of Literary Theory,* 111. In this essay Miller again reproduced the opposition that he critiques; this time between "rhetorical" and "sociological" or "extrinsic" and "intrinsic" modes of reading. Geoffrey Hartman's remarks in the same volume are more compelling ("The State of the Art of Criticism," 97−98). Better still is Tony Bennett, "Texts in History: The Deter-

minations of Readings and Their Texts," in D. Attridge, G. Bennington, and R. Young, eds., *Post-Structuralism and the Question of History.*

16. Here Iser and the deconstructionists meet: see Iser, "Indeterminacy and the Reader's Response in Prose Fiction," in J. Hillis Miller, ed., *Aspects of Narrative.*

17. Maurice Blanchot, "The Essential Solitude," in *The Gaze of Orpheus and Other Literary Essays.*

18. Maurice Blanchot, "Reading," in ibid., 96–97. In this essay Blanchot describes reading as a "light, innocent Yes" which is "ravishing and transparent."

19. Ibid., 94. Mikhail Bakhtin provides an obvious foil: for him all textual activity is precisely a matter of dialogue (e.g., Tzvetan Todorov, *Mikhail Bakhtin: The Dialogical Principle*). A less obvious foil—though, ironically, another profound influence on deconstruction—is Edmond Jabès, for whom everything is textual activity, and all textual activity is a matter of relentless questioning and conversation (e.g., *Le Livre des Questions* and *Le Livre du Dialogue*).

20. See P. Adams Sitney's "Afterword" to Blanchot, *The Gaze of Orpheus*, 169.

21. D. F. McKenzie, *Bibliography and the Sociology of Texts*, 4.

22. Jerome McGann, "Theory of Texts," 20. Cf. McGann's essays in Bakhtinian bibliography, *The Beauty of Inflections*, Parts I and II.

23. See, for instance, the thorough but hostile review by G. Thomas Tanselle in *Studies in Bibliography* XLIV (1991).

24. Although it is a difficult and problematic essay, Peter L. Shillingsburg's "Text as Matter, Concept, and Action" is one such example.

25. John P. Feather, "The Book in History and the History of the Book," 13.

26. David Hall, "The History of the Book: New Questions? New Answers?" 30.

27. Chartier, *Cultural Uses of Print*, 11.

28. Ibid., 6, 183.

29. See M. A. K. Halliday's introduction to *Language as Social Semiotic.* Halliday's approach is highly pragmatic and context-specific: he refuses to recognize a "clear line between the 'what' and the 'how'; all language is language-in-use" (33).

30. George L. Dillon, *Rhetoric as Social Imagination: Explorations of the Interpersonal Function of Language*, 4.

31. Martin Nystrand, *The Structure of Written Communication: Studies in Reciprocity Between Writers and Readers*, 41. Cf. Nystrand's useful introduction to *What Writers Know: The Language, Process, and Structure of Written Discourse*, which discusses the implications of "audience" and "speech community" on "writing, reading, and text."

32. See the essays in James Tully, ed., *Meaning and Context: Quentin Skinner and His Critics;* also David Boucher's study of Skinner, Dunn, and Pocock, *Texts in Context: Revisionist Methods for Studying the History of Ideas.*

33. Chartier, *Cultural Uses of Print*, 5.

34. Carruthers, *The Book of Memory: A Study of Memory in Medieval Culture*, 11, 13; Brian Stock, *The Implications of Literacy: Written Language and Models of*

Interpretation in the Eleventh and Twelfth Centuries; cf. Brian Street, *Literacy in Theory and Practice,* and Gerd Baumann, ed., *The Written Word: Literacy in Transition.*

35. McKenzie, *Bibliography and the Sociology of the Text,* 6–7.

36. Michel de Certeau, *The Practice of Everyday Life,* 166–67.

37. Chartier, *Cultural Uses of Print,* 183, and *Cultural History,* 12.

38. Stephen Greenblatt, *Shakespearean Negotiations,* 1.

39. Gabriel Harvey is the major exception: his extraordinary annotations are the subject of G. C. Moore Smith, *Gabriel Harvey's Marginalia;* Virginia F. Stern, *Gabriel Harvey: His Life, Marginalia and Library;* and Lisa Jardine and Anthony Grafton, " 'Studied for Action': How Gabriel Harvey Read His Livy."

40. Eugene R. Kintgen, "Reconstructing Elizabethan Reading," 13.

41. This is also the starting point of the study I am carrying out with Lisa Jardine and Anthony Grafton, tentatively titled *Reading in the Renaissance* (which focuses primarily on Dee and Harvey), and of a survey of signs of book usage that I carried out in the Huntington's S.T.C. collection.

42. Mary Thomas Crane's work on the gathering and framing of commonplaces in Humanist pedagogy and politics (*Framing Authority*) came to my attention only after I had finished this chapter. I was pleased to discover that while our interests overlap, our accounts are complementary and our material is remarkably distinct. My emphasis in the next few paragraphs corresponds to hers particularly closely: elsewhere I tend to put more weight on reading and on manuscript sources.

43. Joan Simon, *Education and Society in Tudor England,* 109–10.

44. Jardine and Grafton, " 'Studied for Action,' " 30.

45. Walter Ong, Foreword to Sister Joan Marie Lechner, *Renaissance Concepts of the Commonplaces.*

46. Gabriel Naudé, *Instructions Concerning Erecting of a Library* (D2); cf. Richard Schoeck, "Renaissance Guides to Renaissance Learning."

47. I cite this lengthy passage both because it is so explicit and because it is virtually unknown. A better-known set of instructions—to modern and probably to early modern readers—can be found in Jean Bodin's widely disseminated *Methodus ad facilem historiarum cognitionem.*

48. Rudolph Agricola, *De inventione dialectica,* cited in Terence Cave, *The Cornucopian Text,* 14.

49. Naudé, *Instructions Concerning Erecting of a Library,* C7r.

50. Lorna Hutson, *Thomas Nashe in Context,* 45.

51. Folger Library, MS V.a. 381, pp. 86–87; cited in Marion Trousdale's *Shakespeare and the Rhetoricians,* 147.

52. Lorna Hutson, "Fortunate Travelers: Reading for the Plot in Sixteenth-Century England." I am grateful to Lorna Hutson for sharing and discussing several versions of this essay with me.

53. My thesis, on which this book is based, was entitled " 'A Living Library': The Readings and Writings of John Dee."

54. William Barlow, *An Answer to a Catholike English-Man,* 105. Barlow suggests in passing a classical source for this Renaissance trope: he mentions that

the phrase had been applied to "one lesse deserving" by "the *Gretian* Eunapius"—i.e., Eunapius Sardianus, author of the popular *Lives of the Philosophers and Orators*.

55. Northamptonshire Record Office, Finch-Hatton MS F.H.315; reproduced as Fig. 5 in Karl Joseph Holtgen, "Sir Robert Dallington (1561–1637)." By the time the work made it to print in 1613 (when it was published in London by Edward Blount), Dallington's dedicatee had died, and he shuffled his work and his hopes for preferment onto Henry's brother Charles. In the new dedication he once again advised his royal student to turn to examples and precepts. For the former, Charles could still observe James, who was this time pictured as "a liuing and liuely Mirrour vnto you of Pietie, Wisedome, Iustice, Clemencie, and all other regall endowments. . . ."

56. Both cited in Lawrence D. Green, ed. and trans., *John Rainolds's Oxford Lectures on Aristotle's Rhetoric*, 24.

57. It was precisely this pragmatic avenue that a courtly writer like George Chapman—with some hypocrisy—resented: for him "living libraries" were no more than pedantic mercenaries. In his *Euthymiae Raptus* he accused these "*Intellectiue* men" of studying "not to get knowledge, but for meere reward": "And let a Scholler, all earths volumes carrie, / He will be but a walking dictionarie: / A meere articulate Clocke . . ." (cited in Eckhard Auberlen, *The Commonwealth of Wit*, 48).

58. Richard Mulcaster, *Positions* (1581), 254–55. The "politike counsellour," when he does not have information himself, "will enquire [of others] so considerately, and so methodically of the particuler posessour, as he will enter into the very depth of the knowledge . . . and when he hath done so, handle it better, and more for the common good, then the private professour can, for all his cunning in all his particuler: Nay he will direct him in the vse, which enformed him in the skill" (203–4).

59. John Dury, *The Reformed Librarie-Keeper*, 4.

60. Tanner MS 79, fols. 29–30.

61. Printed in W. B. Devereux, *Lives and Letters of the Devereux, Earls of Essex,* I:322–30. Both of these letters were formulaic and similar versions circulated among the Essex and Bacon circles. See Norman K. Farmer, Jr., "Fulke Greville's Letter to a Cousin in France and the Problem of Authorship in Cases of Formula Writing," and Vernon F. Snow, "Francis Bacon's Advice to Fulke Greville on Research Techniques." On the lists of recommended authors that these and related letters also contain see Jardine and Grafton, "'Studied for Action,'" 61 and 73–74.

62. Jardine and Grafton, "'Studied for Action,'" 59 n. 93. Cf. Frederick L. Boersma, *An Introduction to Fitzherbert's Abridgement*, and J. D. Cowley, *Bibliography of Abridgments, Digests, Dictionaries, and Indexes of English Law to 1800*. I am grateful to Jeremy Maule for bringing these works to my attention.

63. V. M. Larminie, *The Godly Magistrate: The Private Philosophy and Public Life of Sir John Newdigate, 1571–1610*, 9. Larminie goes on to suggest that "Newdigate the synthesizer of others' work may be quite as interesting as Newdigate the original thinker."

64. Ann M. Blair, "Restaging Jean Bodin: The *Universae Naturae Theatrum* (1596) in Its Cultural Context."

65. Lawrence Ryan, "Richard Hakluyt's Voyage into Aristotle," 75; I owe this reference to David Armitage.

66. Jardine and Grafton, " 'Studied for Action,' " 75.

67. Dury, *The Reformed Librarie-Keeper*, 5.

68. Bacon, "Of Studies," in *The Essays*, 209.

69. Henry Crosse, *Vertues Common-wealth: or the Highway to Honour*, B3r. One had to strive, in the words and after the example of the "royal reader" Louis Le Roy, "through sight, hearing, reading, and practicing, to acquire knowledge with experience, the one of which is imperfect without the other" (epilogue to *Le Sympose de Platon* [Paris, 1558], cited in Werner L. Gundersheimer, *The Life and Works of Louis Le Roy*).

70. I am extremely grateful to Elisabeth Leedham-Green for both taking and talking me through these books.

71. According to the account given in Volume V of the *Cambridge University Library Catalogue of Manuscripts,* the class contains *all* printed books with manuscript notes by scholars known and unknown. Yet none of the books owned by John Dee is included: I have come across forty-four in the library, at least twenty of which have substantial marginalia.

72. In doing so I pass over many extraordinary volumes, such as those by editors (including Paulus Manutius' copy of the 1521 Aldine Suetonius [Adv.d.13.1] and Thomas North's copy of his own translation of Antonio de Guevara's *Dial of Princes* [Adv.d.14.4]), polemicists (including Walter Haddon's vituperative reading of Osorio's attack on the English church [Adv.c.8.1] and Erasmus' elaborations upon his own *Apologiae* against his detractors [Adv.a.5.1]), and collectors (including Jacobus Colius Ortelianus' copy of Adolphus Occo's treatise on the coins of the Roman emperors [Adv.d.3.22]).

73. Cited in Rosemary O'Day, *Education and Society 1500−1800*, 114. D'Ewes spent two years, from 1617 to 1619, as a fellow-commoner at St. John's College, Cambridge.

74. See Anthony Grafton, "Teacher, Text and Pupil in the Renaissance Class-Room" and Grafton and Lisa Jardine, *From Humanism to the Humanities*, chap. 7. See also Ann Blair's treatment of a similar set of notes in "*Ovidius Methodizatus:* The *Metamorphoses* of Ovid in a Sixteenth-Century Paris College.": Blair's earlier version of this discussion, "Lectures on Ovid's *Metamorphoses*," is worth consulting for its illustrations.

75. Grafton and Jardine, *From Humanism to the Humanities*, 166, and Grafton, "Teacher, Text, and Pupil," 45.

76. David McKitterick, ed., *Andrew Perne: Quatercentenary studies*.

77. See, for instance, the commonplace book of Francis Wilford (Cambridge University Library MS Louard 179a) or the "diary" of George Palfrey (Sidney Sussex College uncatalogued manuscript, on microfilm in Cambridge University Library).

Palfrey's notebook contains a remarkably thorough digest of Jacopo Zabarella's commentaries on Aristotle's *Physics*. Summarizing Zabarella chapter by chapter, and highlighting the contours of the argument with marginal keys (e.g., "Dubium," "Resp.," "Arg.," and "Obiect."), Palfrey's notebook stored a compendium of Aristotelian natural philosophy.

78. Bodleian Library MS Lat. Misc. e 114, fol. 175v; reproduced as Plate XVIIb. in James K. McConica, ed., *The History of the University of Oxford*, vol. 3. These principles are heavily biased toward Ciceronian and Erasmian "copia": they include "elegant phrases" and "learned and weighty *sententiae*."

79. *Statuta Academiae Cantabrigiensis*, 146-47 ("Tempora lectionum et libri praelegendi") and 228 ("De temporibus lectionum et libris praelegendis"). Also see Annabel Patterson, *Hermogenes and the Renaissance*.

80. Dodington uses the symbols "ˆ," "*," and "#." In Adv.b.23.1 (Thomas Wilson and John Rudd's copy of the *Nicomachean Ethics*) the annotator uses the more common practice of sequential numbers.

81. On a blank leaf at the end of the prefatory matter (sig. B4v) the volume is signed "Johannes Rudd hunc librum possidet. teste pecunia / Johannes Rudd hunc librum possidet" and, in Wilson's hand, "John Rudd did me know, / But Tho: Willsonᵈdoth me now owe." Rudd had been a scholar at Caius in 1583-84, but migrated to St. John's in 1584, thus overlapping with Wilson for a short time. It is, of course, possible that the two knew each other—and that the book changed hands—before 1584.

82. There are, in fact, annotations in several hands, but none of them seems to match the elder Wilson's.

83. The second John Bradley is the most likely candidate. The book is also signed by "John Fuliabe," whom I have not been able to trace.

84. For the dates and the details see Isaac Walton's biography in Rev. John Keble, ed., *The Works of Mr. Richard Hooker*.

85. See, for instance, W. D. J. Cargill Thompson, "The Philosopher of the 'Politic Society': Richard Hooker as a Political Thinker," in W. Speed Hill, ed., *Studies in Richard Hooker*.

86. This is the title of a study by Peter Munz.

87. Francis Wilford's commonplace book (mentioned above) also contains such a glossary, although it does not seem to be in his hand. These glossaries are a rich and virtually untapped source for students of historical linguistics and semantics.

88. See Anthony Grafton, "Renaissance Readers and Ancient Texts: Comments on Some Commentaries."

89. They are catalogued in H. Coxe, ed., *Catalogi Codicum Manuscriptorum Bibliothecae Bodleianae*, vol. I, 823-50.

90. Mark Pattison, *Isaac Casaubon, 1559-1614*, 428.

91. This habit is easily observed on the title page of his *Opera Omnia* of Tacitus (Adv.d.3.14).

92. On the similar annotations of Casaubon's friend and colleague Joseph Justus Scaliger—whose *Papyrus* of Melchior Guilandinus is Adv.c.19.1—I defer to the masterful study of Anthony Grafton, *Joseph Scaliger: A Study in the History of Classical Scholarship*.

93. Robert Sidney's copy of the same text, which is heavily and revealingly annotated, is preserved in the British Library [C. 142. e. 13].

94. It was later owned by William Juxon, archbishop of Canterbury from 1660 to 1663, but the notes seem to be in Latewar's hand.

95. See Charles B. Schmitt, *Cicero Scepticus*, 76–77.

96. Lorkin proceeded M.A. (1555) and M.D. (1560) while at Peterhouse and became the Regius Professor of Physic from 1564 to 1591—see the entry in *Alumni Cantabrigiensis*.

97. According to Walter Ong, the Hippocratic tradition was a foundation of Humanist method: "Since the medical tradition had a practical orientation, it tended to generate the notion of a routine of efficiency and to associate this notion with *methodus*" (*Ramus, Method, and the Decay of Dialogue*, 226). If one way it did so was through the *compendium* or the aphoristic "*ars* (in the Stoic tradition a set of precepts directing some sort of practical activity)" (228) that were its written tradition, Lorkin's collection of Hippocratic aphorisms suggests that the same *methodus* could be achieved through active, annotational reading.

98. Peter Murray Jones has discussed another way in which Lorkin used his books—to record details of two dissections (see "Thomas Lorkin's dissections, 1564/5 and 1566/7").

99. This book is now in the library of Eton College [Fc.2.6]. See Vivian Nutton, "'Prisci dissectionum professores': Greek Texts and Renaissance Anatomists," especially 118ff. This text and the one in the Adv. collection are the subjects of Nutton's remarkable study, *John Caius and the Manuscripts of Galen*.

100. Nutton, *John Caius*, 4–6.

101. "Addenda Scriptis Hollerij de Morbis internis. Remedia quae punctum margini affixum habent sunt ea quae G. Butlerus ex Authoribus collegit: et partim in suum Hollerium, partim in alios suos libros scripsit. quae vero sine puncto margini affixo notantur, ea sunt quae nos aliunde congessimus."

102. The paleographical evidence supports this interpretation: none of the hands in the margins and in the "addenda," which look like they were acquired later than Butler's would have been, matches his distinctively messy hand.

103. Mary Dewar, *Sir Thomas Smith: A Tudor Intellectual in Office*.

104. Smith was a student at Queens' and not St. John's College, but he nevertheless had extensive contact with Cheke's circle (Winthrop S. Hudson, *The Cambridge Connection and the Elizabethan Settlement of 1559*, 55).

105. Dewar, *Sir Thomas Smith*, 15, 16. One scholar who has not been deterred is Richard Simpson, who is preparing a study of Smith's library and who, along with Warren Boutcher, first introduced me to its treasures. Dewar apparently approached the Queens' library at a time when its librarians were less hospitable than they are now.

106. Ibid., 149–55; cf. Charles Webster, "Alchemical and Paracelsian Medicine," 304. His own skill in these matters is perhaps indicated by Q[ueens'] C[ollege] L[ibrary] D.1.3, Georgius Agricola's *De re metallica*. It is not certain that this was Smith's copy, but if the hand is his, the annotations reveal his practical interests and technical understanding.

107. Webster, "Alchemical and Paracelsian Medicine," 315–16.

108. There are comparable annotations in his copies of Cinus de Sinibuldis' *Lectura super aureo volumine codicis* (G.11.3) and Sebastian Munster's *Horologiographia* (D.20.39), in which he pays special attention to compasses (A4r).

109. Smith's *Digest. vetus. Digestorum, seu Pandectarum Iuris Ciuilis* (Lyon, 1539) and *Institutiones iuris civilis in graecam linguam . . . cura & studio Viglii Zuichemi* (Basle, 1534) are QCL M.2.11 and H.2.20 respectively.

110. Just as watermarks are evidence of printers' paper stock, and therefore assist in considerations of chronology, the inks used in manuscripts and marginalia are evidence of writers' materials and can be used for similar purposes. Allowing for possible uncertainties (e.g., the use of several inks at once, or the use of the same ink at different times), with those writers who use visibly different inks over time it can provide a crude sense of which readings are contemporary with others—if not a sense of when they were written. See Luigi Michelini Tocci, *In Officina Erasmi*, 32 n. 76.

111. In some instances, Smith used this blank "parchment" to describe the nature of the passage. In a scroll bracket in his copy of Claudius Cantiunculus' *Topica* (QCL 11.2.25) he wrote "Bvdaea Lex" (I1r–v).

112. J. W. Binns, *Intellectual Culture in Elizabethan and Jacobean England*, 337. Given the Continental contacts of the Cheke circle (both teachers and students) it is not unlikely that many of their scholarly techniques—including their reading practices—were learned from their Continental Humanist counterparts.

113. Dewar, *Sir Thomas Smith*, passim; citation from 48; the resulting report was published by Somerset as *An Epitome of the Title that the King's Majesty of England hath to the Sovereignty of Scotland*.

114. Cited in Dewar, *Sir Thomas Smith*, 54, 112.

115. Smith's marginalia give the impression of a reader who read straight through a book, almost always annotating the beginning and end of a text, but clearly lacking the interest (in both of its senses) to sustain attention throughout.

116. As we shall see, Dee's margins also contain many sketches; before seeing the parallel practice in Smith, I was reluctant to attribute them to Dee.

FOUR. DEE'S MARGINALIA

1. See the warnings of Clulee in *John Dee's Natural Philosophy*, 12–13; Roberts and Watson, 3.

2. Clulee, *John Dee's Natural Philosophy*, 16.

3. It is impossible to arrive at a precise figure since less than a third of his printed books have been identified. To take the case of his manuscripts—where the survival rate is much higher—volumes with some annotation outnumber those without by roughly three to one. The reckoning is complicated, however, by the fact that surviving volumes have often been identified on the basis of marginalia alone: many unannotated books may well survive, but with no indication that they belonged to Dee.

4. David McPherson, *Ben Jonson's Library and Marginalia: An Annotated Catalogue*; G. R. Batho, "The Library of the 'Wizard' Earl: Henry Percy Ninth Earl of

Northumberland (1564–1632)," 253; Honor McCusker, "Books and Manuscripts Formerly in the Possession of John Bale," 148; Richard L. DeMolen, "The Library of William Camden," 333; and Nicolas K. Kiessling, *The Library of Robert Burton.*

5. Roberts and Watson, 69.

6. For an exhaustive catalogue of marginal marks, both verbal and nonverbal, see Mario DiGregorio's meticulous edition of *Charles Darwin's Marginalia.*

7. Royal College of Physicians Library D14/1, 48b.

8. BL MS Sloane 2327.

9. Many Renaissance readers corrected by hand the printed addenda or corrigenda in their books; but I have not found this practice in Dee's books.

10. Christ Church (Oxford) Library Wb.5.12. Dee had four manuscript copies for comparison.

11. In a Latin manuscript of the *Leges Walliae* [Merton College (Oxford) Library MS 323], "Liberata" is underlined and glossed "Anglice, Liverie in the court so called" (3r). In a collection of alchemical treatises [Corpus Christi College (Oxford) MS 136] the passage "9 dies in loco frigido & humido" is underlined and connected by a line to the bottom of the page, where Dee wrote, "In a cold and moyst place. Note this secret of the cold place" (manuscript unfoliated). And in a French alchemical work (the "Traité de l'oeuvre de la pierre philosophique" [Bodleian, MS Ashmole 1426]) the word "Teston" is used to describe the thickness of a crucible: Dee translated into English measurements, "A Teston thiknes, is about half a quarter of one of these ynches" (16v).

12. On page 4 of an English manuscript of George Ripley [Wellcome Institute Library MS 239] Dee underlined "groweth owt of one Image" and wrote "vna res" in the margin. In the *Opera* of Arnaldus de Villa Nova [Royal College of Physicians Library D89/6, 8c] he discussed the Hebrew root of the alchemical term "Athanor" (133r).

13. New York Society Library No. 188, B2r.

14. Corpus Christi College (Oxford) MS 125. A variation on the translation note is Dee's practice of writing Arabic numerals in the margin next to a number (usually a date) that the text gives in Roman numerals or Latin longhand.

15. Royal College of Physicians Library D125/7, 17d. Dee's heavily annotated copy of Strabo is now Brussels, Bibliothèque Royale, LP3414c (see Roberts and Watson, no. 112, and A. de Smet, "La Réserve précieuse vent d'acquérir un Exemplaire de la Géographie de Strabo, avec annotations Manuscrites de John Dee").

16. Royal College of Physicians D125/13, 17d.

17. See Jardine and Grafton's reconstruction of Harvey's "book-wheel" ("'Studied for Action,'" 49–51). Although there is little evidence to support it, it is probable that the "furniture" of Dee's library included some kind of large reading space (a desk if not a machine), with room for many books and several readers.

18. Gerard Dorn's *Chemisticum Artificium Naturae, Theoricum, & Practicum*—see Roberts and Watson, no. 1524.

19. Bodleian, MS Ashmole 1451, Pt. 2, 4r.

20. See especially the title page and facing flyleaf in his copy of Ptolemy's *Quadripartitum* (Royal College of Physicians Library D18/8, 48e; Roberts and Watson, no. 37). Dee read this text largely for its treatment of divination, and he wrote out relevant passages from Theophrastus, Cicero, Chrysippus, Ovid, and Propertius.

21. BL C.122.bb.35; Roberts and Watson, no. 1078.

22. Christ Church (Oxford) Library Wb.5.12; Roberts and Watson, no. 601.

23. Pomponius Gauricus, *De Sculptura* (Cambridge University Library M*.5.49(D); Roberts and Watson, no. 468).

24. Royal College of Physicians Library D133/6, 19c; Roberts and Watson no. 629. Similar notes appear on the back flyleaves of Albohaly's *De Iudiciis Nativitatum* (Royal College of Physicians Library D48/6, 46f; Roberts and Watson, no. 693). In this case, however, the notes are closely related to the text: they record planetary positions and observations on the weather (during Dee's stay in Louvain in 1548)—thus apparently testing out Albohaly's theories about the interrelations of astrology and meteorology.

25. Royal College of Physicians Library D40/2, 46b; Roberts and Watson, no. 440. The passage after the one I have quoted seems to suggest that Dee's mother had three sons after him, but I have no further information about them.

26. For the rest of this chapter I will only provide references to entries in Roberts and Watson—information about the text and its current location can be found there.

27. No. M25; this gift was also connected in some way to John Stowe.

28. In 1583 this book was no. 79 in his library catalogue. Dee also acquired no. CM37 during his time with Bonner. Cf. no. 569, the gift of Jacques Goupyl, one of Dee's early Parisian associates; no. D7, which came "Ex Dono Antonij Montague . . . Anno 1602. Septemb.19. apud Cowdrey, Ex Bibliotheca eadem"; no. D16, "ex dono magistri Joannis Baptistae Danielis"; no. DM18, part of which he copied "Ex collectionibus Gulielmi Camdeni"; no. DM20, which was sent by (and purchased from) Jacobus Baptista Hardincurtius; and no. DM161, the gift of "Amico suo Integerrimo Magistro Blomefelde."

29. See Ronald Stearne Wilkinson, "The Alchemical Library of John Winthrop, Jr. (1606-1676) and His Descendants in Colonial America, Part IV." There are four Dee-Winthrop books at the New York Society Library. Wilkinson also claimed that three more were held in the library of the New York Academy of Medicine. I have examined these (Abraham Porto Leonis, *De Auro Dialogi Tres;* Vincent Thornes, *Discorso Della Fisica Sublimatione;* and Jean Liebaut, *Quatre Livres des Secrets de Medicine*), and while they all have marginal annotations, none of them has any connection with Dee.

30. My emphasis; see the similar note in no. 1476—which is reproduced in Wilkinson's article.

31. No. 603: this referred, of course, to the editorial annotations rather than to the text proper. Cf. no. M184.

32. No. DM8; the mention of "santulianhos" may connect this "Blasius" to Dee's friend William Herbert of St. Julian's—with whom he exchanged other employees.

33. No. 1623. In no. M84, a text appears with the title "De essentia rerum": in Dee's catalogue entry it is ascribed to "Thomas Aquinas," but on a blank leaf in the text Dee asserted that "S. Thomas de Essentijs rerum" was written by "frater Thomas" and not "Sanctus Thomas" (59v). And in no. DM81, he altered the title on fol. 22v from "Raymundus Lullius" to "Gaufridus Raymundus."

34. Nos. 208, 603, 662, and 1425.

35. Cf. nos. DM48, DM73, M28, M74, M125, M143, M3, M79, M148, 1482, M194, M53, M84, DM113, M196, M27, DM116, DM129, M33, and DM154. Many of these are collections of fragments or obscure works on alchemy or natural philosophy.

36. See no. 1524.

37. Nos. 1570, M113, and DM94.

38. No. M35.

39. Cf. nos. M196 (99v), DM46 (130v), DM73 (37r), M79 (31r), and DM7 (37v).

40. Cf. no. 1570 (B3v), DM1a, in which he continued the corrupted text along the bottom of fol. 114r, and DM90, in which he noted a discrepancy between the layout of his manuscript copy and its source (p. 28).

41. Dee probably had a better copy of the text: see no. M19.

42. Nos. DM60 (on 96v), M166 (on back flyleaf), and M193 (on first folio, although this faded list may refer to chemicals rather than works).

43. Nos. M28 (1v), M36 (2v), and M75 (ii/v).

44. Dee added several items to the list of sources in Petrus Peregrinus' *De Magnete* (no. 662), E3v–F1v. To the list in Pausanias' *De Tota Graecia* (no. 196) he added one name (a1r).

45. In Dominicus Marius Niger's *Geographiae Commentariorum Libri XI* (no. 111) Dee underlined existing entries and added a few new ones. Cf. no. 360.

46. Nos. DM94, M24, and M84.

47. See the opening folios of his *Summa* (no. M26), fol. 1 of his *Communium Naturalium* (no. M27), and fol. 1 of his *Annotationes super Aristotelis Secretum Secretorum* (no. M56–57).

48. See nos. 86, 301, 553, 597, and 868.

49. See nos. 352, DM113, and M33. In a manuscript of Lulliana (no. DM94) Dee wrote out a long note at the bottom of the first folio, in which he listed three recent printed editions of Lull's works along with one manuscript (all of which he had—nos. 1402, 1406, 1407, and M16). This volume has a remarkable provenance, including (besides Dee) two of the most prominent figures in the history of alchemy—George Ripley in the fifteenth century and Denis Duveen in the twentieth.

50. No. 271. At the bottom of this page, Dee wrote out the titles. Cf. no. M128.

51. Nos. 167 and 198.

52. See nos. 111 and 725.

53. No. M33. In DM105, Dee underlined several items in a list of chemicals with their prices, noting, "Mark how dere these Materialls were then" (37v).

54. For a brilliant discussion of the remarkably similar "genealogical culture"

of sixteenth-century Italy, see Robert Bizzocchi, "Culture généalogique dans l'Italie du XVIe siècle" and " 'Familiae Romanae' Antiche e Moderne." Whereas the Italians fashioned their noble genealogies with reference to the ancient Romans, Dee and other Tudor genealogists turned to the ancient Welsh.

55. See especially Thomas Walsingham's *Historia Brevis* (no. 301); also Mattheus Beroaldus' chronicle (no. 86), Matthew of Westminster's *Flores Historiarum* (no. 290), Geoffrey of Monmouth's *Britanniae vtriusque regum* (no. 601), and John Leland's *Genethliacon illustrissimi Eaduerdi principis Cambriae* (no. 597).

56. Cf. Figure 2, Dee's diary, where he drew a comet along the upper margin.

57. On fol. 153v of no. M194 Dee drew a man with a flowing beard—and another on fol. 160v. On fol. 23r of no. M196, a blank leaf, Dee sketched what appears to be a man in a fool's cap. Cf. no. DM116, fol. 83v; M53 (35r); and 119 (p. 591).

58. No. B154. It is conceivable, of course, that another reader was responsible for this drawing. But it bears a striking resemblance to the shield Dee drew in his genealogical roll (BL Cotton Charter XIV, art. 1), and may be a sketch for that more elaborate rendition.

59. They are quite uniform in appearance, generally having a very large, sharp nose, and small, curly lips. At first I was reluctant to attribute these drawings to Dee: they seemed uncharacteristic and even when the brackets were Dee's, the faces could have been added by subsequent readers. But they occur too often in texts that bear only Dee's hand, and they are too systematic to be ascribed to anyone else.

60. Nos. M79, M91, M160, DM90, M53, DM105, M196, M33, and DM131.

61. This phenomenon, like so many others in Dee studies, seems to have precedent in medieval textual traditions. In a manuscript from c. 1280 a bracket in the margin has been turned into a face in profile—possibly a caricature of Chief Justice Thomas Weyland (see the frontispiece to Richard Eales and David Sullivan, eds., *The Political Context of Law*).

62. Nos. M3, M79, DM90, and M53.

63. Roberts and Watson found only one instance of the delta in a manuscript (23): I have found several more.

64. Clulee (*John Dee's Natural Philosophy,* 36–38) and Roberts and Watson (Introduction, Part I) attempt chronological expositions of his acquisitions and reading practices. These have their merits, but are problematic and must yield to the study of different patterns. Dee's habit of annotating texts several times, often much later than the date of acquisition, and the way materials were *stocked* for future use (not to mention the lack of survival of much of the library), render suspect even the broadest chronological developments.

65. Corpus Christi College (Oxford) MS 191; printed in Roberts and Watson as Appendix 2.

66. Bodleian Library MS Ashmole 1486, art. 5.

67. Cf. Roberts and Watson, 6.

68. In no. DM131 Dee wrote a summary note in English, "Note a day to be for one course of the work" (unfoliated). In the same manuscript he paraphrased,

"I.D. For the red erth is the ende of the first work . . . ," and noted, "How the work must be ordred after that it is comme to white." He drew alchemical apparati in nos. DM1a (137r), 1425 (p. 88), DM90 (p. 25), and M33 (33v and 49r). In DM100, which is in Dee's hand, he added a note of adjustment to one of the diagrams: "My invention for the place of the pipe to yssu at, rather then so nere the Vertex. allso this eg [vase] is 5 good fingers from vtside of the vertex to the vtside of the bottom" (16v–cf. the "eggs" on 17r).

69. No. DM90, p. 61. We can sense the excitement with which Dee repeated this revelation at the end of the text ("Annus Philosophicus est Periodus Luminaris minoris Synodica" [A philosophical year is the period of the conjunction of the moon—i.e., one month]), gracing it with his initials, face brackets, and two quotations from Leviticus. In another manuscript (no. DM131) Dee noted that "lapis albis" could be made in "Anno philosophico vno = Mense vulgari" (unfoliated).

70. "Materialia" is divided into "naturalia" (itself divided into two astrological or chemical symbols, one of which is Dee's hieroglyphical monad) and "contra naturam"; "demonstratiua" consists of the colors (e.g., "Nigredo" and "Albedo"); and for "operatiua" Dee lists four chemical processes.

71. Nos. M184 (13v), M79 (4r), 299 (flyleaf, 336v and 342v), 1425 (passim.), DM94 (passim.), and M53 (17v).

72. No. 1425, p. 122. This text also contains an important astronomical note, providing further evidence that Dee grasped (if not embraced) the Copernican cosmology: he underlined "terram moueri circulariter, & terram esse in coelo vnam ex stellis," and wrote, "Terra moueri circulariter &c vt Copernicus fere" (p. 182).

73. "Albertus ante Arnoldum: sed Arnaldus ante Lullium: et Bachon coaetanens erat Alberti, vt apparet ex sua summa ad Clementem, ergo Bachon erat ante Lullium et arnoldum" (334v).

74. He did this primarily by entering his *monas* in the margins of texts to which he felt it belonged—e.g., no. DM81 (3v).

75. See nos. DM48 (79v; Merlin is also mentioned on 32v), M159 (42v and 71), M94 (passim.), M25 (112v, 113v, and 189v), DM35 (136v), 301 (p. 17), and 1087 (B8r).

76. No. M10—most of these occur in item 8, Geraldus Cambrensis' *Descriptio Cambriae*.

77. No. M25, 155v and 151v.

78. The relevant passages in the text are underlined and annotated.

79. Earlier, on p. 351, he noted the distinction between "Eadgiua," "Eadgitha," and "Eadhilda"; and on p. 200 he noted the etymology of "England" itself.

80. On p. 110 Bale mentions a work on an unknown title by Chancellor: Dee supplied, "I.D. Ego, eius gratia anglice librum scripsit, pro supputandis motibus celestibus ex . . . Tabuli Reinholdi. hic liber nondum mihi constat vbi . . . post Chanceleri calamitosam mortem ex Narfragio, in Scotia." And in Ca[ve]ndish's entry (p. 111), Dee crossed out the epithet "philosophus" and corrected the number of books in his work on Euclid.

81. Mercator's work had appeared less than five years earlier—another indication of Dee's ability to keep pace with Continental developments, and particularly those emanating from his old contacts.

82. Many can be traced to dissolved monasteries and are the result of Dee's efforts at tracking down and acquiring spoiled British antiquities. His most extensive haul came from St. Augustine's, Canterbury, where he picked up between twenty-two and twenty-seven volumes—though 80 percent of these are of a scientific nature. See Roberts and Watson, 14–16 and passim.

83. See no. M125.

84. See q5r. On h6r Dee noted a "Chronographorum error" and elsewhere he attended to discussions of calendars, which no doubt informed his 1582 proposal for the Gregorian reform (see r2 following).

85. These show at least a very rudimentary command of Hebrew grammar— see f6r–v.

86. See nos. DM60 (Eutropius and Orosius) and 196 (Pausanias). In a survey of architectural sites by region (no. 903), Dee annotated only the section on Britain. Especially interesting is Dee's copy of David Chytraeus' ancient history crib (no. 1092), in which Dee noted the evidence of "Bruti in Albion," early literary and navigational achievements, and rulers (including Arthur, Maximilian, and Edward VI, whom he called "Rex incomparabilis").

87. He also noted "The proportion of the Valew of Gold and Siluer: at the tyme" (p. 96)—a subject explored by Sir Thomas Smith and Dee in their writings on exchange rates and the value of money. In general, he was interested in the number of ships that the Trojans had available for navigation and for war (see no. 725, pp. 13–14); and also in any mention of "Oceanum Britannicum" (e.g., no. 1311, p. 18), his collection of which he put to use in the *THALLATOKRATIA BRETTANIKI* of 1597.

88. On the collection see Roberts and Watson, 41.

89. Top of CCXIVr: "I.D. Confusion for lak of distinction betwene Suaben and Sueden Land."

90. The few notes are restricted to the commentaries, which were written by Dee's friend and collaborator Federico Commandino. He did have other copies, however, and we can only assume that he digested these more thoroughly.

91. One reading seems to have a direct relationship with Dee's preface and deserves further study. In Avicenna's treatment of "partibus subalternatis scientiae mathematicae" (in no. 395) Dee provided some unusual names for these applied sciences which are not in Avicenna's text and which evoke similar terms found in the preface (e.g., "Menadica, Statica, Organopoietica, and Catoptrica").

92. See Nicholas Jardine, "The Certainty of Mathematics," in Charles B. Schmitt and Quentin Skinner, eds., *The Cambridge History of Renaissance Philosophy,* 693ff.

93. See Enrico Gamba, "Matematici Urbinati del Cinque-Seicento," in Gamba and Vico Montebelli, *Le Scienze a Urbino nel Tardo Rinascimento:* in his discussion, "Le Discipline Matematiche nella società," he wrote, "Un luogo comune presso i nostri autori e l'esaltazione dell'utilità pratica delle Discipline Matematiche" (88).

94. See Clulee, *John Dee's Natural Philosophy*, 56.

95. Robert Westman, "Proof, Poetics, and Patronage," in David C. Lindberg, ed., *Reappraisals of the Scientific Revolution*, 188.

96. These are reviewed in N. Jardine, "The Certainty of Mathematics," 695.

97. Clulee has reviewed the extensive influence of other medieval mathematical writers on Dee, especially Robert Grosseteste (*John Dee's Natural Philosophy*).

98. W. P. D. Wightman, *Science and the Renaissance*, I:100. Cf. N. Jardine, *The Birth of History and Philosophy of Science*, chap. 7 ("The Status of Astronomy").

99. No. 193, B4v; cf. D3r and Q3r.

100. For example, "Speciales operae planetarum" (A2v) and "Virtus eadem stellarum in vniuersitatibus & particularibus" (A7v).

101. Robert S. Westman, "The Astronomer's Role," 120.

102. Wightman, *Science and the Renaissance*, 100.

103. Such notes are also to be found on the flyleaves of his copy of Galeottus Martius' *De doctrina promiscua* (no. 1235)—see Roberts and Watson, 98.

104. See, for instance, no. M31, passim.

105. This book was one of Dee's earliest acquisitions and, while several of his hands are in evidence, most of the annotations seem to be in an italic that I have tentatively identified with the 1540s and 1550s. He dated his readings October 25th 1545, Christmas Eve 1546, September 6th 1547 at 1:00, and November 8th 1548. One of these readings took place during a visit to Louvain: he must have placed a high value on this book and its notes since it and its companion volume were massive folios.

106. I cite H. Rackham's translation in the Loeb Classical Library edition, 207 and 209.

107. The cosmographers and missionaries of Dee's age (particularly the Jesuits) cited Posidonius as a source of precisely this kind of providence. See F. de Dainville, *Les Jésuites et L'éducation de la Société Française: I. La Géographie des Humanistes*, 154. See also Michael T. Ryan, "The Diffusion of Science and the Conversion of the Gentiles in the Seventeenth Century," in Richard T. Bienvenu and Mordechai Feingold, *In the Presence of the Past*.

FIVE. DEE'S POLITICAL SCIENCE

1. E. G. R. Taylor considered many of Dee's navigational manuscripts; Nicholas H. Clulee discussed Dee's angelic conversations; and Graham Yewbrey looked in detail at the *Brytannicae Reipublicae Synopsis* and the "Brief Remembrance." I. R. F. Calder gave the most extensive treatment of the manuscript works, but molded them to fit his thesis of Dee's Neoplatonism.

2. Chapter VI of Dee's "Compendious Rehearsall." There is an almost identical list in his *Letter . . . apologeticall*, A4v–B2r. A very early version can be found in Dee's dedicatory epistle to Mercator in his *Propaedeumata aphoristica* (1558). This "catalogue," which had been requested by Mercator, contains several works not found in the later lists.

3. Frances Yates, *The Occult Philosophy in the Elizabethan Age*, 86.

4. Aside from those I discuss below, several geometrical and trigonometrical works that seem to answer to descriptions in the "Compendious Rehearsall" survive (at least in part) in BL MS Cotton Vitellius C. VII.

5. Graham Yewbrey, "A Redated Manuscript of John Dee," 249.

6. *Dictionary of Welsh Biography Down to 1940*, 166. For a more general account of Renaissance "manuscript exclusion" see Paul Oskar Kristeller, "In Search of Renaissance Manuscripts."

7. See Harold Love's "Scribal Publication in Seventeenth-Century England."

8. There were many reasons why occult or scientific works would remain in manuscript, and Marie Boas Hall is off the mark when she suggests that Dee was reluctant to publish because this knowledge "should only be imparted to the initiate" ("Science," 476). Ironically, the work for which Dee claimed the most limited—initiated—readership was the *Monas hieroglyphica*, which was among the four that he did publish.

9. French (*John Dee*, 7) and Clulee (*John Dee's Natural Philosophy*, 178 and 288 n. 6) touch on this episode, but Dee scholars have still to assess the content and context of Dee's proposal. For the fullest account of Dee's contribution and its background see J. D. North, "The Western Calendar . . . Four Centuries of Discontent," esp. 102–5. It is ironic, given the nature of the debate, that some confusion has crept into the date of Dee's own proposal: it has been placed in both 1582 and 1583—a confusion that cannot be entirely explained away by the discrepancies between Old Style and New Style dating.

10. There are three copies in the Bodleian Library: MSS Ashmole 1789, fols. 1–40, Smith 35, art. 2, and Ashmole 179, art. 7. The first of these is by far the fullest and most elaborate (not to mention attractive) production. Corpus Christi College (Oxford) MS 254 also contains two copies (in the hands of Dee and Brian Twyne) of parts of the proposal.

11. MS Ashmole 1789, fol. 1r.

12. BL MS Lansdowne 39, item 14 (fol. 28r); see also MS Lansdowne 109, item 27.

13. Fol. 182r.

14. This may well be the earliest evidence of plans for the voyages that John Davis would launch in search of the Northwest Passage from 1585 to 1587: see Kenneth R. Andrews, *Trade, Plunder and Settlement*, 179ff., and my discussion below in Chapter 7.

15. On Dee as antiquary see French, *John Dee*, chap. 8—the most original and reliable chapter in the work.

16. On the collectors and their patrons see May McKisack, *Medieval History in the Tudor Age*, chap. 3. Under Queen Elizabeth, the "Society of Antiquaries" received its charter: see McKisack, chap. 7, and Joan Evans, *A History of the Society of Antiquaries*. The most suggestive accounts of the contexts of Tudor antiquarianism are Kevin Sharpe, *Sir Robert Cotton*, esp. chap. 1; Arthur Ferguson, *Clio Unbound: Perception of the Social and Cultural Past in Renaissance England*, esp. chaps. 4 and 8; and Stan A. E. Mendyk, *'Speculum Britanniae': Regional Study, Antiquarianism, and Science in Britain to 1700*. T. D. Kendrick's

British Antiquity, F. J. Levy's *Tudor Historical Thought*, and F. Smith Fussner's *The Historical Revolution: English Historical Writing and Thought 1580–1640* are still deservedly classics.

17. Joseph M. Levine, *Humanism and History*, 81; cf. McKisack, *Medieval History*, chap. 1. Nicholas Brigham must also be accounted a pioneer: his library was cited as a source for Bale's *Index Brittaniae Scriptorum* seventy-two times (see James Alsop, "Nicholas Brigham [d. 1558], Scholar, Antiquary, and Crown Servant," 65).

18. A copy in Elias Ashmole's hand is Bodleian MS Ashmole 1788, fols. 70–76.

19. Printed in Thomas Smith, ed., *V. Cl. Gulielmi Camdeni, et illustrium virorum ad G. Camdenum Epistolae*, 38.

20. BL MS Harley 374, art. 11; reproduced in French, *John Dee*, as Plate 16.

21. For all of these contacts see French, *John Dee*, 203ff.—although he exaggerates some details.

22. This can perhaps be attributed to his absence from England during its formative years. It is also possible that his social profile was considered unfavorable (he was neither a lawyer nor a landed gentleman, as were virtually all members of the society).

23. BL MS Harley 473. For Dee's itinerary and a brief discussion see French, *John Dee*, 201–2. As French claims, paleographical evidence points to Dee's authorship; but cf. F. Noble, "The Identification of Dr. John Dee as the Author of Harleian MS 473 Based on Its Radnorshire References," 40–42.

24. The title is in the hand of Sir Simonds D'Ewes, who acquired some of Dee's writings and many volumes from his library. On Lambard's *Perambulation of Kent*, see Retha M. Warnicke, *William Lambarde: Elizabethan Antiquary, 1536–1601;* a less detailed but more suggestive account is James D. Alsop and Wesley M. Stevens, "William Lambarde and the Elizabethan Polity," 231–65.

25. French, *John Dee*, 202.

26. An interesting question—though one that is well beyond my scope—is the relation of textual and physical artifacts. We have only begun to understand what is represented by the notebooks of (for instance) Daniel Rogers and Robert Cotton, which are bursting with visual records of ancient monuments and inscriptions. The mimetic, philosophical, and political questions become even more challenging when we shift to the Continent, where the extraordinary collector Cassiano dal Pozzo attempted to create a "Paper Museum"—a comprehensive two-dimensional record of the three-dimensional natural and historical world (see the special issues of *Quaderni Puteani*, released to coincide with the British Museum's 1993 exhibition).

27. Levine, *Humanism and History*, 93.

28. This circle included Stephen Bat[e]man, secretary and author of artistic and theological works. A copy of Dee's *General and Rare Memorials* in his hand survives in the Bodleian Library.

29. McKisack, *Medieval History*, 36–38. The Parker circle's marginalia require further study, especially by someone who does not consider manuscript annotation a "deplorable method" (36).

30. BL MS Cotton Vitellius C.IX, fols. 3–57.

31. The 1513 edition printed the text on its own; the 1566 edition was a collection of four medieval chronicles edited by Simon Schardius.

32. One entry reads, "fol: 59a. Linea 4. In Libro Manuscripto sic habet": In Tertia Francorum, in quarta Wandalorum, in quinta Anglorum, &c." (3r). At that place in the 1566 edition the same line is found, but with the countries listed in a different order. The longest entry in this section of the manuscript cites the same folio and refers to "Britanni sive Britones" and "Britannia Oceani Insulas." This crucial passage for Dee's writings on imperial geography is considerably different in the printed text—hence Dee's desire to copy it out at length.

33. See DNB, s.v. John Harpsfield.

34. RCP D128a/2, 18c; Roberts and Watson no. 290.

35. Another historical manuscript that probably associates the two men is BL MS Cotton Domitian IV (Roberts and Watson, M150), which bears Dee's marginalia and "the name of the scribe, Thos. Harpfeld."

36. In this section I again find myself running along very similar lines to those of Mary Thomas Crane in *Framing Authority*.

37. Terence Cave, *The Cornucopian Text*, 76.

38. Neil Hathaway, "Compilatio: From Plagiarism to Compiling," 19, 41, and 44.

39. A. J. Minnis, *Medieval Theory of Authorship*, passim; cf. Pierre Bourdieu, "Reading, Readers, the Literate, Literature," 94–95, and Deborah N. Losse, "From *Auctor* to *Auteur:* Authorization and Appropriation in the Renaissance."

40. In the Renaissance, "derivative" had different, and often far from pejorative, connotations. See, in general, Harold Ogden White, *Plagiarism & Imitation during the English Renaissance*. David Quint, *Origin and Originality in Renaissance Literature*, is also relevant, but see Marian Rothstein's objections regarding historical literature in "Etymology, Genealogy, and the Immutability of Origins."

41. Minnis, *Medieval Theory*, 14, 30–32.

42. Previous readers of the preface have not adequately conveyed the extent of its similarity (and, in some cases, debt) to the Euclidian prologues and commentaries of (to name only the most important) Peña, Clavius, and—perhaps above all—Proclus. (A noteworthy exception is Enrico Rambaldi's essay, "John Dee and Federico Commandino.") For a thoroughly Yatesian account of Dee's preface, see Alice B. McGinty's thesis, "A Preliminary Analysis of John Dee's Preface to the First English Euclid." It is worth noting, in light of my interests in this chapter, that the translator's short preface—which precedes Dee's—recommends not only natural philosophy, moral philosophy, and the mathematical sciences, but also the reading of history: "The reading likewise of histories, conduceth not a little, to the adorning of the soule & minde of man . . . by it are seene and knowen the artes and doinges of infinite wise men gone before vs" (2r).

43. "Compilatio," 42.

44. Levine, *Humanism and History*, 26 and 32.

45. Arthur Hall, cited in G. R. Elton, "Arthur Hall, Lord Burghley and the

Antiquity of Parliament," in *Studies in Tudor and Stuart Politics and Government,* III:270. Flower-picking was a commonplace trope for the collection of valuable materials: see Crane, *Framing Authority,* 58–59.

46. F. Smith Fussner, *Tudor History and the Historians,* 239.

47. BL MS Cotton Vitellius C.VII.

48. Dee often pairs the terms "ancient" and "credible": he clearly held the historical principle that the more ancient the information the greater its credibility—especially when, as in this text, he was engaged with questions of precedent. But it is also possible to pick up a sense of his awareness that the older the information the greater the need for careful scholarship (particularly in terms of its textual transmission).

49. See his assessments of the writings of Aethicus (219v), Julius Caesar Scaliger (223–24), Mercator and Ortelius (265v), and those touching King Arthur (250ff.).

50. In order "to put some curious Antiquary owt of douwt what other Authors I could or did vse beside the forenamed," Dee—ever source-conscious—went on to provide a further bibliography of "Treatises, Advertisements, Epistles, & depositions of sundry Credible persons."

51. Cf. Thomas Norton, in the introduction to his translation of the *Orations of Arsanes agaynst Philip the trecherous kyng of Macedone* (London, 1560?): ". . . by hearing of other or readyng of bookes hee learneth the state of times past, the doyngs of men, their counsels, their governance, and lastly their successes. By beholding these, as in a glasse, he discerneth and iudgeth rightly of thinges present, and foreseeth wisely of thinges to come" (*3r).

52. Myron Gilmone, "The Renaissance Conception of the Lessons of History," in *Humanists and Jurists,* 20.

53. Norton, *Orations of Arsanes,* *2r–v.

54. Ferguson, *Clio Unbound,* 88. Cf. 424 (on the practical nature of English Humanism) and, on "commonwealth literature" in general, his earlier study, *The Articulate Citizen and the English Renaissance;* also Joseph M. Levine, Kevin Sharpe, and Philip Styles, "Politics and Historical Research in the Early Seventeenth Century," in Fox, *English Historical Scholarship in the Sixteenth and Seventeenth Centuries.*

55. Alsop and Stevens, "Nicholas Brigham," 236. Cf. Stuart Piggott, "Antiquarian Thought in the Sixteenth and Seventeenth Centuries," 98.

56. See especially James K. McConica, *English Humanists and Reformation Politics;* also McKisack, *Medieval History* (on Parker's circle), Ferguson, *Clio Unbound* (chaps. 5 and 6), and Jan van Dorsten, *Poets, Patrons and Professors* (on Daniel Rogers's research into church history).

57. Yates, *The Occult Philosophy,* 75.

58. *Brytanici Imperij Limites,* BL Additional MS 59681, p. 57.

SIX. BRYTANNICAE REIPUBLICAE SYNOPSIS

1. British Library, Cotton Charter XIII, art. 39.

2. The manuscript is written in Dee's clear italic hand and is composed of five

sheets or parts of sheets of paper pasted together with a slight overlap. Three horizontal sheets form the left edge and two vertical sheets (probably one cut in half) form the right. The overlap varies in width, but it does not affect the text since the copying took place after the construction of the sheet. From the creases that are still visible the document appears to have been kept in a folded state in an earlier period: it was mounted on a single sheet of linen backing in the British Museum bindery during the nineteenth century. In addition to the text's premeditated distribution on the constructed page, the relative lack of revisions and the use of rubrics suggest that it was a presentation (as opposed to a working) copy. It is the only copy presently known. (I am grateful to Hilton Kelliher of the British Library for his assistance with the manuscript.)

3. It is worth noting at the outset that Dee's *Synopsis* belongs to a *genre* of political advice: not just that high-profile textual tradition which Arthur Ferguson has termed "the literature of analysis and policy" (*The Articulate Citizen and the English Renaissance,* 4), but more specifically, the group of tightly structured critical accounts of the commonwealth that circulated privately among the Privy Council.

4. See Ralph Sargent, *The Life and Lyrics of Sir Edward Dyer.*

5. E.g., Clulee, *John Dee's Natural Philosophy,* 185, and Yewbrey, "John Dee and the 'Sidney Group,' " chap. 10.

6. Taylor and Calder seem to have believed that one of these manuscripts, the "Atlanticall Discourses" of 1566–68, was identical to the *Synopsis* (see Clulee, *John Dee's Natural Philosophy,* 289 n. 20). Both title and date suggest, however, that it contained Dee's first contributions to the push for a Northwest Passage discovery and was rather related to his maritime writings of 1576–80. Dyer became one of the leading patrons of navigational enterprise: for John Frampton's dedication of Marco Polo's Book (1579) and Hakluyt's praise in the Preface to the *Principal Navigations* (1589) see Taylor, *Tudor Geography,* 255.

7. Dyer himself took an active interest in astrochemical theories and practices: an alchemical treatise entitled "The Epitome of the Treasure of all welth" [Bodleian Library, MS Ashmole 1419, item 4] has been attributed to him. And he was in close contact with Dee and Kelley during their stay in Prague: in 1589 he was sent over to negotiate the release of the imprisoned Kelley and bring him (and, more important, his alchemical tincture) back to England, where the crown was desperately seeking ways to pay off debts from the previous year's military engagements.

8. Furthermore, by 1592 the manuscript had most likely been out of Dee's hands for some time, and was probably unavailable for double-checking.

9. Clulee, *John Dee's Natural Philosophy,* 273; cf. Yewbrey, "John Dee and the 'Sidney Group,' " 42–44.

10. This is written in a large italic hand. Next to it, in a small secretary hand, is written "Brytish Monarchy." This may serve to specify the "kingdome" in question, although that seems rather obvious given the situation. More intriguing is the possibility that it somehow relates the *Synopsis* to the *General and Rare Memorials,* the running title of which is "The Brytish Monarchie." In that text he proclaimed that his work was "vndertaken chiefly, for the Aduancement of the

wonderfull Veritie Philosophicall: And also, for the State Publik of this BRYT-ISH MONARCHIE, to become florishing, in HONOR, WEALTH, and STRENGTH . . ." (△4v).

11. According to French (*John Dee*), this was Dee's motto; cf. British Library MS Additional 19065, fol. 43. It is more likely an appropriate tag from Cicero's *De officiis,* the third book of which is concerned with precisely this issue.

12. There are two points of particular interest in this table. First, the numbers that accompany each region are not sequential and perhaps rank them in order of importance or volume. Second, Dee included as number 7 "Cambalu" and "Quinsai," the chief cities of Cathay (which Dee wrote and then deleted). This was the only region with which trade had not been established, and Dee campaigned vigorously in the following years to initiate it.

13. C. H. Wilson, "Trade, Society and the State," 499.

14. Ibid., 575.

15. Tawney and Power, eds., *Tudor Economic Documents,* III:216.

16. Ibid., 223, 224-25; compare on this point and others Cecil's *Memorandum . . . on the Export Trade in Cloth and Wool (Tudor Economic Documents,* I:45-47). Both Dee and Leake presumably found a legal precedent for the setting of seals on cloth in a statute of 1536 (27 Henry VIII c. 12.) which made cloth marks obligatory. The whole matter of "the searching of cloths" is fully discussed by G. D. Ramsay in *The English Woollen Industry, 1500-1750,* 45-47.

17. Ramsay, *The English Woollen Industry,* 69-70.

18. Christopher Clay, *Economic Expansion and Social Change,* II:13.

19. P. J. Bowden, *The Wool Trade in Tudor and Stuart England,* 160-64; cf. Ramsay, *English Woollen Industry,* 19-21.

20. Indeed, next to a description of Antwerp in Lodovico Guicciardini's *Descriptio Germaniae Inferioris* (Royal College of Physicians Library 125/13, 17d; Roberts and Watson no. 64), Dee admitted that Antwerp was the "Emporium Totius Europae" (C1v).

21. Ramsay, *English Woollen Industry,* 42. Cf. Ramsay's more recent work, *The Queen's Merchants and the Revolt of the Netherlands.*

22. Calder noted (Ch. 8) that Dee penned a short manuscript tract on the rules of the exchange of money in 1578: see *Historical Manuscripts Commission,* Appendix to 7th Report (the MSS of W. M. Molyneux), 632.

23. I cite E. Lamond's edition, 32-33.

24. Cf. Peter H. Ramsey, ed., *The Price Revolution in Sixteenth-Century England,* esp. 5ff.

25. This tag probably derives from Seneca's essay *De vita beata.*

26. Yewbrey, "John Dee and the 'Sydney Group,'" passim.

27. Quentin Skinner, *The Foundations of Modern Political Thought,* I:229. The cardinal virtues were employed, interestingly, in a poem by Dee's student Maurice Kyffin. In *The Blessednes of Brytaine,* written in 1588 in celebration of the queen's Accession Day, Kyffin called Elizabeth a "Large Light of *Sov'raigne Seat,* / Whose *Iustice, Prudence, Temprance, Fortitude,* / Ingrafted yong, are grown foorth spreading Great, / Throughout the world, mong Nations wise & rude" (A3v).

28. C. A. L. Jarrott, "The English Humanists' Use of Cicero's *De Officiis* in their Evaluation of Active and Contemplative Life," and Hans Baron, "Cicero and the Roman Civic Spirit in the Middle Ages and Early Renaissance."

29. Jarrott mentions Dee (citing his "Mathematicall Praeface") as well as, among others, Thomas Digges, Robert Recorde, and William Cunningham ("English Humanists' Use of Cicero").

30. "Compendious Rehearsall," 7.

31. The passage is found on a1v, where there is a printed marginal note reading, simply, "Iustice."

32. Michael Oppenheim, *A History of the Administration of the Royal Navy*, I:118 and 124. Dee's recommendations were spelled out at greater length in the *General and Rare Memorials*.

33. Walter Ong, *Ramus, Method, and the Decay of Dialogue*, 199.

34. In the *General and Rare Memorials* Dee calls himself "the Methodicall Author" (B1v).

35. These descriptions are from, respectively, Lisa Jardine, *Francis Bacon: Discovery and the Art of Discourse*, 46, and Jill Kraye, "Moral Philosophy," in Charles B. Schmitt and Quentin Skinner, eds., *The Cambridge History of Renaissance Philosophy*, 329.

36. Jardine, *Francis Bacon*, 63.

37. Ong, *Ramus*, 202.

38. While the Aristotelian strains in Dee's intellectual approach are un-(dis)missable, he clearly subscribed to Ramist innovations. A recent discussion by E. J. Ashworth offers a useful suggestion why, in the *Synopsis*, Dee would have favored Ramist techniques over traditional Aristotelian (or, for that matter, Platonic) ones: "Ramus emphasized that his Topics are more useful and more natural than Aristotle's Ten Categories. *If we are to discuss war, peace or the state*, it is no use to think in terms of the category of substance. Instead we must appeal to such topics as cause, event, and opposite" ("Logic in Late Sixteenth-Century England: Humanist Dialectic and the New Aristotelianism," 233 [my emphasis]).

39. "Humanist Logic," in Schmitt and Skinner, eds., *The Cambridge History of Renaissance Philosophy*, 186.

40. Ong, *Ramus*, 245. For a more comprehensive treatment of "method" in Ramus' works see Book I of Nelly Bruyère, *Méthode et Dialectique dans l'Oeuvre de La Ramée*.

41. Jardine, "Humanist Logic," 186.

42. Charles Gibbon prefaced his *Remedie of Reason* (1589)—which consisted of 292 aphoristic lessons in dichotomous form—with an extensive *apologia*, since he knew that "there bee many that will vse obiections against the . . . forme of this treatise; because no Arte hath reduced all things (and rightly) to *Dicotomies*" (A3v).

43. Jardine, *Francis Bacon*, 170, 45.

44. They also help to explain why this form was not used by Dee in his better-known works, which were of a more speculative nature (usually into the "area of natural knowledge"). This also suggests that it is because Dee's writings on

"civil business" are generally ignored that his utilizations of dialectic methods seem so strange.

45. Jardine, *Francis Bacon*, 171.

46. Ibid., 169.

47. Walter Ong, *Orality and Literacy*, 177.

48. This could be called "Ong's paradox": despite his call for an attention to specificity and differentiation, Ong clearly subscribes to a "media model" himself and to that universalist model of literacy and orality that Ruth Finnegan has critically labeled "the great divide theory"—see her collection of essays, *Literacy and Orality: Studies in the Technology of Communication.*

49. Ong, "Writing Is a Technology that Restructures Thought," in G. Baumann, ed., *The Written Word*, 48 and 30. For an article that recasts Ong's dictum into a question, see Roy Harris, "How Does Writing Restructure Thought?"

50. D. F. McKenzie, *Bibliography and the Sociology of Texts*, 6–7. The ideological dangers of the media model, which is simultaneously repudiated and co-opted by Ong, are suggestively pictured by Michel de Certeau: "Consumption . . . takes on the appearance of something done by sheep progressively immobilised and 'handled' as a result of the growing mobility of the media as they conquer space"; this is "the ideology of consumption-as-a-receptacle" (*The Practice of Everyday Life*, 165 and 167). Finnegan has also forcefully questioned what she calls the "technological deterministic thesis" (*Literary and Orality*, 37–44; 159–74) found in Ong and—perhaps its source—Marshall McLuhan.

51. Ong, "Writing Is a Technology," 31.

52. Gerd Baumann, *The Written Word: Literacy in Transition*, 16.

53. Brian Street, *Literacy in Theory and Practice*, 1. For a more specific critique of Ong, see Street's essay, "Walter Ong on Literacy," 2–15.

54. Yewbrey, "John Dee and the 'Sidney Group,'" 20 and 19. In the Neoplatonic bent of his "political philosophy" and the prophetic bent of his "religious philosophy," Yewbrey reveals the extent of his debt to Frances Yates.

55. Cicero, *De officiis*, I:153.

56. See Jarrott, "English Humanists' Use of Cicero's *De Officiis*," 10.

57. There is some confusion in Cicero's own account: in the passage cited he simultaneously accords highest virtue to "duties derived from wisdom" and "duties derived from the social instinct" (see the editor's note).

58. For an idea of the complexities involved see Eugene F. Rice, Jr., *The Renaissance Idea of Wisdom*, esp. 93ff.

59. The place of wisdom in Dee's other writings is the subject of chaps. 4–6, of Yewbrey, "John Dee and the 'Sidney Group.'"

60. Here Dee follows the conventions of Tudor commonwealth literature in preserving the status quo.

61. Yewbrey, "John Dee and the 'Sidney Group,'" 53.

62. Dee's analyses of foreign policy are confusingly (but typically) varied: his religious and political ideologies shifted according to the interests he was serving. Thus, at some times he appears to argue for Protestant interventionism; at others a patriotic isolationism; and at still others to proffer a vision of a reformed Europe undivided by national and religious boundaries.

63. A. A. Long and D. N. Sedley refer to "the Stoics' penchant for the expression 'citizen of the world' " and cite a resonant passage from the *Discourses* of Epictetus: "Furthermore you are a citizen of the world and a part of it, not one of the underlings but one of the foremost constituents. For you are capable of attending to the divine government and of calculating its consequences. What then is a citizen's profession? To regard nothing as of private interest, to deliberate about nothing as though one were cut off [i.e., from the whole] . . ." (*The Hellenistic Philosophers*, 1:364).

64. Yewbrey, "John Dee and the 'Sidney Group,' " 21. A major shortcoming of the Yatesian thesis regarding Dee's religious philosophy and prophetic role is its failure to specify the nature, in precise and practical terms, of this "universal reformation."

65. See E. Vernon Arnold, *Roman Stoicism*, 274-75.

66. William Bouwsma, *Concordia Mundi: The Career and Thought of Guillaume Postel*, 130.

67. RCP D144/14, 21b, d5r.

68. See Brendan Bradshaw, "Transalpine Humanism," and Ferguson, *The Articulate Citizen*.

69. W. R. D. Jones, *The Tudor Commonwealth*, 2.

70. G. R. Elton, "Reform and the 'Commonwealth-Men' of Edward VI's Reign," 38. We must, however, avoid an exaggeration of Dee's originality and—even more so—of his agency. His "critique" would not directly influence reform: it would inform potential reformers. And it was not expressed in innovative terms, but those plainly recognizable by his audience.

71. Jones, *The Tudor Commonwealth*, 42, 217, 219.

72. On the tradition of historiographical celebration see Christopher Haigh's introduction to *The Reign of Queen Elizabeth I*.

73. Jones, *The Tudor Commonwealth*, 218.

SEVEN. "THIS BRITISH DISCOVERY AND RECOVERY ENTERPRISE"

1. A. de Smet, "John Dee et sa place dans l'histoire de la cartographie."

2. I borrow the subtitle to Kenneth Andrews's *Trade, Plunder and Settlement*.

3. See, however, Bruce Henry, "John Dee, Humphrey Llwyd, and the Name 'British Empire.' "

4. G. J. Marcus, *A Naval History of England, Vol. I: The Formative Centuries*, chap. 3, "The Age of Expansion," 52.

5. Gwyn Williams, "Welsh Wizard and British Empire," 6.

6. See Yates, *The Occult Philosophy*, 80ff.

7. French, *John Dee*, 180. This is a common assumption in the literature on Dee's imperialism and seems, ironically, to have originated with Taylor. I have not found any evidence for its association with Dee's imperial program.

8. See Marion Leathers Kuntz, "Voyages to the East and Their Meaning in the Thought of Guillaume Postel."

9. Marie-Madeleine Martinet, "Voyages de Découverte et Histoire des Civil-

isations dans L'Angleterre de la Renaissance: De la Monarchie Maritime de Dee à la Quête de L'Eldorado par Ralegh."

10. Charles Merbury, *A Briefe Discourse of Royall Monarchie,* a loose translation of Bodin's *Six Books of a Commonweal* (A2v; my emphasis). Merbury was an English diplomat who had studied at Oxford and served in the household of the lord chamberlain (see the *DNB*).

11. *General and Rare Memorials,* B1v (my emphasis).

12. Ibid., A2r.

13. J. H. Parry, *The Age of Reconnaissance.*

14. Jonathan Haynes, *The Humanist as Traveler;* A. Dupront, "Espace et Humanisme."

15. F. Smith Fussner, *Tudor History and the Historians,* chap. 5 ("Reconnaissance: Tudor Writers and the Expansion of History") passim.

16. A. F. McC. Madden, "1066, 1776 and All That: The Relevance of English Medieval Experience of 'Empire' to Later Imperial Constitutional Issues," 9.

17. *General and Rare Memorials,* A2r.

18. Richard Schoeck, "Renaissance Guides to Renaissance Learning," 241. Cf. Anthony Grafton, *New Worlds, Ancient Texts: The Power of Tradition and the Shock of Discovery.*

19. John Parker, "Samuel Purchas, Spokesman for Empire," 47.

20. Cf. Michel Korinman, "Simon Grynaeus et le 'Novus Orbis': Les Pouvoirs d'une Collection."

21. See Jeffrey Knapp, *An Empire Nowhere: England, America, and Literature from "Utopia" to "The Tempest,"* and Michael Foss, *Undreamed Shores: England's Wasted Empire in America.*

22. Finished in August 1576 and printed in September 1577. Dee's holograph manuscript is preserved in the Bodleian Library (MS Ashmole 1789) and, although there is a facsimile of the printed text, a modern edition—with annotations and collations of manuscript variants—is sorely needed.

23. On this label see French, *John Dee,* 182–86, and Roy Strong, *Gloriana,* 92ff.

24. Dee's sketch for the image is reproduced in French, *John Dee* (plate 14). The classic description of the printed title page is Joseph Ames, *Typographical Antiquities,* I:660–62; a more recent discussion is Margery Corbett and Ronald Lightbown, *The Comely Frontispiece: The Emblematic Title-Page in England 1550–1660,* 49–58. The text owed its lavish production to England's finest printer (on whom see C. L. Oastler, *John Day: The Elizabethan Printer*).

25. Dee uses the term "Monarchie" in a general and loose way, to signify the government or the nation as a whole.

26. See David Gwyn, "John Dee's *Arte of Navigation.*"

27. These tables are now lost, but those printed in Appendix 1 to Taylor's edition of Bourne (*A Regiment for the Sea and Other Writings on Navigation*) may account for some of them. Taylor sheds further light on them and on Dee's invention (which produced more accurate navigational data for the northern regions in particular) in her article, "John Dee and the Nautical Triangle, 1575."

28. A badly burned copy of this manuscript is BL MS Cotton Vitellius C. VII, fols. 26–269, and it is the subject of the next section in this chapter.

29. R. J. Roberts, "John Dee's Corrections to His 'Art of Navigation' "; Clulee, *John Dee's Natural Philosophy*, 195.

30. The "Mechanicien" and the "vnknown Freend," as outlined in the diagram which opens the "Brief Note Scholasticall," both refer to Dee himself.

31. Alice G. Vines, *Neither Fire Nor Steel: Sir Christopher Hatton*, 47. An entry in Dee's diary records that he had an audience with Hatton at Windsor the day he was knighted (1 December).

32. In the 1580s and 1590s Hatton was to become a frequent recipient of dedicatory epistles in works on discovery and navigation. Dee's was (to my knowledge) the first such dedication.

33. In fact, every collation formula I have seen has been slightly off in one way or another. Roberts's version in "John Dee's Correction" (followed by Gwyn in "John Dee's *Arte*") comes closest:

$$\triangle^4 (\triangle_1 + \chi_1, \pm \triangle_3, 4) \, \epsilon^4 \, \epsilon^{*4} \, A^4 \, (\pm A_2) \, B–K^4 \, \underline{L}_2 \, (\pm \underline{L}_2).$$

The only problem is that the interpolation in the "$\triangle$" gathering was originally printed with the "L" gathering (which, then, consists of four leaves—the "Brief Note," the Verse Epistle, the Coat of Arms, and a blank leaf). In other words, all of the additional "Hatton material" was printed together, and then rearranged. The evidence for this is the "perfect" copy in Trinity College, Cambridge, which retains the original "L" grouping.

34. Christopher Clay, *Economic Expansion and Social Change*, II:222–24.

35. Ibid., II:216.

36. Herbert Richmond, *The Navy as an Instrument of Policy 1558–1727*, 8 and chap. 1 passim. On the diffuse "sea war" waged during these decades, see Kenneth Andrews, *Elizabethan Privateering*.

37. The Tudor experience is best described by David Loades in *The Tudor Navy*; for the Stuart period, see B. W. Quintrell, "Charles I and His Navy in the 1630s"; Andrew Thrush, "Naval Finance and the Origins and Development of Ship Money"; and Bernard Capp, *Cromwell's Navy*.

38. G. R. Elton, "Parliament," in Christopher Haigh, ed. *The Reign of Elizabeth I*, 92.

39. See chaps. 5 and 6 in Ada Haeseler Lewis, "A Study of Elizabethan Ship Money 1588–1603." The best general accounts are Roger Schofield, "Taxation and the Political Limits of the Tudor State," and J. D. Alsop, "The Theory and Practice of Tudor Taxation."

40. Lewis, "A Study of Elizabethan Ship Money," 63.

41. E.g., Penry Williams, "The Crown and the Counties," in Haigh, *The Reign of Elizabeth I*, 132. By the last decade of her rule, Elizabeth no longer bothered to look outside London for assistance with shipping, while the capital was taxed eight times (Lewis, "A Study of Elizabethan Ship Money," 72–73).

42. Williams, "The Crown and the Counties."

43. This is a complicated and classic issue of the early modern agricultural economy that is thoroughly discussed by Joan Thirsk in "Enclosing and Engrossing," in *The Agrarian History of England and Wales*, Vol. IV; cf. Eric

Kerridge's concise treatment in *Agrarian Problems in the Sixteenth Century and After,* chap. 4.

44. Shaxton "made a respectable fortune out of the fraudulent export of grain and cloth. His sins were only discovered after he had made sufficient gains . . . to be the owner of eight ships and to have worked his way through the *cursus honorum* of the borough to become mayor of Lynn" (N. J. Williams, *The Maritime Trade of the East Anglian Ports, 1550–1590,* 27).

45. Ibid., 29.

46. C. M. Woodhouse, *George Gemistos Plethon: The Last of the Hellenes.*

47. Much of this activity was carried out in official positions never achieved, and probably never sought, by Dee (Gemistos served as a member of the Senate and a high-ranking judge) and resulted in more direct financial support by the government (he was granted land by five separate rulers).

48. Dee's source was William Canter's edition, printed in Antwerp in 1575—suggesting once again how close was his contact with the European book world.

49. H. F. Tozer, "A Byzantine Reformer," 353.

50. Shelf mark C.21.e.12.

51. The entry from Dee's diary is cited in David B. Quinn, *The Voyages and Colonising Enterprises of Sir Humphrey Gilbert,* I:170; Quinn is far and away the best source on Gilbert.

52. Ibid., I:170–80.

53. G. V. Scammel has characterized the essence of the "economic thought of Hakluyt's time": "We should become stronger whilst foreigners would be reduced to penury" (D. B. Quinn, ed., *Hakluyt Handbook,* I:17).

54. Henry Sheers, *An Essay on Ways and Means . . .* (London, 1701), B1r. BL Additional MS 42075 (fols. 24–29) is Sheers's abridgement of Digges's tract, the basis for this publication. The full text is printed in *Archaeologia* XI (1974), 212–54.

55. See the introduction to E. G. R. Taylor, ed., *The Original Writings and Correspondence of the Two Richard Hakluyts.*

56. The first version of this tract, written in 1570 and dedicated to the earl of Leicester, is BL MS Additional 18035. In the wake of the Armada of 1588 Montgomery penned an "addicion," and a copy of both parts—embellished by some lovely but not always relevant drawings—is BL MS Additional 20042. Another copy of the text, with similar illustrations deriving from John White's American drawings, is Harvard University Library, J. P. R. Lyell Collection, MS Typ. 16. Cf. Helen Wallis, ed., *Raleigh and Roanoke,* 73.

57. "The Life of Sidney," in John Gouws, ed., *The Prose Works of Fulke Greville. Lord Brooke,* 56.

58. A copy in Dee's hand can be found in Bodleian MS Ashmole 1789, fols. 116–17. Aubrey's more famous descendant, John Aubrey, printed the letter in his "Brief Life" of Dee.

59. Recall that it was not printed until September 1577. Aubrey opens the letter by saying that he sends his young cousin—in effect, Dee's baby—back

home in a bag, while his wife carries one of his. He extends his prayer that both "shall come to light, & lyve long: and yo^{rs}, (having *Genium*), for ever" (116r).

60. Shelf mark Sel.2.82. The reason for my unusually messy transcriptions is that the margins have been badly cropped by the razor of a later binder.

61. The evidence for this—again paleographical—has been kindly supplied by R. E. Alton, who subjected the hand to a detailed analysis.

62. On Lumley, his signature and his library, see Sears Jayne and Francis R. Johnson, *The Library of John Lord Lumley: The Catalogue of 1609*.

63. That the reader was not Hitchcock is confirmed by a note on page 24: "Red hichcokes fysshenge plat. Caled his *n*ewe y^rsgyfte to England."

64. Roberts and Watson, 59–61.

65. Henry Stubbe, *A Further Justification of the Present War against the United Netherlands*, 79. I owe this reference to Steve Pincus.

66. In another place, however, Stubbe indicated that he possessed a *manuscript* of Dee's project: see his letter of 8 July 1672 to Sir Joseph Williamson (clerk of the council), *Calendar of State Papers Domestic (CSPD) May–September 1672*, 319–20.

67. James R. Jacob, *Henry Stubbe*, 120–21.

68. See Frances A. Yates, *Astraea: The Imperial Theme in the Sixteenth Century.*

69. The most comprehensive and up-to-date guide to English attitudes and activities in the Age of Discovery is K. R. Andrews, *Trade, Plunder and Settlement;* cf. D. B. Quinn and A. N. Ryan, *England's Sea Empire, 1550–1642*, and—for the purposes of this chapter—D. F. Lach, "The Far East"; H. Wallis, "The Pacific"; and T. E. Armstrong, "The Arctic" in volume 1 of D. B. Quinn, ed., *The Hakluyt Handbook.*

70. The same, it seems, can be said of Columbus himself; see especially Pauline Moffitt Watts, "Prophecy and Discovery: On the Spiritual Origins of Christopher Columbus's 'Enterprise of the Indies,' " 93.

71. R. A. Skeleton, *Explorers' Maps*, 51 and 99.

72. See the maps in ibid., passim., and E. G. R. Taylor, *Tudor Geography,* Fig. 8.

73. The contemporary accounts of these voyages make harrowing reading: see esp. Charles T. Beke, ed., *A True Description of Three Voyages by the North-East Towards Cathay and China, by Gerrit de Veer,* and Thomas Rundall, ed., *Narratives of Voyages Towards the North-West, in Search of a Passage to Cathay and India, 1496–1631.*

74. This phrase is Henry Yule's and is borrowed from his edition of *Cathay and the Way Thither*, a massive compendium of material relating to intercourse between western nations and China in the Middle Ages. Tryggvi J. Oleson's *Early Voyages and Northern Approaches 1000–1632* provides the medieval background to the Renaissance voyages; Donat Pharand's *The Northwest Passage Arctic Straits* is the best technical guide to the navigation of the Northwest Passage; and Helen Wallis's "England's Search for the Northern Passages in the Sixteenth and Early Seventeenth Centuries" is an excellent survey of the relevant cartographic materials. The best general account is George Born Manhart, *The*

English Search for a North-West Passage in the Time of Queen Elizabeth. For more popular works, see Brendan Lehane, *The Northwest Passage;* Philip F. Alexander, *The North-West and North-East Passages 1576–1611;* George M. Thomson, *The North-West Passage;* Leslie N. Neatby, *In Quest of the North-West Passage;* and Vilhjalmur Stefansson, *Northwest to Fortune: The Search of Western Man for a Commercially Practical Route to the Far East.*

75. Andrews, *Trade, Plunder and Settlement,* 166.

76. Ibid., 53–55.

77. Taylor, *Tudor Geography,* 98.

78. Dee's copy, now badly singed, is BL MS Cotton Vitellius C.VII, fols. 344ff.: it was presented to him in 1577. A better copy, with some variants, is BL MS Lansdowne 100, item 7. See Taylor, *Tudor Geography,* 46–48.

79. Taylor, *Tudor Geography,* 91. Taylor suggests that Thomas Digges was also consulted; but if there was a Digges involved it had to be his father Leonard (d. 1559), since at this time Thomas was no more than ten years old.

80. Andrews, *Trade, Plunder and Settlement,* chap. 2. As for Willoughby, a copy of an account of his voyage in Dee's hand survives in BL MS Cotton Otho E.VIII, item 6.

81. In the late 1570s Pet had been occupied with Digges and Borough on the works at Dover Harbour, while Jackman had served under both Christopher Hall and Edward Fenton in Frobisher's voyages to the northwest. Nicholas Chancellor, purser to Hall on the *Gabriel* in Frobisher's 1576 voyage and the son of Richard Chancellor (Dee's former accomplice and Jackman's former master), was made commercial overseer.

82. On that day Dee wrote in his diary, "at the Moscovy howse for the Cathay voyage" (7).

83. Taylor, *Tudor Geography,* 126–27. Dee's autograph copy, again partially damaged by fire, is BL MS Cotton Otho E.VIII, fols. 77–79. A complete contemporary transcript is BL MS Lansdowne 122, art. 5.

84. The Chancellor narrative is also in BL MS Cotton Otho E.VIII. The Smith map, found on fol. 73 of the same volume, is reproduced as Fig. 2 in Andrews, *Trade, Plunder and Settlement.* The interview and the preparation of the map probably took place on 23 March 1581 when Smith visited Dee at Mortlake (*Diary,* 11).

85. *Diary,* 18.

86. On Davis, his voyages, and his writings see Albert Hastings Markham, ed., *The Voyages and Works of John Davis.* According to Markham, Dee's diary contains the first recorded mention of his name (in 1579). Davis, no doubt with Dee's tuition, became an accomplished cosmographer—see his works, *The worldes hydrographical description* (an attempt to prove "that from England there is a short and speedie passage into the South Seas, to China, Molucca, Philippina, and India, by Northerly Navigation"), and *The Seamans Secrets* (a textbook on navigation). Judging by the books that Davis stole from Dee circa 1585, he absorbed many of Dee's nonmaritime interests as well (see Roberts and Watson). "Mr. Townson" is William Towerson, on whom see J. D. Alsop, "The Career of William Towerson, Guinea Trader."

87. *Diary*, 18, 19.

88. Much of the following account is based on Andrews, *Trade, Plunder and Settlement*, 167–79.

89. Gilbert's was not the only pro-Cathay voice in these years. It was around this time that Dee prepared, at the request of Edward Dyer, his "Atlanticall Discourses": these do not survive but were undoubtedly aligned with this early phase of the Northwest Campaign. And Taylor prints extracts from two anonymous proposals for the Northwest Passage which date from the same period (*Tudor Geography*, 265–67).

90. For a parallel project Richard Grenville produced (in 1574–75) "A discourse concerninge a Straighte to be discovered towarde the Northweste passinge to Cathaia and the Orientall Indians . . ." (BL MS Lansdowne 100, item 4).

91. Seventy thousand pounds, according to Quinn and Ryan, *England's Sea Empire*, 34.

92. Andrews, *Trade, Plunder and Settlement*, 178.

93. BL MS Cotton Otho E. VIII, fol. 44r–v: this account is (except for fol. 45) a copy in Dee's hand. The document is printed in Taylor, *Tudor Geography*, 269–70; her transcription is not entirely accurate, however, and she fails to distinguish between the two sections of the account, dating the whole 1577.

94. *Calendar of State Papers, Colonial Series, East Indies, China and Japan, 1513–1616*, 13, 29, 30, 33–34, 43, and 54.

95. See Taylor, *Tudor Geography*, 108–9.

96. BL MS Cotton Vitellius C. VII, fols. 26–269.

97. The manuscript lacks the first five chapters, but these are summarized in Samuel Purchas, *Hakluytus Posthumus, or Purchas his Pilgrims*, I:93, 97, 105–6, and 108–16.

98. At the top of a page (588) discussing Solomon's voyages, Dee entered the heading "Classis Salomonis" (Royal College of Physicians Library D19/3, 49a; Roberts and Watson no. 111). Dee's copy also included Hieronymus Gemusaeus' *Strabonis Epitome*.

99. For a stimulating guide see G. Gliozzi, *Adamo e il nuovo mondo*, pt. I, chap. IV.

100. Colin Jack-Hinton, *The Search for the Islands of Solomon, 1567–1838*, chap. I.

101. BL MS Harley 167, item 13 (dated 12 December 1586).

102. Jack-Hinton, *Search for the Islands of Solomon*, 21; Taylor, *Tudor Geography*, 114–19.

103. There are some interesting references to the Swedish archbishops-cum-historiographers Johannes and Olaus Magnus: Dee admired their works (on which see Kurt Johannesson, *The Renaissance of the Goths*) and was inclined to support their claims over those of the Germans.

104. Taylor, *Tudor Geography*, 131ff.

105. Skelton, *Explorers' Maps*, 14.

106. *Discoveries*, 86r–v; *Diary*, 3.

107. E. G. R. Taylor, "A Letter Dated 1577 from Mercator to John Dee."

108. Skelton, *Explorers' Maps*, passim.

109. Dee's copy of Scaliger's text is now RCP D129/2, 18c: the section in question (around fol. 283) is annotated.

110. An unidentified work of Pliny (Roberts and Watson no. 237) was among those stolen by John Davis. Dee had five different editions of Ptolemy's *Geographia*, two of which (nos. 166 and 1301) were stolen by Davis. The copy that survives (no. 402) has disappointingly sparse marginalia. Dee's copy of Strabo's *Geographia* is currently Brussels, Bibliothèque Royale, class-mark LP3414c (Roberts and Watson, no. 112), and apparently contains more than two thousand notes, including one that refers to Frobisher's voyage of 1576. Dee had two editions of Arrian's *Periplus*. One (no. 36) was stolen by Davis; the other (no. 405) is copiously annotated. Dee had two copies of Simler's edition of Aethicus's *Cosmographia* (nos. 1219 and 1994), neither of which has been traced; and neither has his copy of Herberstein's *Historia Moscovita* (no. 84). Dee's copy of the 1555 edition of Olaus Magnus's *Historia de rebus septentrionalibus* (no. 283) was stolen by Davis. Dee had four different works by Krantzius (nos. 29, 1760, 1761, and 1960), none of which seems to survive.

Dee owned an Italian edition of Barros's *Asia* (no. 553), which can now be found at the Royal College of Physicians Library. It is very heavily annotated. Dee paid special attention to such practical issues as the cost of running a mine, the ethics of taking prisoners, the importance of interpreters and geographical guides, the manner of claiming territorial possessions, the accuracy of maritime distances, the "forse of presents and gifts." It is here that we find Dee's clearest statements on the conversion of natives ("The Principall Intent of Discovery among Infidells [is] The Conversion of them to Chryst"—see the bottom of E8r) and the queen's jurisdiction over Scotland (next to an assertion of the Portuguese king's dominion over Guinea, he wrote "So is the Quene of England superior Dominions over Scotland"—O4r). Despite his intention to apply these practices in the name of the British Empire he had to admit that "Portugall [is] first and chief towards . . . Artificiall Nauigation" (margin of H7r).

Dee seems to have owned only Belleforest's French edition of Muenster's *Cosmographie universelle* (no. 205), but he owned three of Thevet's cosmographical works (nos. 238, 346, and 1096). While the first two survive at the Royal College of Physicians Library, only the first of these is annotated. Not surprisingly, the sections on Cathay and Quinsay are especially full of marginalia. As in the Barros volume, Dee attended to the practical matters of the exploration and exploitation of the New World. But—more so than in the Barros—he was also interested in the curiosities Thevet retailed, such as a cure for leprosy (n6v), the fact that the men of Madagascar live to the age of 140 or 160 (o1r), the "first Invention of Letters Hieroglyphic" (z2r), and the people of "Zipangu" who "eat flyes as [Dee added mysteriously] I haue seen them full oft" (HH6r).

111. In order "to put some curious Antiquary owt of douwt what other Authors I could or did vse beside the forenamed," Dee went on to list further "Treatises, Advertisements, Epistles, & depositions of sundry Credible persons."

112. In the introduction to his edition of Frampton's Elizabethan translation,

N. M. Penzer speaks of the "labyrinthine intricacies of Polian manuscript tradition' and helpfully reviews the early textual history of the Book (*The Most Noble and Famous Travels of Marco Polo,* xix).

113. In making this point Dee provided another traditional rationale (one that he could find in early Renaissance writers such as Gemistos and late Renaissance writers such as Bodin): "vndowtedly neith[er the] Portingale or Spanyard can abide the cold Clymate so well as we" (175r).

114. This proposal was incongruous with that which preceded it: by 1577 the regions mentioned were all well known to other "Conquerous Christians." The Portuguese in particular were well established: their first ambassador had reached Peking (Cambalu) in 1520; by 1557 they had a base at Macao for the China trade; and in 1571 they opened trade with Japan at Nagasaki (Skelton, *Explorers' Maps,* 19).

115. Such practical sentiments, which seem to parallel developments in empirical science, did not convince William Borough, who resented the application of mathematical theories to navigation without adequate experience at sea (see Taylor, *Tudor Geography,* 97).

116. In *Discoveries* Dee referred to an "apter tyme & place" where he would attempt to prove the "marveilous agreement of the historyes of Antiquit[y]" and the present and outline the "great vnlooked for light & Credit" that would be "restored to the Originalls of *BRVTVS*" (206v). This may well have been one of the purposes of a manuscript he wrote in 1583 entitled *The Originals, and chiefe points, of our auncient Brytish Histories, discoursed vpon, and examined* (see item 45 in the inventory of his works in the "Letter Apologeticall").

117. BL Additional MS 59681. Dee scholars have not yet taken this volume into account: Taylor and Gwyn Williams, the two most serious students of Dee's maritime activities, claimed that the text did not survive; Yewbrey clearly did not know of it; and it is not included in French's and Clulee's bibliographies.

118. *Diary,* 4. The involvement of Walsingham and the northern Atlantic position of these islands suggests that these claims were connected with the voyages to the northwest discussed in the previous section.

119. Ibid.

120. John Nichols, *The Progresses and Public Processions of Queen Elizabeth,* II:5ff.

121. *Diary,* 5. Dee seems to have had detailed knowledge of the queen's whereabouts and frequently records her movements in his diary. An even stronger indication of his access to news of the court is his knowledge that, on 16 August 1579, "Monsieur [the Duke of Alençon] cam secretly to the court from Calays" and, ten days later, "went back agayn to France" (6).

122. Dee served the queen in a medical capacity, and this conference was related to the queen's ill health. As Dee recalled in his "Compendious Rehearsall," he met with Dr. Bayly, the queen's physician, and then undertook (at the command of Leicester and Walsingham) a "very painefull and dangerous winter journey, about a thousand five hundred myles by sea and land . . . to consult with the learned physitians and philosophers beyond the seas for her Majesties health-recovering and preserving" (22).

123. *Diary*, 9. They are repeated, almost verbatim, in the "Compendious Rehearsall," 18–19.

124. According to the "Compendious Rehearsall" the queen had charged Burghley "to peruse the whole thinge accordingly, and to make report to her Majestie, what he findeth therein" (18). It is possible to learn just what he found: among the Burghley papers at the British Library there is a memorial in his hand entitled "A Summary of Mr. Dee's book" (MS Lansdowne 94, art. 51). Interestingly, it abstracts only Dee's most contentious arguments—the genealogy of Elizabeth, tracing her descent from the early Welsh kings, and the conclusion "That Arthur King of Britain was the conqueror of these Cuntryes . . ." (fol. 121).

125. They are the only sections of the manuscript that are entirely in Latin. I am extremely grateful to Elisabeth Leedham-Green for her advice on translations.

126. Gliozzi's *Adamo e il nuovo mondo* is illuminating on the use of the term *Atlantis* in the Renaissance (see pt. II, chap. I).

127. Gwyn A. Williams, *Madoc: The Legend of the Welsh Discovery of America*, 38; cf. Richard Henry Major, *The Voyages of the Venetian Brothers Nicolo & Antonio Zeno, to the Northern Seas in the XIVth Century*. The Zeno narrative was published in Ramusio's *Viaggi*, which Dee cited so extensively in *Discoveries*. In Miller Christy's *The Silver Map of the World*, there are two maps that are indispensable for making sense of the confused cartography Dee adopted. The first (facing p. 24) is a chart of the North Atlantic, with a superimposition of the Zeno chart of 1558, showing the real and the supposed routes sailed by Frobisher; the second (facing p. 54) shows the result of adjusting the Zeno chart's erroneous latitudes.

128. My emphasis. This conclusion is also supported by the word *appinximus* ["we have here depicted"], used on the next page.

129. The passage continues, "As most evidently, and at large it is declared in the great Volum of famous, and riche discoveris, very latlie Collected. . . ."

130. BL MS Cotton Augustus I.i.1. The top section of this map is reproduced as Fig. 1 in E. G. R. Taylor, "A Letter Dated 1577 from Mercator to John Dee." In this version the seventeen numbered claims from *Limites* are condensed to twelve, and a few passages are omitted. According to Roberts and Watson, a third version—in Dee's own hand—could be found in BL MS Cotton Otho C. VII, until it was destroyed by fire (see no. DM29a).

131. Graham Yewbrey, "A Redated Manuscript of John Dee," 249–53.

132. Confusingly, Dee assigned the date "1578" to "*Britannici Imperii Limites*" in his 1592 inventory. This could be, like other dates seem to be, a simple mistake. Or it could refer to the entire collection, including the "Brief Remembrance," which could have been assembled from May 1578.

133. The reference to *Memorials*'s printing "last yeare" indicates that this section was written in 1578: it was probably added to the original material on the occasion of a conference with the queen.

134. A final piece of evidence in favor of this conclusion is Burghley's "Summary of Mr. Dee's Book." The material he abstracted was based on the rolls

Dee presented to the queen; and everything contained in his summary can be found in the pages of *Limites*.

135. *Limites* ("Brief Remembrance"), 13. Along the right margin of the list of numbered claims Dee noted the regions concerned. Their cumulative effect is staggering.

136. Williams, *Madoc*, 38.

137. T. D. Kendrick, *British Antiquity*, chap. 6.

138. A similar passage prefaces a similar effort in *Discoveries* (chaps. 27–28).

139. Thomas Wemyss Fulton, *The Sovereignty of the Sea*, 25.

140. Kendrick, *British Antiquity*, 78.

141. Williams, *Madoc*, 66. Chap. 3, "Imperial Madoc," is a compelling summary of the imperial efforts of Welsh scholars on behalf of the Tudors.

142. Cited in ibid., 42.

143. BL MS Lansdowne 100, item 6. There is another copy in Lansdowne 105 (item 21). The former is undated and anonymous, but the latter is endorsed "Digges" and connects it to a case between the queen and a Mr. Chute, who claimed land left by the receding seas as his own.

144. *DNB*, s.v. Thomas Digges.

145. A general account of Dee's cartographic activities is Antoine de Smet, "John Dee et sa place dans l'histoire de la cartographie."

146. J. B. Harley, "Meaning and Ambiguity in Tudor Cartography," 22. Harley's essay also includes a very useful table of six types of maps with their practical uses, symbolic meanings, and social functions (31).

147. J. B. Harley, "Silences and Secrecy: The Hidden Agenda of Cartography," 71.

148. Skelton, *Explorers' Maps*, 78.

149. See Peter Barber, "Pageantry, Defense, and Government: Maps at Court to 1550" and "Monarchs, Ministers, and Maps, 1550–1625," in David Buisseret, ed., *Monarchs, Ministers, and Maps*.

150. Victor Morgan, "The Cartographic Image of 'The Country.'"

151. See Skelton's remarkable account, "The Maps of a Tudor Statesman," in Skelton and Summerson, *A Description of the Maps and Architectural Drawings in the Collection . . . at Hatfield House*. One of these volumes, a copy of the 1570 Ortelius *Theatrum Orbis Terrarum* (now at Burghley House), is interleaved with manuscript maps. Among them is a beautiful chart prepared by Dee for Burghley in 1580: it covers the areas and arguments concerning the polar regions of the Northeast Passage.

152. Richard Helgerson, "The Land Speaks," in *Forms of Nationhood*.

153. Anna Maria Crinò and Helen Wallis, "New Researches on the Molyneux Globes," 15, 14 (my emphasis). I am grateful to Helen Wallis (former librarian of the British Museum Map Room) for directing me to this source and for discussing with me Dee's imperial geography.

154. Curiously, as they are mapped onto the queen, the four places (and therefore Elizabeth) appear upside down. This puzzle is solved, however, if we look at a map with a polar projection—like the one that Dee seems to have

prepared for Sir Humphrey Gilbert (Skelton, *Explorers' Maps,* 102). From this perspective, the western half of the Northern Hemisphere does indeed appear upside down. The mapping is not, however, as exact as Dee's precision suggests. I would suggest that this precision is meant to work on a social rather than a geographical register: it rhetorically enhances Dee's intimacy with the queen (as well, of course, as making his argument seem that much closer to "manifest destiny").

155. Roy Strong, *Portraits of Queen Elizabeth I,* Plate E 32. Cf. Strong's *Gloriana: The Portraits of Queen Elizabeth I,* and Helgerson, "The Land Speaks."

156. There are three known copies of this manuscript. Two are in Dee's hand: a draft, in BL MS Harley 249 (later owned by Sir Simonds D'Ewes), and a later copy, bound with Dee's *Memorials* in BL C.21.e.12. The third, roughly contemporary, copy is BL MS Royal 7 C.XVI, fols. 158-65. I cite the Harleian copy, but silently incorporate the revisions apparent in the other copies.

157. Dee suspected that Dyer was no longer in possession of a copy of *Memorials* and so, as his postscript indicates, he sent a copy along with the letter (105r).

158. In returning to *Memorials* and following Dee's directions, his discovery and recovery enterprise clearly emerges from that text's more limited concerns. Without exception, the passages to which Dyer was directed not only addressed the law of sea sovereignty but advocated the pursuit of Dee's aggressive program.

159. Dee's library was not well stocked in legal books, and he seems to have gathered most of his material out of Bartolus, whom he puts at the head of his list. He recommended to Dyer, "yf you haue any better writers, vppon the forsaid Lawyers intents, you will, or may haue pleasure, to consider their discoursinges . . ." (96r).

160. 95r-96v; cf. Fulton, *Sovereignty of the Sea,* chaps. 1 and 3.

161. He gives this point particular stress and repeats the "pithy words" from *Memorials,* "That all those who pass with in our Sea Iurisdiction, and therein commit any Notable offense, against vs, may Lawfully and iustly be PONISHED, as yf on our Land Territorie . . ." (97v). Here Dee has in mind foreign fishermen in particular.

162. Fulton, *Sovereignty of the Sea,* 19ff. Fulton reproduces Selden's map, which was p. 122 (sig. R1v) in the first edition of 1635.

163. *The Parliamentary History of England,* ed. W. Cobbett and J. Wright, I:902, 903. The fact that there was a parliament in session may well be related to Dyer's request for material from Dee.

164. Here Dee referred Dyer to *Limites,* in which he had written of "her Maties Title, not onely to the Superioritie, over the king of Scotes, and the whole kingdome, but allso of her right . . . to the kingdome it selfe" (100r).

165. A. E. Nordenskiold, *Periplus,* chap. 10.

166. He quoted the following pages from *Rerum Germanicarum Historici Clariss. Regnorum Aquilonarium, Daniae, Sueciae, Noruagiae, Chronica: Daniae Lib.IIII, Cap.20* (g6r), *Norvagiae Lib.I, Cap.39* (G2r), *Daniae Lib.I, Cap.1* (a1v), and *Daniae Lib.I, Cap.38* (c1r).

167. From his *Chronica Slauorum, seu Annales* he quoted A2r, A2v, and B2r.

168. *Batavia,* 6, 17, 112, and 251.

169. See Mercator's map of Europe (Duysburg, 1595), Hondius' world map (Amsterdam, 1595), and the relevant maps in Rodney W. Shirley, *The Mapping of the World.* For advice on this question I am grateful to the staff of the map rooms in the British Museum and the Cambridge University Library.

170. See T. H. Lloyd, *England and the German Hanse, 1157–1611,* chap. 6; C. G. A. Clay, *Economic Expansion and Social Change,* II:183–84; and E. P. Cheney, "International Law under Queen Elizabeth." The relevant primary sources are scattered throughout the State Papers: see esp. the letters from Christopher Parkins (English ambassador to Denmark) to Robert Cecil in the *CSPD* and the letters of Giacomo and Francesco Vendramin to the doge and Senate of Venice in the *CSPF Venetian;* also Uncalendared State Papers Foreign Hamburg and Hanse Towns (SP82), passim.

171. See, for instance, the papers regarding traffic with the Hanse towns in SP12/126.

172. For the text of the decree and a concise account of its background see Francesco Vendramin's letter of 10 September 1597 in *CSPF Venetian* (284–85).

173. SP12/265, no. 71.

174. Ibid., no. 145.

Bibliography

I. PRIMARY

A. Books

Bacon, Roger. *Epistolae . . . de secretis operibus artis et naturae et de nullitate magiae.* Hamburg: ex bibliopolio Frobeniano, 1618.

Barlow, William. *An Answer to a Catholike English-Man.* London: Thomas Haveland, 1609.

Bodin, Jean. *Methodus ad facilem historiarum cognitionem.* Paris, 1566.

Byshop, John. *Beautifull Blossomes.* London: Henrie Cockyn, 1577.

Camerarius, Philipp. *The Living Librarie, or, Meditations and Observations Historical, Natural, Moral, Political, and Poetical.* Translated by John Molle. London: Adam Islip, 1621.

Dallington, Robert. *Aphorismes Civill and Militarie.* London: Edward Blount, 1613.

Darrell, John. *A True Narration of the Strange and Grievous Vexation by the Devil of 7. Persons in Lancashire.* London, 1600.

Dee, John. *General and Rare Memorials pertayning to the Perfect Arte of NAVIGATION.* London: John Daye, 1577.

———. *A Letter, containing a most briefe discourse apologeticall.* London: P. Short, 1599.

———. *The "Mathematicall Praeface" to Euclid's Elements.* Translated by Henry Billingsly. London: John Daye, 1570.

———. *Monas hieroglyphica.* Antwerp: Willem Sylvius, 1564.

———. *A True and Faithfull Relation of what passed for many years between Dr. John Dee and Some Spirits.* Edited by Meric Casaubon. London, 1659.

Dury, John. *The Reformed Librarie-Keeper.* London: William Du-Gard, 1650; repr. Augustan Reprint Society No. 220, 1983.

Euclid. *Elementa.* Edited by Federico Commandino. Pisa: Camillo Francischini, 1572.

Fletcher, Giles. *Of the Russe Commonwealth.* London: T. D. for T. Charde, 1591.

Gibbon, Charles. *The Remedie of Reason.* London: Thomas Orwin, 1589.

Gilbert, Humphrey. *A Discourse of a Discovery for a new Passage to Cataia.* London: H. Middleton for R. Jones, 1576.

Hakluyt, Richard. *Divers voyages touching the discouerie of America.* London: T. Dawson for T. Woodcocke, 1582.

———. *Principal Navigations.* London: G. Bishop and R. Newberie, 1589.

Harvey, Richard. *An Astrological Discourse.* London: Henry Binneman, 1583.

Hearne, Thomas, ed. *Johannis Glastoniensis Chronica.* 2 vols. Oxford, 1726.

———. *Reliquiae Bodleianae.* London: J. Harley, 1703.

Hitchcock, Robert. *A Pollitique Platt.* London: John Kingston, 1580.

———, trans. *The Quintesence of Wit, being a corrant comfort of Conceites, Maximes,*

253

and poleticke deuises, selected and gathered together by Francisco Sansouino. London: Edward Allde, 1590.

Hondius, Jodocus. *Vera Totius Expeditionis Nauticae.* . . . Amsterdam?, c. 1595.

Johnson, Samuel. *A Dictionary of the English Language.* 2 vols. London: W. Strahan, 1755.

Junius, Hadrianus. *Batavia.* Louvain: apud Franciscum Raphelengium, 1588.

Krantzius, Albertus. *Rerum Germanicarum Historici Clariss. Regnorum Aquilonarium, Daniae, Sueciae, Noruagiae, Chronica.* Frankfurt: Andreas Wechelus, 1575.

Kyffin, Maurice. *The Blessednes of Brytaine.* London: J. Wolfe, 1588.

Merbury, Charles. *A Briefe Discourse of Royall Monarchie, as of the Best Common Weale.* London: Thomas Vautrollier, 1581.

Mercator, Gerard. Map of Europe. Duysburg, 1595.

Mulcaster, Richard. *Positions.* London: Thomas Vautrollier, 1581.

Naudé, Gabriel. *Instructions Concerning Erecting of a Library.* Translated by John Evelyn. London: for G. Bedle, T. Collins, and J. Crook, 1661.

―――. *News from France.* London: Timothy Garthwait, 1652. Reprint. Chicago: A. C. McClurg, 1907.

Norton, Thomas, trans. *Orations of Arsanes agaynst Philip the trecherous kyng of Macedone.* London: John Daye, 1560?

Pflacher, Moses. *Analysis Typica Omnium cum Veteris tum Noui Testamenti Librorum Historicorum.* London: Edmund Bollifant, 1587.

Possevinus, Antonius. *Bibliotheca selecta.* Rome: Ex Typographia Apostolica Vaticana, 1593.

Powel, David, ed. *The Historie of Cambria.* London: R. Newberie, 1584.

Presbyterus, Helmoldus. *Chronica Slauorum, seu Annales.* Frankfurt: Andreas Wechelus, 1581.

Recorde, Robert. *The Ground of Artes.* London: H. Bynneman, 1582.

Schardius, Simon, ed. *Germanicarum rerum quatuor celebriores vetustioresque chronographi.* Frankfurt: Apud G. Coruinum, S. Feyrabend, & haered. W. Galli, 1566.

Selden, John. *Of the Dominion, Or, Ownership of the Sea.* Translated by Marchamont Nedham. London: William Du-Gard, 1652.

Sheers, Henry. *An Essay on Ways and Means.* . . . London, 1701.

Sigebertus. *Gemblacensis. Chronicon ab anno 381 ad 1113.* Paris: Henricus Stephanus, 1513.

Smith, Thomas. *De Republica Anglorum.* London: Henri Midleton, 1583.

Smith, Thomas, ed. *V. Cl. Gulielmi Camdeni, et illustrium virorum ad G. Camdenum Epistolae.* London: Richard Chiswell, 1691.

Statuta Academiae Cantabrigiensis. Cambridge, 1785.

Stubbe, Henry. *A Further Justification of the Present War Against the United Netherlands.* London: Henry Hills and John Starkey, 1673.

Ursus, Nicolas Raymarus Dithmarsus. *Fundamentaum Astronomicum.* Argentorati: Excudebat Bernhardus Iobin, 1588.

Vaughan, Edward. *Ten Introductions: How to read . . . the holie Bible.* London: A. Islip, 1594.

B. Manuscripts

Cambridge

Cambridge University Library

    Louard 179a.

    Microfilm deposit of Sidney Sussex uncatalogued mss.

Pembroke College

    2.113.

London

British Library

    Additional 18035.

    Additional 19065.

    Additional 20042.

    Additional 42075.

    Additional 59681.

    Cotton Augustus I.i.1.

    Cotton Charter XIII, art. 38.

    Cotton Charter XIII, art. 39.

    Cotton Charter XIII, art. 48.

    Cotton Charter XIV, art. 1.

    Cotton Otho E.VIII.

    Cotton Tiberius B.IX.

    Cotton Vitellius C.VII.

    Cotton Vitellius C.IX.

    Harley 94.

    Harley 167.

    Harley 249.

    Harley 374.

    Harley 473.

    Harley 1879.

    Harley 5835.

    Harley 6485.

    Lansdowne 39.

    Lansdowne 94.

    Lansdowne 100.

    Lansdowne 105.

    Lansdowne 109.

    Lansdowne 121.

    Lansdowne 122.

    Lansdowne 229.

    Royal 7.C.XVI.

    Royal 8.B.XX.

    Sloane 3188.

Public Record Office

    SP12/126.

    SP12/196.

SP12/265, no. 71.
SP12/265, no. 145.
Uncalendared State Papers Foreign Hamburg and Hanse Towns (SP82).

Oxford

Bodleian Library
   Ashmole 179.
   Ashmole 487.
   Ashmole 488.
   Ashmole 1419.
   Ashmole 1486.
   Ashmole 1788.
   Ashmole 1789.
   Dugdale 24.
   Smith 35.
   Smith 96.
   Tanner 79.

Corpus Christi College
   254.
   255.

C. Adversaria*

1. JOHN DEE

Cambridge

University Library

H*.8.22(C)	Dionysius the Areopogite, *De mystica Theologia.* {271}
M*.5.49(D)	Pomponius Gauricus, *De sculptura.* {468}
U.3.59	Diogenes Laertius, *Peri Bion . . .* {502}
Inc.4.D.2.17	Jean Ganivet, *Amicus medicorum.* {569}
C*.6.57(E)	Georgius Fabricius Chemnicensis, *In paeanas tres, prudentii, sedulii, fortunati.* {934}
A*.8.55(F)	Saint Diadochus, *Capita centum de perfectione spirituali.* {1570}
R*.5.27(F)	Iacobus a Saa, *De Navigatione.* {B154}
MS Ff. 6.50	Alchemica. {DM1a}

Magdalene College Pepys Library

MS 2329	Scientific miscellany. {M91}

St. John's College Library

MS 171	William de Conchis, *Philosophia.* {M160}

* I devote a separate section to the large number of primary volumes with marginal annotations that I cite, since they refer to particular *copies* of works. Within this section I have separated books and manuscripts only within the listings of each collection. In the subsection on Dee, the numerals in brackets following the descriptions refer to entry numbers in Roberts and Watson's edition of his library catalog. I follow their spelling (and not Dee's) for authors' names.

Trinity College Library

Adv.d.1.23	Ptolemy, *De geographia*. {402}
Adv.d.1.26	Ramus, *Prooemium Mathematicum*. {805}
O.2.50	Miscellany. {M3}
O.2.47	Alchemica. {M79}
O.8.30	St. Thomas Aquinas, *De veritate theologica*. {M148}
O.8.9	Medica. {DM7}
O.8.28	Ps. Lull, *Liber experimentorum*. {DM8}
O.2.21	Geoffrey of Monmouth.

London

British Library

616.m.2	Conrad Gesner, *Appendix Bibliothecae*. {210}
531.k.6(3)	Paulo Crusio, *Doctrina revolutionum solis*. {546}
C.107.d.22	Pliny the Elder, *De mundi historia*. {603}
C.54.bb.6	Petrus Peregrinus Maricurtensis, *De Magnete*. {662}
C.122.bb.35	Euclid, *Elements*. {1078}
8461.b.13	Cicero, *Tusculanae Quaestiones*.
Cot.Vesp.A.X.	Historical miscellany. {M10}
Cot.Gal.E.VII	Chronicles. {M25}
Cot.Tib.C.V	Roger Bacon, *Summa*. {M26}
MS Harley 1	Scientific miscellany. {M28}
MS Harley 3	Johannes de Mirfeld, *Breviarum Bartholomaei*. {M31}
MS Sloane 2327	Alchemica. {M35}
MS Harley 267	Astronomica. {M36}
Cot.Tib.B.IX	Miscellany. {M72 etc.}
MS Harley 80	Roger Bacon, *Scientia perspectiva*. {M72}
MS Royal 15.B.9	Miscellany. {M74}
MS Add. 48178	Martinus Polonus, *Chronicon*. {M75}
Cot.Dom.I	Historical miscellany. {M94 etc.}
Cot.Cleo.B.II	Ecclesiastical history. {M113}
MS Harley 315	*Vita sanctorum*. {M125}
MS Harley 624	*Vita sanctorum*. {M125}
Cot. Nero C.VII	*Vita sanctorum*. {M125}
MS Royal 12.B.22	Chalcidius, *In Timaeum Platonis*. {M143}
Cot.Dom.IV	Historical miscellany. {M150}
Cot.Vesp.AII	Miscellany. {M159 etc.}
MS Royal 7.D.2	Miscellany. {M166}
MS Sloane 2128	Alchemica. {M184}
Cot.Jul.D.V	Roger Bacon, *Opus maius* etc. {DM29}
Cot.Ot.E.VIII	Papers re: voyages of discovery. {DM30}
Cot.Tit.D.IX	Hywel Dda, *Laws*. {DM30a}
Cot.Vit.C.IX	Miscellany. {DM35}
MS Harley 54	Roger Hovedon, *Chronica*. {DM43}
MS Harley 200	Historical miscellany. {DM46}
MS Harley 218	Miscellany. {DM48}

MS Harley 654   Ancient histories. {DM60}
MS Sloane 336   Medica. {DM72}
MS Sloane 338   Chemica. {DM73}
MS Sloane 2006 Alchemica. {DM74}
MS Stowe 1070   Alchemica. {cM81}

Royal College of Physicians Library

D18/8, 48e   Ptolemy, *Quadripartitum.* {37}

D125/13, 17d   Lodovico Guicciardini, *Descriptio Germaniae Inferioris.* {64}

D125/13, 17d   Jean Lemaire, *Les illustrations de Gaule et singularitez de Troye.* {72}

D14/1, 48b   Andreas Alexander, *Mathemalogia.* {79}

D126/6, 17e   Matthaeus Beroaldus, *Chronicum.* {86}

D19/3, 49a   Dominicus Marius Niger, *Geographiae commentariorum libri XI.* {111}

D128a/4, 18c Suetonius et al., *Historia Romanae scriptores.* {119}

D10/1, 47d   Archimedes, *Opera non nulla.* {167}

D125/7, 17d   Franciscus Irenicus, *Germaniae exegeseos volumina exarata.* {184}

D15/5, 48b   Cyprianus von Leowitz, *Eclipsum omnium.* {193}

D121/5, 16a   Pausanias, *De tota Graecia.* {196}

D5/8, 48f   Andre Thevet, *La cosmographie universelle.* {238}

D121/17, 16b Cicero, *Opera.* {246}

D126/4, 17e   Herodotus' histories. {257}

D128a/2, 18c Matthew of Westminster, *Flores Historiarum.* {290}

D89/6, 8c   Arnaldus de Villa Nova, *Opera.* {299}

D124/11, 17c Thomas Walsingham, historical works. {301, 301A}

D25/5, 49e   Alphonso X, *Astronomicae tabulis.* {340}

D129/5, 18c   Pierre d'Oudegherst, *Les chroniques et annales de Flandres.* {348}

D30/15, 45c   Antoine Mizauld, *Planetologia.* {352}

D133/1, 19c   Rene Chopin, *De domanio Franciae.* {360}

D40/2, 46b   Girolamo Cardano, *Libri quinque.* {440}

D129/2, 18c   Julius Caesar Scaliger, *Exotericarum exercitationum . . . de subtilitate, ad Hieronymum Cardanum.* {476}

D131/14, 19b Christophe de Roffignac, *Commentarii omnium a creato orbe historiarum.* {531}

D130/17, 19a Joao de Barros, *L'Asia.* {553}

D133/6, 19c   Walther Hermann Ryff, *In Caii Plinii Secundi naturalis historiae commentarius.* {629}

D48/6, 46f   Albohaly, *De iudiciis nativitatum.* {693}

D139/7, 20c   Dictys Cretensis et al., *Belli Troiani scriptores praecipui.* {725}

D144/14, 21b Guillaume Postel, *De originibus.* {868}

(o) 937   Onofrio Panvinio, *Reipublicae Romanae Commentariorum.* {903}

D150/3, 21d   Gildas, *De excidio & conquestu Britanniae.* {1087}

D146/4, 21c David Chytraeus, *Chronologia Historiae Herodoti et Thu-cydidis.* {1092}

D145b/3, 21b Paulus Orosius, *Adversus Paganos Historiarum.* {1311}

D107/3, 7c Petrus Bonus Lombardus, chemical works. {1425}

MS 398 Ranulph Higden, *Polychronicon.* {M121}

Wellcome Institute Library

MS 239 George Ripley, *Practica et accurtaciones Georgij Rypley et Raimundi.* {DM90}

MS 693 George Ripley, *Rotulum heroglyphicum.* {DM91}

2644(I) Galen, *Mathematices scientiae prognostica de decubitu infirmorum.* {951}

New Haven

Yale University Beinecke Library

MS Mellon 12 Ramon Lull, various works. {DM94}

New York

New York Society Library

189 Paracelsus, *De balneis.* {1476}

188 Paracelsus, *Das Buch Meteororum.* {1482}

86 Gerard Dorn, *Chemisticum artificium naturae, theoricum et practicum.* {1524}

Oxford

Bodleian Library

40 A Art.Seld. Avicenna, *Compendium de anima.* {395}

MS Ashm. 1471 Natural philosophical miscellany. {M24}

MS Digby 237 Roger Bacon, *Communium naturalium.* {M27}

MS Ashm. 1451 Alchemica. {M53}

MS Digby 71 Natural philosophical miscellany. {M84}

MS Ashm. 341 Alchemica. {M194}

MS Digby 119 Natural philosophical miscellany. {M196}

MS Ashm. 1426 Alchemica. {DM100}

MS Ashm. 1503 Alchemica. {DM105}

MS Digby 76 Natural philosophical miscellany. {DM113}

MS Digby 190 Natural philosophical miscellany. {DM116}

All Souls College Library

SR 59.b.23 Giorgio Valla, *Commentationes in Ptolomei Quadripartitum. . . .* {21}

SR 17.d.3 Guillaume Postel, *Linguarum duodecim characteribus differentium Alphabetum.* {1623}

Christ Church Library

Wb.4.8 John Bale, *Illustrium maioris Brytanniae scriptorum . . . summarium.* {274}

Wb.5.13 John Leland, *Opuscula.* {597}

Wb.5.12 Geoffrey of Monmouth, *Britanniae utriusque regum origo.* {601}

Corpus Christi College Library

MS 125	Natural philosophical miscellany. {M33}
MS 149	Roger Bacon, *Annotations super Aristotelis secretum secretorum*. {M56-7}
MS 277	Alchemica. {M193}
MS 127	Roger Bacon, *De erroribus medicorum*. {DM129}
MS 136	Alchemica. {DM131}
MS 244	Alchemica. {DM148}
MS 254	Mathematical miscellany. {DM154}

Merton College Library

MS 323	Hywel Dda, *Leges Walliae*. {DM160}

2. SIR THOMAS SMITH

Queens' College (Cambridge) Library

D.1.3	Georgius Agricola, *De re metallica*.
F.10.20	Paracelsus, *Chirurgia magna*.
G.11.3	Cinus de Sinibuldis, *Lectura super aureo volumine codicis*.
D.20.39	Sebastian Muenster, *Hologiographia*.
M.2.11	Justinian, *Digests*.
H.2.20	*Institutiones iuris civilis*.
11.2.25	Claudius Cantinculus, *Topica*.
D.10.22	Albertus Krantzius, *Chronica*.
G.3.19	Paulus Aemylius Veronensis, *Historici clarissimi de rebus gestis Francorum*.
F.1.4	Tacitus, *Historia*.

3. OTHERS

Cambridge University Library

Adv.a.3.1	Isaac Casaubon's Pliny.
Adv.a.3.2	Isaac Casaubon's Herodotus.
Adv.a.5.1	Erasmus' copy of his own *Apologiae*.
Adv.a.6.1–2	Petrus Faber's Cicero.
Adv.b.22.1	Vivessotius' *Ars medica* of Galen.
Adv.b.23.1	Thomas Wilson's *Nicomachean Ethics*.
Adv.c.2.1	John Bradley's *Nicomachean Ethics*.
Adv.c.8.1	Walter Haddon's *Hieronymus Osorius in Gualterum Haddonum Magistrum Libellorum Supplicum*.
Adv.c.8.4	Richard Hooker's *Logics* of Aristotle.
Adv.c.19.1	Joseph Justus Scaliger's copy of Melchior Guilandinus' *Papyrus*.
Adv.d.2.1	Hollerius, *De morbis internis*.
Adv.d.3.1	John Caius' Galen.
Adv.d.3.5	Isaac Casaubon's Arrian.
Adv.d.3.14	Isaac Casaubon's Tacitus.
Adv.d.3.22	Jacobus Colius Ortelianus' *Imperatorum Romanorum Numismata* of Adolphus Occo.

Adv.d.4.4	Bartholomew Dodington's Hermogenes.
Adv.d.12.1	Richard Latewar's Tacitus.
Adv.d.13.1	Paulus Manutius' Aldine Suetonius.
Adv.d.14.1	Anthony Nicholaus' Latin grammar of Linacre.
Adv.d.14.4	Sir Thomas North's own copy of his translation of Antonio de Guevara, *The Dial of Princes*.
Adv.e.3.1	Isaac Casaubon's Terence.
Adv.e.12.1	Thomas Lorkin's Galen and Hippocrates.
Sel.2.82	Lumley's copy of Dee's *General and Rare Memorials*.

British Library

C.21.e.12	Hitchcock's copy of *General and Rare Memorials* with notes and *THALATTOKRATIA BRETANNIKI*.
C.60.f.8	Gabriel Harvey's copy of Bourne's *Regiment for the Sea*.
C.142.e.13	Robert Sidney's Tacitus.

II. SECONDARY

Alexander, Philip F. *The North-West and North-East Passages 1576–1611*. Cambridge: Cambridge University Press, 1915.

Alsop, J. D. "The Career of William Towerson, Guinea Trader." *International Journal of Maritime History* 4:2 (December 1992), 45–82.

———. "Nicholas Brigham (d.1558), Scholar, Antiquary, and Crown Servant." *Sixteenth Century Journal* 12:1 (Spring 1981), 49–67.

———. "The Theory and Practice of Tudor Taxation." *English Historical Review* 97 (1982), 1–30.

Alsop, J. D., and Wesley M. Stevens. "William Lambarde and the Elizabethan Polity." *Studies in Medieval and Renaissance History* 8 (1986), 231–65.

Ames, Joseph. *Typographical Antiquities*. London: T. Payne & Son, 1785–90.

Andrews, Kenneth R. *Elizabethan Privateering: English Privateering during the Spanish War, 1585–1603*. Cambridge: Cambridge University Press, 1964.

———. *Ships, Money and Politics: Seafaring and Naval Enterprise in the Reign of Charles I*. Cambridge: Cambridge University Press, 1991.

———. *Trade, Plunder and Settlement: Maritime Enterprise and the Genesis of the British Empire, 1480–1630*. Cambridge: Cambridge University Press, 1984.

Arnold, E. Vernon. *Roman Stoicism*. London: RKP, 1911. Reprint. 1958.

Asch, R. G., and A. M. Birke, eds. *Princes, Patronage, and the Nobility: The Court at the Beginning of the Modern Age c.1450–1650*. Oxford: Oxford University Press, 1991.

Ashworth, E. J. "Logic in Late Sixteenth-Century England: Humanist Dialectic and the New Aristotelianism." *Studies in Philology* 88:2 (Spring 1991), 224–36.

Attridge, D., G. Bennington, and R. Young, eds. *Post-Structuralism and the Question of History*. Cambridge: Cambridge University Press, 1987.

Auberlen, Eckhard. *The Commonwealth of Wit: The Writer's Image and His Strategies of Self-Representation in Elizabethan Literature*. Tübingen: Gunter Narr Verlag, 1984.

Bacon, Francis. *The Essays*. Edited by John Pitcher London: Penguin, 1985.

Barnes, Barry. *Interests and the Growth of Knowledge*. London: RKP, 1977.

Barnes, Barry, and Donald MacKenzie. "On the Role of Interests in Scientific Change." In *On the Margins of Science: The Social Construction of Rejected Knowledge,* edited by Roy Wallis. Keele: University of Keele, 1979.

Baron, Hans. "Cicero and the Roman Civic Spirit in the Middle Ages and Early Renaissance." *Bulletin of the John Rylands Library* 22 (1938), 72–97.

Baron, Samuel. "Herberstein and the English 'Discovery' of Muscovy." *Terrae Incognitae* 18 (1986), 43–54.

Barone, R. W. "The Reputation of John Dee: A Critical Appraisal." Ph.D. thesis, Ohio State University, 1989.

Batho, G. R. "The Library of the 'Wizard' Earl: Henry Percy Ninth Earl of Northumberland (1564–1632)." *The Library,* 5th ser., 15 (1960), 246–61.

Baumann, Gerd, ed. *The Written Word: Literacy in Transition*. Oxford: Oxford University Press, 1986.

Beke, Charles T., ed. *A True Description of Three Voyages by the North-East Towards Cathay and China, by Gerrit de Veer*. London: The Hakluyt Society, 1853.

Biagioli, Mario. "Galileo's System of Patronage." *History of Science* 28 (1990), 1–62.

———. "Scientific Revolution, Social Bricolage, and Etiquette." In Porter and Teich, *The Scientific Revolution in National Context*.

———. "The Social Status of Italian Mathematicians, 1450–1600." *History of Science* 27 (1989), 41–95.

Bienvenu, Richard T., and Mordechai Feingold, eds. *In the Presence of the Past: Essays in Honor of Frank Manuel*. Dordrecht: Kluwer, 1991.

Binns, J. W. *Intellectual Culture in Elizabethan and Jacobean England: The Latin Writings of the Age*. Leeds: Francis Cairns, 1990.

Biondi, Albano. "La *Bibliotheca Selecta* di Antonio Possevino: un progetto di egemonia culturale." In *La 'Ratio Studiorum': Modelli culturali e pratiche educative dei Gesuiti in Italia tra Cinque e Seicento,* edited by Gian Paolo Brizzi. Roma: Bulzoni Editore, 1981.

Bizzocchi, Roberto. "Culture généalogique dans l'Italie du XVIe siècle. *Annales ESC* (1991).

———. " 'Familiae Romanae' Antiche e Moderne." *Rivista Storica Italiana* 103 (1991), 355–97.

Blair, Ann M. "Lectures on Ovid's *Metamorphoses:* The Class Notes of a Sixteenth-Century Paris Schoolboy." *Princeton University Library Chronicle* 59 (1989), 117–44.

———. "*Ovidius Methodizatus*: The *Metamorphoses* of Ovid in a Sixteenth-Century Paris College." *History of Universities* 9 (1990), 73–118.

———. "Restaging Jean Bodin: The *Universae Naturae Theatrum* (1596) in Its Cultural Context." Ph.D. thesis, Princeton University, 1990.

Blanchot, Maurice. *The Gaze of Orpheus and Other Literary Essays*. Translated by Lydia Davis. Barrytown, N.Y.: Station Hill, 1981.

Bodley, Thomas. *The Life of Sir Thomas Bodley Written by Himself*. Chicago: A. C. McClurg, 1906.

Boersma, Frederick L. *An Introduction to Fitzherbert's Abridgement.* Abingdon: Professional Books, 1981.

Bolzoni, Lina. "Il segretario neoplatonico." In *La Corte e il 'Cortegiano': II—Un modello europeo,* edited by Adriano Prosperi. Roma: Bulzoni Editore, 1980.

Boucher, David. *Texts in Context: Revisionist Methods for Studying the History of Ideas.* Dordrecht: D. Reidel, 1985.

Bourcier, Elisabeth. *Les journaux privés en Angleterre de 1600 à 1660.* Paris: Publications de la Sorbonne, 1976.

Bourdieu, Pierre. "Reading, Readers, the Literate, Literature." In *In Other Words,* translated by Matthew Adamson. Cambridge: Polity Press, 1990.

Bourdieu, Pierre, and Roger Chartier. "La lecture: une pratique culturelle." In Roger Chartier, *Pratiques de la lecture.*

Bouwsma, William J. *Concordia Mundi: The Career and Thought of Guillaume Postel (1510–1581).* Cambridge, Mass.: Harvard University Press, 1957.

Bowden, P. J. *The Wool Trade in Tudor and Stuart England.* London: Macmillan, 1971.

Bradshaw, Brendan. "Transalpine Humanism." In *The Cambridge History of Political Thought, 1450–1700* edited by J. H. Burns and Mark Goldie. Cambridge: Cambridge University Press, 1991.

Brayley, E. W. *A Topographical History of Surrey.* 4 vols. The Victoria County Histories. London: University of London, 1902.

Bruyère, Nelly. *Méthode et Dialectique dans l'Oeuvre de la Ramée.* Paris: Librairie Philosophique J. Vrin, 1984.

Buisseret, David, ed. *Monarchs, Ministers, and Maps: The Emergence of Cartography as a Tool of Government in Early Modern Europe.* Chicago: University of Chicago Press, 1992.

Butler, E. M. *The Myth of the Magus.* Cambridge: Cambridge University Press, 1948.

Calder, I. R. F. "John Dee Studied as an English Neoplatonist." Ph.D. thesis, The Warburg Institute, University of London, 1952.

Calendar of State Papers, Colonial Series, East Indies, China and Japan, 1513–1616. Edited by W. Noel Sainsbury. London: Longman, Green, Longman & Roberts, 1862.

Calendar of Treasury Papers, 1556/7–1696.

Cambridge University Library Catalogue of Manuscripts. Cambridge: Cambridge University Press, 1864.

Capp, Bernard. *Cromwell's Navy: The Fleet and the English Revolution, 1648–1660.* Oxford: Clarendon Press, 1989.

Carruthers, Mary. *The Book of Memory: A Study of Memory in Medieval Culture.* Cambridge: Cambridge University Press, 1990.

Casciato, M., M. G. Ianniello, and M. Vitale, eds. *Enciclopedismo in Roma Barocca: Athanasius Kircher e il Museo del Collegio Romano tra Wunderkammer e Museo Scientifico.* Venice: Marsilio Editore, 1986.

Cave, Terence. *The Cornucopian Text: Problems of Writing in the French Renaissance.* Oxford: Oxford University Press, 1979.

Ceard, Jean, and Jean-Claude Margolin, eds. *Voyager à la Renaissance*. Paris: Editions Maisonneauve et Larose, 1987.

Certeau, Michel de. *The Practice of Everyday Life*. Translated by Steven Rendall. Berkeley: University of California Press, 1984.

Chartier, Roger. *Cultural History: Between Practices and Representations*. Translated by Lydia G. Cochrane. Cambridge: Polity Press, 1988.

———. *The Cultural Uses of Print in Early Modern France*. Translated by Lydia G. Cochrane. Princeton: Princeton University Press, 1987.

———, ed. *A History of Private Life, Volume 3*. Cambridge, Mass.: The Belknap Press, 1989.

———, ed. *Pratiques de la lecture*. Marseille: Rivages, 1985.

Cheney, E. P. "International Law under Queen Elizabeth." *EHR* 20 (1905), 659–72.

Christy, Miller. *The Silver Map of the World: A Contemporary Medallion Commemorative of Drake's Great Voyage*. London: Henry Stevens, 1900.

Cicero, Marcus Tullius. *De Natura Deorum*. Translated by H. Rackham, The Loeb Classical Library Edition. London: William Heinemann, 1933.

———. *De Officiis*. Translated by Walter Miller, The Loeb Classical Library Edition. Cambridge, Mass.: Harvard University Press, 1913.

Clark, J. W. *Libraries in the Medieval and Renaissance Periods*. Cambridge: Macmillan and Bowes, 1894.

Clay, C. G. A. *Economic Expansion and Social Change: England, 1500–1700*. 2 vols. Cambridge: Cambridge University Press, 1984.

Clucas, Stephen. "Samuel Hartlib's Ephemerides, 1635–59, and the Pursuit of Scientific and Philosophical Manuscripts: The Religious Ethos of an Intelligencer." *The Seventeenth Century* 6:1 (Spring 1991), 33–55.

———. Book review. *Renaissance Studies* 6 (1992), 96–101.

Clulee, Nicholas H. *John Dee's Natural Philosophy: Between Science and Religion*. London: Routledge, 1988.

Cohen, Ralph, ed. *The Future of Literary Theory*. London: Routledge, 1989.

Collinson, Patrick. "De Republica Anglorum: Or, History with the Politics Put Back." Inaugural Lecture as Regius Professor of Modern History. Cambridge: Cambridge University Press, 1990.

———. "Puritans, Men of Business, and Elizabethan Parliaments." *Parliamentary History* 7:2 (1988), 187–211.

Comito, Terry. *The Idea of the Garden in the Renaissance*. New Brunswick, N.J.: Rutgers University Press, 1978.

Corbett, Margery, and Ronald Lightbown. *The Comely Frontispiece: The Emblematic Title-Page in England 1550–1660*. London: RKP, 1979.

Cormack, Lesley. Book review. *ISIS* 82 (1991), 134–35.

Cowley, J. D. *Bibliography of Abridgments, Digests, Dictionaries, and Indexes of English Law to 1800*. London: Selden Society, 1932.

Coxe, H., ed. *Catalogi Codicum Manuscriptorum Bibliothecae Bodleianae*. Vol. 1. Oxford, 1853.

Crane, Mary Thomas. *Framing Authority: Sayings, Self, and Society in Sixteenth-Century England*. Princeton: Princeton University Press, 1993.

Crinò, Anna Maria, and Helen Wallis. "New Researches on the Molyneux Globes." In *Der Globusfreund: Report on the VIth International Symposium of Coronelli Society.* Wien, 1987.

Crowley, John. *Aegypt.* New York: Bantam Books, 1987.

Curry, Patrick. "Revisions of Science and Magic." *History of Science* 23 (1985), 299–325.

Dainville, F. de. *Les Jésuites et L'éducation de la Société Française: I. La Géographie des Humanistes.* Paris: Beauchesne, 1940.

Darnton, Robert. "First Steps Toward a History of Reading." *Australian Journal of French Studies* 23:1 (1986), 5–30.

Dee, John. "The Compendious Rehearsall." In *The Autobiographical Tracts of Dr. John Dee,* edited by James Crossley. Manchester: *Chetham Miscellanies,* Vol. I, 1851.

———. *John Dee on Astronomy: 'Propaedeumata aphoristica' (1558 and 1568), Latin and English.* Translated by Wayne Shumaker. Berkeley: University of California Press, 1978.

———. *The Private Diary of Dr. John Dee, and the Catalogue of his Library of Manuscripts.* Edited by J. O. Halliwell. London: The Camden Society, 1842.

——— (spurious). *The Rosie Crucian Secrets.* Edited by E. J. Langford Garstin. Wellingborough: The Aquarian Press, 1985.

DeMolen, Richard L. "The Library of William Camden." *Proceedings of the American Philosophical Society* 128 (1984), 326–409.

Desan, Philippe, ed. *Humanism in Crisis: The Decline of the French Renaissance.* Ann Arbor: University of Michigan Press, 1991.

Devereux, W. B. *Lives and Letters of the Devereux, Earls of Essex.* London: John Murray, 1853.

Dewar, Mary. *Sir Thomas Smith: A Tudor Intellectual in Office.* London: Athlone Press, 1964.

Dictionary of Welsh Biography Down to 1940. London: The Cymmrodorion Society, 1959.

DiGregorio, Mario. *Charles Darwin's Marginalia.* New York: Garland, 1990.

Dillon, George L. *Rhetoric as Social Imagination: Explorations of the Interpersonal Function of Language.* Bloomington: Indiana University Press, 1986.

Dionisotti, C., A. Grafton, and J. Kraye, eds. *The Uses of Greek and Latin: Historical Essays.* London: The Warburg Institute, 1988.

Dodge, Ernest S. *Northwest by Sea.* New York: Oxford University Press, 1961.

Dorsten, Jan A. van. *Poets, Patrons and Professors: Sir Philip Sidney, Daniel Rogers, and the Leiden Humanists.* London: Oxford University Press, 1962.

Dupront, A. "Espace et Humanisme." *Bibliothèque D'Humanisme et Renaissance* 8 (1946), 7–104.

Durling, Richard J. "Conrad Gesner's *Liber Amicorum* 1555–1565." *Gesnerus* 22 (1965), 134–59.

Eales, Richard, and David Sullivan, eds. *The Political Context of Law.* London: Hambledon Press, 1987.

Eco, Umberto. *Foucault's Pendulum.* Translated by William Weaver. London: Secker & Warburg, 1989.

Elton, G. R. "Reform and the 'Commonwealth-Men' of Edward VI's Reign." In *The English Commonwealth, 1547–1640,* edited by P. Clark, A. G. R. Smith, and N. Tyacke. New York: Barnes and Noble, 1979.

———. *Studies in Tudor and Stuart Politics and Government.* 3 vols. Cambridge: Cambridge University Press, 1983.

Escarpit, Robert. *Sociology of Literature.* Translated by Ernest Pick. 2d ed. London: Frank Cass, 1971.

Evans, Joan. *A History of the Society of Antiquaries.* Oxford: Oxford University Press, 1956.

Evans, R. J. W. *Rudolf II and His World: A Study in Intellectual History 1576–1612.* Oxford: Clarendon Press, 1973.

Farmer, Norman K., Jr. "Fulke Greville's Letter to a Cousin in France and the Problem of Authorship in Cases of Formula Writing." *Huntington Library Quarterly* 22:2 (Summer 1969), 140–47.

Feather, John P. "The Book in History and the History of the Book." *Journal of Library History* 21:1 (Winter 1986), 12–26.

Feingold, Mordechai. *The Mathematician's Apprenticeship: Science, Universities, and Society in England, 1560–1640.* Cambridge: Cambridge University Press, 1984.

———. "The Occult Tradition in the English Universities of the Renaissance: A Reassessment." In *Occult and Scientific Mentalities in the Renaissance,* edited by Brian Vickers. Cambridge: Cambridge University Press, 1984.

Ferguson, Arthur. *The Articulate Citizen and the English Renaissance.* Durham, N.C.: Duke University Press, 1966.

———. *Clio Unbound: Perception of the Social and Cultural Past in Renaissance England.* Durham, N.C.: Duke University Press, 1979.

Figurovski, N. A. "The Alchemist and Physician Arthur Dee (Artemii Ivanovich Dii)." *Ambix* 13 (1965), 35–51.

Findlen, Paula. "The Economy of Scientific Exchange in Early Modern Italy." In Bruce Moran, *Patronage and Institutions.*

———. "The Museum: Its Classical Etymology and Renaissance Genealogy." *Journal of the History of Collections* 1 (1989), 59–78.

Finnegan, Ruth. *Literacy and Orality: Studies in the Technology of Communication.* Oxford: Basil Blackwell, 1988.

Fisch, Menachem, and Simon Schaffer, eds. *William Whewell: A Composite Portrait.* Oxford: Oxford University Press, 1991.

Foss, Michael. *Undreamed Shores: England's Wasted Empire in America.* New York: Charles Scribner's Sons, 1974.

Foster, C. W., ed. *Lincoln Episcopal Records 1571–84.* Canterbury and York Society Vol. II. London: Canterbury and York Society, 1913.

Fowden, Garth. *The Egyptian Hermes: A Historical Approach to the Late Pagan Mind.* Cambridge: Cambridge University Press, 1987.

Fox, Levi, ed. *English Historical Scholarship in the Sixteenth and Seventeenth Centuries.* Oxford: Oxford University Press, 1956.

French, Peter J. *John Dee: The World of an Elizabethan Magus.* London: RKP, 1972.

Freund, Elizabeth. *The Return of the Reader: Reader-Response Criticism.* London: Methuen, 1987.

Fritze, Ronald Harold. " 'Truth hath lacked witnesse, tyme wanted light': The Dispersal of the English Monastic Libraries and Protestant Efforts at Preservation, c. 1535–1625." *Journal of Library History* 18:3 (Summer 1983), 274–91.

Fulton, Thomas Wemyss. *The Sovereignty of the Sea: An Historical Account of the Claims of England to the Dominion of the British Seas, and of the Evolution of the Territorial Waters.* Edinburgh and London: William Blackwood and Sons, 1911.

Fussner, F. Smith. *The Historical Revolution: English Historical Writing and Thought 1580–1640.* London: RKP, 1962.

———. *Tudor History and the Historians.* New York: Basic Books, 1970.

Gamba, Enrico, and Vico Montebelli. *Le Scienze a Urbino nel Tardo Rinascimento.* Urbino: QuattroVenti, 1988.

Gent, Lucy. *Picture and Poetry 1560–1620.* Leamington Spa: J. Hall, 1981.

Gilmore, Myron. *Humanists and Jurists: Six Studies in the Renaissance.* Cambridge, Mass.: Harvard University Press, 1963.

Gingerich, Owen, and Robert S. Westman. *The Wittich Connection: Conflict and Priority in Late Sixteenth-Century Cosmology.* Transactions of the American Philosophical Society 78. 1988.

Gliozzi, Giuliano. *Adamo e il nuovo mondo: La nascita dell'antropologia come ideologia coloniale . . . (1500–1700).* Firenze: La Nuova Italia Editrice, 1976.

Gouws, John, ed. *The Prose Works of Fulke Greville, Lord Brooke.* Oxford: Clarendon Press, 1986.

Grafton, Anthony. *Defenders of the Text: The Traditions of Scholarship in an Age of Science, 1450–1800.* Cambridge, Mass.: Harvard University Press, 1991.

———. "Humanism, Magic, and Science." In *The Impact of Humanism on Western Europe,* edited by Grafton and Angus MacKay. London: Longman, 1992.

———. *Joseph Scaliger: A Study in the History of Classical Scholarship.* Vol. 1. Oxford: Clarendon Press, 1983.

———. *New Worlds, Ancient Texts: The Power of Tradition and the Shock of Discovery.* Cambridge, Mass.: Harvard University Press, 1992.

———. "Renaissance Readers and Ancient Texts: Comments on Some Commentaries." *Renaissance Quarterly* 38:4 (1985), 615–49.

———. "Teacher, Text and Pupil in the Renaissance Class-Room: A Case Study from a Parisian College." *History of Universities* 1 (1981), 37–70.

———. "The World of the Polyhistors: Humanism and Encyclopedism." *Central European History* 18:1 (March 1985), 31–47.

Grafton, Anthony, and Lisa Jardine. *From Humanism to the Humanities: Education and the Liberal Arts in Fifteenth- and Sixteenth-Century Europe.* London: Duckworth, 1986.

Green, Lawrence D., ed. and trans. *John Rainolds's Oxford Lectures on Aristotle's Rhetoric.* London: Associated University Presses, 1986.

Greenblatt, Stephen. *Shakespearean Negotiations.* Berkeley: University of California Press, 1988.

Gundersheimer, Werner L. *The Life and Works of Louis Le Roy.* Geneva: Librairie Droz, 1966.

Gwyn, David. "John Dee's *Arte of Navigation.*" *The Book Collector* 34 (1985), 309–22.

Haigh, Christopher, ed. *The Reign of Queen Elizabeth I.* London: Macmillan, 1984.

Hall, David. "The History of the Book: New Questions? New Answers?" *Journal of Library History* 21:1 (Winter 1986), 27–38.

Hall, Marie Boas. "Science." In *The New Cambridge Modern History,* vol. 3, edited by R. B. Wernham. Cambridge: Cambridge University Press, 1968.

Halliday, M. A. K. *Language as Social Semiotic: The Social Interpretation of Language and Meaning.* London: Edward Arnold, 1978.

Halliwell-Phillipps, J. O., ed. *Rara Mathematica.* London: John William Parker, 1839.

Hankins, James. *Plato in the Italian Renaissance.* 2 vols. Leiden: E. J. Brill, 1990.

Hannaway, Owen. *The Chemist and the Word: The Didactic Origins of Chemistry.* Baltimore: Johns Hopkins University Press, 1975.

———. "Laboratory Design and the Aim of Science: Andreas Libavius versus Tycho Brahe," *ISIS* 77 (1986), 586–610.

Harley, J. B. "Meaning and Ambiguity in Tudor Cartography." In *English Map-Making 1500–1650,* edited by Sarah Tyacke. London: The British Library, 1983.

———. "Silences and Secrecy: The Hidden Agenda of Cartography." *Imago Mundi* 40 (1988), 57–76.

Harris, Roy. "How Does Writing Restructure Thought?" *Language and Communication* 9:2/3 (1989), 99–106.

Hartman, Geoffrey. "The State of the Art of Criticism." In Ralph Cohen, *The Future of Literary Theory.*

Hatfield, Gary. "Metaphysics and the New Science." In David C. Lindberg, *Reappraisals of the Scientific Revolution.*

Hathaway, Neil. "Compilatio: From Plagiarism to Compiling." *Viator* 20 (1989), 19–44.

Haynes, Jonathan. *The Humanist as Traveler: George Sandys' Relation of a Journey begun An. Dom. 1610.* Rutherford, N.J.: Fairleigh Dickinson University Press, 1986.

Heekelingen, H. de Vries de, ed. *Correspondance de Bonaventura Vulcanius.* The Hague: Martinus Nijhoff, 1923.

Helgerson, Richard. *Forms of Nationhood: The Elizabethan Writing of England.* Chicago: University of Chicago Press, 1992.

Hellman, C. Doris. *The Comet of 1577: Its Place in the History of Astronomy.* New York: Columbia University Press, 1944.

Henry, Bruce. "John Dee, Humphrey Llwyd, and the Name 'British Empire.'" *Huntington Library Quarterly* 35 (1971–72), 189–90.

Hessels, J. H., ed. *Abrahami Ortelii . . . epistulae.* Cambridge: Cambridge University Press, 1887.

Hill, Christopher. *The Intellectual Origins of the English Revolution*. Oxford: Oxford University Press, 1965.

Hill, W. Speed, ed. *Studies in Richard Hooker*. Cleveland: Case Western Reserve University Press, 1972.

Hippocrates Junior. *The Predicted Plague*. London: Simpkin, Marshall, Hamilton, Kent, & Co., 1900.

Hobson, Anthony. "English Library Buildings of the 17th and 18th Century." *Wolfenbütteler Forschungen*. Band 2. Bremen and Wolfenbüttel: Jacobi Verlag, 1977. 63–74.

Holtgen, Karl Joseph. "Sir Robert Dallington (1561–1637): Author, Traveler, and Pioneer of Taste." *Huntington Library Quarterly* 4 (1984), 147–77.

Holub, Robert C. *Reception Theory: A Critical Introduction*. London: Methuen, 1984.

Hudson, Winthrop. *The Cambridge Connection and the Elizabethan Settlement of 1559*. Durham, N.C.: Duke University Press, 1980.

Hutson, Lorna. "Fortunate Travelers: Reading for the Plot in Sixteenth-Century England." *Representations* 41 (1993), 83–103.

———. *Thomas Nashe in Context*. Oxford: Clarendon Press, 1989.

Impey, Oliver, and Arthur MacGregor, eds. *The Origins of Museums: The Cabinet of Curiosities in Sixteenth- and Seventeenth-Century Europe*. Oxford: Clarendon Press, 1985.

Irwin, Raymond. *The English Library*. London: George Allen & Unwin, 1966.

Iser, Wolfgang. *The Act of Reading: A Theory of Aesthetic Response*. London: RKP, 1978.

———. *The Implied Reader: Patterns of Communication in Prose Fiction from Bunyan to Beckett*. Baltimore: Johns Hopkins University Press, 1974.

———. "Indeterminacy and the Reader's Response in Prose Fiction." In J. Hillis Miller, *Aspects of Narrative*.

———. "Interaction between Text and Reader." In Susan R. Suleiman and Inge Crosman, *The Reader in the Text*.

Jabès, Edmond. *Le livre des questions*. Paris: Editions Gallimard, 1963.

———. *Le livre du dialogue*. Paris: Editions Gallimard, 1984.

Jack-Hinton, Colin. *The Search for the Islands of Solomon, 1567–1838*. Oxford: Clarendon Press, 1969.

Jacob, James R. *Henry Stubbe: Radical Protestantism and the Early Enlightenment*. Cambridge: Cambridge University Press, 1983.

Jardine, Lisa. *Francis Bacon: Discovery and the Art of Discourse*. Cambridge: Cambridge University Press, 1974.

———. "Humanist Logic." In Charles B. Schmitt and Quentin Skinner, *The Cambridge History of Renaissance Philosophy*.

———. Review essay. *History Workshop* 21 (Spring 1986), 179–81.

Jardine, Lisa, and Anthony Grafton. " 'Studied for Action': How Gabriel Harvey Read his Livy." *Past and Present* 129 (November 1990), 30–78.

Jardine, N. *The Birth of History and Philosophy of Science: Kepler's 'A Defense of Tycho against Ursus' with Essays on Its Provenance and Significance*. Cambridge: Cambridge University Press, 1984.

Jarrott, C. A. L. "The English Humanists' Use of Cicero's *De Officiis* in Their Evaluation of Active and Contemplative Life." Ph.D. thesis, Stanford University, 1954.

Jayne, Sears, and Francis R. Johnson, eds. *The Library of John, Lord Lumley: The Catalogue of 1609*. London: The British Museum, 1956.

Jesi, Furio. "John Dee e il suo sapere." *Comunita* 166 (April 1972).

Johnson, Francis R. *Astronomical Thought in Renaissance England: A Study of the English Scientific Writings from 1500 to 1645*. Baltimore: The Johns Hopkins Press, 1937. Reprint. Octagon Books, 1968.

Jones, Gareth Lloyd. *The Discovery of Hebrew in Tudor England: A Third Language*. Manchester: Manchester University Press, 1983.

Jones, Peter Murray. "Thomas Lorkin's Dissections, 1564/5 and 1566/7." *Transactions of the Cambridge Bibliographical Society* 9:3 (1988), 209–29.

Jones, W. R. D. *The Tudor Commonwealth, 1529–1559*. London: Athlone Press, 1970.

Josten, C. H., ed. *Elias Ashmole's Autobiographical and Historical Notes, His Correspondence, and Other Contemporary Sources Relating to His Life and Work*. 5 vols. Oxford: Clarendon Press, 1966.

Keble, Rev. John, ed. *The Works of Mr. Richard Hooker*. Oxford: Clarendon Press, 1888.

Kelley, Donald R., and Richard H. Popkin, eds. *The Shapes of Knowledge from the Renaissance to the Enlightenment*. Dordrecht: Kluwer, 1991.

Kendrick, T. D. *British Antiquity*. New York: Barnes & Noble, 1950.

Kerridge, Eric. *Agrarian Problems in the Sixteenth Century and After*. London: George Allen and Unwin, 1969.

Kiessling, Nicolas K. *The Library of Robert Burton*. Oxford Bibliographical Society Monographs, n.s. XXII. Oxford: Oxford Bibliographical Society, 1988.

Kintgen, Eugene R. "Reconstructing Elizabethan Reading." *Studies in English Literature* 30:1 (Winter 1990), 1–18.

Klose, Wolfgang. *Corpus Alborum Amicorum*. Stuttgart: Anton Hiersmann, 1988.

Knapp, Jeffrey. *An Empire Nowhere: England, America, and Literature from "Utopia" to "The Tempest."* Berkeley: University of California Press, 1991.

Korinman, Michel. "Simon Grynaeus et le 'Novus Orbis': Les Pouvoirs d'une Collection." In Jean Ceard and Jean-Claude Margolin, *Voyager à la Renaissance*.

Kraye, Jill. "Moral Philosophy." In Charles B. Schmitt and Quentin Skinner, *The Cambridge History of Renaissance Philosophy*.

Kristeller, Paul Oskar. "In Search of Renaissance Manuscripts." *The Library*, Sixth Series 10:4 (December 1988), 291–303.

Kuntz, Marion Leathers. "Voyages to the East and Their Meaning in the Thought of Guillaume Postel." In Jean Ceard and Jean-Claude Margolin, *Voyager à la Renaissance*.

Larminie, V. M. *The Godly Magistrate: The Private Philosophy and Public Life of Sir John Newdigate, 1571–1610*, Dugdale Society Occasional Papers No. 28. Oxford, 1982.

Latour, Bruno. *Science in Action: How to Follow Scientists and Engineers through Society.* Milton Keynes: The Open University Press, 1987.

Lechner, Sister Joan Marie. *Renaissance Concepts of the Commonplaces.* New York: Pageant Press, 1962.

Leedham-Green, Elisabeth. *Books in Cambridge Inventories: Book-lists from Vice-Chancellor's Court Probate Inventories in the Tudor and Stuart Periods.* 2 vols. Cambridge: Cambridge University Press, 1986.

Lehane, Brendan. *The Northwest Passage.* Alexandria, Va.: Time-Life Books, 1981.

Levine, Joseph M. *Humanism and History: Origins of Modern English Historiography.* Ithaca: Cornell University Press, 1987.

Levy, F. J. *Tudor Historical Thought.* San Marino: The Huntington Library, 1967.

Lewis, Ada Haeseler. "A Study of Elizabethan Ship Money 1588–1603." Ph.D. Thesis, Philadelphia, 1928.

Lindberg, David C., ed. *Reappraisals of the Scientific Revolution.* Cambridge: Cambridge University Press, 1990.

Lipsius, Justus. *A Brief Outline of the History of Libraries.* Translated by John Cotton Dana. Chicago: A. C. McClurg, 1907.

Lloyd, T. H. *England and the German Hanse, 1157–1611: A Study of Their Trade and Commercial Diplomacy.* Cambridge: Cambridge University Press, 1991.

Loades, David M. *The Tudor Navy: An Administrative, Political, and Military History.* Aldershot: Scolar, 1992.

Long, A. A., and D. N. Sedley. *The Hellenistic Philosophers.* 2 vols. Cambridge: Cambridge University Press, 1987.

Losse, Deborah N. "From *Auctor* to *Auteur:* Authorization and Appropriation in the Renaissance." *Medievalia et Humanistica* n.s. 16 (1988), 153–63.

Love, Harold. "Scribal Publication in Seventeenth-Century England." *Transactions of the Cambridge Bibliographical Society* 9 (1987), 130–54.

Lytle, Guy Fitch, and Stephen Orgel, eds. *Patronage in the Renaissance.* Princeton: Princeton University Press, 1981.

McConica, James K. *English Humanists and Reformation Politics.* Oxford: Clarendon Press, 1965.

———, ed. *The History of the University of Oxford.* Vol. 3. Oxford: Oxford University Press, 1986.

McCusker, Honor. "Books and Manuscripts formerly in the possession of John Bale." *The Library* 4th ser., 16 (1936), 144–65.

McGann, Jerome J. *The Beauty of Inflections: Literary Investigations in Historical Method & Theory.* Oxford: Clarendon Press, 1988.

———. "Theory of Texts." *London Review of Books* 10:4 (18 February 1988), 20.

McGinty, Alice B. "A Preliminary Analysis of John Dee's Preface to the First English Euclid." M. A. thesis, Tufts University, 1970.

MacGregor, Arthur, ed. *Tradescant's Rarities: Essays on the Foundation of the Ashmolean Museum.* Oxford: Clarendon Press, 1983.

McKenzie, D. F. *Bibliography and the Sociology of Texts.* The Panizzi Lectures. London: The British Library, 1985.

McKisack, May. *Medieval History in the Tudor Age.* Oxford: Clarendon Press, 1971.

McKitterick, David, ed. *Andrew Perne: Quatercentenary Studies.* Cambridge: Cambridge Bibliographical Society, 1991.

McLean, Antonia. *Humanism and the Rise of Science in Tudor England.* London: Heinemann, 1972.

McPherson, David. *Ben Jonson's Library and Marginalia: An Annotated Catalogue, Studies in Philology Texts and Studies,* 1974.

Maçzak, Antoni, ed. *Klientelsysteme im Europa der Fruhen Neuzeit.* München: R. Oldenbourg, 1988.

Madden, A. F. McC. "1066, 1776 and All That: The Relevance of English Medieval Experience of 'Empire' to Later Imperial Constitutional Issues." In *Perspectives of Empire: Essays Presented to Gerald S. Graham,* edited by John E. Flint and Glyndwr Williams. London: Longman, 1973.

Major, Richard Henry. *The Voyages of the Venetian Brothers Nicolo & Antonio Zeno, to the Northern Seas in the XIVth Century.* London: The Hakluyt Society, 1873.

Marcus, G. J. *A Naval History of England,* vol. 1: *The Formative Centuries.* London: Longmans, 1961.

Markham, Albert Hastings, ed. *The Voyages and Works of John Davis.* London: The Hakluyt Society, 1880.

Martin, Julian. *Francis Bacon, the State, and the Reform of Natural Philosophy.* Cambridge: Cambridge University Press, 1992.

Martinet, Marie-Madeleine. "Voyages de Decouverte et Histoire des Civilisations dans L'Angleterre de la Renaissance: De la Monarchie Maritime de Dee à la Quête de L'Eldorado par Ralegh." In Jean Ceard and Jean-Claude Margolin, *Voyager à la Renaissance.*

Mebane, John S. *Renaissance Magic and the Return of the Golden Age: The Occult Tradition and Marlowe, Jonson, and Shakespeare.* Lincoln: University of Nebraska Press, 1989.

Mendyk, Stan A. E. *'Speculum Britanniae': Regional Study, Antiquarianism, and Science in Britain to 1700.* Toronto: University of Toronto Press, 1989.

Miller, J. Hillis. *The Ethics of Reading.* The Wellek Library Lectures. New York: Columbia University Press, 1987.

———. "The Function of Literary Theory at the Present Time." In Ralph Cohen, *The Future of Literary Theory.*

———, ed. *Aspects of Narrative.* New York: Columbia University Press, 1971.

Minnis, A. J. *Medieval Theory of Authorship: Scholastic Literary Attitudes in the Later Middle Ages.* 2d ed. Aldershot: Scolar Press, 1988.

Moran, Bruce. *The Alchemical World of the German Court: Occult Philosophy and Chemical Medicine in the Circle of Moritz of Hessen (1572–1632), Sudhoff's Archiv* Beiheft 29. Stuttgart: Franz Steiner Verlag, 1991.

———. "Privilege, Communication, and Chemiatry: The Heremetic-Alchemical Circle of Moritz of Hessen-Kassel." *Ambix* 32:3 (November 1985), 110–26.

———, ed. *Patronage and Institutions: Science, Technology, and Medicine at the European Court, 1500–1750.* Suffolk: Boydell Press, 1991.

Morgan, Victor. "The Cartographic Image of 'The Country' in Early Modern England." *Transactions of the Royal Historical Society,* 5th ser. 29 (1979).

Morson, Gary Saul, and Caryl Emerson. *Mikhail Bakhtin: Creation of a Prosaics.* Stanford: Stanford University Press, 1990.

Mullaney, Steven. *The Place of the Stage: License, Play, and Power in Renaissance England.* Chicago: University of Chicago Press, 1988.

Munz, Peter. *The Place of Hooker in the History of Thought.* London: RKP, 1952.

Neatby, Lesley N. *In Quest of the North West Passage.* London: Constable & Co., 1958.

Nichols, John. *The Progresses and Public Processions of Queen Elizabeth.* 2 vols. London: The Society of Antiquaries, 1788.

Noble, F. "The Identification of Dr. John Dee as the Author of Harleian MS 473 Based on Its Radnorshire References." *Transactions of the Radnorshire Society* 26 (1956), 40–42.

Nordenskiold, A. E. *Periplus.* Translated by F. A. Bather. Stockholm: P. A. Norstedt & Soner, 1897.

Norlind, Wilhelm. *Tycho Brahe: En Levnadsteckning.* Lund: C. W. K. Gleerup, 1970.

North, J. D. "The Western Calendar—'Intolerabilis, Horribilis, et Derisibilis' . . . Four Centuries of Discontent." In *Gregorian Reform of the Calendar,* edited by G. V. Coyne, M. A. Hoskin, and O. Pedersen. The Vatican: Pontificia Acedemia Scientiarum, 1983.

Nutton, Vivian. *John Caius and the Manuscripts of Galen.* Cambridge: Cambridge Philological Society, 1987.

———. " 'Prisci dissectionum professores': Greek Texts and Renaissance Anatomists." In C. Dionisotti, A. Grafton, and J. Kraye, *The Uses of Greek and Latin.*

Nystrand, Martin. *The Structure of Written Communication: Studies in Reciprocity Between Writers and Readers.* New York: Academic Press, 1986.

———, ed. *What Writers Know: The Language, Process, and Structure of Written Discourse.* New York: Academic Press, 1982.

Oastler, C. L. *John Day: The Elizabethan Printer.* Oxford: Oxford Bibliographical Society, 1975.

O'Day, Rosemary. *Education and Society 1500–1800.* London: Longman, 1982.

Oleson, Tryggvi J. *Early Voyages and Northern Approaches 1000–1632.* London: Oxford University Press, 1964.

Ong, Walter. *Orality and Literacy: The Technologizing of the Word.* London: Methuen, 1982.

———. *Ramus, Method, and the Decay of Dialogue.* Cambridge, Mass.: Harvard University Press, 1958. Reprint 1983.

Ophir, Adi. "A Place of Knowledge Re-Created: The Library of Michel de Montaigne," *Science in Context* 4:1 (Spring 1991), 163–189.

Oppenheim, Michael. *A History of the Administration of the Royal Navy.* 2 vols. London: The Bodley Head, 1896.

Parker, John. "Samuel Purchas, Spokesman for Empire." In *Theatrum Orbis Librorum: Liber Amicorum presented to Nico Israel on the Occasion of His Seventieth*

Birthday, edited by T. C. van Uchelen, K. van der Horst, and G. Schilder. Utrecht: HES Publishers, 1989.

Parkes, M. B. "The Influence of the Concepts of *ordinatio* and *compilatio* on the Development of the Book." In *Scribes, Scripts and Readers: Studies in the Communication, Presentation and Dissemination of Medieval Texts*. London: Hambledon Press, 1991.

The Parliamentary History of England. Edited by W. Cobbett and J. Wright. 36 vols. London, 1806–20.

Parry, J. H. *The Age of Reconnaissance: Discovery, Exploration and Settlement 1450–1650*. Berkeley: University of California Press, 1963.

Patterson, Annabel. *Hermogenes and the Renaissance*. Princeton: Princeton University Press, 1970.

Pattison, Mark. *Isaac Casaubon, 1559–1614*. 2d ed. Oxford: Clarendon Press, 1892.

Peck, Linda Levy. *Court Patronage and Corruption in Early Stuart England*. Boston: Unwin Hyman, 1990.

Penzer, N. M., ed. *The Most Noble and Famous Travels of Marco Polo*. Translated by John Frampton. London: Adam and Charles Black, 1937.

Pharand, Donat. *The Northwest Passage Arctic Straits*. Dordrecht: Martinus Nijhoff, 1984.

Piggott, Stuart. "Antiquarian Thought in the Sixteenth and Seventeenth Centuries." In Levi Fox, *English Historical Scholarship*.

Pocock, J. G. A. *The Machiavellian Moment: Florentine Political Thought and the Atlantic Republican Tradition*. Princeton: Princeton University Press, 1975.

Pomian, Krzysztof. *Collections and Curiosities: Paris and Venice 1500–1800*. Translated by Elizabeth Wiles-Portier. Cambridge: Polity Press, 1990.

Porter, Roy, and Mikulas Teich, eds. *The Scientific Revolution in National Context*. Cambridge: Cambridge University Press, 1992.

Puraye, Jean, et al., eds. *Abraham Ortelius' Album Amicorum*. Amsterdam: A. L. van Gendt & Co., 1969.

Purchas, Samuel. *Hakluytus Posthumus, or Purchas his Pilgrims*. 20 vols. Glasgow: James MacLehose & Sons, 1905–7.

Quinn, David B. *The Voyages and Colonising Enterprises of Sir Humphrey Gilbert*, 2 vols. London: The Hakluyt Society, 1940.

———, ed. *The Hakluyt Handbook*. 2 vols. London: The Hakluyt Society, 1974.

Quinn, David B., and A. N. Ryan. *England's Sea Empire, 1550–1642*. London: George Allen & Unwin, 1983.

Quint, David. *Origin and Originality in Renaissance Literature: Versions of the Source*. New Haven: Yale University Press, 1983.

Quintrell, B. W. "Charles I and His Navy in the 1630s." *The Seventeenth Century* 3 (1988), 159–79.

Rambaldi, Enrico I. "John Dee and Federico Commandino: An English and an Italian Interpretation of Euclid During the Renaissance." In *Italy and the English Renaissance*, edited by S. Rossa and D. Savoia. Milano: Edizioni Unicopli, 1989.

Ramsay, G. D. *The English Woollen Industry, 1500–1750*. London: Macmillan, 1982.

———. *The Queen's Merchants and the Revolt of the Netherlands: The End of the Antwerp Mart, Part 2*. Manchester: Manchester University Press, 1986.

Ramsey, Peter H., ed. *The Price Revolution in Sixteenth-Century England*. London: Methuen, 1971.

Regond-Bohat, A. and A. Loechel. "Les Cabinets de curiosités au XVIe siècle." In *La Curiosité à la Renaissance*, edited by Jean Ceard. Paris: Société d'Edition d'Enseignement Superieur, 1986.

Regosin, Richard L. *The Matter of My Book: Montaigne's 'Essais' as the Book of the Self*. Berkeley: University of California Press, 1977.

Rice, Eugene F., Jr. *The Renaissance Idea of Wisdom*. Cambridge, Mass.: Harvard University Press, 1958.

Richmond, Herbert. *The Navy as an Instrument of Policy 1558–1727*. Edited by E. A. Hughes. Cambridge: Cambridge University Press, 1953.

Roberts, R. J. "John Dee's Corrections to his 'Art of Navigation.'" *The Book Collector* 24 (Spring 1975), 70–75.

Roberts, R. J., and A. G. Watson. *John Dee's Library Catalogue*. London: The Bibliographical Society, 1990.

Ronan, Colin. *Their Majesties' Astronomers: A Survey of Astronomy in Britain between the Two Elizabeths*. London: The Bodley Head, 1967.

Rose, Paul Lawrence. "Commandino, John Dee, and the *De superficierum divisionibus* of Machometus Bagdedinus." *Isis* 63 (1972), 88–93.

———. *The Italian Renaissance of Mathematics: Studies on Humanists and Mathematicians from Petrarch to Galileo*. Geneva: Librarie Droz, 1976.

Rosen, Edward. *Three Imperial Mathematicians: Kepler Trapped Between Tycho Brahe and Ursus*. New York: Abaris Books, 1986.

Rothstein, Marian. "Etymology, Genealogy, and the Immutability of Origins." *Renaissance Quarterly* 43:2 (Summer 1990), 332–47.

Rundall, Thomas, ed. *Narratives of Voyages Towards the North-West, in Search of a Passage to Cathay and India, 1496–1631*. London: The Hakluyt Society, 1849.

Ryan, Lawrence. "Richard Hakluyt's Voyage into Aristotle." *Sixteenth Century Journal* 12:3 (Fall 1981), 73–84.

Säljo, Roger, ed. *The Written Word: Studies in Literate Thought and Action*. Berlin: Springer-Verlag, 1988.

Sargent, Ralph. *The Life and Lyrics of Sir Edward Dyer*. Oxford: Oxford University Press, 1968.

Schmidt-Biggemann, Wilhelm. *Topica Universalis: Eine Modellgeschichte humanistischer und barocker Wissenschaft*. Hamburg: Felix Meiner Verlag, 1983.

Schmitt, Charles B. *Cicero Scepticus: A Study of the Influence of the 'Academica' in the Renaissance*. The Hague: Martinus Nijhoff, 1972.

———. "Reappraisals in Renaissance Science." Review of Westman and McGuire's *Hermeticism and the Scientific Revolution. History of Science* 16 (1978), 200–214.

Schmitt, Charles B., and Quentin Skinner, eds. *The Cambridge History of Renaissance Philosophy*. Cambridge: Cambridge University Press, 1988.

Schoeck, Richard. "Renaissance Guides to Renaissance Learning." In *Acta Conventus Neo-Latini Turonensis*, edited by Jean-Claude Margolin. 2 vols. Paris: Librarie Philosophique J. Vrin, 1980.

Schofield, Roger. "Taxation and the Political Limits of the Tudor State." In *Law and Government under the Tudors*, edited by Claire Cross, David Loades, and J. J. Scarisbrick. Cambridge: Cambridge University Press, 1988.

Serres, Michel. *Hermes: Literature, Science, Philosophy*. Edited and translated by Josue V. Harari and David F. Bell. Baltimore: Johns Hopkins University Press, 1983.

Shackleford, Jole. "Tycho Brahe, Laboratory Design, and the Aim of Science: Reading Plans in Context." *ISIS* 84:2 (June 1993), 211–30.

Shakespeare, William. *The Tempest*. Edited by Frank Kermode. London: Methuen, 1958.

Shapin, Steven. "The House of Experiment in Seventeenth-Century England." *ISIS* 79 (1988), 373–404.

———. " 'The Mind is its Own Place': Science and Solitude in Seventeenth-Century England." *Science in Context* 4:1 (Spring, 1991), 191–218.

———. " 'A Scholar and a Gentleman': The Problematic Identity of the Scientific Practitioner in Early Modern England." *History of Science* 29 (1991), 279–327.

Shapin, Steven, and Simon Schaffer. *Leviathan & the Air-Pump: Hobbes, Boyle, & the Experimental Way of Life*. Princeton: Princeton University Press, 1989.

Shapiro, Barbara. "History and Natural History in Sixteenth- and Seventeenth-Century England: An Essay on the Relationship Between Humanism and Science." In *English Scientific Virtuosi in the 16th and 17th Centuries*, edited by Shapiro and Robert G. Frank. Los Angeles: Clark Memorial Library, 1979.

Sharpe, J. A. *Early Modern England: A Social History, 1550–1760*. London: Edward Arnold, 1987.

Sharpe, Kevin. *Sir Robert Cotton, 1586–1631: History and Politics in Early Modern England*. Oxford: Oxford University Press, 1979.

Sherman, William H. " 'A Living Library': The Readings and Writings of John Dee." Ph.D. thesis, Cambridge University, 1992.

Shillingsburg, Peter L. "Text as Matter, Concept, and Action." *Studies in Bibliography* 44 (1991), 31–82.

Shirley, Rodney W. *The Mapping of the World: Early Printed World Maps, 1472–1700*. London: The Holland Press, 1983.

Simon, Joan. *Education and Society in Tudor England*. Cambridge: Cambridge University Press, 1966.

Skelton, R. A. *Explorers' Maps: Chapters in the Cartographic Record of Geographical Discovery*. London: RKP, 1958. Reprint Spring Books, 1970.

Skelton, R. A., and J. Summerson. *A Description of the maps and architectural drawings in the collection . . . at Hatfield House*. Oxford: Roxburghe Club, 1971.

Skinner, Quentin. *The Foundations of Modern Political Thought*. 2 vols. Cambridge: Cambridge University Press, 1978.

Smet, Antoine de. "La Réserve précieuse vent d'acquérir un Exemplaire de la

Géographie de Strabo, avec annotations Manuscrites de John Dee," *Bulletin-Bibliothèque Royale de Belgique* 11 (1967), 109–14.

———. "John Dee et sa place dans l'histoire de la cartographie." In *My Head Is a Map: Essays & Memoirs in Honour of R. V. Tooley,* edited by Helen Wallis and Sarah Tyacke. London: Francis Edwards and Carta Press, 1973.

Smith, G. C. Moore. *Gabriel Harvey's Marginalia.* Stratford-upon-Avon, 1913.

Smith, Thomas (probable). *Discourse of the Common Weal.* Edited by E. Lamond. Cambridge: Cambridge University Press, 1954.

Smolka, Josef. "The Scientific Revolution in Bohemia." In Roy Porter and Mikulas Teich, *The Scientific Revolution in National Context.*

Snow, Vernon F. "Francis Bacon's Advice to Fulke Greville on Research Techniques." *Huntington Library Quarterly* 23:4 (August 1970), 369–78.

Solomon, Julie Robin. " 'To Know, To Fly, To Conjure': Situating Baconian Science at the Juncture of Early Modern Modes of Reading." *Renaissance Quarterly* 44 (1991): 513–58.

Stefansson, Vilhjalmur. *Northwest to Fortune: The Search of Western Man for a Commercially Practical Route to the Far East.* London: George Allen & Unwin, 1958.

Stegmann, André. "Comment constituer une bibliothèque en France au début du XVIIe siecle." In *Le Livre dans l'Europe de la Renaissance,* edited by Pierre Aquilon and Henri-Jean Martin. Actes du XXVIIIe Colloque international d'Etudes humanistes de Tours. Nantes: Promodis, 1988.

Stern, Virginia F. *Gabriel Harvey: His Life, Marginalia and Library.* Oxford: Oxford University Press, 1979.

Stock, Brian. *The Implications of Literacy: Written Language and Models of Interpretation in the Eleventh and Twelfth Centuries.* Princeton: Princeton University Press, 1983.

Street, Brian V. *Literacy in Theory and Practice.* Cambridge: Cambridge University Press, 1984.

———. "Walter Ong on Literacy." *Aspects* 1:1 (1986), 2–15.

Strong, Roy. *Gloriana: The Portraits of Queen Elizabeth I.* London: Thames & Hudson, 1987.

———. *Portraits of Queen Elizabeth I.* Oxford: Oxford University Press, 1963.

———. *The Renaissance Garden in England.* London: Thames and Hudson, 1979.

Styles, Philip. "Politics and Historical Research in the Early Seventeenth Century." In Levi Fox, *English Historical Scholarship.*

Suleiman, Susan R., and Inge Crosman, eds. *The Reader in the Text: Essays on Audience and Interpretation.* Princeton: Princeton University Press, 1980.

Tanselle, G. Thomas. Review essay. *Studies in Bibliography* 44 (1991), 83–143.

Tawney, R. H., and E. Power, eds. *Tudor Economic Documents.* 3 vols. London: Longmans, 1924.

Taylor, Archer. *Renaissance Guides to Books: An Inventory and Some Conclusions.* Berkeley: University of California Press, 1945.

Taylor, E. G. R. "John Dee and the Nautical Triangle, 1575." *Journal of the Institute of Navigation* 8 (1955), 318–25.

————. "A Letter Dated 1577 from Mercator to John Dee." *Imago Mundi* 13 (1956), 56–68.

————. *Tudor Geography, 1485–1583.* London: Methuen, 1930.

————, ed. *The Original Writings and Correspondence of the two Richard Hakluyts.* 2 vols. London: The Hakluyt Society, 1935.

————, ed. *A Regiment for the Sea and Other Writings on Navigation by William Bourne.* Cambridge: Cambridge University Press, 1963.

Theutenberg, Bo Johnson. "*Mare Clausum et Mare Liberum.*" *Arctic* 37:4 (December, 1984), 481–92.

Thirsk, Joan. "Enclosing and Engrossing." In *The Agrarian History of England and Wales.* Vol. 4. Cambridge: Cambridge University Press, 1967.

Thomson, George M. *The North-West Passage.* London: Secker & Warburg, 1975.

Thrower, N. J. W., ed. *Sir Francis Drake and the Famous Voyage, 1577–1580.* Berkeley: University of California Press, 1984.

Thrush, Andrew. "Naval Finance and the Origins and Development of Ship Money." In *War and Government in Britain, 1598–1650,* edited by Mark C. Fissel. Manchester: Manchester University Press, 1991.

Tocci, Luigi Michelini. *In Officina Erasmi: L'Apparato Autografo di Erasmo per L'Edizione 1528 degli Adagia. . . .* Roma: Edizioni de Storia e Letteratura, 1989.

Todorov, Tzvetan. *Mikhail Bakhtin: The Dialogical Principle.* Translated by Wlad Godzich. Minneapolis: University of Minnesota Press, 1984.

Tozer, H. F. "A Byzantine Reformer." *Journal of Hellenic Studies* 7 (1886), 353–80.

Trousdale, Marion. *Shakespeare and the Rhetoricians.* London: Scolar Press, 1982.

Tully, James, ed. *Meaning and Context: Quentin Skinner and his Critics.* Cambridge: Polity, 1988.

Vines, Alice G. *Neither Fire Nor Steel: Sir Christopher Hatton.* Chicago: Nelson-Hall, 1978.

Wallis, Helen. "England's Search for the Northern Passages in the Sixteenth and Early Seventeenth Centuries." *Arctic* 37:4 (December 1984), 453–72.

————, ed. *Raleigh and Roanoke.* London and Raleigh: The British Library, 1985.

Warnicke, Retha M. *William Lambarde: Elizabethan Antiquary, 1536–1601.* London: Phillimore & Co., 1973.

Warren, William Thorn, ed. *St. Cross Hospital, Near Winchester: Its History and Buildings.* Winchester: Warren and Son, 1899.

Watts, Pauline Moffitt. "Prophecy and Discovery: On the Spiritual Origins of Christopher Columbus's 'Enterprise of the Indies.'" *American Historical Review* 90 (1985), 73–102.

Webster, Charles. "Alchemical and Paracelsian Medicine." In *Health, Medicine and Mortality in the Sixteenth Century,* edited by C. Webster. Cambridge: Cambridge University Press, 1979.

————. *The Great Instauration: Science, Medicine and Reform, 1626–1660.* London: Duckworth, 1975.

Welfare, Simon, and John Fairley. *The Cabinet of Curiosities*. London: Weidenfeld and Nicolson, 1991.

Wernham, R. B. "The Public Records in the Sixteenth and Seventeenth Centuries." In Levi Fox, *English Historical Scholarship*.

Westman, Robert S. "The Astronomer's Role in the Sixteenth Century: A Preliminary Study." *History of Science* 18 (1980), 105–47.

———. "Humanism and Scientific Roles in the Sixteenth Century." In *Humanismus und Naturwissenschaften*, edited by R. Schmitz and F. Krafft. Boppard: Harald Boldt Verlag, 1980.

———. "Proof, Poetics, and Patronage: Copernicus's Preface to *De Revolutionibus*." In David C. Lindberg, *Reappraisals of the Scientific Revolution*.

Whitby, C. L. *John Dee's Actions with Spirits*. 2 vols. New York: Garland, 1991.

———. "John Dee and Renaissance Scrying." *Bulletin of the Society for Renaissance Studies* 3:2 (October 1985), 25–37.

White, Harold Ogden. *Plagiarism & Imitation during the English Renaissance: A Study in Critical Distinctions*. New York: Octagon 1973.

Wightman, W. P. D. *Science in the Renaissance*. 2 vols. Edinburgh and London: Oliver and Boyd, 1962.

Wilkinson, Ronald Stearne. "The Alchemical Library of John Winthrop, Jr. (1606–1676) and His Descendants in Colonial America, Part IV." *Ambix* 13 (1966), 139–86.

Williams, Gwyn A. *Madoc: The Legend of the Welsh Discovery of America*. Oxford: Oxford University Press, 1987.

———. "Welsh Wizard and British Empire: Dr. John Dee and a Welsh Identity." The Gwyn Jones Lecture. Cardiff: University College Cardiff Press, 1980.

Williams, N. J. *The Maritime Trade of the East Anglian Ports, 1550–1590*. Oxford: Oxford University Press, 1988.

Williams, Raymond. *Marxism and Literature*. Oxford: Oxford University Press, 1977.

Wilson, C. H. "Trade, Society and the State." *The Cambridge Economic History of Europe*, vol. 4. Cambridge: Cambridge University Press, 1967.

Woodcock, Thomas, and John Martin Robinson. *The Oxford Guide to Heraldry*. Oxford: Oxford University Press, 1988.

Woodhouse, C. M. *George Gemistos Plethon: The Last of the Hellenes*. Oxford: Clarendon Press, 1986.

Wright, C. E. "The Dispersal of Monastic Libraries." *Transactions of the Cambridge Bibliographical Society* 1 (1947–53), 208–37.

Yates, Frances A. *The Art of Memory*. London: RKP, 1966.

———. *Astraea: The Imperial Theme in the Sixteenth Century* London: RKP, 1975.

———. *Giordano Bruno and the Hermetic Tradition*. Chicago: University of Chicago Press, 1964.

———. *Ideas and Ideals in the North European Renaissance: Collected Essays*. Vol. 3. London: RKP, 1984.

———. *The Occult Philosophy in the Elizabethan Age*. London: RKP, 1979.

————. *The Rosicrucian Enlightenment*. London: RKP, 1972.

————. *Shakespeare's Last Plays: A New Approach*. London: RKP, 1975.

————. *Theatre of the World*. London: RKP, 1969.

Yewbrey, Graham. "John Dee and the 'Sidney Group': Cosmopolitics and Protestant 'Activism' in the 1570s." Ph.D. thesis, University of Hull, 1981.

————. "A Redated Manuscript of John Dee." *Bulletin of the Institute of Historical Research* 50 (1977), 249–53.

Yule, Henry. *Cathay and the Way Thither*. 4 vols. London: The Hakluyt Society, 1913–16.

Index

Numbers in italic indicate pages having illustrations.